Just War Theory

READINGS IN SOCIAL AND POLITICAL THEORY

Edited by William Connolly and Steven Lukes

Authority *edited by Joseph Raz*
Feminism and Equality *edited by Anne Phillips*
Interpreting Politics *edited by Michael T. Gibbons*
Just War Theory *edited by Jean B. Elshtain*
Language and Politics *edited by Michael J. Shapiro*
Legitimacy and the State *edited by William Connolly*
Liberalism and Its Critics *edited by Michael J. Sandel*
Power *edited by Steven Lukes*
Rational Choice *edited by Jon Elster*
The Self and the Political Order *edited by Tracy B. Strong*
Social Contract Theory *edited by Michael Lessnoff*

Just War Theory

Edited by JEAN BETHKE ELSHTAIN

NEW YORK UNIVERSITY PRESS
Washington Square, New York

© Jean Bethke Elshtain, 1992

First published in the U.S.A. in 1992 by
NEW YORK UNIVERSITY PRESS
Washington Square
New York, NY 10003

Library of Congress Cataloging-in-Publication Data

Just war theory / edited by Jean Bethke Elshtain.
     p.   cm. — (Readings in social and political theory)
   Includes index.
   ISBN 0−8147−2186−9 (cloth) — ISBN 0−8147−2187−7 (pbk.)
   1. Just war doctrine. I. Elshtain, Jean Bethke. 1941−
II. Series.
B105.W3J87 1991
172′.42−dc20.   91−465
                                        CIP

Manufactured in Great Britain

'Great ideas, it has been said, come into the world as gently as doves. Perhaps then, if we listen attentively, we shall hear, amid the uproar of empires and nations, a faint flutter of wings, the gentle stirring of life and hope. Some will say that this hope lies in a nation; others, in a man. I believe rather that it is awakened, revived, nourished by millions of solitary individuals whose deeds and works every day negate frontiers and the crudest implications of history. As a result, there shines forth fleetingly the ever threatened truth that each and every man, on the foundation of his own sufferings and joys, builds for all.'

Albert Camus

Contents

Contributors

Paul Ramsey was Harrington Spear Paine Professor of Religion at Princeton University.

Michael Howard is Regius Professor of History, Oxford University.

Michael Walzer is Professor of Social Science at the Institute for Advanced Study, Princeton University.

James Turner Johnson is Professor of Religion at Rutgers University and Director of International Programs.

William V. O'Brien is Professor of Theology and Ethics at Georgetown University.

Robert L. Holmes is Professor of Philosophy, University of Rochester.

Susan Khin Zaw is Lecturer in Philosophy at the Open University and has been active on nuclear issues.

Jean Bethke Elshtain is the Centennial Professor of Political Science and Professor of Philosophy at Vanderbilt University.

Stephen Toulmin is a professor at the University of Chicago and a member of the Committee on Social Thought.

Stanley Hauerwas is Director of Graduate Studies in Religion at Duke University.

Introduction

JEAN BETHKE ELSHTAIN

For political and social theorists, just war is back on the agenda. Although international relations theorists have for years tracked alternatives to so-called 'realist' or *realpolitik* thinking about matters of war and peace and located just war doctrine and theory inside what they dubbed the 'idealist' frame, few turned their attention to the transformations, complexities, and continuing resonance of just war as a mode of discourse and a language of justification and evaluation. That was left to theologians, predominantly but not exclusively Catholic. It was they who kept this particular tradition – one situated complicatedly in a history and a set of assumptions which are neither 'realist' nor 'pacifist' but partake of both – alive and brought it to bear on the great dilemmas of modern total warfare – saturation bombing of civilian centres; blurring of the line between combatants and noncombatants in polities whose economies were geared entirely towards war-making; the creation and use of such 'ultimate' weapons of terror as the atomic bomb, and so on.

International lawyers and military professionals were two other groups that grappled with claims and concepts emerging from the just war tradition as they attempted to root relations between states on a more predictably rule-governed basis (the lawyers) or pondered whether consideration of fair play ideals, emerging from medieval warrior civilization and the chivalric code, were at all applicable to modern battlefield conditions (the soldiers). Just war also continued to serve as a general way men and women in the West justified war and, at the same time, attempted to limit its destructive effects. One can, then, speak of a just war tradition, thick with life, that evolved out of just war as canonical doctrine. Just war is a set of essentially contested concepts around which political life is focused. Contests over the range of applicability of just war precepts generate and focus political debate. Just war as political theory touches both the deontological and consequentialist poles of moral reasoning. By embracing both dimensions, just war theory cuts across the usual lines of fault in moral philosophy just as it does in international relations as political theory by refusing to fit (so to speak) inside the realist—idealist dichotomy.

Just war as political theory received a new lease on life with the publication of Michael Walzer's *Just and Unjust Wars* in 1977. Reminding political theorists long dominated by realist presumptions that, in fact, it is nearly impossible to sustain a debate over war, peace and the use and abuse of violence without recourse to categories lodged within or emerging from the just war tradition, Walzer helped to put just war back on the map of contemporary social and political thought. He had plenty of help — some of it from morally murky events such as the Vietnam War, particularly traumatic for Americans, and some from modern guerrilla warfare and 'terrorism' variously defined that cried out for complex and nuanced evaluations of the sort just war thinkers had been engaged in for decades. (Some have argued the thinking got too finely tuned and lost its moral edge — but that's a debate played out in this volume.)

Walzer's volume had been preceded by several years by James Turner Johnson's *Ideology, Reason, and the Limitation of War* (Princeton, 1975), written within a horizon framed by historical and theological concerns. Johnson's follow-up volume, *Just War Tradition and the Restraint of War*, (Princeton, 1981), took account of Walzer's work but tackled as well emergent narrative approaches, attuned to literary conventions and the tropes of war, the diminution of heroic tales and the rise of bitter and ironic 'war stories', and stressing the inability of humans to achieve moral clarity over the ambiguous and unpredictable events of war. Johnson brought the historic narrative approach into a relation with the more legalistic case-study tack, showing how each illumines aspects of war and war making and how each takes off from a starting point in elaborate structures of argumentation and rhetoric.

Debates within the world of academic political theory and moral philosophy also gave an added boost to the return of just war as political theory. I refer to earlier volumes in this series (for example, *Interpreting Politics* and *Language and Politics*) which alerted us to the inescapability of interpretation, the contestability of political concepts, the fixity *and* fluidity of our language(s) of political and moral contestation. Any rigid line between morality and politics; between religious and other modes of thinking, became less defensible. Theologians turned to political theory. Political thinkers found themselves debating bishops. This brings us to the current moment in the long history of just war.

This volume displays both the continuities and breaks in the just war tradition, alerting readers to on-going *theoretical* debates by drawing upon thinkers who either defend or attack just war with reference to some alternative perspective or engage one another *within* a horizon framed by the just war tradition broadly defined. Both the *jus in bello* or law of war and the *jus ad bellum* or right and justice of making war, come into play. One critical theme echoing through the readings has to do with public/private or external/internal rules and political moralities. As all students of political thought know, justice governed relations between citizens within the *polis* for the Greeks. But force came into play, sometimes more readily than at other times, between, say, Athenians and 'others'. This meant that what would be counted a wrong against a citizen was not necessarily so adjudged if it pertained between citizens collectively and some external group. The *locus classicus* of this tendency is the so-called Melian dialogue in Thucydides' *History of the Peloponnesian War* in which the Athenian generals proclaim might the right that reigns. Just war, tapping at one and the same time universalist presumptions (whether Christian or natural law) and historically particular identities (this *civitas*, this commonwealth), blurred but did not eliminate the external—internal distinction with its attendant moralities and notions of justice.

This is but one of the many moments when just war and political theory find themselves deeply entangled. Perhaps the best way to put it is this: debates over nuclear strategy and the justice or injustice of it; questions concerning just how far the range of human moral reason and consequent action can and should be presumed to extend; ruminations surrounding a preferred vision of peace or tranquillity in contrast to a condition of war or warfulness or warlikeness — all presuppose the continued viability of just war discourse or, even more strongly, display its inevitability. In light of the vitality of these debates, and the continuing flood of interesting discussion, it is appropriate to include a volume on just war in this series on readings in social and political thought. For just war is not *just* about war: it is an account of politics that aims to be non-utopian yet to place the political within a set of moral concerns and considerations, within an ethically shaped framework. It is important to see just war thinking in its full elaboration as a theory of international *and* domestic politics.

We begin more or less at the beginning with Paul Ramsey's discussion of St Augustine's just war thinking. Ramsey, one of the most distinguished Protestant theologians and civic thinkers of the last four decades, working in the grand tradition of Reinhold

Niebuhr, demonstrates that Augustine's just war thinking locates his discourse in the heart of political theory. For Augustine does not offer a system of rules for the classification of 'hard cases' any war throws up; rather, especially in his famous assault on the Roman *imperium* in Chapter XIX of *The City of God*, Augustine presents a vision of earthly justice, order, and peace and a definition of a commonwealth that goes much beyond notions of self-interest. People are united by what they love in common, not simply by the rules they abide by. Importantly, Augustine extols *justice*, not *peace* as the highest value, the most noble good. Peace may, in fact, be an *unjust* order – the peace of the *Pax Romana*, for example, for it was a *pax-ordo* of compulsion. Just war must be understood within a larger frame of justice. As Ramsey unpacks Augustine's position, he reminds us of Augustine's unblinking anti-Manicheanism. Augustine refuses to locate all good in one side, all evil in another – even, or most especially, in time of war.

Michael Howard, an important contemporary realist in the classical mould, is sceptical of attempts to impose moral strictures on war-making from outside the business of war itself. War, after all, is conducted by states or legitimated authorities. Men (and women, from time to time) fight as members of states, not as private persons. For Howard, the hey-day of just war as a set of categorical imperatives designed to limit war had passed by the end of the sixteenth century with the crack-up of Western Christiandom. Subsequent attempts to limit war were not particularly successful and the twentieth century gave us war at its most total and most terrible, war as a zero-sum game of obliteration. Although not a just war thinker, Howard nevertheless evokes the 'dictates of humanity' and 'transcendent moral values' in his discussion even as he claims that there is no reason to suppose the military 'economy of force' and such values need coincide.

Michael Walzer would suggest to Howard that the fact he cannot do without some such notion as the 'dictates of humanity' is powerful support for his own insistence that the principle of force is not a world unto itself, a world with its own laws. There is a 'moral reality of war' and the 'opinions of mankind' are in part constitutive of that reality. Those opinions, in turn, can be tracked genealogically to just war presumptions whose continuing resonance affords ordinary citizens a language in and through which to make judgements about the violence of their states. James Turner Johnson agrees that just war is inevitable, for it is the way Western culture and history have responded to questions of whether values can or ought to be protected by force. Just war holds that there *are* cases where force can appropriately be used to protect values − say, defence of the innocent − and that the sorting out of a scale of values is a feature of any ethic, anywhere, at any time. That Churches, especially the Catholic Church, have been at the forefront of recent debates over nuclear deterrence should not surprise us, for a complex dialectic between yearnings for peace and commitments to justice has, for centuries, defined the life and thought of Christian bodies in the West. Contrary to pacifist or peace-church arguments, however, those indebted to just war discourse leave open the possibility that 'values must be protected and preserved by force'.

That possibility is called into question for the nuclear age by the United States Catholic Bishops in their 1983 pastoral, 'The Challenge of Peace', which, more than any single document, has generated the most energetic, even acrimonious, debate over just war in the post-Second World War era. The Bishops assert the universally binding nature of a few moral principles, most importantly the 'dignity of the human person'. They affirm the goodness of a pluralistic society. But, getting down to brass tacks, they shift just war thinking more towards the 'peace' than the 'justice' pole. Perhaps, better put, they insist that genuine justice cannot be achieved until the arms race is ended. For the Bishops, just war and pacifism are edged closer to one another but not collapsed for they continue to insist that Christians may be enjoined to resist unjust aggression. (Though this need not mean an automatic call to arms; perhaps, instead, a call to militant non-violent resistance.) The Bishops accept the doctrine of nuclear deterrence reluctantly and provisionally and *only* if it can be clearly shown to be a way-station on the road to a nuclear arms build-down. But they reject unequivocally any first use of nuclear weapons or any resort to nuclear weapons to counter a conventional attack.

This is all too much for William V. O'Brien who describes his own position as 'Christian realism', an amalgam of *realpolitik* and just war presumptions. The bishops' pastoral unleashed a storm of protest, from the 'right' and the 'left'. O'Brien insists that by shifting the focus of their discourse to *peace* above all, the Bishops changed the subject of just war, for just war does not locate peace as the highest value, as does pacifism. O'Brien deploys standard realist categories (realism vs. idealism) to sort out his criticism of the Bishops. But O'Brien himself seems to shift the focus from justice to the 'defense of freedom', with freedom the highest value to be upheld and deterrence morally acceptable to the extent it helps us (we in the West but in the United States especially) to do just that. Robert Holmes criticizes the Bishops, and all just war thinking, from yet another perspective. Arguing that realists, like O'Brien, have not decisively answered just war argument, Holmes works on the topic by forcing just war within a set of philosophic considerations which lead him to conclude that the fact that moral constraints are invariably violated in war negates or, in some sense, shows how deeply defective is the just war tradition. He treats just war theory as a set of law-like propositions within the frame of an empirical theory. Other just war thinkers (Walzer, Johnson, Ramsey) would argue that just war is not such a theory — that it is necessarily morally ambiguous and that conflict is inescapable.

The final four essays in the volume show just how inescapable that conflict really is. Susan Khin Zaw puts fundamental just war questions along the lines of: Can one threaten to do something wrong 'even for the sake of avoiding actually having to do it?' She offers no explicit description of just war, but her essay testifies to the sort of debates that can and do occur *only* because contemporary political philosophers and theorists share a cluster of concerns and assumptions — 'familiar moral lines' she calls them — including the insistence that justice matters even in the face of military strategy and necessity. With just war thinkers, she insists that the debate about morality cannot be sanitized, stripped of passion and emotion. Jean Bethke Elshtain rehearses the realist and just war positions, showing the ways in which representations of gender (by their presence or absence) have served to constitute these perspectives as theories of politics and social life. She presses just war discourse into service as a wider theory of politics, elaborating what she takes to be its strengths and weaknesses in light of a politics for our difficult times, 'dark times', Hannah Arendt called them. Stephen Toulmin's rethinking of the question of citizen allegiance is prompted by just war's long commitment to limiting obedience to the state. For the citizen is to respond to the state's call to arms only if a war is being conducted in a just manner. Toulmin insists that we cannot do without just war as a starting point but that, in these nuclear times, we need to rethink state sovereignty (which means rethinking the starting point for both realism and just war) and, as well, the nature of our loyalties as citizens, professional men and women, and members of a wider humanity. Toulmin supports multiple loyalties as a check on state demands — this is part of his 'recognition of new realities'. Stanley Hauerwas, one of the most prolific and provocative of contemporary theologians, offers sober reminders of the difficulties which inhere in any call to radical disenthrallment from previous ways of thinking and being. Culturally, Hauerwas insists, we lack a coherent morality to sustain any anti-nuclear position, whether just war or pacifist. Any position needs concrete embodiment 'in the lives and habits of an actual community' and Hauerwas is deeply pessimistic about the ability of contemporary American society (or any advanced Western society) to hold on to a moral position that, with just war, does not locate survival but justice as its highest value. Elshtain's epilogue is an exercise in disillusioned hope that the civic values and imperatives internal to just war are, if not robust, at least still breathing and still prodding us to moral debate on questions of force and the use of force and its relation to justice.

1

The Just War According to St Augustine

PAUL RAMSEY

Whoever wishes to understand the theory of the *justum bellum* (which should perhaps be translated the 'justified war' rather than the 'just war') must understand, in the writings of St Augustine, the similarity between his critique of the pagan personal virtues and his critique of the social justice of any of the nations or empires of this world, in defense of which participation in warfare still could, he believed, be justified in Christian conscience. Augustine is not more severe in his criticism and rejection of the natural personal virtues as only 'splendid vices' than he is in his analysis of the actual nature of that justice which prevails in the common life of a nation. Yet he was the first great formulator of the theory that war might be 'just', which thereafter has mainly directed the course of Western Christian thinking about the problem of war. A brief inspection of Augustine's views will show that most later formulations of the theory of the *justum bellum* and, as a consequence, the verdict that no actual war can meet the conditions of the just-war theory, are radically un-Augustinian. It will show that the political experience and ethical analysis summarized in the so-called just war theory cannot be dealt with all in one lump, as if it were a simple system of moral rules for the classification of cases, subject to no significant historical development, freighted with few ambiguities, there to be accepted or rejected as a single, if ancient or 'classical', formulation of one possible position in Christian ethics, with no significant decisions to be taken *within* this tradition itself.

It is well known that, according to Augustine, the 'four-fold division' of personal virtue (i.e., the cardinal virtues of prudence,

Reprinted with permission from Paul Ramsey, *War and the Christian Conscience. How Shall Modern War Be Conducted Justly?* (The Lily Endowment Research Program in Christianity and Politics, Duke University Press, Durham, N. Carolina, 1961), pp. 15–33.

justice, courage, and temperance) is 'taken from four *forms* of love';[1] and that these dependable structures in human behavior or character 'arise from' a man's loves,[2] as their habitual actualization, in order that the desired end (be it health, wealth, pleasure, or honor) may better be served and more steadily attained. These *ends* Augustine criticized, because, as temporal, they perish and can be lost against the will; and this judgment, in turn, was based on his analysis that all men in their desiring desire not only some good, not even a good higher than all others, but also the permanent enjoyment of it. A man necessarily wills and loves more than he gets in this world. Thou hast made us *toward* Thyself, and our hearts are restless until they rest in Thee. Until it rests in God, something was sought in the desire of the soul, no matter to what it was directed, that was not obtained.

These earthly *loves* Augustine criticized as not only vain but also selfish; and he was equally severe in his criticism of the love wherewith men love whatever they love, no matter how high it may be on some scale or in the order of natures Augustine derived from Neo-Platonism. The height of the value makes no essential difference; and, for all his respect for the typical Roman or Stoic virtues, arising from love of honor and informed by this love, in comparison with the Epicurean 'virtues', Augustine wrote that 'he has the soundest perception who recognizes that even the love of praise is a vice,'[3] and that 'though that glory be not a luxurious woman [i.e., pleasure], it is nevertheless puffed up, and has much vanity in it'.[4] Even when men pursue virtue for its own sake, and, as they say, for no other reward or benefit than virtue itself, still virtue is the form to which their secret love gives the substance: 'For although some suppose that virtues which have a reference only to themselves, and are desired only on their own account, are yet true and genuine virtues, the fact is that even then they are inflated with pride, and are therefore to be reckoned vices rather than virtues.' If Augustine believed that Roman morality was 'less base' than some of the types of character he knew to be cultivated under the sun, this can only mean that he paid it paradoxical tribute as more splendidly vicious than others. 'Where there is no true religion' — bringing the soul to rest in the one good End that eternally endures, and converting, transforming, and redirecting the love wherewith a man loves every good — 'there can be no true virtue'.[5] Upright pagans have the form but not the substance of true virtue. As to this, there can be no distinction among men.

The word 'form' is Augustine's own, but not the word 'substance', in the foregoing statement of his theory of moral virtue. The latter term, and the distinction to follow between the mere form and the real substance of justice, is used, not in the somewhat different sense in which later scholasticism may have used 'form–substance', but to direct attention to that charity which makes virtue virtuous. The heart of the matter of virtue or of justice consists in a matter of the heart. The right inner intention or direction of the will alone 'rightwises' every virtue, regardless of the 'formal' identity there may be between one 'justice' and another 'justice', warranting the use of the same word to point to patterns of behavior, character, or relationships which arise from and are informed by quite different sorts of love.

What Augustine says about social justice and the nature of the state in Book XIX of *The City of God* can best be comprehended by means of this distinction between form and substance. Moreover, his radical critique of such justice as characterizes, has characterized, or ever will characterize, the kingdoms of this world should be held firmly in mind whenever the question arises concerning the theory of a *justum bellum*, of which he was the primary architect. Properly grasped, even more than when improperly grasped, Augustine's views on political justice are apt today to occasion considerable puzzlement in a person who holds idealistic and universalistic conceptions of justice, and consternation in the Christian who may want *real* justice on the side he supports in war and who may have been informed that the theory of a just war is supposed to tell him clearly when this is the case and when not.

Here it is necessary to oppose and reject Ernest Barker's interpretation of St Augustine's political theory, and especially of Book XIX, set forth in his Introduction to the Temple Classics edition of *The City of God*.[6] Barker's key distinction is only a relative one, between 'absolute' and 'relative' righteousness. By the latter he means 'a system of right relations mainly in the legal sphere' or 'a system of right relations reckoning with, and adjusted to, the sinfulness of human nature'.[7] The State has relative justice (relative natural law?); the City of God, absolute justice (absolute natural law?); and the terrene city, absolute unrighteousness.[8] Absolute righteousness goes further than the relative justice of states, but it does not fundamentally challenge this justice. Any flaw there may be in worldly justice is not intrinsically a flaw in the *morality* of it; and, on Barker's showing, love of God would, theoretically, only add to earthly justice a religious dimension. Such an interpretation does not take seriously into account Augustine's belief that there can be no justice, or rendering man his due, unless God is given His due.

In passing, it should be pointed out that Barker makes a similar *donum superadditum* analysis of Augustine's treatment of the personal moral virtues. 'One by one,' he writes, 'St Augustine examines the four cardinal virtues of ancient theory ... and of each in turn he proves that so long as it is a merely moral virtue, without the comfort of faith in God and the corroboration of the hope of eternal life, it must necessarily absent itself from felicity.'[9] Love of God adds 'comfort', 'corroboration', and saving 'felicity' to virtues that are already intrinsically, even if 'merely', moral. Surely Augustine meant and said more than this. Moral virtue without charity not ony 'must necessarily absent itself from felicity'; it also, and primarily, necessarily absents itself from virtuousness and lacks the very essence of virtue.

Barker's eloquent words of tribute to the significance of St Augustine fail, therefore, to communicate the full measure of the tumult and dialectical encounter that was going on in his mind. 'It is the great fascination of *The City of God* (and particularly perhaps of the nineteenth book) that we see the two men ["the antique man of the old classical culture, and the Christian man of the New Gospel"] at grips with one another. This is what makes the work one of the greatest turning points in the history of human destiny: it stands on the confines of two worlds, the classical and the Christian, and it points the way into the Christian'.[10] Or again: 'The nineteenth book particularly illustrates this sentinel attitude.'[11] Augustine is not only a sentinel on the ramparts. He not only points the way into the Christian world. He also attacks, in order to capture and, afterward, to conserve. His critique and rejection of the humanistic autonomy of classical moral achicvement — the substance of its virtue — was most thoroughgoing and severe (as Charles Cochrane has shown), in order that that world might be torn from its foundations, and turn if possible and be converted. The new direction of morality required more of a transformation than an addition, and Augustine's new direction in moral and political analysis proceeds not by distinctions in degree. Given man's citizenship in the City of God, his citizenship elsewhere is not merely relatively inferior; it must be seen as radically deprived of the ethical substance formerly attributed to it before that which is new had come. We may now turn to see confirmation of this Book XIX, *contra* Barker.

Notice first that Barker insists on translating *Justitia* always as 'righteousness' (even though, in the reverse, he notes the fact that the term for righteousness in Plato and in the New Testament was 'received in the Latin' as *Justitia*, with large and sometimes disastrous consequences in the field of theology and of moral philosophy).[12] The idea of 'righteousness' was, for Plato, St Paul, and St Augustine, without much distinction, according to Barker, 'a moral idea (which at its highest seemed to pass into a religious idea) rather than an idea of law'.[13] This means that in the thought of Augustine, Platonic 'righteousness is lifted to a higher plane' rather easily and smoothly. Righteousness simply 'ceases to be a system of right relations between men, based on the idea of social stations, and it becomes a system of right relations between man and God (but also, and consequently, between man and man)'.[14] If righteousness already seemed about to pass over into a religious idea, this higher plane has already been envisioned and in some degree attained. On this interpretations, there would be no mounting of an attack upon the will (or love) that governs, directs, and determines the innermost nature of the systems of justice and relationships within and among the nations.

Consequently, Barker affirms that the State 'has its own "order": it has its own relative "righteousness". It is not a *magnum latrocinium*; for you *cannot* remove righteousness from it and St Augustine only said that kingdoms were great bands of brigands if you remove righteousness.'[15] However, it befalls this interpretation that Augustine also said that you cannot remove justice from a band of brigands! You would have left neither band nor brigands, for there is nothing so clearly contrary to nature as to display no order and no remnant of interrelationships that may be termed 'due', by common consent or habitual acceptance.[16]

Barker affirms not only that states have 'a sort of *Justitia*' of their own, but also that 'the citizens of the heavenly city avail themselves of this *Justitia* in the course of their pilgrimage, so that the State is thus, in its way, a coadjutor of the City of God'.[17] Now, it is significant that this is precisely what Augustine avoids saying, even when he might have done so, in the formal sense of the existing legal system or system of social relationships, not in the sense of substantive justice. One passage that Barker cites says not this, but that the children of God make use of earthly *peace*,[18] and Augustine ordinarily describes this as an '*unjust* peace'.[19] The Heavenly City also uses the 'order' of the world in the course of its pilgrimage. Augustine explicitly says *pax-ordo*, not *justitia*, in this connection. Barker places the term in the text, because what he wants to be able to take out of it is his own scheme of continuous religio-political concepts, e.g.: '*Ordo* is a great word in St Augustine; and *ordo* is closely allied to what I have called a "system of right relations," and that in turn is closely allied to, and indeed identical with, the idea of Righteousness.'[20] Augustine would not have said the relations were 'right'. Instead, he might have said that it is an 'unjust order' as well as an 'unjust peace' that the Heavenly City uses in its pilgrimage. That City does not rescind or destroy, rather it preserves and pursues those orders, *different though they be in different nations*, by which earthly peace, doubtless an unjust peace and a just endurable order, is maintained. It seeks ever 'agreement of human wills in matters pertaining to the mortal nature of man'. The Heavenly City, therefore, preserves, pursues, and uses the forms of justice, different though they may be in different nations, for that is but a necessary part of their *pax-ordo*, and the agreement of human wills about goods that are mortal, in the midst of which it continues on its journey. There is continuity among *pax, ordo,* and justitia in this sense; but a great gulf is fixed between these and either ultimate Righteousness or justice that is the substance of right human relations. Human wills are in themselves divided and sinful wills, and of course the same is the case also in their agreements of will, no matter how inclusive these may be.

In summary, Barker elevates *Justitia* by translating it as 'righteousness'; yet at the same time he continues to regard it as closely associated with the concrete order or system of relations that necessarily exists in any State. This brings about a seemingly smooth Christianization of classical politics. Such an interpretation is incapable of appreciating the passages in which Augustine evacuates the ethical idealism from Graeco—Roman definitions of the commonwealth before and in the course of pointing the way to the Christian world. To Barker, this — the most startling thesis of Book XIX — seems to be only a matter of language, a *tour de force*, or an unwarranted quarrel resulting from purely religious (i.e., non-political, non-moral) preconceptions on Augustine's part. The point here has to do with Cicero's definition of *res publica* as 'an assemblage associated by a common acknowledgment of right (*jus*) and by a community of interests'.[21] Barker comments:

> It is the word Right, or *Jus*, which offends St Augustine. In the Latin usage *Jus* is a legal term; and it signifies simply the body of legal rules which is recognized, and can be enforced, by a human authority. On the basis of this significance of *Jus* there is little in Cicero's definition with which we need quarrel. It might, perhaps, go farther; but it is correct enough so far as it goes. But St Augustine has his own preconceptions; and they made him resolve to quarrel with Cicero's definition. With his mind full of the idea of Righteousness (the Greek

dikaiosune, as it appears in Plato and in St Paul), he twists the sense of *jus*. He identifies *jus* with *justitia*; he identifies *Justitia* with *vera justitia*; and he argues accordingly that 'where there is no true righteousness, there cannot be a union of men associated by a common acknowledgement of Right.'[22]

On the surface, of course, Barker is correct. In Cicero, and else-where in Latin political writings, *jus* signifies simply the body of legal rules recognized and enforced by the State. But when Augustine moves quickly on to the assertion that where there is no true justice (*justitia*) there can be no right (*jus*), more is involved than the mistaken replacement of one word for another. Augustine goes behind the words, behind the system of legal rules, to the common assumption of Graeco—Roman political theory that justice is the ethical substance of a commonwealth. This he gets a grip on; and, therefore, it is a theoretical *argument*, not a mere logomachy, when he contends that 'where there is no true justice there can be no assemblage of men associated by a common acknowledgment of right, and therefore there can be no people ...; and if no people, then no weal of the people' – and therefore "there never was a Roman republic." Whether contained in the term *jus*, or not, there is a real difference between Augustine's and the classical conception of the State; and this difference is at the level of the analysis of the actual justice present in the commonwealth. When Augustine writes that the virtues which a soul or a State seems to possess 'are rather vices than virtues, so long as there is no reference to God in the matter',[23] he is not calling for a mere religious addendum, or for a State that goes further than its existent, intrinsic justice to become a denominationally Christian State. Rather he is making a judgment in political analysis itself, a judgment upon such seeming justice. When, therefore, Barker rejoins that 'this has only been proved on the basis of assumptions about the significance of *Jus* which Cicero would never have admitted,'[24] he may be correct so far as this word alone is concerned; but the challenge to Cicero's assumptions, not about religion, or *jus*, but about secular *justitia*, remains. Incidentally, if Augustine's meaning in himself using *Justitia* (despite its translation as Righteousness) was to signify a system of right legal relations; if, as Barker contends, the word *ordo* is closely allied with such a system of relationships or functions in society, and this in turn is 'closely allied to, and indeed identical with the idea of Righteousness', then one wonders what led him to make the mistake, even verbally,

of objecting at all to Cicero's definition. He did this because
behind *jus* he seemed to discern pretentions to a quality of justice
he could not allow to be the case in any earthly kingdom.

By discarding the definition of a commonwealth which was so
idealistic as to be a logical class without any members, and adopting
another, Augustine reaches the conclusion that Rome, after all,
was a 'people'. If only there is an assemblage of reasonable beings,
and not of beasts, and they are bound together by an agreement as
to the objects of love, it can reasonably be called a people. Thus
Augustine demoralizes *res publica*. For the word 'love' as used
here has no specially laudable denotation or connotation. It simply
means the activity of 'will'. 'An assemblage of reasonable beings
bound together by a common agreement as to the objects of their
love, ... whatever it loves';[25] or, as Barker translates, 'a reasoning
multitude associated by an agreement to pursue in common the
objects which it desires'.[26] Neither a common language nor a
common ethnic origin nor common and universal conceptions of
the norms of justice nor the substance of justice in the common
life constitute a people, but a common will or love. 'This is
practically Cicero's definition', the Carlyles comment, 'but with
the elements of law and justice left out. No more fundamental
difference could well be imagined, although St Augustine seems to
take the matter lightly; for Cicero's whole conception of the State
turns upon the principle that it is a means of attaining and preserving
justice ... It would appear, then, that the political theory of St
Augustine is materially different in several respects from that of St
Ambrose and other Fathers, who represent the ancient tradition
that justice is the essential quality, as it is also the end, of the
State.'[27]

As with justice as a personal virtue, so with social justice.
'When a man does not serve God what justice can we ascribe to
him ...? And if there is no justice in such an individual, certainly
there can be none in a community of such persons.'[28] Indeed,
what justice can be ascribed to such communities? The forms of
justice, lacking the inner rectitude that makes justice just or relationships right among men.

Then should be kept clearly in mind the justice of which Augustine
was speaking when he wrote of wars in which Christian engagement
was justified.

How many great wars, how much slaughter and bloodshed,
have provided this unity [of the imperial city]! And though
those are past, the end of these miseries has not yet come.

For though there have never been wanting, nor are yet wanting, hostile nations beyond the empire, against whom wars have been and are waged, yet, supposing there were no such nations, the very extent of the empire itself has produced wars of a more obnoxious description – social and civil wars – and with these the whole race has been agitated, either by the actual conflict or fear of a renewed outbreak. If I attempted to give an adequate description of these manifold disasters, these stern and lasting necessities, though I am quite unequal to the task, what limit could I set? But, say they, the wise man will wage just wars. As if he would not all the rather lament the necessity of just wars, if he remembers that he is a man; for if they were not just he would not wage them, and would therefore be delivered from all wars. [For it is the wrongdoing of the opposing party which compels the wise man to wage just wars; and this wrongdoing, even though it give rise to no war, would still be matter of grief to man because it is man's wrong-doing.] Let every one, then, who thinks with pain on all these great evils, so horrible, so ruthless, acknowledge that this is misery. And if any one either endures or thinks of them without mental pain, this is a more miserable plight still, for he thinks himself happy because he has lost human feeling.[29]

Notice that Augustine writes of 'the wrong-doing of the opposing party which compels the wise man to wage just wars,' as incidental to his stress upon the mental pain this misery should cause every man to feel. It is not made incidental to justifying the right side specifically in terms of universal standards of justice. The same is true of his statement that 'even when we wage just war, our adversaries must be sinning': this is prefatory to pointing to the fact that 'every victory, even though gained by wicked men, is a result of the first judgment of God, who humbles the vanquished either for the sake of removing or punishing their sins.'[30] It is a lively sense of man's common plight in wrongdoing and of the judgment of God that overarches the justified war, and not – except perhaps as an incidental implication of what Augustine says – a sense of or clarity about the universal ethical standards that are to be applied. On the face of it, therefore, the statement of the Calhoun Commission (in the course of outlining 'three main attitudes toward participation in war which developed in the life of the Christian Church': pacifism, the just war, and the holy war) that 'the just war was carefully defined, in such terms that only one side could be regarded as fighting justly',[31] cannot certainly be read back as far in this tradition as Augustine's first statement of it.

If Augustine believed that there is always only one side that can be regarded as fighting justly in the wars in which a Christian will find himself responsibly engaged, he should not have believed this. For his own analysis of the *pax-ordo*-formal *justitia* or *jus* of nations gives no ground for any such conclusion in every case, perhaps not in most cases. Justice is the form of men's loves; in the State it is the form of that love or agreement to pursue in common the objects which a 'people' desire. Moreover, social justice arises from a common agreement as to the objects of their love (will); and, since the agreement would break down and the people become a mere multitude without minimum or greater degrees of participation in the life of a nation, accepted schemes of justice serve to strengthen that common will or love which constitutes *res publica*. The Christian has reason to endeavor to strengthen 'the combination of men's wills to attain the things which are helpful to this life'. The 'heavenly city, while it sojourns on earth . . ., not scrupling about diversities in the manners, laws, and institutions whereby earthly peace is secured and maintained, but recognizing that, however various these are, they all tend to one and the same end of earthly peace . . . [is] so far from rescinding and abolishing these diversities, that it even preserves and adopts them . . . Even the heavenly city, therefore, while in its state of pilgrimage, avails itself of the peace of earth, and . . . desires and maintains a common agreement among men regarding the acquisition of the necessities of life . . .'[32] Thus, a Christian in this life finds his own life and will bound up inextricably with such a common agreement among men as to the objects of their political purposes, and he is bound to foster the combination of men's wills to attain the things which are helpful to this life. Doubtless he seeks not only to preserve but also to enlarge such agreements of will and the scope of peaceful orders on this earth. But is it not likely that there will be occasions on which the love or will informing secular justice cannot be extended into greater combinations, that appeal must then be made the *ultima ratio* of war, and that the existing justice Augustine has in mind when speaking of the 'just' war may tragically be on both sides? In any case, all Augustine's language about the purpose that lies at the root of the State, and his severe castigation of the resulting justice which still must be what justifies warfare, brings us remarkably close to that remarkable statement in the best book about 'limited warfare' that has appeared in recent years, to the effect that 'nations might better renounce the use of war as an instrument of *anything but* national policy'.[33]

In elevating a better peace as one criterion of the just war (we may also say the limited war), Augustine was not unaware that there slips into the national policy which constitutes the multitude a people, an attitude according to which 'even those whom they make war against they wish to make their own, and impose on them the laws of their peace'.[34] And so the 'just' war which seeks peace, in the sense of a larger and better and more stable agreement of wills, has its own intrinsic limits which it may overstep. Nations may seek to extend *pax-ordo* by mere compulsion, and not by agreement of wills. Yet Augustine could not have supposed that warfare is justified only on the part of the side which is driven by none of the desire to impose the laws of its own peace. Such a supposition would be contrary to his basic analysis of the reality of States, and of the love basic to their nature. Whether of individuals or of communities of individuals who are agreed to be a people, the love for temporal goods and for those material things necessary for individual or collective life must of necessity be a love in which *men must fear to have colleagues*. All men's loves, for any other good than the *bonum summum et commune*, is of its nature fratricidal. That is why Cain, who killed his brother, is the founder of the earthly city. If it be said, quite correctly, that the earthly city is an 'ideal negation' and that actual societies are not necessarily like that, then we must remember Remus and point to Romulus, who was the founder of Rome. The truth is that, according to Augustine, fratricidal love and brotherly love based on love of God are always commingled in human history. There is no heart, no people, and no public policy so redeemed or so clearly contrary to nature as to be without both. Communities are built over fratricidal love by men with divided hearts. We must not only say that, according to the doctrine of the divided will, Augustine was unable to will entirely, and with a whole heart, to love God, because at the same moment he nilled this for the will (or love) of his 'ancient mistresses' (the adjective I understand to indicate the span of time that had elapsed, not to characterize his mistresses when he had them).[35] We must also say that he was equally unable to will entirely to love his mistresses with a whole heart, because of the foundation of the love of God that was laid in him. Them he also nilled for the love of God, for God had made him for himself.[36] The same complex analysis must be given of the love or will in common which makes a people. It, too, cannot will any finite thing entirely. Something is sought in every human desire, no matter to what it is directed, that is not obtained. That is the created good, and at the same time the misdirected evil of it; for men and States necessarily will and love more than they get in this world. They desire not only some good, or even a good higher that all others, but also the permanent enjoyment of it. An unrectified *nisus* toward the eternal disturbs every people's purpose: that is why they see in their good *the* Good, in the laws of their peace the conditions of universal peace, and are resolved that this too shall not pass away. Yet Augustine, who saw all this so clearly, not as an aloof spectator of the human scene or of the rise and fall of empires but as one who was content to dwell in the midst of this since God had placed him there, was almost the first thinker known in our literature to justify Christian participation in wars. The just war theory cannot have meant for him the presence of justice (i.e., the temporary order and form of these divided loves) on one side, its absence on the other.

These conclusions, then, have been demonstrated from a review of St Augustine's views of political justice and the *justum bellum*. At least at the outset, the just war theory did not rest upon the supposition that men possess a general competence to discriminate with certainty between social orders at large by means of clear, universal principles of justice, so as to be able to declare (without sin's affecting one's judgment of his own nation's cause) one side or social system to be just and the others unjust. This was not the premise by which Augustine came to a confident enough judgment as to a Christian's responsibility in justifiable (if not unambiguously just) war. My contention is that Christian ethics may attribute to ordinary men, and to their political leaders, a capacity to know more clearly and certainly the moral limits pertaining to the armed action a man or a nation is about to engage in, than they are likely to know enough to compare unerringly the over-all justice of regimes and nations. There is still more reason to believe that men know something of moral significance about proper conduct than to believe that they are able to count up all the remote effects of their actions, so as to measure their actions by the standards of any consequentialist system of ethics.

Two main alterations of the just war doctrine took place between Augustine and Aquinas. First, a shift from voluntarism to rationalism in understanding the nature of political community, and therefore an increasing emphasis upon the natural-law concept of justice in analysis of the cause that justifies participation in war. This is what is usually meant by the doctrine of the just war. I shall reject this, in the belief that Augustine was more correct and realistic in believing people to be bound together more by agreement of will and purpose than by agreement in their general conceptions of justice. Secondly, rules for the right *conduct* of war were drawn up, particularly for the protection of non-combatants. This is usually dismissed as the weakest part of the traditional theory of the just war. I propose, however, that we seriously reconsider this question of the just conduct of war. For, it may well be the case that natural reason falters in attempting to make large comparison of the justice inherent in great regimes in conflict but is quite competent to deliver verdict upon a specific action that is proposed in warfare. It is striking that Christian theories of justified war in the past have directed attention at least as much to the conduct as to the ultimate and large-scale consequences of military action ...

NOTES

1 'On the Morals of the Catholic Church', (italics added) xv. Except where otherwise indicated, citations to the works of St Augustine are from *Basic Writings of Saint Augustine*, ed. Whitney J. Oates. (Two vols.; New York: Random House, 1948).
2 Ibid., xxv.
3 *The City of God*, V, 13.
4 Ibid., V, 20.
5 Ibid., XIX, 25.
6 Trans. John Healey. (one volume ed.; London: Dent; New York: E. P. Dutton, 1931, 1934, 1940).
7 Ibid., p. xxvi. The objection to this definition of the justice of nations is that it states only that the sinfulness of human nature is reckoned with and adjusted to. There is no suggestion that this 'system of right relations' itself gives form to unrectified love and participates in the sin it represses.
8 'The earthly city, like the heavenly city, is an ideal conception; or rather, and to speak more exactly, it may be called the ideal negation, or antithesis, of the ideal ... The actual State, as it really exists, is something different. It is not absolutely unrighteous. On the contrary, it has a sort of Justitia of its own ...' Ibid., p. xxv. This is not to be denied. But the question is whether this sort of justice ought properly to be called 'relative', or merely formal.
9 Ibid., pp. xxv–xxvi.
10 Ibid., p. iv.
11 Ibid., p. xxxiii.
12 Ibid., pp. xx–xxi.
13 Ibid., p. xxi.
14 Ibid., p. xxiii.

15 Ibid., p. xxxviii.
16 The same point may be stated in terms of 'peace'. When discussing peace as the end of 'just' wars, Augustine clinches his point by saying, 'Even robbers take care to maintain peace with their comrades'. An earthly kingdom, while it abhors 'the just peace of God and loves its own unjust peace', 'cannot help loving peace of one kind or other. For there is no vice so clean contrary to nature that it obliterates the faintest traces of nature' (XIX, 12). 'There may be peace without war, but there cannot be war without some kind of peace, because war supposes the existence of some nature, to wage it, and these natures cannot exist without peace of one kind or other' (XIX, 13, [bold] italics added).
17 Barker's *Introduction*, p. xxv.
18 'Therefore the heavenly city rescinds and destroys none of those things by which earthly peace is attained or maintained: rather it preserves and pursues that which, different though it be in different nations, is yet directed to the one and selfsame end of earthly peace ... Therefore, again, the heavenly city uses earthly peace in its pilgrimage: it preserves and seeks the agreement of human wills in matters pertaining to the mortal nature of man ...' *The City of God*, XIX, 17; quoted by Barker, p. xxvii. See also XIX, 26.
19 Ibid., XIX, 12.
20 Barker's *Introduction*, p. xxiii.
21 *The City of God*, XIX, 21.
22 Barker's *Introduction*, p. xlvii.
23 *The City of God*, XIX, 25.
24 Barker's *Introduction*, p. xlviii.
25 *The City of God*, XIX, 24.
26 Barker's *Introduction*, p. xlix. Yet it was Augustine who first fully formulated the 'justice' of Christian participation in war to preserve earthly pax-ordo! One may compare this with the way C. C. Morrison, in a remarkable series of editorials in the *Christian Century*, removed clear judgments of greater justice from among the grounds for a Christian's positive involvement in his nation's cause in World War II (*The Christian and the War*, Willett, Clark & Co., 1942); and with Reinhold Niebuhr's wonderfully ironic and self-analytic remark about the occasion he has to thank God for placing him on the just side in three years in one lifetime.
27 R. W. Carlyle and A. J. Carlyle: *A History of Medieval Political Theory in the West* (Edinburgh and London: W. Blackwood & Sons, 1903–36), 1, 166, 170.
28 *The City of God*, XIX, 21.
29 Ibid., XIX, 7.
30 Ibid., XIX, 15.
31 'The Relation of the Church to the War in Light of the Christian Faith', *Social Action*, Dec. 1944, p. 61.

32 *The City of God*, XIX, 17.
33 Robert Osgood: *Limited War: The Challenge to American Strategy* (Chicago: The University of Chicago Press, 1957), p. 21.
34 *The City of God*, XIX, 12.
35 *The Confessions*, VIII, 26.
36 Ibid., VIII, 20−22.

2

Temperamenta Belli: Can War be Controlled?

MICHAEL HOWARD

The assumption is very generally made that control and restraint are alien to the very nature of war. Clausewitz opened his *On War* with a statement to this effect, 'War' he wrote, 'is an act of force to compel our enemy to do our will ... Attached to force are certain self-imposed, imperceptible limitations hardly worth mentioning, known as international law and custom, but they scarcely weaken it ... To introduce the principle of moderation into the theory of war itself would always lead to logical absurdity.'[1]

Much depends on the meaning one attaches to such terms as 'limitation', 'control', 'restraint', and 'moderation'. But the proposition that war is in its essence 'uncontrollable' is an untenable one, as Clausewitz himself recognized elsewhere in his text.[2] War, at least as the term has been understood in western societies since the Middle Ages, is not the condition of generalized and random violence pictured by Thomas Hobbes as 'the state of nature'. It is on the contrary a highly social activity – an activity indeed which demands from the groups which engage in it a unique intensity of societal organization and control. It involves the reciprocal use of organized force between two or more social groups, directed according to an overall plan or series of plans for the achievement of a political object. Rousseau was surely right when he stated, in contradiction to Hobbes, that war without social organization is inconceivable; that it is only as a member of a state, or comparable social organism, that man makes war.[3] Indeed the requirement for social control imposed by the necessities of war has normally been a major element, if not *the* major element, in the development of state structures.

Reprinted with permission from Michael Howard (ed.) *Restraints on War: Studies in the Limitation of Armed Conflict* (Oxford University Press, 1979), pp. 1–15.

All this predicates a distinction between 'war' on the one hand and riot, piracy, brigandage, generalized insurrection and random violence on the other. The wars of which we speak consist of the purposive and instrumental use of force by legitimized authorities. It is a discrete condition with a certain coherent and orderly predictability of its own. Members of belligerent armed forces normally operate according to orders transmitted through a highly structured hierarchy. They may legitimately kill members of opposing armed forces in battle unless the latter explicitly surrender, and there is a distinct risk that they will kill them even then. The persons and property of civilians in zones of military operations or within reach of military projectiles are at risk even if they are totally non-combatant. In areas occupied by military forces engaged in combat civilians are subject to the legal authority of those forces, whether they be friendly or hostile. Enemy nationals in a country at war are likely to be put under severe constraints. None of this may be agreeable, but it is all highly *predictable*, and comes about as the result of conscious decision by effective authorities.

The state of war indeed involves at every level of government and society the imposition of authoritative control. Governments, in so far as they are able, will control the production, allocation, and utilization of resources, including human resources. Individual freedom of movement, of expression, of communication and of consumption will be controlled in 'the national interest'. The military authorities will use the resources at their disposal to achieve an objective according to a planned strategy implemented through a coherent and authoritative hierarchy which possesses exceptional sanctions for the enforcement of obedience. One still occasionally comes across the old-fashioned liberal stereotype of the soldier as a stupid and brutal *Untermensch* dedicated to random violence. Such characters can indeed be found in most armies, but equally most armies go to great lengths to discipline and if possible eliminate them. In reality the military, at least in 'advanced' countries, constitute highly motivated, well organized and cohesive groups, educated, technologically sophisticated, with a professional obsession with order, discipline, and channels of command. Even in the least developed societies they are likely to exhibit these traits to a greater degree than the rest of the population.[4]

The prime characteristic of the military is not that they use violence, nor even that they use violence legitimized by virtue of their function as instruments of the state. It is that they use that violence with great *deliberation*. Such violence, purposeful, deliberate, and legitimized is normally known as *force*, and the use of force between states is what we mean by war. War consists of such deliberate, controlled, and purposeful acts of force combined and harmonized to attain what are ultimately political objectives. That such acts may be horrifying in their consequences goes without saying. Their object is quite precisely the infliction of destruction, suffering, and death, 'the trial of moral and physical forces', to quote Clausewitz again, 'through the medium of the latter'.[5] But strategy consists in determining how, where, and upon whom that destruction is to be inflicted. Such destruction can be random, as was German and British 'area' bombing in 1940–3, for lack of technical means to make it precise. It can also be random as the result of a deliberate decision, as when in seventeenth- and eighteenth-century warfare the territory of an opponent was ravaged, or in more recent conflicts hostages were shot or towns burned by occupation forces in retaliation for *franc tireur* activity; or, in the contemporary world, urban guerrillas detonate bombs in cities to demonstrate their ubiquity and effectiveness. Such decisions and the consequences which flow from them normally are the result of deliberate choice and explicit orders, and they require for their implementation, even in the case of guerrilla activities, a highly articulated structure of control. When random violence is the result of the breakdown of such control, as in the notorious My Lai massacre of Vietnamese civilians by US forces in 1969, when troops lapse from disciplined and discriminating use of force into purposeless and indiscriminate violence, the result is as repugnant to military professionalism as it is to transcendent ethical values.[6]

Military activity thus carries an intrinsic imperative towards control; an imperative derived from the need to maintain order and discipline, to conserve both moral and material forces and ensure that these are always responsive to direction. These military criteria however will not necessarily coincide with the dictates of humanity. For example, the military case against area bombing would be, not that it was inhumane, but that it was ineffective in achieving its objective of demoralizing the civilian population and reducing war production; that it was psychologically 'counterproductive' and materially wasteful.[7] General William T. Sherman's very comparable strategy in 1864 however, no less ferociously indiscriminate in the destruction it inflicted on the Confederacy, could by the same criteria be adjudged a military success: it did effectively reduce the civil population of the Confederacy to a state of near-despair. The military principle of 'economy of force' may sometimes conveniently coincide with the dictates of transcendent moral values, but there is little historical justification for assuming that this will always be the case.

To control and limit the conduct of war is thus not inherently impossible; indeed without controls and limitations war cannot be conducted at all. The difficulty lies in introducing and maintaining controls and limits derived from criteria other than those inherent in sound strategy and the requirement for 'good order and military discipline'. Such criteria can normally be grouped under two heads. There are the categorical imperatives derived from the general value-systems of the culture concerned; and there are the prudential considerations which demand that, to put it at its lowest, the costs of war do not in the long run outweigh its benefits.

The first of these criteria dominated thinking about war during the era of ecclesiastical dominance which lasted in Europe until the sixteenth century, as clerical apologists, attempting to accommodate the necessities of warfare to the ethical imperatives of the Christian religion, refined the concept of 'the just war'. The second became dominant from the seventeenth to the nineteenth centuries, the age of Grotius; when it was assumed, in the words of Montesquieu, that 'the law of nations is naturally founded on this principle, that different nations ought in time of peace to do one another all the good they can, and in time of war as little injury as possible without prejudicing their real interests.[8] This second approach concentrated on what was and was not permissible in wars between states without concerning itself about the rights and wrongs of any particular war. The first, without ignoring this question of *jus in bello*, was primarily concerned with *jus ad bello* — the justice or injustice of the cause for which one fought. And this concern was to reappear in a yet stronger form in the wars of 'national self-determination' or 'national liberation' of the nineteenth and twentieth centuries.

During this period, war in western societies passed, broadly speaking, through three phases.[9] From about the eleventh century war ceased to be the struggle for physical survival it had been during the 'barbarian' invasions and became gradually a ritualized conflict within a warrior culture, partly agonistic, partly juristic. Wars were agonistic in so far as they were extensions of competitive games and tournaments, juristic in so far as they were an appeal to a 'higher tribunal' where no legal remedy was available. In both capacities highly formalized 'rules of war' were appropriate and indeed necessary. But in general the restraints observed in warfare within Christendom did not apply in the 'just wars' which Christians fought to defend, to purify, or to extend their faith. To submit to restraints which prejudiced ones chances of victory when fighting in a righteous cause, to accept the concept of *jus in bello* when one had an unquestionable *jus ad bellum*, was a paradox which few warring communities, then or since, found it easy to accept.

The 'Grotian' period, during which jurists explicitly abjured any interest in the cause of a conflict and concerned themselves only with its conduct, stretched approximately from the Peace of Westphalia in 1648 to the Hague Conferences on the eve of the First World War, and was the golden age of the *jus in bello*, of formal, positive constraints on the conduct of war. But such behaviour postulated a very stable structure of society and a highly homogeneous culture shared to an equal degree by all its members. It required on the part of governments an overriding concern for the maintenance of social and political stability, and a capacity to maintain that stability within their own domestic systems. Since war was always an instrument of state policy, as Clausewitz discerned, it would be 'limited' in so far as that policy was limited; but once a state decided to pursue a policy of revolution and conquest and was no longer prepared to be bound by established norms, it would fight 'absolute' and unconstrained war. No restraints would be imposed other than those arising out of the nature of war itself.[10]

Such, unfortunately, was the way in which warfare has developed in the third of our periods, the twentieth century, when the concept of 'the just war' has re-emerged with renewed vehemence; whether in the assertion of national identities, or of ideological absolutes, or a combination of the two. Such conflicts of their nature tend to be 'zero-sum games' in which each side considers itself to be fighting for the preservation of all its cultural values, for its very survival, against an alien and irreconcilable adversary. Nor are such perceptions necessarily false. In the Second World War Hitler attacked both Poland and the Soviet Union with the intention of destroying their societies and reconstructing them as German colonies.[11] As an outcome of that war both German and Japanese cultural values were completely transformed by their victorious enemies. So, as an outcome of the thirty-years' war in South-East Asia, have been the cultural values of the societies of Cambodia and Vietnam. There is little reason to expect anything different as the result of a comparable conflict in Southern Africa. Wars today can be irreversible in their consequences. There is thus little inclination to conduct them with restraint.

A strong case can indeed be made for the argument that if war *can* be limited, if the belligerents can be reasonable enough to accept extraneous limitations on its conduct and regard the enemy almost as a *frère adversaire*, they should be reasonable enough to avoid fighting altogether. This sentiment became widespread towards the end of the eighteenth century: a reaction against the formal and artificial constraints of European warfare which simply provided a life-style for a parasitic warrior-aristocracy, a growing feeling that one should not fight at all except in extreme situations, and then do so with no holds barred. This was the view that Tolstoy put into the mouth of Prince Andrei on the eve of the Battle of Borodino in *War and Peace*

> We have been playing at war that's what's vile! We play at magnanimity and all the rest of it ... if there was none of this magnanimity business in warfare, we should never go to war, except for something worth facing certain death for, as now ... War is not a polite recreation but, the vilest thing in life, and we ought to understand that and not play at war. Our attitude towards the fearful necessity of war ought to be stern and serious. It boils down to this: we should have done with humbug and let war be war and not a game.[12]

Agreed limitations on warfare imply rational understandings with an enemy who, if he can be reasoned with, should not be an enemy. 'Laws of war', *jus in bello*, do imply a rather sophisticated warrior culture in which adversaries are conscious of an overriding common interest in preserving the rules of the game; and it may be precisely this kind of aristocratic society that a war is being fought to destroy.

In any case, two developments over the past hundred years have combined to introduce into wars, at least between industrialized states, an increasing element of *totality*. The first of these has been the development of mass democracy, the erosion of those aristocratic élites whose kinship, cultural if not actual, across national boundaries had strengthened the kind of constraints to which Andrei objected and whose chivalric concepts of honour could occasionally be found mitigating the ruthlessness of the First and even the Second World War.[13] The growth of mass societies and the possibility of government control of communications made total alienation between belligerent societies, their mutual perceptions as figures of total evil, all too easy. The fundamental tragedy of the First World War was that what was to a very large extent an old-style 'war of policy' to readjust the balance of power in Europe, another War of Austrian Succession, became seen, because of mass participation and mass propaganda, as a total war between incompatible and mutually exclusive cultures, when in fact it need have been nothing of the kind.

Linked with this development in society has been the simultaneous development in technology which created new modes of destruction of an indiscriminate kind: the submarine at sea, which could not possibly operate within the old restrictions of Prize Law and, more significant still, air power in its earlier and cruder manifestations. Finally with the advent of thermonuclear weapons total war threatens total destruction on a scale incompatible with any criterion either of political calculation or of military necessity. For the first time the Clausewitzian analysis is put in question: nuclear war, if it came, could be total, not because of the political objectives of the belligerents, but because of the military tools and their disposal. Western strategists plan for the mass destruction of Soviet cities, and vice versa, not because their political masters have any serious political motive for extirpating the societies of their adversaries, but because in a grotesque inversion of logic the means now dictate the ends. Both on moral and on prudential grounds therefore it has seemed increasingly clear, as the twentieth century has pursued its course, that war should not simply be limited; it should be abolished, outlawed.

This was something new. The existence of war was until the nineteenth century accepted as inevitable by everyone except a few Christian sects. The problem was to determine the limitations upon its conduct. Aquinas and others in the Middle Ages had defined the nature of a 'just war': a war waged by a legitimate authority, for a cause in itself just, to make reparation for an injury or to restore what had been wrongly seized, and with the intention of advancing good and avoiding evil. To this sixteenth-century jurists like Suarez and Vitoria added prudential considerations. There should be a reasonable prospect of victory. Every attempt should have been made to reconcile the differences by peaceful means. No direct attack should be made against non-combatants. The amount of force used should not be disproportionate to the end to be achieved.[14] By the time of Grotius more prudential considerations began, as we have seen, to predominate. By the eighteenth century the concept of the 'just war' had disappeared. 'War waged in its right form must be ragarded as just on both sides' stated the great Swiss jurist Eméric Vattel. This was the heyday of 'limited war'; and as the technical developments of the nineteenth century widened the destructive scope of warfare and made such limits seem ever more difficult to maintain, new conventions had to be drawn up (The Declaration of Paris of 1856, the Geneva Convention of 1864, the Declaration of Brussels of 1874, the Hague Conventions of 1899 and 1907) in an attempt to rescue and reassert them.

Even during this era of 'limited wars', however, a significant cleavage persisted between the attitude of continental and of British jurists. From the eighteenth century onwards continental jurists accepted the distinction made by Rousseau, that war is a conflict not between individuals but between *states*, and assumed that individuals took part in it only in so far as they voluntarily abandoned their private status and, by taking up arms, became the agents of the state. This meant that not only the lives and the property of private individuals, so far as possible, should be protected from belligerent acts, but their economic activities as well; which effectively meant their trade. This doctrine, of course, long antedated Rousseau. Its great protagonist was Hugo Grotius himself[15], and its most stubborn champions were the Dutch; whose capacity to carry on their struggle for independence in the sixteenth and seventeenth centuries depended entirely on their freedom to trade, including freedom to trade with their enemies. But for the British during the same period blockade of commerce became a major weapon of war; blockade which, however narrowly defined, inflicted inevitable and deliberate hardship upon enemy civilians. So from John Selden onwards[16] British jurists argued that the economic activities of civilians, in so far as they made possible the belligerent acts of governments, were a perfectly legitimate target for military activity. The British in fact looked beyond the immediate conflict of armed forces to the war-fighting capabilities of the states which sustained them, and took a consistently hard line over such matters as the definition of contraband, the rights of neutrals, and the right of search.[17]

It was to be the British doctrine that prevailed. As the nineteenth century progressed, virtually every economic, intellectual, and political development in Europe eroded the distinction between 'society' and 'state'. Even if private individuals did not become formal 'agents of the state' through compulsory military service, the extension of political and emotional participation in national affairs left ever fewer areas of pure 'privacy'. Nineteenth-century conflicts such as the American Civil War and the Franco-Prussian War gave a foretaste of the lesson of the First World War: that no military victories, however spectacular, were likely to be decisive so long as civil society retained the will and the capacity to carry on the war. Paradoxically, at the time when the Geneva and the Hague Conventions were mitigating the horrors of the battlefield to the extent almost of giving the military a privileged status, the scope of armed conflict was being inexorably extended far beyond that battlefield. The lessons of the First World War were summed up in a paper which the British Naval Staff presented in 1921 to the Committee of Imperial Defence: 'Nothing can be clearer than the fact that modern war resolves itself into an attempt to throttle the national life. Waged by the whole power of the nation, its ultimate object is to bring pressure on the mass of the enemy people, distressing them by every possible means, so as to compel the enemy's government to submit to terms.[18]

But if the objective of military effort was *not* the opposing armed forces but 'the mass of the enemy people', the most direct and economical way of deploying that effort was surely to strike directly at that mass, and air forces, particularly the Royal Air Force, justified their claims to institutional independence by their capacity to do just that. There was some talk of 'surgical strikes' against arms factories and centres of government, but a generation was to pass before technology made this practicable, and even those who advocated such strikes regarded the 'morale' of the enemy working population to be a entirely legitimate objective.[19]
. . .

It was very largely this growing destructiveness of war, the damage mutually inflicted by armed forces even before the advent of air power placed the whole social structure in hazard, the led governments to give support, after 1918, to the movement to 'outlaw' war itself and to create, not a *jus ad bellum*, but a *jus contra bellum*. In the Covenant of the League of Nations, in the Pact of Paris (the Kellogg−Briand Pact) of 1928, and in the United Nations Charter, the initiation of war for any purpose was condemned. The signatories of the Kellogg−Briand Pact 'condemn [ed] recourse to war for the solution of international controversies and re-nounce[d] it as an instrument of national policy in their relations with one another.[20] The creation by this Pact of a *jus contra bellum* was made one of the bases for the charges levelled against the defendants before the International Military Tribunal at Nuremberg in 1946 for 'crimes against peace', as the Hague and Geneva Conventions were made the basis of the charges of 'war crimes'. An entirely new category of law had to be created to encompass their 'crimes against humanity'.[21] It is interesting in this context to note that the United Nations Charter avoids refe-rence to the term 'war' altogether. It refers only to 'acts of aggress-ion', 'breaches of the peace' and 'threats to peace'; while all signatories, by Article 2 para. 4, pledged themselves to 'refrain in their international relations from the threat or use of force against the territorial integrity or political independence of any state.'[22]

Having abolished war, it might be considered paradoxical, not to say pessimistic, to continue to make regulations for controlling it. This thought clearly crossed the collective mind of the International Law Commission of the United Nations in 1949 when it came to consider the codification of the Laws of War. 'It was considered that, if the Commission, at the very beginning of its work, were to undertake this study, public opinion might interpret its action as showing lack of confidence in the efficiency of the means at the disposal of the United Nations for maintaining peace.[23] But as Professor Hersch Lauterpacht drily observed, 'The phenomenon of war does not fully admit of treatment in accordance with the canons of logic. Banished as a legal institution, war now remains an *event*, calling for legal regulation for the sake of humanity and the dignity of man'.[24] So in 1949 a further Geneva Convention was signed, extending to civilians the rights which previous conventions had recognized as inhering in members of the armed forces with respect to humane treatment at the hands of belligerents.

... But perhaps of yet greater significance in the nuclear age have been the *prudential* attempts to impose restraints on conflict; attempts initiated not so much from humanitarian concern with the belligerents themselves, whether military or civilian, as out of the realization that technology has now given mankind the capacity quite literally to destroy itself. Little could be done to mitigate the totality of wars when that totality was caused by the deliberate policy of the belligerents. But if destructiveness is the consequence not of the object aimed at but of the means employed, then military and moral restraints are not necessarily incompatible. The concept of 'limited war' between advanced industrial communities becomes not simply possible but necessary, if the use of force is to serve any political object; including that of defending one's own territory or that of one's allies. ... Such restraints can no longer be regarded as an intrusion from the moral into the military sphere. They belong to the category of those purely military constraints considered at the beginning of this chapter, in the absence of which war becomes mere indiscriminate and inconclusive violence.

During the quarter of a century which has passed since strategic analysts began to refine the concept of 'limited war', the world has mercifully been spared the experience of major conflicts between industrialized states. It has however witnessed widespread conflicts of a different kind; struggles subsumed under the title of 'wars of national liberation', usually fought by indigenous groups against European colonial authorities or, as in Southern Africa, regimes asserting a racial hegemony. These groups seldom had any status in international law: they were rebels against the jurisdiction of governments enjoying full state sovereignty. Nevertheless at the International Conference on Human Rights held in Tehran in 1968 a resolution was passed demanding that persons struggling against 'racist or colonial regimes' should be protected against 'inhuman or brutal treatment and treated as prisoners of war': that 'freedom fighters', in fact, should be afforded the protection of international law.[25] A further conference of experts was convened in Geneva to implement this resolution, which in 1977 agreed on a Convention . . .

Such a demand of course goes to the root of the international system itself. There has been a long history concerning the award of belligerent status to insurgent forces in civil war. There has been . . . an equally historic and acrimonious controversy over the rights and duties of civilians taking up arms against an invader. But the principle that only 'legitimate authorities', states and their agents, have the right to make war and to claim recognition and protection in war, has been the basis of the whole system of rational, controllable, inter-state conflict. Naturally such a system is biased in favour of the *status quo* and places independent, non-state actors at a considerable disadvantage. But it is easy to forget what an enormous advance was made in the direction of a just, peaceable and orderly society when the chaotic permissiveness of violence in fourteenth- and fifteenth-century Europe was codified and limited, over the centuries, into orderly relations between 'perfect states'. The problem is to extend the traditional system to encompass and humanize this new kind of conflict. But it can be done only if the objectives of both sides are moderate and compatible. No amount of legal draftsmanship can prevent a quest for total victory from leading to total war.

War, as we said at the beginning, involves inherent constraints. It is carried out by men making conscious choices and obedient to hierarchical commands. Orders can be given to spare as well as to destroy. Whatever the objective aimed at or the weapons used, the plea of military necessity has to be brought into focus with two other requirements, arising from the nature of man as a moral and as a social being. The first imposes an ethical rule: one does not cease to be a moral being when one takes up arms, even if required by military necessity to commit immoral acts. There are other tribunals to which one may be called to account. And the second imposes a prudential rule: one should not behave to one's adversary in such a way as to make subsequent reconciliation impossible. War is instrumental, not elemental: its only legitimate object is a better peace.

NOTES

1   Carl von Clausewitz, *On War* (Princeton, 1977). p. 75.
2   War is simply the continuation of political intercourse . . . war cannot be divorced from political life; and whenever this occurs in our thinking about war, the many links that connect the two elements are destroyed and we are left with something pointless and devoid of sense.' Ibid., p. 605.
3   J.-J. Rousseau, *The State of War*. Reprinted in M. G. Forsyth *et al.* (eds.), *The Theory of International Relations* (London, 1970), p. 167.
4   See Stanislav Andreski, *Military Organization and Society* (London, 1954) and Gavin Kennedy, *The Military in the Third World* (London, 1974), *passion*.
5   Clausewitz, *On War*, p. 127.
6   A distinction must be made in the case of siege-warfare, when cities were quite deliberately 'put to the sack', involving indiscriminate massacre, looting and rapine, if they refused summonses to surrender *en regle*.
7   Against this, its protagonists reasonably argue that it threw the German Air Force on to the defensive and enabled allied air forces to join command of the air over the battlefields in 1942–5, See Noble Frankland, *The Bombing Offensive Against Germany: Outlines and Perspective* (London, 1965) for a balanced discussion.
8   Montesquieu, *The Spirit of the Laws* (New York, 1940), p. 5.
9   A similar but not identical tripartite division is to be found in Robert E. Osgood and Robert W. Tucker, *Force, Order and Justice* (Baltimore, Md., 1967). For an extended treatment see Michael Howard, *War in European History* (Oxford, 1976).
10 Clausewitz, *On War*, p. 606.
11 Norman Rich, *Hitler's War Aims: the Establishment of the New Order* (London, 1974).
12 Leo Tolstoy, *War and Peace* (Harmondsworth, 1957), p. 921.
13 For a radical attack on such constraints see Thorstein Veblen, *An Inquiry into the Nature of Peace* (New York, 2nd edn., 1919).
14 There is a brief and useful summary in Sydney D. Bailey, *Prohibitions and Restraints on War* (Oxford, 1972), pp. 1–16.
15 Hugo Grotius, *The Freedom of the Seas* (trans. J. B. Scott, New York, 1916).

16 John Selden, *Mare Clausum: the Right and Dominion of the Sea* (London, 1663).

17 See especially G. N. Clark, *The Dutch Alliance and the War Against French Trade* (Manchester, 1923).

18 CAB 16. 46/47. CID 131 c.

19 See Sir Charles Webster and Noble Frankland, *The Strategic Air Offensive Against Germany* (London, 1961. 4 vols.), vol. IV, Appendix 2.

20 Texts in James T. Shotwell, *War as an Instrument of National Policy and its Renunciation in the Peace of Paris* (New York, 1929), p. 302.

21 Bailey, *Prohibitions*, p. 158. Ian Brownlie, *International Law and the Use of Force by States* (Oxford, 1963), pp. 167–95.

22 II. G. Nicholas, *The United Nations as a Political Institution* (Oxford, 1967), p. 208.

23 Bailey, *Prohibitions*, p. 91

24 Quoted in Lothar Kotsch, *The Concept of War in Contemporary History and International Law* (Geneva, 1956), p. 294.

25 Bailey, *Prohibitions*, p. 92

3

Against 'Realism'

MICHAEL WALZER

For as long as men and women have talked about war, they have talked about it in terms of right and wrong. And for almost as long, some among them have derided such talk, called it a charade, insisted that war lies beyond (or beneath) moral judgment. War is a world apart, where life itself is at stake, where human nature is reduced to its elemental forms, where self-interest and necessity prevail. Here men and women do what they must to save themselves and their communities, and morality and law have no place. *Inter arma silent leges*: in time of war the law is silent.

Sometimes this silence is extended to other forms of competitive activity, as in the popular proverb. 'All's fair in love and war.' That means that anything goes — any kind of deceit in love, any kind of violence in war. We can neither praise nor blame; there is nothing to say. And yet we are rarely silent. The language we use to talk about love and war is so rich with moral meaning that it could hardly have been developed except through centuries of argument. Faithfulness, devotion, chastity, shame, adultery, seduction, betrayal; aggression, self-defense, appeasement, cruelty, ruthlessness, atrocity, massacre — all these words are judgments, and judging is as common a human activity as loving or fighting.

It is true, however, that we often lack the courage of our judgments, and especially so in the case of military conflict. The moral posture of mankind is not well represented by that popular proverb about love and war. We would do better to mark a contrast rather than a similarity: before Venus, censorious; before Mars, timid. Not that we don't justify or condemn particular attacks, but we do so hesitantly and uncertainly (or loudly and recklessly), as if we were not sure that our judgments reach to the reality of war.

Reprinted with permission from Michael Walzer, *Just and Unjust Wars* (Basic Books, New York, 1977), pp. 3–20.

THE REALIST ARGUMENT

Realism is the issue. The defenders of *silent leges* claim to have discovered an awful truth: what we conventionally call inhumanity is simply humanity under pressure. War strips away our civilized adornments and reveals our nakedness. They describe that nakedness for us, not without a certain relish: fearful, self-concerned, driven, murderous. They aren't wrong in any simple sense. The words are sometimes descriptive. Paradoxically, the description is often a kind of apology: yes, our soldiers committed atrocities in the course of the battle, but that's what war does to people, that's what war is like. The proverb, all's fair, is invoked in defense of conduct that appears to be unfair. And one urges silence on the law when one is engaged in activities that would otherwise be called unlawful. So there are arguments here that will enter into my own argument: justifications and excuses, references to necessity and duress, that we can recognize as forms of moral discourse and that have or don't have force in particular cases. But there is also a general account of war as a realm of necessity and duress, the purpose of which is to make discourse about particular cases appear to be idle chatter, a mask of noise with which we conceal, even from ourselves, the awful truth. It is that general account that I have to challenge before I can begin my own work, and I want to challenge it at its source and in its most compelling form, as it is put forward by the historian Thucydides and the philosopher Thomas Hobbes. These two men, separated by 2,000 years, are collaborators of a kind, for Hobbes translated Thucydides' *History of the Peloponnesian War* and then generalized its argument in his own *Leviathan*. It is not my purpose here to write a full philosophical response to Thucydides and Hobbes. I wish only to suggest, first by argument and then by example, that the judgment of war and of wartime conduct is a serious enterprise.

The Melian Dialogue

The dialogue between the Athenian generals Cleomedes and Tisias and the magistrates of the island state of Melos is one of the high points of Thucydides' *History* and the climax of his realism. Melos was a Spartan colony, and its people had 'therefore refused to be subject, as the rest of the islands were, unto the Athenians; but rested at first neutral; and afterwards, when the Athenians put them to it by wasting of their lands, they entered into open war.'[1]

This is a classic account of aggression, for to commit aggression is simply to 'put people to it' as Thucydides describes. But such a description, he seems to say, is merely external; he wants to show us the inner meaning of war. His spokesmen are the two Athenian generals, who demand a parley and then speak as generals have rarely done in military history. Let us have no fine words about justice, they say. We for our part will not pretend that, having defeated the Persians, our empire is deserved; you must not claim that having done no injury to the Athenian people, you have a right to be let alone. We will talk instead of what is feasible and what is necessary. For this is what war is really like: 'they that have odds of power exact as much as they can, and the weak yield to such conditions as they can get.'

It is not only the Melians here who bear the burdens of necessity. The Athenians are driven, too; they must expand their empire, Cleomedes and Tisias believe, or lose what they already have. The neutrality of Melos 'will be an argument of our weakness, and your hatred of our power, among those we have rule over.' It will inspire rebellion throughout the islands, wherever men and women are 'offended with the necessity of subjection' — and what subject is not offended, eager for freedom, resentful of his conquerors? When the Athenian generals say that men 'will everywhere reign over such as they be too strong for,' they are not only describing the desire for glory and command, but also the more narrow necessity of inter-state politics: reign or be subject. If they do not conquer when they can, they only reveal weakness and invite attack; and so, 'by a necessity of nature' (a phrase Hobbes later made his own), they conquer when they can.

The Melians, on the other hand, are too weak to conquer. They face a harsher necessity: yield or be destroyed. 'For you have not in hand a match of valor upon equal terms ... but rather a consultation upon your safety ...' The rulers of Melos, however, value freedom above safety: 'If you then to retain your command, and your vassals to get loose from you, will undergo the utmost danger: would it not in us, that be already free, be great baseness and cowardice, if we should not encounter anything whatsoever rather than suffer ourselves to be brought into bondage?' Though they know that it will be a 'hard matter' to stand against the power and fortune of Athens, 'nevertheless we believe that, for fortune, we shall be nothing inferior, as having the gods on our side, because we stand innocent against men unjust.' And as for power, they hope for assistance from the Spartans, 'who are of necessity obliged, if for no other cause, yet for consanguinity's sake and for their own honor to defend us.' But the gods, too, reign where they can, reply the Athenian generals, and consanguinity and honor have nothing to do with necessity. The Spartans will (necessarily) think only of themselves: 'most apparently of all men, they hold for honorable that which pleaseth and for just that which profiteth'.

So the argument ended. The magistrates refused to surrender; the Athenians laid siege to their city; the Spartans sent no help. Finally, after some months of fighting, in the winter of 416 BC Melos was betrayed by several of its citizens. When further resistance seemed impossible, the Melians 'yielded themselves to the discretion of the Athenians: who slew all the men of military age, made slaves of the women and children; and inhabited the place with a colony sent thither afterwards of 500 men of their own'.

The dialogue between the generals and the magistrates is a literary and philosophical construction of Thucydides. The magistrates speak as they well might have done, but their conventional piety and heroism is only a foil to what the classical critic Dionysius calls the 'depraved shrewdness' of the Athenian generals.[2] It is the generals who have often seemed unbelievable. Their words, writes Dionysius, 'were appropriate to oriental monarchs . . . but unfit to be spoken by Athenians . . .'[3] Perhaps Thucydides means us to notice the unfitness, not so much of the words but of the policies they were used to defend, and thinks we might have missed it had he permitted the generals to speak as they probably in fact spoke, weaving 'fair pretenses' over their vile actions. We are to understand that Athens is no longer itself. Cleomedes and Tisias do not represent that noble people who fought the Persians in the name of freedom and whose politics and culture, as Dionysius says, 'exercised such a humanizing influence on everyday life.' They represent instead the imperial decadence of the city state. It is not that they are war criminals in the modern sense; that idea is alien to Thucydides. But they embody a certain loss of ethical balance, of restraint and moderation. Their statesmanship is flawed, and their 'realistic' speeches provide an ironic contrast to the blindness and arrogance with which the Athenians only a few months later launched the disastrous expedition to Sicily. The *History*, on this view, is a tragedy and Athens itself the tragic hero.[4] Thucydides has given us a morality play in the Greek style. We can glimpse his meaning in Euripides' *The Trojan Women*, written in the immediate aftermath of the conquest of Melos and undoubtedly intended to suggest the human significance of slaughter and slavery — and to predict a divine retribution:

> How ye are blind
> Ye treaders down of cities, ye that cast
> Temples to desolation, and lay waste
> Tombs, the untrodden sanctuaries where lie
> The ancient dead; yourselves so soon to die![5]

But Thucydides seems in fact to be making a rather different, and a more secular, statement than this quotation suggests, and not about Athens so much as about war itself. He probably did not mean the harshness of the Athenian generals to be taken as a sign of depravity, but rather as a sign of impatience, toughmindedness, honesty — qualities of mind not inappropriate in military commanders. He is arguing, as Werner Jaeger has said, that 'the principle of force forms a realm of its own, with laws of its own,' distinct and separate from the laws of moral life.[6] 'This is certainly the way Hobbes read Thucydides, and it is the reading with which we must come to grips. For if the realm of force is indeed distinct and if this is an accurate account of its laws, then one could no more criticize the Athenians for their wartime policies than one could criticize a stone for falling downwards. The slaughter of the Melians is explained by reference to the circumstances of war and the necessities of nature; and again, there is nothing to say. Or rather, one can *say* anything, call necessity cruel and war hellish; but while these statements may be true in their own terms, they do not touch the political realities of the case or help us understand the Athenian decision.

It is important to stress, however, that Thucydides has told us nothing at all about the Athenian decision. And if we place ourselves, not in the council room at Melos where a cruel policy was being expounded, but in the assembly at Athens where that policy was first adopted, the argument of the generals has a very different ring. In the Greek as in the English language, the word *necessity* 'doubles the parts of indispensable and inevitable'.[7] At Melos, Cleomedes and Tisias mixed the two of these, stressing the last. In the assembly they could have argued only about the first, claiming, I suppose, that the destruction of Melos was necessary (indispensable) for the preservation of the empire. But this claim is rhetorical in two senses. First, it evades the moral question of whether the preservation of the empire was itself necessary. There were some Athenians, at least, who had doubts about that, and more who doubted that the empire had to be a uniform system of domination and subjection (as the policy adopted for Melos suggested). Secondly, it exaggerates the knowledge and foresight of the generals.

They are not saying with certainty that Athens will fall unless Melos is destroyed; their argument has to do with probabilities and risks. And such arguments are always arguable. Would the destruction of Melos really reduce Athenian risks? Are there alternative policies? What are the likely costs of this one? Would it be right? What would other people think of Athens if it were carried out?

Once the debate begins, all sorts of moral and strategic questions are likely to come up. And for the participants in the debate, the outcome is not going to be determined 'by a necessity of nature,' but by the opinions they hold or come to hold as a result of the arguments they hear and then by the decisions they freely make, individually and collectively. Afterwards, the generals claim that a certain decision was inevitable; and that, presumably, is what Thucydides wants us to believe. But the claim can only be made afterwards, for inevitability here is mediated by a process of political deliberation, and Thucydides could not know what was inevitable until that process had been completed. Judgments of necessity in this sense are always retrospective in character — the work of historians, not historical actors.

Now, the moral point of view derives its legitimacy from the perspective of the actor. When we make moral judgments, we try to recapture that perspective. We reiterate the decision-making process, or we rehearse our own future decisions, asking what we would have done (or what we would do) in similar circumstances. The Athenian generals recognize the importance of such questions, for they defend their policy certain 'that you likewise, and others that should have the same power which we have, would do the same'. But that is a dubious knowledge, especially so once we realize that the 'Melian decree' was sharply opposed in the Athenian assembly. Our standpoint is that of citizens debating the decree. What *should* we do?

We have no account of the Athenian decision to attack Melos or of the decision (which may have been taken at the same time) to kill and enslave its people. Plutarch claims that it was Alcibiades, chief architect of the Sicilian expedition, who was 'the principal cause of the slaughter ... having spoken in favor of the decree'.[8] He played the part of Cleon in the debate that Thucydides does record, that occured some years earlier, over the fate of Mytilene. It is worth glancing back at the earlier argument. Mytilene had been an ally of Athens from the time of the Persian War; it was never a subject city in any formal way, but bound by treaty to the Athenian cause. In 428, it rebelled and formed an alliance with the

Spartans. After considerable fighting, the city was captured by Athenian forces, and the assembly determined 'to put to death ... all the men of Mytilene that were of age, and to make slaves of the women and children: laying to their charge the revolt itself, in that they revolted not being in subjection as others were ...' [9] But the following day the citizens 'felt a kind of repentance ... and began to consider what a great and cruel decree it was, that not the authors only, but that the whole city should be destroyed.' It is this second debate that Thucydides has recorded, or some part of it, giving us two speeches, that of Cleon upholding the original decree and that of Diodotus urging its revocation. Cleon argues largely in terms of collective guilt and retributive justice; Diodotus offers a critique of the deterrent effects of capital punishment. The assembly accepts Diodutus' position, convinced apparently that the destruction of Mytilene would not uphold the force of treaties or ensure the stability of the empire. It is the appeal to interest that triumphs — as has often been pointed out — though it should be remembered that the occasion for the appeal was the repentance of the citizens. Moral anxiety, not political calculation, leads them to worry about the effectiveness of their decree.

In the debate over Melos, the positions must have been reversed. Now there was no retributivist argument to make, for the Melians had done Athens no injury. Alcibiades probably talked like Thucydides' generals, though with the all-important difference I have already noted. When he told his fellow citizens that the decree was necessary, he didn't mean that it was ordained by the laws that govern the realm of force; he meant merely that it was needed (in his view) to reduce the risks of rebellion among the subject cities of the Athenian empire. And his opponents probably argued, like the Melians, that the decree was dishonorable and unjust and would more likely excite resentment than fear throughout the islands, that Melos did not threaten Athens in any way, and that other policies would serve Athenian interests and Athenian self-esteem. Perhaps they also reminded the citizens of their repentance in the case of Mytilene and urged them once again to avoid the cruelty of massacre and enslavement. How Alcibiades won out, and how close the vote was, we don't know. But there is no reason to think that the decision was predetermined and debate of no avail: no more with Melos than with Mytilene. Stand in imagination in the Athenian assembly, and one can still feel a sense of freedom.

But the realism of the Athenian generals has a further thrust. It is not only a denial of the freedom that makes moral decision possible; it is a denial also of the meaningfulness of moral argument. The second claim is closely related to the first. If we must act in accordance with our interests, driven by our fears of one another, then talk about justice cannot possibly be anything more than talk. It refers to no purposes that we can make our own and to no goals that we can-share with others. That is why the Athenian generals could have woven 'fair pretenses' as easily as the Melian magistrates; in discourse of this sort anything can be said. The words have no clear references, no certain definitions, no logical entailments. They are, as Hobbes writes in *Leviathan*, 'ever used with relation to the person that useth them,' and they express that person's appetites and fears and nothing else. It is only 'most apparent' in the Spartans, but true for everyone, that 'they hold for honorable that which pleaseth them and for just that which profiteth.' Or, as Hobbes later explained the names of the virtues and vices are of 'uncertain signification'.

> For one calleth wisdom, what another calleth fear; and one cruelty what another justice; one prodigality, what another magnanimity . . . etc. And therefore such names can never be true grounds of any ratiocination.[10]

Never' — until the sovereign, who is also the supreme linguistic authority, fixes the meaning of the moral vocabulary; but in the state of war, '*never*' without qualification, because in that state, by definition, no sovereign rules. In fact, even in civil society, the sovereign does not entirely succeed in bringing certainty into the world of virtue and vice. Hence moral discourse is always suspect, and war is only an extreme case of the anarchy of moral meanings. It is generally true, but especially so in time of violent conflict, that we can understand what other people are saying only if we see through their 'fair pretenses' and translate moral talk into the harder currency of interest talk. When the Melians insist that their cause is just, they are saying only that they don't want to be subject; and had the generals claimed that Athens deserved its empire, they would simply have been expressing the lust for conquest or the fear of overthrow.

This is a powerful argument because it plays upon the common experience of moral disagreement — painful, sustained, exasperating, and endless. For all its realism, however, it fails to get at the realities of that experience or to explain its character. We can see this clearly, I think, if we look again at the argument over the Mytilene decree. Hobbes may well have had this debate in mind when he wrote, 'and one [calleth] cruelty what another justice . . .' The Athenians repented of their cruelty, writes Thucydides, while Cleon told them that they had not been cruel at all but justly severe. Yet this was in no sense a disagreement over the meaning of words. Had there been no common meanings, there could have been no debate at all. The cruelty of the Athenians consisted in seeking to punish not only the authors of the rebellion but others as well, and Cleon agreed that that would indeed be cruel. He then went on to argue, as he had to do given his position, that in Mytilene there were no 'others'. 'Let not the fault be laid upon a few, and the people absolved. For they have all alike taken arms against us . . .'

I cannot pursue the argument further, since Thucydides doesn't, but there is an obvious rejoinder to Cleon, having to do with the status of the women and children of Mytilene. This might involve the deployment of additional moral terms (innocence, for example); but it would not hang — any more than the argument about cruelty and justice hangs — on idiosyncratic definitions. In fact, definitions are not at issue here, but descriptions and interpretations. The Athenians shared a moral vocabulary, shared it with the people of Mytilene and Melos; and allowing for cultural differences, they share it with us too. They had no difficulty, and we have none, in understanding the claim of the Melian magistrates that the invasion of their island was unjust. It is in applying the agreed-upon words to actual cases that we come to disagree. These disagreements are in part generated and always compounded by antagonistic interests and mutual fears. But they have other causes, too, which help to explain the complex and disparate ways in which men and women (even when they have similar interests and no reason to fear one another) position themselves in the moral world. There are, first of all, serious difficulties of perception and information (in war and politics, generally), and so controversies arise over 'the facts of the case'. There are sharp disparities in the weight we attach even to values we share, as there are in the actions we are ready to condone when these values are threatened. There are conflicting commitments and obligations that force us into violent antagonism even when we see the point of one another's positions. All this is real enough, and common enough: it makes morality into a world of good-faith quarrels as well as a world of ideology and verbal manipulation.

In any case, the possibilities for manipulation are limited. Whether or not people speak in good faith, they cannot say just anything they please. Moral talk is coercive; one thing leads to another.

Perhaps that's why the Athenian generals did not want to begin. A war called unjust is not, to paraphrase Hobbes, a war misliked; it is a war misliked for particular reasons, and anyone making the charge is required to provide particular sorts of evidence. Similarly, if I claim that I am fighting justly, I must also claim that I was attacked ('put to it', as the Melians were), or threatened with attack, or that I am coming to the aid of a victim of someone else's attack. And each of these claims has its own entailments, leading me deeper and deeper into a world of discourse where, though I can go on talking indefinitely, I am severely constrained in what I can say. I must say this or that, and at many points in a long argument this or that will be true or false. We don't have to translate moral talk into interest talk in order to understand it; morality refers in its own way to the real world.

Let us consider a Hobbist example. In Chapter XXI of *Leviathan*, Hobbes urges that we make allowance for the 'natural timorousness' of mankind. 'When armies fight, there is on one side, or both a running away; yet when they do it not out of treachery, but fear, they are not esteemed to do it unjustly, but dishonorably.' Now, judgments are called for here: we are to distinguish cowards from traitors. If these are words of 'inconstant signification', the task is impossible and absurd. Every traitor would plead natural timorousness, and we would accept the plea or not depending on whether the soldier was a friend or an enemy, on obstacle to our advancement or an ally and supporter. I suppose we sometimes do behave that way, but it is not the case (nor does Hobbes, when it comes to cases, suppose that it is) that the judgments we make can only be understood in these terms. When we charge a man with treason, we have to tell a very special kind of story about him, and we have to provide concrete evidence that the story is true. If we call him a traitor when we cannot tell that story, we are not using words inconstantly, we are simply lying.

STRATEGY AND MORALITY

Morality and justice are talked about in much the same way as military strategy. Strategy is the other language of war, and while it is commonly said to be free from the difficulties of moral discourse, its use is equally problematic. Though generals agree on the meaning of strategic terms — entrapment, retreat, flanking maneuver, concentration of forces, and so on — they nevertheless disagree about strategically appropriate courses of action. They argue about what ought to be done. After the battle, they disagree about what happened, and if they were defeated, they argue about who was to blame. Strategy, like morality, is a language of justification.[11] Every confused and cowardly commander describes his hesitations and panics as part of an elaborate plan; the strategic vocabulary is as available to him as it is to a competent commander. But that is not to say that its terms are meaningless. It would be a great triumph for the incompetent if they were, for we would then have no way to talk about incompetence. No doubt, 'one calleth retreat what another calleth strategic redeployment . . .' But we do know the difference between these two, and though the facts of the case may be difficult to collect and interpret, we are nevertheless able to make critical judgments.

Similarly, we can make moral judgments: moral concepts and strategic concepts reflect the real world in the same way. They are not merely normative terms, telling soldiers (who often don't listen) what to do. They are descriptive terms, and without them we would have no coherent way of talking about war. Here are soldiers moving away from the scene of a battle, marching over the same ground they marched over yesterday, but fewer now, less eager, many without weapons, many wounded: we call this a retreat. Here are soldiers lining up the inhabitants of a peasant village, men, women, and children, and shooting them down: we call this a massacre.

It is only when their substantive content is fairly clear that moral and strategic terms can be used imperatively, and the wisdom they embody expressed in the form of rules. Never refuse quarter to a soldier trying to surrender. Never advance with your flanks unprotected. One might construct out of such commands a moral or a strategic war plan, and then it would be important to notice whether or not the actual conduct of the war conformed to the plan. We can assume that it would not. War is recalcitrant to this sort of theoretical control – a quality it shares with every other human activity, but which it seems to possess to an especially intense degree. In *The Charterhouse of Parma*, Stendhal provides a description of the battle of Waterloo that is intended to mock the very idea of a strategic plan. It is an account of combat as chaos, therefore not an account at all but a denial, so to speak, that combat is accountable. It should be read alongside some strategic analysis of Waterloo like that of Major General Fuller, who views the battle as an organized series of maneuvers and counter-maneuvers.[12] The strategist is not unaware of confusion and disorder in the field; nor is he entirely unwilling to see these as aspects of war itself, the natural effects of the stress of battle. But he sees them also as matters of command responsibility, failures of discipline or control. He suggests that strategic imperatives have been ignored; he looks for lessons to be learned.

The moral theorist is in the same position. He too must come to grips with the fact that his rules are often violated or ignored — and with the deeper realization that, to men at war, the rules often don't seem relevant to the extremity of their situation. But however he does this, he does not surrender his sense of war as a human action, purposive and premeditated, for whose effects someone is responsible. Confronted with the many crimes committed in the course of a war, or with the crime of aggressive war itself, he searches for human agents. Nor is he alone in this search. It is one of the most important features of war, distinguishing it from the other scourges of mankind, that the men and women caught up in it are not only victims, they are also participants. All of us are inclined to hold them responsible for what they do (though we may recognize the plea of duress in particular cases). Reiterated over time, our arguments and judgments shape what I want to call *the moral reality of war* — that is, all those experiences of which moral language is descriptive or within which it is necessarily employed.

It is important to stress that the moral reality of war is not fixed by the actual activities of soldiers but by the opinions of mankind. That means, in part, that it is fixed by the activity of philosophers, lawyers, publicists of all sorts. But these people don't work in isolation from the experience of combat, and their views have value only insofar as they give shape and structure to that experience in ways that are plausible to the rest of us. We often say, for example, that in time of war soldiers and statesmen must make agonizing decisions. The pain is real enough, but it is not one of the natural effects of combat. Agony is not like Hobbist fear; it is entirely the product of our moral views, and it is common in war only insofar as those views are common. It was not some unusual Athenian who 'repented' of the decision to kill the men of Mytilene, but the citizens generally. They repented, and they were able to understand one another's repentance, because they shared a sense of what cruelty meant. It is by the assignment of such meanings that we make war what it is — which is to say that it could be (and it probably has been) something different.

What of a soldier or statesman who does not feel the agony? We say of him that he is morally ignorant or morally insensitive,

much as we might say of a general who experienced no difficulty
making a (really) difficult decision that he did not understand the
strategic realities of his own position or that he was reckless and
insensible of danger. And we might go on to argue, in the case of
the general, that such a man has no business fighting or leading
others in battle, that he ought to know that his army's right flank,
say, is vulnerable, and ought to worry about the danger and take
steps to avoid it. Once again, the case is the same with moral
decisions: soldiers and statesmen ought to know the dangers of
cruelty and injustice and worry about them and take steps to
avoid them.

HISTORICAL RELATIVISM

Against this view, however, Hobbist relativism is often given a
social or historical form: moral and strategic knowledge, it is said,
changes over time or varies among political communities, and so
what appears to me as ignorance may look like understanding to
someone else. Now, change and variation are certainly real enough,
and they make for a tale that is complex in the telling. But the
importance of that tale for ordinary moral life, and, above all, for
the judgment of moral conduct is easily exaggerated. Between
radically separate and dissimilar cultures, one can expect to find
radical dichotomies in perception and understanding. No doubt
the moral reality of war is not the same for us as it was for
Genghis Khan; nor is the strategic reality. But even fundamental
social and political transformations within a particular culture
may well leave the moral world intact or at least sufficiently whole
so that we can still be said to share it with our ancestors. It is rare
indeed that we do not share it with our contemporaries, and by
and large we learn how to act among our contemporaries by
studying the actions of those who have preceded us. The assumption
of that study is that they saw the world much as we do. That is
not always true, but it is true enough of the time to give stability
and coherence to our moral lives (and to our military lives). Even
when world views and high ideals have been abandoned — as the
glorification of aristocratic chivalry was abandoned in early modern
times — notions about right conduct are remarkably persistent:
the military code survives the death of warrior idealism. I shall say
more about this survival later on, but I can demonstrate it now in
a general way by looking at an example from feudal Europe, an
age in some ways more distant from us than Greece of the city

states, but with which we nevertheless share moral and strategic perceptions.

Three Accounts of Agincourt

Actually, the sharing of strategic perceptions is in this case the more dubious of the two. Those French knights so many of whom died at Agincourt had notions about combat very different from our own. Modern critics have still felt able to criticize their 'fanatical adherence to the old method of fighting' (King Henry, after all, fought differently) and even to offer practical suggestions: the French attack, writes Oman, 'should have been accompanied by a turning movement around the woods . . .'[13] Had he not been 'overconfident' the French commander would have seen the advantages of the move. We can talk in a similar way about the crucial moral decision that Henry made toward the end of the battle, when the English thought their victory secure. They had taken many prisoners, who were loosely assembled behind the lines. Suddenly, a French attack aimed at the supply tents far in the rear seemed to threaten a renewal of the fighting. Here is Holinshed's sixteenth century account of the incident (virtually copied from an earlier chronicle):

> . . . certain Frenchmen on horseback . . . to the number of six hundred horsemen, which were the first that fled, hearing that the English tents and pavilions were a good way distant from the army, without any sufficient guard to defend the same . . . entered upon the king's camp and there . . . robbed the tents, broke up chests, and carried away caskets and slew such servants as they found to make any resistance . . . But when the outcry of the lackeys and boys which ran away for fear of the Frenchmen . . . came to the king's ears, he doubting lest his enemies should gather together again, and begin a new field; and mistrusting further that the prisoners would be an aid to his enemies . . . contrary to his accustomed gentleness, commanded by sound of trumpet that every man . . . should incontinently slay his prisoner.'

The moral character of the command is suggested by the words 'accustomed gentleness' and 'incontinently'. It involved a shattering of personal and conventional restraints (the latter well-established by 1415), and Holinshed goes to some lengths to explain and excuse it, stressing the king's fear that the prisoners his forces held were about to rejoin the fighting. Shakespeare, whose *Henry V* closely follows Holinshed, goes further, emphasizing the slaying of the English servants by the French and omitting the chronicle's assertion that only those who resisted were killed:

> *Fluellen*, Kill the [b]oys and the baggage! 'Tis expressly against the law of arms. 'Tis as arrant a piece of knavery, mark you now, as can be offert.

At the same time, however, he cannot resist an ironical comment:

> *Gower* ... they have burned and carried away all that was in the king's tent, wherefore the king most worthily hath caused every soldier to cut his prisoner's throat. O, 'tis a gallant king![15]

A century and a half later, David Hume gives a similar account, without the irony, stressing instead the king's eventual cancellation of his order:

> ... some gentlemen of Picardy ... had fallen upon the English baggage, and were doing execution on the unarmed followers of the camp, who fled before them. Henry, seeing the enemy on all sides of him, began to entertain apprehensions from his prisoners: and he thought it necessary to issue a general order for putting them to death; but on discovering the truth, he stopped the slaughter, and was still able to save a great number.[16]

Here the moral meaning is caught in the tension between 'necessary' and 'slaughter'. Since slaughter is the killing of men as if they were animals — it 'makes a massacre', wrote the poet Dryden, 'what was a war' — it cannot often be called necessary. If the prisoners were so easy to kill, they were probably not dangerous enough to warrant the killing. When he grasped the actual situation, Henry, who was (so Hume wants us to believe) a moral man, called off the executions.

French chroniclers and historians write of the event in much the same way. It is from them that we learn that many of the English knights refused to kill their prisoners — not, chiefly, out of humanity, rather for the sake of the ransom they expected; but also 'thinking of the dishonor that the horrible executions would reflect on themselves'.[17] English writers have focused more, and more worriedly, on the command of the king; he was, after all, their king. In the later nineteenth century, at about the same time as the rules of war with respect to prisoners were being codified, their criticism grew increasingly sharp: 'a brutal butchery', 'cold-blooded wholesale murder'[18] Hume would not have said that, but the difference between that and what he did say is marginal, not a matter of moral or linguistic transformation.

To judge Henry ourselves we would need a more circumstantial account of the battle than I can provide here.[19] Even given that account our opinions might differ, depending on the allowance we were willing to make for the stress and excitement of battle. But this is a clear example of a situation common in both strategy and morality, where our sharpest disagreements are structured and organized by our underlying agreements, by the meanings we share. For Holinshed, Shakespeare, and Hume — traditional chronicler, Renaissance playwright, and Enlightenment historian — and for us too, Henry's command belongs to a category of military acts that requires scrutiny and judgment. It is *as a matter of fact* morally problematic, because it accepts the risks of cruelty and injustice. In exactly the same way, we might regard the battle plan of the French commander as strategically problematic, because it accepted the risks of a frontal assault on a prepared position. And, again, a general who did not recognize these risks is properly said to be ignorant of morality or strategy.

In moral life, ignorance isn't all that common; dishonesty is far more so. Even those soldiers and statesmen who don't feel the agony of a problematic decision generally know that they should feel it. Harry Truman's flat statement that he never lost a night's sleep over his decision to drop the atomic bomb on Hiroshima is not the sort of thing political leaders often say. They usually find it preferable to stress the painfulness of decision-making; it is one of the burdens of office, and it is best if the burdens appear to be borne. I suspect that many officeholders even experience pain simply because they are expected to. If they don't, they lie about it. The clearest evidence for the stability of our values over time is the unchanging character of the lies soldiers and statesmen tell. They lie in order to justify themselves, and so they describe for us the lineaments of justice. Wherever we find hypocrisy, we also find moral knowledge. The hypocrite is like that Russian general in Solzhenitsyn's *August 1914*, whose elaborate battle reports barely concealed his total inability to control or direct the battle. He knew at least that there was a story to tell, a set of names to attach to things and happenings, so he tried to tell the story and attach the names. His effort was not mere mimicry; it was, so to speak, the tribute that incompetence pays to understanding. The case is the same in moral life: there really is a story to tell, a way of talking about wars and battles that the rest of us recognize as morally appropriate. I don't mean that particular decisions are necessarily right or wrong, or simply right or wrong, only that there is a way of seeing the world so that moral decision-making makes sense. The hypocrite knows that this is true, though he may actually see the world differently.

Hypocrisy is rife in wartime discourse, because it is especially important at such a time to appear to be in the right. It is not only that the moral stakes are high: the hypocrite may not understand that; more crucially, his actions will be judged by other people, who are not hypocrites, and whose judgments will affect their policies toward him. There would be no point to hypocrisy if this were not so, just as there would be no point to lying in a world where no one told the truth. The hypocrite presumes on the moral understanding of the rest of us, and we have no choice, I think, except to take his assertions seriously and put them to the test of moral realism. He pretends to think and act as the rest of us expect him to do. He tells us that he is fighting according to the moral war plan: he does not aim at civilians, he grants quarter to soldiers trying to surrender, he never tortures prisoners, and so on. These claims are true or false, and though it is not easy to judge them (nor is the war plan really so simple), it is important to make the effort. Indeed, if we call ourselves moral men and women, we must make the effort, and the evidence is that we regularly do so. If we had all become realists like the Athenian generals or like Hobbists in a state of war, there would be an end alike to both morality and hypocrisy. We would simply tell one another, brutally and directly, what we wanted to do or have done. But the truth is that one of the things most of us want, even in war, is to act or to seem to act morally. And we want that, most simply, because we know what morality means (at least, we know what it is generally thought to mean)

... I am going to assume throughout that we really do act within a moral world; that particular decisions really are difficult, problematic, agonizing, and that this has to do with the structure of that world; that language reflects the moral world and gives us access to it; and finally that our understanding of the moral vocabulary is sufficiently common and stable so that shared judgments are possible ...

NOTES

1 This and subsequent quotations are from *Hobbes' Thucydides*, ed. Richard Schlatter (New Brunswick, N. J., 1975), pp. 377–85 (*The History of The Peloponnesian War*, 5:84–116).

2 Dionysius of Halicarnassus, *On Thucydides*, trans. W. Kendrick Pritchett (Berkeley, 1975), pp. 31–3.

3 Even oriental monarchs are not quite so toughminded as the Athenian generals. According to Herodotus, when Xerxes first disclosed his plans for an invasion of Greece, he spoke in more conventional terms: 'I will bridge the Hellespont and march an army through Europe into Greece, and punish the Athenians for the outrage they committed upon my father and upon us.' (*The Histories*, Book 7, trans. Aubrey de Scelincourt) The reference is to the burning of Sardis, which we may take as the pretext for the Persian invasion. The example bears out Francis Bacon's assertion that 'there is that justice imprinted in the nature of men that they enter not upon wars (whereof so many calamities do ensue) but upon some, at least specious, grounds and quarrels' (Essay 29, 'Of the True Greatness of Kingdoms' and Estates')

4 See F. M. Cornford, *Thucydides Mythistoricus* (London, 1907), esp. ch. XIII.

5 *The Trojan Women*, trans. Gilbert Murray (London, 1905), p. 16.

6 Werner Jaeger, *Paideia: the Ideals of Greek Culture*, trans. Gilbert Highet (New York, 1939), I, 402.

7 H. W. Fowler, *A Dictionary of Modern English Usage*, second ed., rev. Sir Ernest Gowers (New York, 1965), p. 168; cf. Jaeger, I, 397.

8 *Plutarchs Lives*, trans. John Dryden, rev. Arthur Hugh Clough (London, 1910), I, 303. Alcibiades also 'selected for himself one of the captive Melian women ...'

9 *Hobbes' Thucydides*, pp. 194–204. (*The History of the Peloponnesian War*, 3:36–49).

10 Thomas Hobbes *Leviathan*, ch. IV.

11 Hence we can 'unmask' strategic discourse just as Thucydides did with moral discourse. Imagine that the two Athenian generals, after their dialogue with the Melians, return to their camp to plan the coming battle. The senior in command speaks first: 'Don't give me any fine talk about the need to concentrate our forces or the importance of strategic surprise. We'll simply call for a frontal assault; the men will organize themselves as best they can; things are going to be confused anyway. I need a quick victory here, so that I can return to Athens covered with glory before the debate on the Sicilian campaign begins. We'll have to accept some risks; but that doesn't matter since the risks will be yours, not mine. If we are beaten, I'll contrive to blame you. That's what war is like.' Why is strategy the language of hard-headed men? One sees through it so easily ...

12 *The Charterhouse of Parma*, I, chs. 3 and 4; J. F. C. Fuller, *A Military History of the Western World* (n.p., 1955), II, ch. 15.

13 C. W. C. Oman. *The Art of War in the Middle Ages* (Ithaca, N.Y., 1968), p. 137.

14 Raphael Holinshed, *Chronicles of England, Scotland, and Ireland*, excerpted in William Shakespeare. *The Life of Henry V* (Signet Classics, New York, 1965), p. 197.

15 *Henry V*, 4:7, II, 1–11.

16 David Hume, *The History of England* (Boston, 1854), II, 358.

17 René de Belleval, *Azincourt* (Paris, 1865), pp. 105–6.

18 See the summary of opinions in J. H. Wylie, *The Reign of Henry the Fifth* (Cambridge, England, 1919), II, 171ff.

19 For an excellent and detailed account, which suggests that Henry's action cannot be defended, see John Keegan, *The Face of Battle* (New York, 1976), pp. 107–12.

4

Threats, Values, and Defense: Does the Defense of Values by Force Remain a Moral Possibility?

JAMES TURNER JOHNSON

THE JUST WAR TRADITION

Two deep and broad streams of moral reflection on war run through Western history. These streams have their thematic origin in a single fundamental question: Is it ever morally allowable to employ force in the protection and preservation of values? The moral tradition of pacifism has resulted from a negative response to this question, given in various ways under various historical circumstances. A positive answer, given in ways no less conditioned by historical circumstances yet with a similar depth of underlying consistency and wholeness, has produced the other moral tradition on force and violence, which it is both convenient and proper to call by a familiar name: *just war tradition*. We should note two characteristic facts about this tradition.

First, it is a moral response to the question of value and force that is not only historically deep but is a product of reflection and action across the whole breadth of this culture's experience. It is not a moral doctrine in the narrow sense, reflecting the attitudes only of those sectors of the culture, like religion, often conceived as having a specialized function of moralizing cut off from the rest of human existence. To be sure, this tradition has often found expression in church law and theological reflection; yet it also appears in codifications and theories of international law, in military manuals on how rightly to conduct war, and — as Michael

Reprinted with permission from William V. O'Brien and John Langan S. J. (eds) *The Nuclear Dilemma and the Just War Tradition* (Lexington Books, Lexington, Mass., 1986), pp. 31–48.

Walzer has shown in *Just and Unjust Wars* — in the judgments and reactions of common people.[1] In short, this tradition encapsulates something of how we in this culture respond morally to the question of protection of value by force. It is not the only response — pacifist rejection of force parallels it through history — but it is a fundamental one, revealing how we characteristically think about morality and war and defining the terms for our reflections in new or changing circumstances.

The second characteristic fact about just war tradition is that it preserves not one but two kinds of moral response to the question of value and force: limitation always accompanies justification. The response that says, yes, here are some conditions in which it is morally right to use force to protect value, goes on to set limits to what may rightly be done toward that end. This second element in the response is determined by the nature of the value or values to be protected; thus the need for limitation is built into the need to protect value as a necessary correlate. This means in general that unlimited or even disproportionately large amounts of force are not what is justified when the use of force to protect values is itself justified. Just war tradition, as recognized by such contemporary commentators as Paul Ramsey, William V. O'Brien, and Walzer, is a moral tradition of justifiable and limited war.[2] What has come to be known as the *jus ad bellum* has to do with the question of justification; that of limitation is addressed by the *jus in bello*. These are interconnected areas, but the priority, logical as well as historical, is with the former: only after the fundamental question is answered about the moral justification of employing force to protect values does the second question, about the morally requisite limits governing the use of that force, arise in turn. Problems arising in the *jus in bello* context may cause us to want to reflect further about the nature of the values we hold, the threat against them, and the means we may use to defend them; yet such further reflection means only that we must again enter the arena of the 'war decision', the *jus ad bellum*.[3]

It is often claimed that the development of nuclear weapons has made this traditional way of thinking about morality and war obsolete and irrelevant.[4] From what I have said, it should be clear that I think this is not the case. Indeed, my claim is that we naturally think in the same terms that are encountered in the tradition, whether we want to or not. A pacifist critic like James Douglass employs one part of the tradition to reject the whole of it.[5] No sooner has another critic, Stanley Hoffmann, rejected it than he reinvents it point by point.[6] Such phenomena should be instructive. We would do well not to repudiate this tradition of moral reflection from the past; to do so merely isolates us from the wisdom of others surely no less morally or intellectually acute than we — others who in their own historical contexts have faced problems analogous to our own about whether and how to employ force in the defense of values. It is thus better to use this tradition consciously — trying to learn from it and with it, even in the nuclear age — than to forget it and subsequently have to reinvent it.

DEFENSE OF VALUES BY FORCE AS A MORAL POSSIBILITY

To protect and preserve values is the only justifying cause for the use of force that is admitted in Western moral tradition. Classically, the use of force in response to a threat to values was justified in four ways: to protect the innocent, to recover something wrongly taken, to punish evil, and to defend against a wrongful attack in progress. Let us look briefly at each of these and inquire what we may derive from them in our present context.

Defense of the innocent is an idea that can be traced at least as far as Augustine in Christian thought.[7] It also has a history in military traditions back through the code of chivalry into the customs of premedieval Germanic societies.[8] By itself it implies an interventionist model of the justified use of military force and, more broadly, of national power. This not only flies in the face of much contemporary moralizing but also challenges such neoisolationists as Laurence Beilenson who argue for a retreat from foreign involvement by this country and the creation of a new 'fortress America'.[9] It is also at odds with the individualistic ethics fostered domestically in our society with the demise of close ties of community, an ethic that implies 'not getting involved' perhaps even in extreme cases like mugging or rape.[10] Granted that it is extremely dangerous to throw military power around in a world that has the capability of destroying itself by global war; granted also that national *hubris*, if unrestrained, could use defense of others as an unwarranted excuse for a new round of imperialistic conquests,[11] there still, I submit, remain in the contemporary world cases in which limited and proportionate use of force may be the appropriate means to preserve the value referred to in the phrase 'defense of the innocent'. The case of Grenada was not morally the same as that of Afghanistan; intervention in Hungary by the West at the time of the 1956 uprising would not have been the moral equivalent of the Soviet invasion that did in fact occur; intervention in Uganda by neighboring Tanzania to depose Idi Amin and put an end to his bloodthirsty and self-aggrandizing rule was not the same as would have been an invasion aimed simply at increasing Tanzanian territory. Clearly, not every case where the rights of innocent persons need to be protected should become an occasion for military intervention; the case of Hungary offers a clear instance when following out this line of implication from just war tradition to the exclusion of other considerations would have led to the wrong decision. But my point is that the moral distinctions assumed by the classical formulation of just war tradition still remain, and the necessity to tread warily (which was no less an obligation in any previous age of human history) does not remove either the moral outrage that comes from violation of the innocent,[12] the obligation to prevent or stop such violation if at all possible,[13] or the possibility that among all the means available, military ones may be the best.

The recovery of something wrongly taken is a necessary counterpart to the idea of defense against aggression in progress.[14] If such after-the-fact reaction were not allowed, the result would be that expansion or other aggressive acts would, if speedy and effective, be tacitly accepted. There must be, of course, some consistent and agreed-on means of identifying what belongs to one society or one polity and what to another; but even in the absence of complete consensus on this, it is not necessary to reduce everything to a matter of different ideological or national perspective, so that what is one's own is simply whatever one says is one's own. The Falklands conflict provides an instructive contemporary example of the relevance of such reflection. The Argentine claim to the islands was not without some merit, but this was hardly of sufficient value to justify military invasion and occupation against the will of the inhabitants. The principle of self-determination, often cited to protect weak nations against military and other forms of aggression by stronger ones, though not the only meaningful principle here, was certainly violated by Argentina's action. If only defense against an aggression in progress were justified, then Britain and the British inhabitants of the islands, would have had no recourse, after the failure of the intensively pursued negotiations, but to accept the newly established status quo of Argentine military rule. The allowance of after-the-fact use of force to regain something wrongly taken is the source of moral justification for Britain's military actions in the Falkalands war.

The punishment of evil is, in my judgment, the least useful of the classic formulations of just cause in the present context.[15] One reason for this is the prevalence of ideological divisions in the contemporary world. This line of justification for the use of force to protect value is all too easily changed into a justification for ideological warfare by one's own 'forces of light' against the 'forces of darkness' with their different ideological beliefs. This problem is not as acute among the superpowers as it once was, although it still exists and might still be fanned back to its former heat; more pressing immediate instances are to be found in the conflicts of the Middle East and Northern Ireland. Yet classically the punishment of differences of *belief was not what was implied by this idea of just cause; what was to be punished was the kind of action* identified in the other three kinds of justifying cause.[16]

What is unique to this concept of punishment taken alone is that it implicitly allows going beyond what these other concepts justify to further action aimed at insuring that the same thing does not happen again. Because such an allowance can easily be pushed too far, we should be cautious in citing this reason to justify force for the protection of value in the present age. Nuclear deterrence depends on the threat of punishment above all else; yet the use of current types of strategic nuclear weapons kept for deterrence purposes could itself threaten the very values such use would ostensibly seek to preserve. This is, of course, the heart of the nuclear dilemma, and I will return to it later. For now, my only point is that the justification of force as punishment for wrong done must not be allowed to become isolated from the general question of the protection of value or from the other justifying moral reasons for the use of force to protect value. Yet even with this caveat, if the goal of permitted military action is, as another part of just war tradition insists, the end of peace, then it is not proper to rule out the morality of punishment entirely.

If we had begun with twentieth-century international law and some other aspects of contemporary moral, political, and legal thought, we would have started with the justification of *defense against aggression in progress* – and perhaps got no further.[17] By keeping this classic idea of justifying cause for the use of force until last, I mean to symbolize that this idea is not as fundamental over the whole history of Western moral reflection on war as it has become in contemporary thought. Indeed, when we set this justification for the use of force alongside the others just identified and discussed, we discover that the right of self-defense is not in fact a moral absolute. One may oneself be in the wrong in a particular conflict. Rather than to exalt one's own righteousness and well-being over that of others, the better moral course is to deflate somewhat this allowance of self-defense to more appropriate proportions alongside the other *jus ad bellum* provisions.

In short, self-defense is not an absolute right, and the means of self-defense may therefore not be unlimited; there are other values to consider than the integrity of the self or one's own national polity. It is this consideration from just war tradition that points to the wrongness of schemes of national defense based on a threat of catastrophic annihilation, even if that threat is mutual. The irony of the present situation is that the very legal and moral efforts that attempt to restrict the incidence of the use of force by allowing only its defensive use − I am thinking of the Kellogg-Briand Pact of 1928 and Article 2 of the United Nations Charter, as well as current ostensibly moral arguments that the more terrible the deterrent threat, the less likelihood there will be of war − have the effect of insuring that should war come, despite these efforts, it will be of the most immoral and value-destructive kind attainable through military technology. That is, concentrating solely on the rightness of defense against aggression, though admittedly a moral justification for the use of force, has led us to think of strategic nuclear deterrence by threat of catastrophe as morally right, while ruling out lesser levels of force as possible responses to threats to value, even when these latter are more justifiable from the broader perspectives of just war tradition.[18]

In short, we would do well to remember what many in our present debate have either forgotten or systematically ignored: that circumstances may come into being in human history in which the use of force, at appropriate levels and discriminatingly directed, may be the morally preferable means for the protection and preservation of values. In forgetting or ignoring this, sometimes in the name of ostensibly moral considerations, those who would reject such a use of force are in fact choosing a less moral course than the one historically given form in the tradition that says that just war must also be limited war.

THE QUESTION OF VALUES

May values ever be defended by forceful means? Answering this question requires us to think, first, about the nature of the values to be protected and the interrelation among values. We do this normally not by reflection but by affirmation. Hence the following from John Stuart Mill:

War is an ugly thing, but not the ugliest of things. The decayed and degraded state of moral and patriotic feeling which thinks nothing *worth* a war, is worse. ... A man who has nothing which he cares about more than he does about his personal safety is a miserable creature who has no chance of being free, unless made and kept so by the existing of better men than himself.[19]

Mill in this context alludes to the values from which he speaks, but the salient fact about this statement is his ranking of relative values. He does not deny the value of personal safety; yet it is not for him the *highest* value. He does not deny the ugliness of war; he only affirms that in the ranking of priorities it is not the *worst* evil. Mill was, of course, a utilitarian in ethics; yet such priority ranking of values is not a feature unique to utilitarianism and to be dismissed by all nonutilitarians. Such ranking is indeed a feature of *any* ethic, for the service of one value often conflicts with the service of another, and there must be some way of deciding among them. Consider the following from Erasmus, a figure who was anything but a utilitarian:

Think ... of all the crimes that are committed with war as a pretext, while 'good lawes fall silent amid the clash of arms' — all the instances of sack and sacrilege, rape, and other shameful acts, such as one hesitates even to name. And even when the war is over, this moral corruption is bound to linger for many years. Now assess for me the cost — a cost so great that, even if you win the war, you will lose much more than you gain. Indeed, what realm ... can be weighed against the life, the blood, of so many thousand men.[20]

This passage is replete with priority ranking of values. Erasmus begins by identifying war rhetorically with criminal activity, thus locating it at the bottom of the value scale. He then turns explicitly to proportional counting of relative costs: 'even if you win the war, you will lose much more than you gain'; 'what realm ... can be weighed against the life, the blood, of so many thousand men?' Such comparative weighting of goods is as central to the ethics of Erasmian humanism as it is to Mill's utilitarianism; indeed, it appears as a core feature of moral argument as such. Ultimately, there is no way to get to the truth or falsity of various perceptions of value. This is why, finally, there can be no real argument between absolute pacifists, who reject all possibility of the use of force to protect value, and those who accept some possibility of such use of force.[21] But this is not a problem in most of the current defense debate, which is a debate over ranking of values among persons who weight their values as differently as do Mill and Erasmus.

Recognizing values where they exist and sorting them according to priorities where there are conflicts among them is the function of moral agency, an art learned in one's community of moral discourse.[22] Without going into a full theory of moral agency, which is far beyond the scope of this chapter, the most we can say here is that affirmations like those of Mill and Erasmus allow us to glimpse the structure of relative values held by each participant in a moral debate and to relate those structures of value both to a larger normative conception of common life and to our own personal rankings of value. For our present purposes this is enough.

One interesting thing about Erasmus and Mill on war is how contemporary they sound; by thinking about them, we may learn something about ourselves. Erasmus counted costs both great and small in his rejection of war. A glimpse of the latter appears elsewhere in the letter quoted earlier, where he complains that preparations for war have dried up the sources of patronage on which he depended for support.[23] This was purely personal injury, but the complaint is not unlike contemporary arguments against military spending as subtracting from resources available for feeding the hungry, healing the sick and — in direct continuity with Erasmus — supporting humanistic scholarship. The value ranking is obvious.

The real meat of Erasmus' objection to war is found, however, in his idealistic vision of world community, which he conceived as both good in itself beyond the goods of any national community and achievable by the right kind of human cooperative interaction.[24] Again, this way of thinking has parallels in current debate, where rejection of force to protect values associated with the nation-state is coupled to a new vision of world order in which the nation-state system has no place.[25] The preservation of peace among nations, both in Erasmus and in contemporary debate, appears as the highest instrumental value, on which the maintenance of all other values depends. This is a different sort of reasoning from that of the pacifism of absolute principle; even the latter, however, may engage in priority ranking, as in these words of Mennonite theologian John Howard Yoder: "'Thou shalt not kill' ... is an absolute ... immeasurably more human, more personalistic, more genuinely responsible than the competitive absolute, "Thou shalt not let Uncle Sam down" or "Thou shalt fight for freedom" or "Never give up the ship".'[26] What we may note here is the tendency to diminish rhetorically the values being downgraded; similarly, Erasmus in all his works against war represents war-making as nothing more than the result of frivolous and misguided rivalry among sovereigns. War, Yoder and Erasmus alike suggest, may never be anything more than frivolous and misguidèd; the possibility that it might be an instrumental means of protecting value is dismissed out of hand. Contemporary examples of such reasoning abound, centering around the dismissal of any form of military preparedness as 'militarism' and rejection of 'war-fighting' strategic planning as opposed to deterrence strategy.[27]

The influence of Erasmian humanistic pacifism on contemporary debate runs deep, and I cannot here chart its full extent, but one more example of this presence must be noted for what it is. Erasmus rejects war as the *summum malum*, assimilating it to criminality; in contemporary debate the counterpart is the assimilation of all war to the evil of catastrophic nuclear holocaust. Erasmus cites 'sack, sacrilege, and rape'; Jonathan Schell, in the idiom of our own age, cites 'the biologic effects of ultraviolet radiation with emphasis on the skin',[28] while piling up evidence of 'the likely consequences of a holocaust for the earth'[29] — as if anyone had to be reminded that a holocaust is, by definition, evil.

It should be clear that Erasmus, Schell, and Yoder are simply moving in a different sphere from Mill and the main line of just war thinking (which I also share). It is simply impossible, given the assimilation of war to criminality and holocaust, for Erasmus and Schell to share Mill's judgment that '[w]ar is an ugly thing, but not the ugliest of things'. No more could Yoder, for whom the use of force is trivialized into the maxim, 'Never give up the ship', or those who, like Erasmus, regard war as the result of frivolous self-assertion by political leaders or, in the current phrase, 'militarism'. Between these and the position represented by Mill there would seem to be an impassible gulf. Yet it is possible at least to see across that gulf, if not to bridge or remove it. And from the perspective of just war tradition, there is something fundamentally wrong with the perception of value found on the other side.

First, although there is no need to deny the charm of an idealistic vision of world community, such a conception of an ideal that is not yet a reality (and may never become one) should not subtract from the quite genuine value to be found in the nation-state system or, more particularly, in a national community like our own. Historically, the roots of the nation-state system lie in the need to organize human affairs so as to minimize conflict while preserving the unique cultural identities of different peoples. It can be argued plausibly that it still fulfills these functions — imperfectly, to be sure, but with nothing better currently at hand. Likewise, the personal security, justice, freedom, and domestic peace provided in a liberal democratic nation-state like the United States are not to be dismissed lightly by reference to a utopian vision in which these and other values would all be present in greater measure. We must always, as moral beings, measure reality against our ideals; yet to reject the penultimate goods secured by the real because they do not measure up to the ultimate goods envisioned in the ideal is to ensure the loss of even the penultimate goods that we now enjoy. The ultimate would certainly be better; yet in the meantime, we have the obligation to hold as fast as possible to the value at hand, even though doing so must inevitably incur costs. A positive response to the original just war question recognizes this, as did Mill; Erasmus and his contemporary idealistic descendants did not.

Second, if force is to be used to protect values, it is not trivia that are to be protected but values of fundamental worth. Mill's allusion to the value of 'being free' is on a quite different level from Yoder's maxim, 'Never give up the ship', or Erasmus' collapsing of all reasons for war into the venality of princes. Equally, I believe, not to be reduced to the trivial or frivolous is Walzer's perception, expressed throughout *Just and Unjust Wars*, that the justification for fighting lies in the recognition of evil and revulsion against it.[30] Walzer's negative way of putting the matter is important for another reason: it reminds us that we do not have to be able to give an extensive and comprehensive listing of all values that may be protected and in what ranking in order to know *that there are* such values; they will be apparent when they are violated or threatened with violation.

Third, knowing that some wars have resulted from the aggressively self-assertive characters of rulers does not mean that war may never be anything else. It is doubtful that Erasmus was right even about the rulers of his own time. In our own age we must surely make a distinction between, for example, the war made by Hitler and that made by Churchill; nor is it particularly useful to reduce the rise and fall of relations between the United States and the Soviet Union to the personalities of a Carter and a Brezhnev, Gorbachev and a Reagan. A manichaean dismissal of everything military as 'militaristic' is also an uncalled for reductionism that makes military preparedness itself an evil, not an instrument for good or ill in ways to be determined by human choices.

Finally, neither Erasmus' time nor in our own is it right to represent war as the irreducible *summum malum*. I have already suggested why I think Erasmus was wrong in making this claim; more important for our current context is the wrongness of assimilating all contemporary war to catastrophic nuclear war. Let us dwell on this for a moment.

Who could want a nuclear holocaust? Yet the effort to avoid such a catastrophe is not itself justification for rejection of the possibility that lower levels of force may justifiably be employed to protect value. This is, nonetheless, the clear import of the argument when limited conventional war is collapsed into limited nuclear war by reference to the threat of escalation and when nuclear war of any extent is collapsed into catastrophic holocaust on a global scale.[31] Such an argument has the effect of making any contemporary advocate of the use of force to protect values an advocate instead of the total destruction of humankind or even of all life on earth. It should hardly need to be said that such rhetorical hyperbole is unjustified; no one who argues from just war tradition, with its strong emphasis on counting the costs and estimating the probability of success of any projected military action, should be represented as guilty of befriending the idea of nuclear holocaust.

Yet this collapsing of categories is also wrong historically. War in the nuclear age has not been global catastrophe but a continuation of conventional warfare limited in one or several ways – by geography, goals, targets, means. This arena of contemporary limited warfare is one in which traditional moral categories for judging war are very much at home, as such different writers as William V. O'Brien and Michael Walzer have, in their respective ways, both recognized. The issue, then, is not of the prohibition of all means of defense in the nuclear age, because the assimilation of all contemporary war to the *summum malum* of nuclear holocaust is invalid; it is, rather, the perennial question of when and how force may be used for the defense of values.[32] We will return to this question later.

THE PROBLEM OF THREATS TO VALUES

For there to be a need to defend values, there must be a threat to those values. To anyone with a modicum of objectivity, however, it must be apparent that in the current defense debate there is no agreement about the nature of the threat, and so there can be little hope of agreement about the means of preserving values in the face of the menace identified. Speaking broadly, I find in the present debate three distinct identifications of the threat to values that must be met. For some, there is no danger worth mentioning beyond that of nuclear holocaust, which is defined as threatening everything that is of value. For others the principal challenge to the values that matter for them is the arms race as such, with its diversion of resources to military ends and a perceived transformation of values toward those of militarism. Finally, a third perspective identifies the principal threat to values in the rivalry between the United States and the Soviet Union, West and East, two different and competing social, economic, political, and moral systems. This last is the most easily identifiable in terms of traditional interstate political analysis and in terms of just war tradition. All three perspectives have many forms and are somewhat fluid, so that in painting them with broad strokes of the brush I cannot render the inner details of each. Yet the broadly painted pictures of these different perspectives are themselves interesting morally, and it is on these that I will focus in this brief context.

Let us begin by exploring what is distinctive about each of the first two positions I have identified. These clearly overlap, but their emphases are importantly different, as are their respective histories and implicit value commitments. One way of recognizing this quickly is by noting that the anti-nuclear-holocaust position can be expressed in a commitment to increased military spending for a strengthened deterrent, quite contrary to the anti-arms race position, which finds typical expression in the nuclear freeze movement and support for disarmament programs. Similarly, part of the historical case for tactical and theater nuclear weapons has been that they cost less to provide than equivalent conventional forces, thus tending to free economic and manpower resources for nonmilitary purposes; yet many from the anti-nuclear-holocaust position view such war-fighting weapons as inherently destabilizing and dangerously likely to lead to catastrophic nuclear war.[33] Within the anti-nuclear-holocaust position, opposition to the arms race and military spending is but an instrumentality, whereas within the anti-arms race position opposition to nuclear arms is only an instrumentality. When there is convergence between these two positions (as there has been in the most recent stage of the defense debate), it is a mixed marriage that is as likely to end in divorce as in conversion of one or both partners.

These two positions also have different historical and ideological roots. The anti-nuclear-holocaust position is, of course, a product of the nuclear age and specifically of the period in which the

United States and the Soviet Union have practiced strategic nuclear deterrence against each other. It is thus the child of nuclear deterrence theory and finds a characteristic expression in one such theory, the deterrence-only position. Clearly, however, there has been a transformation of values from parent to offspring. Thus when Philip Green wrote *Deadly Logic* in the mid-1960s, he cited 'resistence to Communism' as the fundamental 'ethical root of deterrence theory',[34] but the ethical root of the contemporary deterrence-only position is the perception of *nuclear warfare*, not the menace to values posed by a totalitarian political system, as the evil to be avoided by the possession of a nuclear deterrent.[35]

The historical roots of the anti-arms race position are at least a century old; they lie in opposition to the increasing practice in nineteenth-century European states of sustaining a standing army built up by universal or nearly universal conscription, and in opposition to the social and economic costs of sustaining such armies. Religious groups have been the chief enunciators of this position and they are so today. A direct line runs between the *Postulata* on war prepared for Vatican Council I in 1870, which deplored the 'intolerable burden' of defense spending and the social costs of 'huge standing and conscript armies',[36] and the 1983 pastoral of the US Catholic bishops with its deploring of the 'economic distortion of priorities' due to the 'billions readily spent for destructive instruments',[37] or, to take a Protestant example, the 1980 statement on the arms race by the Reformed Church in America decrying 'the devastating social and personal consequences of the arms race'.[38] Two ethical roots of this position are visible in the sources cited: an opposition to war and weapons as contrary to the biblical vision of peace, and an identification with the needs of the poor as best expressing Christian conformity to Christ. Both themes have secular counterparts in contemporary debate, and the first obviously parallels the utopian vision of Erasmian humanism.

If nuclear holocaust is the danger against which values must be protected, then deterrence theory is one rational response, but so would be general nuclear disarmament. If the arms race itself is the menace to values that must be defended against, then a freeze on military expenditures followed by a general scaling down of military establishments is the clear implication. Both these perspectives on the contemporary threat to values incorporate truths about the present historical situation; both are rooted in important perceptions of moral value; each offers, in its own way, a response to the problem of threat to values as it perceives that threat. Yet neither of these perspectives is really about the question with which we began this chapter, the fundamental question that is the root of our moral tradition on war: When and how may force justifiably be employed for the defense of values? Rather than approaching seriously the problem of possible moral justification of force, each of these perspectives has, in its own way, *defined that possibility out of existence* in the search for a general rejection of the use of force as a moral option in the contemporary age. The reason is that neither of these perspectives is able to comprehend the possibility of significant threats to value alongside the one on which each of them is fixed.

The problem, however, is that what is thus ignored does not for this reason cease to exist. International rivalries persist, as they did in the prenuclear era; ideologies and realistic perceptions of national interest continue to influence the actions of nations, and these actions are often played out through projections of force. Terrorism, civil war, and international war continue to be plain realities of our present era, and there is no reason to suppose either that aggression will no longer take place in human history or that it can effectively be opposed by means other than military ones.[39] Indeed, prospective victims of aggression today might reflect with Clausewitz: 'The aggressor is always peace-loving; he would prefer to take over our country unopposed.'[40] The just war perspective, the third perspective in the contemporary debate, views the problem of threats to value in this light, in continuity with the main line of statecraft over history, and conceives the problem of defense against such threats also in terms continuous with that historical experience.

Let it be clear: the rivalry between the Soviet Union and the United States is not the only source of danger to American values; yet it would be blindness to wish away the existence of this rivalry, which is rooted in more than common possession of mutual annihilative power; more than competing ideologies; more than national interest; more than global competition for friends, allies, and trading partners — and yet in all of these. And this rivalry is more than simply a product of adverse perceptions; it is real. Where it takes military form, as for example most unambiguously along the NATO—Warsaw Pact border, thinking about the menace to values must go beyond efforts to avoid catastrophic nuclear war and to end the arms race to include efforts to define and mount a credible, effective, and moral defense against the particular military threat manifest there.

At the same time, however, potential military defense of values is not limited to this confrontation or to the global East—West rivalry; it may be a matter of attempting to secure a weak Third World nation against the power of a nearby predator, of deterring or responding to terrorist attacks, or of maintaining the traffic of oil tankers through the Strait of Hormuz. All these possible uses of force involve the defense of value; all are, in general terms, the kind of resort to force regarded as justified in just war tradition. This third perspective on the threat to values, then, is the one I wish to address in my concluding section.

THE PROBLEM OF DEFENSE AGAINST THREATS TO VALUE

I wish now to return to a reflection with which this chapter began — that in general the nature of values to be protected and the threats against them are such that unlimited or even disproportionate amounts of force are not what is justified when the use of force to defend values is justified. When defense of values by force appears to require transgressing the boundaries set by the *jus in bello* concepts of proportionality and discrimination, this necessitates that we look again to see whether this is an occasion when the defense of values by force is morally justified. The answer may be no; yet it may also be yes, and this is the possibility I wish to explore in this section.

In fact there are two directions of thought, not one, that lead toward a renewal of the justification of value protection by force in such a situation. The first drives toward restructuring the application of force and beyond that to creating new kinds of force capabilities suited to limited application in the defense of value. The second leads into the far more dangerous consideration of whether values may ever be protected by means that themselves violate important values. I will discuss these in turn.

Clausewitz in his time understood well the difference between 'absolute war' — war pushed to the limits of the destructive capacities of the belligerents — and 'real' wars carried on by less than absolute means for limited purposes as an extension of politics. In the twentieth century many others have forgotten or ignored this difference.[41] Typically, the values threatened by war are less than ultimate, and so the threat; it is wrong to defend these values against such challenges by totalistic means disproportionate to both the values to be defended and the evil that menaces them. When we add that total war implies also the indiscriminate targeting of noncombatants, a violation of the fundamental idea of protection of the innocent, the indictment of such use of force in response to threats against values grows yet more damning.

Nevertheless, the problem of limitation of force in contemporary warfare is different from that which existed earlier. Today limitation must be accomplished first and foremost by human choice; in previous ages such limitation was also a product of the nature of weapons available, the restraints imposed by the seasons of the year, and the economic and social bases on which war was waged. Limitation in the use of force was relatively easy when the means were battle-axes or smooth-bore muskets, when three-quarters of the year was closed to military actions, and when soldiers were themselves units of economic production who could not be in arms year round. Today the problem is more complex: the structuring of force capabilities to defend against possible menaces to value must at the same time provide an effective deterrent and an effective means of active defense while still honoring the moral identity manifest in the society or culture in which the threatened values are known and maintained. Among the recent nuclear strategies that did not meet this dual test is massive retaliation, conceived as a strategy for use, since it allowed so-called brush-fire wars to erupt unchecked and threatened disproportionate and indiscriminate nuclear devastation as a response to aggression on a much lower scale. Nor does contemporary mutual assured destruction doctrine, for reasons already given. But the issue is not simply one of the disproportionateness of nuclear arms. The same moral problems exist, for example, with the strategic conventional air strikes against population centers of World War II. Similarly, in the context of current history one of the most acute problems is how to frame a moral response against terrorist activity without oneself being forced into the characteristic patterns of terrorism.

Though complicated, this problem is not insoluble. If the use of force is justified in response to threats against value, but the only means of force available are such that they contravene important values themselves, then the preferred moral alternative is the development of different means of force. If tactical and theater nuclear weapons are judged too destructive to use or deemed too likely to result in escalation to all-out nuclear war if employed, then the moral choice is to devise nonnuclear defenses to replace them and to pay the costs, economic and social, of such defenses.[42] If the strategic nuclear deterrent is deemed immoral to employ, then the right response is not to engage in the self-deception of deterrence-only reasoning but to explore possible means of defense against nuclear strikes that would not require a preemptive first strike by this nation or a possibly indiscriminate and dispropor- tionate punitive second strike.[43] The justification of using force to defend value certainly means, as I have said earlier, more than *defense* in its narrow sense, the warding off of attacks in progress; yet it certainly also means at least that, and to claim the moral high ground for a rejection of steps toward creating such defense is simply to twist moral reasoning out of shape.

Finally, however, there remains the possibility that values must be protected and preserved by force, and by force that itself contravenes at least some of the values it intends to protect and preserve. This is the possibility that, at the extreme, has been called 'supreme emergency',[44] and only at this extreme is it a morally unique case. Must one fight honorably and die, even knowing that one's ultimate moral values will thus die also? Or may one sin for the moment in order to defeat the evil that threatens, hoping for time to repent later and making the commit- ment to pass on undiluted to future generations the values that have been transgressed in the emergency?[45] Some of the lines of argument already advanced bear on this dilemma. I have suggested that ideological claims ought not to be inflated to the point of seeming to justify unlimited warfare; I have argued against dispro- portionate and indiscriminate warfare as morally evil in themselves; and I have suggested that part of the trouble in responding to an immoral form of warfare like terrorism is that in making such a response one's own humanity may be diminished to the level of that of the terrorist. In short, I tend to be dubious of supreme- emergency claims and am inclined to hold the moral line for preservation of value in the means chosen as well as in the decision to offer a defense. Even so there remains a possibility of a genuine supreme-emergency situation. What is to be said about this?

First, it is not a newly recognized kind of situation. In the early Middle Ages Christian soldiers were required to do penance after participating in war because of the possibility that they might have acted sinfully in that war, killing perhaps out of malice toward the enemy rather than with a feeling of regretful duty in the service of justice. Here we encounter a case in which the possibility is admit- ted that protection of values may involve violation of values. When in the sixteenth century Vitoria considered what might be done in a just war, he allowed that a militarily necessary storming of a city could be undertaken even though this would inevitably result in violations of the rights of noncombatants in the city.[46] Such historical evidence suggests a moral acceptance of the possibility of preserving value by wrong means; yet this evidence also implies the limits on that acceptance.

Second, the transgression of value in the service of value must be approached through the general recognition that value conflicts are the stuff with which human moral agency has to deal. Every moral system provides means for handling such conflicts, and that a genuine supreme emergency might come to exist is by definition such a conflict, in which higher values must in the last analysis be favored over lower ones. The values constituting the *jus ad bellum*, having priority over those of the *jus in bello*, would on my reasoning have to be honored in such a case, even at some expense to the latter.

I have thus brought this discussion to the brink of morally admissible possibility so that we might look over and see what lies below. The view is not a pretty one. Having seen it, though, we may the more purposefully return to the other line of implication sketched before: the development of military capabilities suited to our moral commitments. We may still yearn — and work — for a world without war, for an end to the menace of catastrophic nuclear war, for an end to the arms race; yet with such military capabilities we would be the better prepared to meet morally the threats to value that may be expected to be inevitable so long as these ideals are not achieved.

NOTES

1 Michael Walzer, *Just and Unjust Wars* (New York: Basic Books, 1977).

2 See Paul Ramsey, *War and the Christian Conscience* (Durham, N. C.: Duke University Press, 1961), and *The Just War* (New York: Charles Scribner's Sons, 1968); William V. O'Brien, *The Conduct of Just and Limited War* (New York: Praeger, 1981).

3 The term is O'Brien's and is meant by him to emphasize the difference in order of priority between the *jus ad bellum* and the *jus in bello*, which has to do with war-fighting once the initial decision to make war has been made. See O'Brien, *Just and Limited War*, esp. chaps. 1–3.

4 Cf. Stanley Hoffmann, *Duties beyond Borders* (Syracuse, N.Y.: Syracuse University Press, 1981), pp. 46–55, and James Douglass, *The Non-Violent Cross* (New York: Macmillan 1968).

5 Cf. Ramsey's criticism in *The Just War*, pp. 259–78.

6 Hoffmann, *Duties*, p. 59ff.

7 For an example of such tracing in contemporary argument, see Ramsey, *War and the Christian Conscience*, pp. 34–7.

8   For discussion, see James Turner Johnson, *Just War Tradition and the Restraint of War* (Princeton, N.J.: Princeton University Press, 1981), pp. 131–50.

9   See Laurence Beilenson, *Survival and Peace in the Nuclear Age* (Chicago: Regnery and Company, 1980).

10 On the loss of community and its implications, see James Sellers, *Warming Fires* (New York: Seabury Press, 1975), and Thomas Luckmann, *The Invisible Religion* (New York: Macmillan, 1967).

11 This is a familiar theme in the thought of Reinhold Niebuhr. Cf. his *Christianity and Power Politics* (New York: Charles Scribner's Sons, 1940), and *The Structure of Nations and Empires* (New York: Charles Scribner's Sons, 1959).

12 Cf. Walzer, *Just and Unjust Wars*, pp. 133–5.

13 Cf. Ramsey, *The Just War*, pp. 141–7.

14 This concept, taken over from Roman law by Augustine and Isidore of Seville, was central to the definition of just war given in medieval canon law. See *Corpus Juris Canonici*, Pars Prior, *Decretum Magistri Gratiani*, Pars Secunda, Causa XXIII, Quaest. II, Can. II.

15 This is another *jus ad bellum* criterion that came from Roman law through Augustine into church law; see ibid. But it had a more central place in the thought of Thomas Aquinas, who connected it to the words of Paul in Romans 13:4: '[The prince] is the minister of God to execute his vengeance against the evildoer.' See Thomas Aquinas, *Summa Theologica*, II/II, Quaest. XL, Art. 1.

16 I make this judgment cognizant of the minority tradition in Christian just war theory from Augustine forward that allowed some forms of war for religion; in Augustine's words, repeated for canon law by Gratian, 'The enemies of the church are to be coerced even by war' (*Decretum Magistri Gratiani*, Quaest. VIII, Can. XLVIII). In fact, however, efforts to justify wars in Western cultural history, even those clearly involving some benefit or detriment to religion, have generally been justified by appeal to the other reasons already given: protection of the innocent, retaking of something lost, punishment of evil. For discussion of this issue of religious war – and by extension ideological war – see James Turner Johnson, *Ideology, Reason, and the Limitation of War* (Princeton, N.J.: Princeton University Press, 1975), chaps. I–III.

17 Ibid., pp. 266–70.

18 An early version of this kind of argument undergirded massive retaliation strategy, which Robert W. Tucker in *The Just War* (Baltimore, Md.: The Johns Hopkins Press, 1960) regards as an expression of a general American moral attitude justifying all-out responses to injustice received rather than limited uses of force proportionate to harm done to US interests. But suppose that this opposition to limited warfare is retained while all-out retaliation is itself denied as immoral (although the use of deterrence as a *threat* continues to be accepted); then the argument changes shape, though its fundamentals remain. Such a new version of the moral argument for deterrence and against

limited warfare can be found in the 1983 Pastoral Letter of the US Catholic bishops. (See National Conference of Catholic Bishops, *The Challenge of Peace* (Washington, D.C.: United States Catholic Conference, 1983). The purpose of deterrence, as defined here, is 'only to prevent the *use* of nuclear weapons by others' (par. 188, emphasis in original). 'War-fighting strategies', including even *planning* for fighting nuclear war at a limited level over a protracted period, are explicitly rejected (pars. 184, 188, 189). The reason is the prudential judgment that limited nuclear warfare can be expected to escalate to 'mass destruction' (pars. 151–61, 184). Although this suggests heavier reliance on conventional weapons (par. 155), even a conventional war 'could escalate to the nuclear level' (par. 156). Although the resultant position is not *explicitly* a deterrence-only one, it is difficult to find in the pessimism toward limited war and war-fighting strategies expressed in the bishops' letter any room for limited and proportionate responses to limited levels of harm done, such as the traditional *jus in bello* implies.

19 John Stuart Mill, 'The Contest in America', in *Dissertations and Discussions* (Boston: William V. Spencer, 1867), pp. 208–9. The full text of the passage in question,' written to oppose England's siding with the Confederacy in the American Civil War, is as follows:

> War is an ugly thing, but not the ugliest of things: the decayed and degraded state of moral and patriotic feeling which thinks nothing *worth* a war, is worse. When a people are used as mere human instruments for firing cannon or thrusting bayonets, in the service and for the selfish human instruments for firing cannon or thrusting bayonets, in the service and for the selfish purposes of a master, such war degrades a people. A war to protect other human beings against tyrannical injustice; a war to give victory to their own ideas of right and good, and which is their own war, carried on for an honest purpose by their own free choice – is often the means of their regeneration. A man who has nothing which he cares about more than he does about his personal safety is a miserable creature who has no chance of being free, unless made and kept so by the existing of better men than himself. As long as justice and injustice have not terminated their ever renewing fight for ascendancy in the affairs of mankind, human beings must be willing, when need is, to do battle for the one against the other.

20 Desiderius Erasmus, Letter to Antoon van Bergen, Abbot of St. Bertin, dated London, 14 March 1514; number 288 in *The Correspondence of Erasmus, Letters 142 to 297*, trans. R. A. B. Minors and D. F. S. Thomson, annotated by Wallace K. Ferguson (Toronto and Buffalo: University of Toronto Press, 1975), lines 47–63.

21 That is, for such pacifists the rejection of force has itself become a value, or it is necessarily implied by some other value (for example, Christian love in some forms of religious pacifism); in either case it is unassailable from outside the moral system in which this value is held. Other forms of pacifism, of course, reach their judgment against the use of force by argument based not on the evil of force as such but on the harm to some higher good that the use of force may entail. The contemporary position sometimes called *just-war pacifism*, which is based on a prudential calculation of proportionality, is such a form of pacifism.

22 See, further, James Turner Johnson 'On Keeping Faith: The Uses of History for Religious Ethics', *Journal of Religious Ethics* 7, no. 1 (Spring 1979): 98–116.

23 Erasmus, Letter, 14 March 1514, lines 17–24.

24 See, further, Roland H. Bainton, *Christian Attitudes toward War and Peace* (New York and Nashville: Abingdon Press, 1960), p. 131, and Lester K. Born, *The Education of a Christian Prince by Desiderius Erasmus* (New York: Octagon Books, 1965), pp. 1–26.

25 See, for example, Richard A. Falk, *A Study of Future Worlds* (New York: Macmillan/The Free Press, 1975).

26 John Howard Yoder, *Nevertheless* (Scottdale, Penna., and Kitchener, Ont.: Herald Press, 1976), p. 33.

27 Condemnation of 'militarism' has become a common feature of the public policy statements of many Protestant denominations. See, for example, the statements by The Christian Church (Disciples of Christ) and the Reformed Church in America in Robert Heyer, ed., *Nuclear Disarmament* (New York and Ramsey, N.J.: Paulist Press, 1982), pp. 245–6, 251–2, 267. A prominent example of condemnation of war-fighting strategic planning is the US Catholic bishops' pastoral; see National Conference of Catholic Bishops, *The Challenge of Peace*, paragraphs 184–90. Such thinking is far more like the traditional pacifism represented by Yoder and Erasmus than it is like the reasoning of just war tradition.

28 Jonathan Schell, *The Fate of the Earth* (New York: Avon Books, 1982), p. 85.

29 Ibid., p. 78.

30 See, for example, the discussions of noncombatant immunity found in Walzer, chaps. 8–10. Despite the criticisms I have earlier directed at the US Catholic bishops' letter, it clearly embodies an understanding that the values that might be endangered by an enemy are not trivial; they include 'those key values of justice, freedom and independence which are necessary for personal dignity and national integrity' (National Conference of Catholic Bishops, *The Challenge of Peace*, paragraph 175).

31 See, for example, Louis Rene Beres, *Mimicking Sisyphus* (Lexington, Mass.: Lexington Books, D.C. Heath and Company, 1983), pp. 15–24; cf. the argument of the US Catholic bishops, note 18.

32 O'Brien, *Just and Limited War*, chap. 1.

33 Cf. National Conference of Catholic Bishops, *The Challenge of Peace*, pars. 188, 190.

34 Philip Green, *Deadly Logic* (New York: Schocken Books, 1968), pp. 249–51.

35 Cf. National Conference of Catholic Bishops, *The Challenge of Peace*, pars. 175, 188. This document, on my reading, is only a whisker away from the deterrence-only position on nuclear weapons; that whisker is the ambiguity maintained in the threat of strategic nuclear retaliation, specifically in the possible difference between 'declaratory policy' and 'action policy' (par. 164). Paragraph 148 denies counter-population retaliation; paragraph 184 repeats this and also under-cuts the possibility of counterforce strategic retaliation. These themes recur elsewhere in section II of the document as well. Is the 'conditional acceptance of nuclear deterrence' (par. 198) in this Pastoral Letter then anything more than a 'conditional acceptance' of the *possession* of such weapons (not making any distinctions among types, purposes, or relative destructive power, but treating all nuclear weapons the same), and does not the 'no first use' position taken in the letter (par. 150 and *passim*) in practical terms collapse into a policy of 'no use at all'?

36 See John Eppstein, *The Catholic Tradition of the Law of Nations* (Washington, D.C.: Catholic Association for International Peace, 1935), p. 132.

37 National Conference of Catholic Bishops, *The Challenge of Peace*, par. 134.

38 Heyer, *Nuclear Disarmament*, p. 266.

39 Cf. Walzer, *Just and Unjust Wars*, pp. 329–35.

40 Carl von Clausewitz, *On War*, ed. and trans. Michael Howard and Peter Paret (Princeton, N.J.: Princeton University Press, 1976), p. 370.

41 See, for example, Paul Fussell's argument in *The Great War and Modern Memory* (New York and London: Oxford University Press, 1975), passim, that modern war is inevitably totalistic, chaotic, beyond human control, and disproportionately destructive of values.

42 Cf. National Conference of Catholic Bishops, *The Challenge of Peace*, pars. 155, 215–16.

43 See, further, Sam Cohen, 'Rethinking Strategic Defense', in Robert W. Poole, Jr., ed., *Defending a Free Society* (Lexington, Mass.: Lexington Books, D.C. Heath and Company, 1984), pp. 99–122.

44 Walzer, *Just and Unjust Wars*, chap. 16.

45 See, further, my discussion of Walzer on this matter in *Just War Tradition*, pp. 24–8.

46 Franciscus de Vitoria, *De Jure Belli*, section 37, in Franciscus de Vitoria, *De Indis et De Jure Belli Relectiones*, ed. Ernest Nys (Washington, D.C.: Carnegie Institute, 1917). Vitoria makes clear, however, that he thought few wars meet the test of an unambiguous conflict of justice against injustice.

5

The Challenge of Peace: God's Promise and Our Response

THE PASTORAL LETTER ON WAR AND PEACE

'The whole human race faces a moment of supreme crisis in its advance toward maturity.' Thus the Second Vatican Council opened its treatment of modern warfare.[1] Since the council, the dynamic of the nuclear arms race has intensified. Apprehension about nuclear war is almost tangible and visible today. As Pope John Paul II said in his message to the United Nations concerning disarmament: 'Currently the fear and preoccupation of so many groups in various parts of the world reveal that people are more frightened about what would happen if irresponsible parties unleash some nuclear war.'[2]

As bishops and pastors ministering in one of the major nuclear nations, we have encountered this terror in the minds and hearts of our people — indeed, we share it. We write this letter because we agree that the world is at a moment of crisis, the effects of which are evident in people's lives. It is not our intent to play on fears, however, but to speak words of hope and encouragement in time of fear. Faith does not insulate us from the challenges of life; rather, it intensifies our desire to help solve them precisely in light of the good news which has come to us in the person of Jesus, the Lord of history. From the resources of our faith we wish to provide hope and strength to all who seek a world free of the nuclear threat. Hope sustains one's capacity to live with danger without being overwhelmed by it; hope is the will to struggle against obstacles even when they appear insuperable. Ultimately our hope rests in the God who gave us life, sustains the world by his power and has called us to revere the lives of every person and all peoples.

The crisis of which we speak arises from this fact: nuclear war threatens the existence of our planet; this is a more menacing threat than any the world has known. It is neither tolerable nor necessary that human beings live under this threat. But removing it will require a major effort of intelligence, courage and faith. As Pope John Paul II said at Hiroshima: 'From now on it is only through a conscious choice and through a deliberate policy that humanity can survive.'[3]

As Americans, citizens of the nation which was first to produce atomic weapons, which has been the only one to use them and which today is one of the handful of nations capable of decisively influencing the course of the nuclear age, we have grave human, moral and political responsibilities to see that a 'conscious choice' is made to save humanity. This letter is therefore both an invitation and a challenge to Catholics in the United States to join with others in shaping the conscious choices and deliberate policies required in this 'moment of supreme crisis'.

PEACE IN THE MODERN WORLD: RELIGIOUS PERSPECTIVES AND PRINCIPLES

. . .

The nuclear threat transcends religious, cultural and national boundaries. To confront its danger requires all the resources reason and faith can muster. This letter is a contribution to a wider common effort meant to call Catholics and all members of our political community to dialogue and specific decisions about this awesome question.

The Catholic tradition on war and peace is a long and complex one, reaching from the Sermon on the Mount to the statements of Pope John Paul II. Its development cannot be sketched in a straight line, and it seldom gives a simple answer to complex questions. It speaks through many voices and has produced multiple forms of religious witness. As we locate ourselves in this tradition, seeking to draw from it and develop it, the document which provides profound inspiration and guidance for us is the Pastoral Constitution on the Church in the Modern World of Vatican II, for it is based on doctrinal principles and addresses the relationship of the church to the world with respect to the most urgent issues of our day.[4]

A rule of interpretation crucial for the pastoral constitution is equally important for this pastoral letter, although the authority inherent in these two documents is quite distinct. Both documents use principles of Catholic moral teaching and apply them to specific contemporary issues. The bishops at Vatican II opened the pastoral constitution with the following guideline on how to relate principles to concrete issues.

'In the first part, the church develops her teaching on man, on the world which is the enveloping context of man's existence, and on man's relations to his fellow men. In Part II, the church gives closer consideration to various aspects of modern life and human society; special consideration is given to those questions and problems which, in this general area, seem to have a greater urgency in our day. As a result, in Part II the subject matter which is viewed in the light of doctrinal principles is made up of diverse elements. Some elements have a permanent value; others, only a transitory one. Consequently, the constitution must be interpreted according to the general norms of theological interpretation. Interpreters must bear in mind — especially in Part II — the changeable circumstances which the subject matter, by its very nature, involves.'[5]

In this pastoral letter too we address many concrete questions concerning the arms race, contemporary warfare, weapons systems and negotiating strategies. We do not intend that our treatment of each of these issues carry the same moral authority as our statement of universal moral principles and formal church teaching. Indeed, we stress here at the beginning that not every statement in this letter has the same moral authority. At times we reassert universally binding moral principles (e.g., non-combatant immunity and proportionality). At still other times we reaffirm statements of recent popes and the teaching of Vatican II. Again, at other times we apply moral principles to specific cases.

When making applications of these principles we realize — and we wish readers to recognize — that prudential judgments are involved based on specific circumstances which can change or which can be interpreted differently by people of good will (e.g., the treatment of 'no first use'). However, the moral judgments that we make in specific cases, while not binding in conscience, are to be given serious attention and consideration by Catholics as they determine whether their moral judgments are consistent with the Gospel.

We shall do our best to indicate, stylistically and substantively, whenever we make such applications. We believe such specific judgments are an important part of this letter, but they should be interpreted in light of another passage from the pastoral constitution:

'Often enough the Christian view of things will itself suggest some specific solution in certain circumstances. Yet it happens rather frequently, and legitimately so, that with equal sincerity some of the faithful will disagree with others on a given matter. Even against the intention of their proponents, however, solutions proposed on one side or another may be easily confused by many people with the gospel message. Hence it is necessary for people to remember that no one is allowed in the aforementioned situations to appropriate the church's authority for his opinion. They should always try to enlighten one another through honest discussion, preserving mutual charity and caring above all for the common good.'[6]

This passage acknowledges that on some complex social questions the church expects a certain diversity of views even though all hold the same universal moral principles. The experience of preparing this pastoral letter has shown us the range of strongly held opinion in the Catholic community on questions of war and peace. Obviously, as bishops we believe that such differences should be expressed within the framework of Catholic moral teaching. We urge mutual respect among different groups in the church as they analyze this letter and the issues it addresses. Not only conviction and commitment are needed in the church, but also civility and charity.

The pastoral constitution calls us to bring the light of the Gospel to bear upon 'the signs of the times'. Three signs of the times have particularly influenced the writing of this letter. The first, to quote Pope John Paul II at the United Nations, is that 'the world wants peace, the world needs peace'.[7] The second is the judgment of Vatican II about the arms race: 'The arms race is one of the greatest curses on the human race and the harm it inflicts upon the poor is more than can be endured.'[8] The third is the way in which the unique dangers and dynamics of the nuclear arms race present qualitatively new problems which must be addressed by fresh applications of traditional moral principles. In light of these three characteristics, we wish to examine Catholic teaching on peace and war.

The Catholic social tradition as exemplified in the pastoral constitution and recent papal teachings is a mix of biblical, theological and philosophical elements which are brought to bear upon the concrete problems of the day. The biblical vision of the world, created and sustained by God, scarred by sin, redeemed in Christ and destined for the kingdom, is at the heart of our religious heritage. This vision requires elaboration, explanation and application in each age; the important task of theology is to penetrate ever more adequately the nature of the biblical vision of peace and relate it to a world not yet at peace. Consequently, the teaching about peace examines both how to construct a more peaceful world and how to assess the phenomenon of war.

At the center of the church's teaching on peace and at the center of all Catholic social teaching, are the transcendence of God and the dignity of the human person. The human person is the clearest reflection of God's presence in the world; all of the church's work in pursuit of both justice and peace is designed to protect and promote the dignity of every person. For each person not only reflects God, but is the expression of God's creative work and the meaning of Christ's redemptive ministry. Christians approach the problem of war and peace with fear and reverence. God is the Lord of life, and so each human life is sacred; modern warfare threatens the obliteration of human life on a previously unimaginable scale. The sense of awe and 'fear of the Lord' which former generations felt in approaching these issues weighs upon us with new urgency. In the words of the pastoral constitution: 'Men of this generation should realize that they will have to render an account of their warlike behavior; the destiny of generations to come depends largely on the decisions they make today.'[9]

Catholic teaching on peace and war has had two purposes: to help Catholics form their consciences and to contribute to the public policy debate about the morality of war. These two purposes have led Catholic teaching to address two distinct but overlapping audiences. The first is the Catholic faithful, formed by the premises of the Gospel and the principles of Catholic moral teaching. The second is the wider civil community, a more pluralistic audience, in which our brothers and sisters with whom we share the name Christian, Jews, Moslems, other religious communities, and all people of good will also make up our polity. Since Catholic teaching has traditionally sought to address both audiences, we intend to speak to both in this letter, recognizing that Catholics are also members of the wider political community.

The conviction, rooted in Catholic ecclesiology, that both the community of the faithful and the civil community should be addressed on peace and war has produced two complementary but distinct styles of teaching. The religious community shares a specific perspective of faith and can be called to live out its implications.

The wider civil community, although it does not share the same vision of faith, is equally bound by certain key moral principles. For all men and women find in the depth of their consciences a law written on the human heart by God.[10] From this law reason draws moral norms. These norms do not exhaust the gospel vision, but they speak to critical questions affecting the welfare of the human community, the role of states in international relations and the limits of acceptable action by individuals and nations on issues of war and peace.

. . .

We propose, therefore, to discuss both the religious vision of peace among peoples and nations and the problems associated with realizing this vision in a world of sovereign states devoid of any central authority and divided by ideology, geography and competing claims . . .

Building peace within and among nations is the work of many individuals and institutions; it is the fruit of ideas and decisions taken in the political, cultural, economic, social, military and legal sectors of life. We believe that the church as a community of faith and social institution, has a proper, necessary and distinctive part to play in the pursuit of peace.

. . .

Because peace, like the kingdom of God itself, is both a divine gift and a human work, the church should continually pray for the gift and share in the work. We are called to be a church at the service of peace, precisely because peace is one manifestation of God's word and work in our midst. Recognition of the church's responsibility to join with others in the work of peace is a major force behind the call today to develop a theology of peace. Much of the history of Catholic theology on war and peace has focused on limiting the resort to force in human affairs; this task is still necessary and is reflected later in this pastoral letter, but it is not a sufficient response to Vatican II's challenge 'to undertake a completely fresh reappraisal of war'.[11]

. . .

A theology of peace should ground the task of peacemaking solidly in the biblical vision of the kingdom of God, then place it centrally in the ministry of the church. It should specify the obstacles in the way of peace, as these are understood theologically and in the social and political sciences. It should both identify the specific contributions a community of faith can make to the work of peace and relate these to the wider work of peace pursued by other groups and institutions in society. Finally, a theology of peace must include a message of hope. The vision of hope must be available to all, but one source of its content should be found in a church at the service of peace.

. . .

Peace and the Kingdom

For us as believers, the sacred scriptures provide the foundation for confronting the dilemma of war and peace today. Any use of scripture in this area is conditioned by three factors. *First*, the term 'peace' has been understood in different ways at various times and in various contexts. For example, peace can refer to an individual's sense of well-being or security, or it can mean the cessation of armed hostility, producing an atmosphere in which nations can relate to each other and settle conflicts without resorting to the use of arms. For men and women of faith, peace will imply a right relationship with God, which entails forgiveness, reconciliation and union. Finally, the scriptures point to eschatological peace, a final, full realization of God's salvation when all creation will be made whole. Among these various meanings, the last two predominate in the scriptures and provide direction to the first two.

Second, the scriptures as we have them today were written over a long period of time and reflect many varied historical situations, all different from our own. Our understanding of them is both complicated and enhanced by these differences, but not in any way obscured or diminished by them. *Third*, since the scriptures speak primarily of God's intervention in history, they contain no specific treatise on war and peace. Peace and war must always be seen in light of God's intervention in human affairs and our response to that intervention. Both are elements within the ongoing revelation of God's will for creation.

Acknowledging this complexity, we still recognize in the scriptures a unique source of revelation, a word of God which is addressed to us as surely as it has been to all preceding generations. We call upon the Spirit of God who speaks in that word and in our hearts to aid us in our listening. The sacred texts have much to say to us about the ways in which God calls to live in union with and in fidelity to the divine will. They provide us with direction for our lives and hold out to us an object of hope, a final promise, which guides and directs our actions here and now.

The Old Testament   War and peace are significant and highly complex elements within the multilayered accounts of the creation and development of God's people in the Old Testament.

(1)   War   Violence and war are very much present in the history of the people of God, particularly from the Exodus period to the monarchy. God is often seen as the one who leads the Hebrews in battle, protects them from their enemies, makes them victorious over other armies (see, for example, Dt. 1:30; 20:4; Jos. 2:24; Jgs. 3:28). The metaphor of warrior carried multifaceted connotations for a people who knew themselves to be smaller and weaker than the nations which surrounded them. It also enabled them to express their conviction about God's involvement in their lives and his desire for their growth and development. This metaphor provided the people with a sense of security; they had a God who would protect them even in the face of overwhelming obstacles. It was also a call to faith and to trust; the mighty God was to be obeyed and followed. No one can deny the presence of such images in the Old Testament nor their powerful influence upon the articulation of this people's understanding of the involvement of God in their history. The warrior God was highly significant during long periods of Israel's understanding of its faith. But this image was not the only image, and it was gradually transformed, particularly after the experience of the exile, when God was no longer identified with military victory and might. Other images and other understandings of God's activity became predominant in expressing the faith of God's people.

(2)   Peace   Several points must be taken into account in considering the image of peace in the Old Testament. First, all notions of peace must be understood in light of Israel's relation to God. Peace is always seen as gift from God and as fruit of God's saving activity. Second, the individual's personal peace is not greatly stressed. The well-being and freedom from fear which result from God's love are viewed primarily as they pertain to the community and its unity and harmony. Furthermore, this unity and harmony extend to all of creation; true peace implied a restoration of the

right order not just among peoples, but within all of creation. Third, while the images of war and the warrior God become less dominant as a more profound and complex understanding of God is presented in the texts, the images of peace and the demands upon the people for covenantal fidelity to true peace grow more urgent and more developed.

(3) Peace and Fidelity to the Covenant   If Israel obeyed God's law, God would dwell among them. 'I will walk among you and will be your God and you shall be my people' (Lv. 26:12). God would strengthen the people against those who opposed them and would give peace in the land. The description of life in these circumstances witnesses to unity among peoples and creation, to freedom from fear and to security (Lv. 26:3 – 16). The right relationship between the people and God was grounded in and expressed by a covenantal union. The covenant bound the people to God in fidelity and obedience; God was also committed in the covenant to be present with the people, to save them, to lead them to freedom. Peace is a special characteristic of this covenant; when the prophet Ezekiel looked to the establishment of the new, truer covenant, he declared that God would establish an everlasting covenant of peace with the people (Ez. 37:26).

. . .

(4) Hope for Eschatological Peace   Experience made it clear to the people of God that the covenant of peace and the fullness of salvation had not been realized in their midst. War and enmity were still present, injustices thrived, sin still manifested itself. These same experiences also convinced the people of God's fidelity to a covenant which they often neglected. Because of this fidelity, God's promise of a final salvation involving all peoples and all creation and of an ultimate reign of peace became an integral part of the hope of the Old Testament. In the midst of their failures and sin, God's people strove for greater fidelity to him and closer relationship with him; they did so because believing in the future they had been promised, they directed their lives and energies toward an eschatological vision for which they longed. Peace is an integral component of that vision.

The final age, the Messianic time, is described as one in which the 'Spirit is poured on us from on high'. In this age creation will be made whole, 'justice will dwell in the wilderness' the effect of righteousness will be peace, and the people will 'abide in a peaceful

habitation and in secure dwellings and in quiet resting places'
(Is. 32:15–20). There will be no need for instruments of war
(Is. 2:4; Mi. 4:3),[12] God will speak directly to the people and
'righteousness and peace will embrace each other' (Ps. 85:10–11).
A Messiah will appear, a servant of God upon whom God has
placed his spirit and who will faithfully bring forth justice to the
nations: 'He will not cry or lift up his voice, or make it heard in
the street; a bruised reed he will not break and a dimly burning
wick he will not quench; he will faithfully bring forth justice' (Is.
42:2–3).

The Old Testament provides us with the history of a people
who portrayed their God as one who intervened in their lives, who
protected them and led them to freedom, often as a mighty leader
in battle. They also appear as a people who longed constantly for
peace. Such peace was always seen as a result of God's gift which
came about in fidelity to the covenantal union. Furthermore, in
the midst of their unfulfilled longing, God's people clung tenaciously
to hope in the promise of an eschatological time when, in the
fullness of salvation, peace and justice would embrace and all
creation would be secure from harm. The people looked for a
Messiah, one whose coming would signal the beginning of that
time. In their waiting, they heard the prophets call them to love
according to the covenantal vision, to repent and to be ready for
God's reign.

New Testament   As Christians we believe that Jesus is the Messiah
or Christ so long awaited. God's servant (Mt. 12:18–21), prophet
and more than a prophet (Jn. 4:19–26), the one in whom the
fullness of God was pleased to dwell, through whom all things in
heaven and on earth were reconciled to God, Jesus made peace by
the blood of the cross (Col. 1:19–20). While the characteristics of
the *shalom* of the Old Testament (gift from God, inclusive of all
creation, grounded in salvation and covenantal fidelity, inextricably
bound up with justice) are present in the New Testament traditions,
all discussion of war and peace in the New Testament must be
seen within the context of the unique revelation of God that is
Jesus Christ and of the reign of God which Jesus proclaimed and
inaugurated.

(1)   War   There is no notion of a warrior God who will lead the
people in a historical victory over its enemies in the New Testament.
The only war spoken of is found in apocalyptic images of the final
moments, especially as they are depicted in the Book of Revelation.
Here war stands as image of the eschatological struggle between

God and Satan. It is a war in which the Lamb is victorious (Rv. 17:14).

Military images appear in terms of the preparedness which one must have for the coming trials (Lk. 14:31; 22:35−38). Swords appear in the New Testament as an image of division (Mt. 12:34; Heb. 4:12); they are present at the arrest of Jesus, and he rejects their use (Lk. 22:51 and parallel texts); weapons are transformed in Ephesians, when the Christians are urged to put on the whole armor of God which includes the breastplate of righteousness, the helmet of salvation, the sword of the Spirit, 'having shod your feet in the equipment of the gospel of peace' (Eph. 6:10−17; cf. 1 Thes. 5:8−9). Soldiers too are present in the New Testament. They are at the crucifixion of Jesus, of course, but they are also recipients of the baptism of John, and one centurion receives the healing of his servant (Mt. 8:5−13 and parallel texts; cf. Jn. 4:46−53).

Jesus challenged everyone to recognize in him the presence of the reign of God and to give themselves over to that reign. Such a radical change of allegiance was difficult for many to accept and families found themselves divided, as if by a sword. Hence, the Gospels tell us that Jesus said he came not to bring peace but rather the sword (Mt. 10:34). The peace which Jesus did not bring was the false peace which the prophets had warned against. The sword which he did bring was that of the division caused by the word of God, which like a two-edged sword 'pierces to the division of soul and spirit, of joints and marrow, and discerns the thoughts and intentions of the heart' (Heb. 4:12).

All are invited into the reign of God. Faith in Jesus and trust in God's mercy are the criteria. Living in accord with the demands of the kingdom rather than those of one's specific profession is decisive.[13]

(2)   Jesus and Reign of God   Jesus proclaimed the regin of God in his words and made it present in his actions. His words begin with a call to conversion and a proclamation of the arrival of the kingdom. 'The time is fulfilled, and the kingdom of God is at hand; repent, and believe in the Gospel' (Mt. 1:15; Mt. 4:17). The call to conversion was at the same time an invitation to enter God's reign. Jesus went beyond the prophets' cries for conversion when he declared that, in him, the reign of God had begun and was in fact among the people (Lk. 17:20−21; 12:32).

His words, especially as they are preserved for us in the Sermon on the Mount, describe a new reality in which God's power is manifested and the longing of the people is fulfilled. In God's reign the poor are given the kingdom, the mourners are comforted, the meek inherit the earth, those hungry for righteousness are satisfied, the merciful know mercy, the pure see God, the persecuted know the kingdom and peacemakers are called the children of God (Mt. 5:3–10).

Jesus' words also depict for us the conduct of one who lives under God's reign. His words call for a new way of life which fulfills and goes beyond the law. One of the most striking characteristics of this new way is forgiveness. All who hear Jesus are repeatedly called to forgive one another and to do so not just once, but many, many times (Mt. 6:14–15; Lk. 6:37; Mt. 18:21–22; Mk. 11:25; Lk. 11:4; 17:3–4). The forgiveness of God, which is the beginning of salvation, is manifested in communal forgiveness and mercy.

Jesus also described God's reign as one in which love is an active, life-giving, inclusive force. He called for a love which went beyond family ties and bonds of friendship to reach even those who were enemies (Mt. 5:44–48; Lk. 6:27–28). Such a love does not seek revenge, but rather is merciful in the face of threat and opposition (Mt. 5:39–42; Lk. 6:29–31). Disciples are to love one another as Jesus has loved them (Jn. 15:12).

. . .

Most characteristic of Jesus' actions are those in which he showed his love. As he had commanded others, his love led him even to the giving of his own life to effect redemption. Jesus' message and his actions were dangerous ones in his time, and they led to his death — a cruel and viciously inflicted death, a criminal's death (Gal. 3:13). In all of his suffering, as in all of his life and ministry, Jesus refused to defend himself with force or with violence. He endured violence and cruelty so that God's love might be fully manifest and the world might be reconciled to the One from whom it had become estranged. Even at his death Jesus cried out for forgiveness for those who were his executioners: 'Father, forgive them' (Lk. 23:34).

The resurrection of Jesus is the sign to the world that God indeed does reign, does give life in death and that the love of God is stronger even than death (Rom. 8:36–39).

Only in light of this, the fullest demonstration of the power of God's reign, can Jesus' gift of peace — a peace which the world cannot give (Jn. 14:27) — be understood. Jesus gives that peace to his disciples, to those who had witnessed the helplessness of the crucifixion and the power of the resurrection (Jn. 20:19, 20, 26). The peace which he gives to them as he greets them as their risen Lord is the fullness of salvation. It is the reconciliation of the world and God (Rom. 5:1–2; Col. 1:20); the restoration of the unity and harmony of all creation which the Old Testament spoke of with such longing. Because the walls of hostility between God and humankind were broken down in the life and death of the true, perfect servant, union and well-being between God and the world were finally fully possible (Eph. 2:13–22; Gal. 3:28).

(3) Jesus and the Community of Believers   As his first gift to his followers, the risen Jesus gave his gift of peace. This gift permeated the meetings between the risen Jesus and his followers (Jn. 20:19–29). So intense was that gift and so abiding was its power that the remembrance of that gift and the daily living of it became the hallmark of the community of faith. Simultaneously, Jesus gave his Spirit to those who followed him. These two personal and communal gifts are inseparable. In the Spirit of Jesus the community of believers was enabled to recognize and to proclaim the Savior of the world.

Gifted with Jesus' own Spirit, they could recognize what God had done and know in their own lives the power of the One who creates from nothing. The early Christian communities knew that this power and the reconciliation and peace which marked it were not yet fully operative in their world. They struggled with external persecution and with interior sin, as do all people. But their experience of the Spirit of God and their memory of the Christ who was with them nevertheless enabled them to look forward with unshakable confidence to the time when the fullness of God's reign would make itself known in the world. At the same time, they knew that they were called to be ministers of reconciliation (2 Cor. 5:19–20), people who would make the peace which God had established visible through the love and the unity within their own communities.

. . .

Conclusion   Even a brief examination of war and peace in the scriptures makes it clear that they do not provide us with detailed answers to the specifics of the questions which we face today. They do not speak specifically of nuclear war or nuclear weapons, for these were beyond the imagination of the communities in which the scriptures were formed. The sacred texts do, however, provide us with urgent direction when we look at today's concrete realities.

. . .

Kingdom and History

The Christian understanding of history is hopeful and confident but also sober and realistic. 'Christian optimism based on the glorious cross of Christ and the outpouring of the Holy Spirit is no excuse for self-deception. For Christians, peace on earth is always a challenge because of the presence of sin in man's heart.'[14] Peace must be built on the basis of justice in a world where the personal and social consequences of sin are evident.

. . .

'Although Christians put all their best energies into preventing war or stopping it, they do not deceive themselves about their ability to cause peace to triumph nor about the effect of their efforts to this end. They therefore concern themselves with all human initiatives in favor of peace and very often take part in them. But they regard them with realism and humility. One could almost say that they relativize them in two senses: They relate them both to the self-deception of humanity and to God's saving plan.'[15] Christians are called to live the tension between the vision of the reign of God and its concrete realization in history. The tension is often described in terms of 'already but not yet': i.e., we already live in the grace of the kingdom, but it is not yet the completed kingdom. Hence, we are a pilgrim people in a world marked by conflict and injustice. Christ's grace is at work in the world; his command of love and his call to reconciliation are not purely future ideals but call us to obedience today.

With Pope Paul VI and Pope John Paul II we are convinced that 'peace is possible'.[16] At the same time experience convinces us that 'in this world a totally and permanently peaceful human society is unfortunately a utopia, and that ideologies that hold up that prospect as easily attainable are based on hopes that cannot be realized, whatever the reason behind them'.[17]

This recognition — that peace is possible but never assured and that its possibility must be continually protected and preserved in the face of obstacles and attacks upon it — accounts in large measure for the complexity of Catholic teaching on warfare. In the kingdom of God peace and justice will be fully realized. Justice is always the foundation of peace. In history, efforts to pursue both peace and justice are at times in tension, and the struggle for justice may threaten certain forms of peace.

It is within this tension of kingdom and history that Catholic teaching has addressed the problem of war. Wars mark the fabric of human history, distort the life of nations today and, in the form of nuclear weapons, threaten the destruction of the world as we know it and the civilization which has been patiently constructed over centuries. The causes of war are multiple and not easily identified. Christians will find in any violent situation the consequences of sin: not only sinful patterns of domination, oppression or aggression, but the conflict of values and interests which illustrate the limitations of a sinful world. The threat of nuclear war which affects the world today reflects such sinful patterns and conflicts.

In the 'already but not yet' of Christian existence, members of the church choose different paths to move toward the realization of the kingdom in history. As we examine both the positions open to individuals for forming their consciences on war and peace and the Catholic teaching on the obligation of the state to defend society, we draw extensively on the pastoral constitution for two reasons.

First, we find its treatment of the nature of peace and the avoidance of war compelling, for it represents the prayerful thinking of bishops of the entire world and calls vigorously for fresh new attitudes while faithfully reflecting traditional church teaching. Second, the council fathers were familiar with more than the horrors of World Wars I and II. They saw conflicts continuing 'to produce their devastating effect day by day somewhere in the world,' the increasing ferocity of warfare made possible by modern scientific weapons, guerrilla warfare 'drawn out by new methods of deceit and subversion' and terrorism regarded as a new way to wage war.[18] The same phenomena mark our day.

For similar reasons we draw heavily upon the popes of the nuclear age, from Pope Pius XII through Pope John Paul II. The teaching of popes and councils must be incarnated by each local church in a manner understandable to its culture. This allows each local church to bring its unique insights and experience to bear on the issues shaping our world. From 1966 to the present, American bishops, individually and collectively, have issued numerous statements on the issues of peace and war, ranging from the Vietnam War to conscientious objection and the use of nuclear weapons. These statements reflect not only the concerns of the hierarchy, but also the voices of our people, who have increasingly expressed to us their alarm over the threat of war. In this letter we wish to continue and develop the teaching on peace and war which we have previously made and which we have previously made and which reflects both teaching of the universal church and the insights and experience of the Catholic community of the United States.

It is significant that explicit treatment of war and peace is reserved for the final chapter of the pastoral constitution. Only after exploring the nature and destiny of the human person does the council take up the nature of peace, which it sees not as an end in itself, but as an *indispensable condition* for the task 'of constructing for all men everywhere a world more genuinely human'.[19] An understanding of this task is crucial to understanding the church's view of the moral choices open to us as Christians.

The Moral Choices for the Kingdom

In one of its most frequently quoted passages the pastoral constitution declares that it is necessary 'to undertake a completely fresh reappraisal of war'.[20] ...

It is clear then that to evaluate war with a new attitude, we must go far beyond an examination of weapons systems or military strategies. We must probe the meaning of the moral choices which are ours as Christians. In accord with the vision of Vatican II, we need to be sensitive to both the danger of war and the conditions of true freedom within which moral choices can be made.[21] Peace is the setting in which moral choice can be most effectively exercised. How can we move toward that peace which is indispensable for true human freedom? How do we define such peace?

The Nature of Peace   The Catholic tradition has always understood the meaning of peace in positive terms. Peace is both a gift of God and a human work. It must be constructed on the basis of central human values: truth, justice, freedom and love. The pastoral constitution states the traditional conception of peace.

'Peace is not merely the absence of war. Nor can it be reduced solely to the maintenance of a balance of power between enemies. Nor is it brought about by dictatorship. Instead, it is rightly and appropriately called 'an enterprise of justice' (Is. 32:7). Peace results from that harmony built into human society by its divine founder and actualized by men as they thirst after ever greater justice.'[22]

Pope John Paul II has enhanced this positive conception of peace by relating it with new philosophical depth to the church's teaching on human dignity and human rights. The relationship was articulated in his 1979 Address to the General Assembly of the United Nations and also in his World Day of Peace Message of 1982.

'Unconditional and effective respect for each one's unprescriptable and unalienable rights is the necessary condition in order that peace may reign in a society. *Vis-à-vis* these basic rights, all others are in way derivatory and secondary. In a society in which these rights are not protected, the very idea of universality is dead as soon as a small group of individuals set up for their own exclusive advantage a principle of discrimination whereby the rights and even the lives of others are made dependent on the whim of the stronger.'[23]

As we have already noted, however, the protection, of human rights and the preservation of peace are tasks to be accomplished in a world marked by sin and conflict of various kinds. The church's teaching on war and peace establishes a strong presumption against war which is binding on all; it then examines when this presumption may be overriden, precisely in the name of preserving the kind of peace which protects human dignity and human rights.

The Presumption Against War and the Principle of Legitimate Self-Defense Under the rubric 'curbing the savagery of war', the council contemplates the 'melancholy state of humanity'. It looks at this world as it is, not simply as we would want it to be. The view is stark: ferocious new means of warfare threatening savagery surpassing that of the past, deceit, subversion, terrorism, genocide. This last crime in particular is vehemently condemned as horrendous, but all activities which deliberately conflict with the all-embracing principles of universal natural law, which is permanently binding, are criminal, as are all orders commanding such action. Supreme commendation is due the courage of those who openly and fearlessly resist those who issue such commands. All individuals, especially government officials and experts, are bound to honor and improve upon agreements which are 'aimed at making military activity and its consequences less inhuman' and which 'better and more workably lead to restraining the frightfulness of war'.[24]

This remains a realistic appraisal of the world today. Later in this section the council calls for us 'to strain every muscle as we work for the time when all war can be completely outlawed by international consent'. We are told, however, that this goal requires the establishment of some universally recognized public authority with effective power 'to safeguard, on the behalf of all, security,

regard for justice and respect for rights'.[25] *But what of the present?*
The council is exceedingly clear, as are the popes.

'Certainly war has not been rooted out of human affairs. As
long as the danger of war remains and there is no competent and
sufficiently powerful authority at the international level, governments cannot be denied the right to legitimate defense once every
means of peaceful settlement has been exhausted. Therefore, government authorities and others who share public responsibility have
the duty to protect the welfare of the people entrusted to their care
and to conduct such grave matters soberly.

'But it is one thing to undertake military action for the just
defense of the people, and something else again to seek the subju-
gation of other nations. Nor does the possession of war potential
make every military or political use of it lawful. Neither does the
mere fact that war has unhappily begun mean that all is fair
between the warring parties.'[26]

The Christian has no choice but to defend peace, properly understood, against aggression. This is an inalienable obligation. It is
the *how* of defending peace which offers moral options. We stress
this principle again because we observe so much misunderstanding
about both those who resist bearing arms and those who bear
them. Great numbers from both traditions provide examples of
exceptional courage, examples the world continues to need.

Of the millions of men and women who have served with
integrity in the armed forces, many have laid down their lives.
Many others serve today throughout the world in the difficult and
demanding task of helping to preserve that 'peace of a sort' of
which the council speaks.

We see many deeply sincere individuals who, far from being
indifferent or apathetic to world evils, believe strongly in conscience
that they are best defending true peace by refusing to bear arms.
In some cases they are motivated by their understanding of the
Gospel and the life and death of Jesus as forbidding all violence.
In others, their motivation is simply to give personal example of
Christian forbearance as a positive, constructive approach toward
loving reconciliation with enemies. In still other cases, they propose
or engage in 'active non-violence' as programed resistance to thwart
aggression or to render ineffective any oppression attempted by
force of arms. No government, and certainly no Christian, may
simply assume that such individuals are mere pawns of conspira-
torial forces or guilty of cowardice.

Catholic teaching sees these two distinct moral responses as
having a complementary relationship in the sense that both seek to

serve the common good. They differ in their perception of how the common good is to be defended most effectively, but both responses testify to the Christian conviction that peace must be pursued and rights defended within moral restraints and in the context of defining other basic human values.

In all of this discussion of distinct choices, of course, we are referring to options open to individuals. The council and the popes have stated clearly that governments threatened by armed, unjust aggression *must* defend their people. This includes defense by armed force if necessary as a last resort. We shall discuss below the conditions and limits imposed on such defense. Even when speaking of individuals, however, the council is careful to preserve the fundamental *right* of defense. Some choose not to vindicate their rights by armed force and adopt other methods of defense, but they do not lose the right of defense nor may they renounce their obligations to others. They are praised by the council, as long as the rights and duties of others or of the community itself are not injured.

Pope Pius XII is especially strong in his conviction about the responsibility of the Christian to resist unjust aggression:

> *A people threatened with an unjust aggression, or already its victim, may not remain passively indifferent, if it would think and act as befits a Christian.* All the more does the solidarity of the family of nations forbid others to behave as mere spectators, in any attitude of apathetic neutrality. Who will ever measure the harm already caused in the past by such indifference to war of aggression, which is quite alien to the Christian instinct? How much more keenly has it brought any advantage in recompense? On the contrary, it has only reassured and encouraged the authors and fomentors of aggression, while it obliges the several peoples, left to themselves, to increase their armaments indefinitely . . .
>
> Among (the) goods (of humanity) some are of such importance for society that it is perfectly lawful to defend them against unjust aggression. *Their defense is even an obligation for the nations as a whole, who have a duty not to abandon a nation that is attacked.*[27]

None of the above is to suggest, however, that armed force is the only defense against unjust aggression, regardless of circumstances. Well does the council require that grave matters concerning the protection of peoples be conducted *soberly*. The council fathers were well aware that in today's world, the 'horror and perversity of war are immensely magnified by the multiplication of scientific weapons. For acts of war involving these weapons can inflict massive and indiscriminate destruction far exceeding the bounds of legitimate defense.'[28] Hence we are warned: 'Men of our time must realize that they will have to give a somber reckoning for their deeds of war. For the course of the future will depend largely on the decisions they make today.'[29] There must be serious and continuing study and efforts to develop programmed methods for both individuals and nations to defend against unjust aggression without using violence.

. . .

Christians are aware that plans based on aggression, domination and the manipulation of others lurk in human hearts, and sometimes even secretly nourish human intentions in spite of certain declarations or manifestations of a pacifist nature. For Christians know that in this world a totally and permanently peaceful human society is unfortunately a utopia and that ideologies that hold up that prospect as easily attainable are based on hopes that cannot be realized, whatever the reason behind them.

It is a question of a mistaken view of the human condition, a lack of application in considering the question as a whole; or it may be a case of evasion in order to calm fear, or in still other cases a matter of calculated self-interest. Christians are convinced, if only because they have learned from personal experience, that these deceptive hopes lead straight to the *false peace* of totalitarian regimes. But this realistic view in no way prevents Christians from working for peace: instead, it stirs up their ardor, for they also know that Christ's victory over deception, hate and death gives those in love with peace a more decisive motive for action than what the most generous theories about man have to offer; Christ's victory likewise gives a hope more surely based than any hope held out by the most audacious dreams.

This is why Christians, even as they strive to resist and prevent every form of warfare, have no hesitation in recalling that, in the name of an elementary requirement of justice, peoples have a right and even a duty to protect their exist-

ence and freedom by proportionate means against an unjust
aggressor.[30]

. . .

The Just-War Criteria The moral theory of the 'just war' or
'limited-war' doctrine begins with the presumption which binds all
Christians: We should do no harm to our neighbors; how we treat
our enemy is the key test of whether we love our neighbor; and
the possibility of taking even one human life is a prospect we
should consider in fear and trembling. How is it possible to move
from these presumptions to the idea of a justifiable use of lethal
force?

Historically and theologically the clearest answer to the question
is found in St Augustine. Augustine was impressed by the fact and
the consequences of sin in history — the 'not yet' dimension of the
kingdom. In his view war was both the result of sin and a tragic
remedy for sin in the life of political societies. War arose from
disordered ambitions, but it could also be used in some cases at
least to restrain evil and protect the innocent. The classic case
which illustrated his view was the use of lethal force to prevent
aggression against innocent victims. Faced with the fact of attack
on the innocent, the presumption that we do no harm even to our
enemy yielded to the command of love understood as the need to
restrain an enemy who would injure the innocent.

The just war argument has taken several forms in the history
of Catholic theology, but this Augustinian insight is its central
premise.[31] In the twentieth century, papal teaching has used the
logic of Augustine and Aquinas[32] to articulate a right of self-
defense for states in a decentralized international order and to
state the criteria for exercising that right. The essential position
was stated by Vatican II: 'As long as the danger of war persists
and there is no international authority with the necessary competence and power, governments cannot be denied the right of
lawful self-defense, once all peace efforts have failed'.[33] We have
already indicated the centrality of this principle for understanding
Catholic teaching about the state and its duties.

Just war teaching has evolved, however, as an effort to prevent
war; only if war cannot be rationally avoided does the teaching
then seek to restrict and reduce its horrors. It does this by establishing a set of rigorous conditions which must be met if the decision
to go to war is to be morally permissible. Such a decision, especially

today, requires extraordinarily strong reasons for overriding the presumption *in favor of peace* and *against* war. This is one significant reason why valid just war teaching makes provision for conscientious dissent. It is presumed that all sane people prefer peace, never *want* to initiate war and accept even the most justifiable defensive war only as a sad necessity. Only the most powerful reasons may be permitted to override such objection. In the words of Pope Pius XII:

'The Christian will for peace . . . is very careful to avoid recourse to the force of arms in the defense of rights which, however legitimate, do not offset the risk of kindling a blaze with all its spiritual and material consequences.'[34]

The determination of *when* conditions exist which allow the resort to force in spite of the strong presumption against it is made in light of *jus ad bellum* criteria. The determination of *how* even a justified resort to force must be conducted is made in light of the *jus in bello* criteria. We shall briefly explore the meaning of both.[35]

Jus ad Bellum: Why and when recourse to war is permissible.

(1) Just Cause War is permissibly only to confront 'a real and certain danger', i.e., to protect innocent life, to preserve conditions necessary for decent human existence and to secure basic human rights. As both Pope Pius XII and Pope John XXIII made clear, if war of retribution was ever justifiable, the risks of modern war negate such a claim today.

(2) Competent Authority In the Catholic tradition the right to use force has always been joined to the common good; war must be declared by those with responsibility for public order, not by private groups or individuals.

The requirement that a decision to go to war must be made by competent authority is particularly important in a democratic society. It needs detailed treatment here since it involves a broad spectrum of related issues. Some of the bitterest divisions of society in our own nation's history, for example, have been provoked over the question of whether or not a president of the United States has acted constitutionally and legally in involving our country in a *de facto* war, even if − indeed, especially if − war was never formally declared. Equally perplexing problems of conscience can be raised for individuals expected or legally required to go to war even though our duly elected representatives in Congress have in fact voted for war.

The criterion of competent authority is of further importance in a day when revolutionary war has become commonplace. Historically, the just war tradition has been open to a 'just revolution' position, recognizing that an oppressive government may lose its claim to legitimacy. Insufficient analytical attention has been given to the moral issues of revolutionary warfare. The mere possession of sufficient weaponry, for example, does not legitimize the initiation of war by 'insurgents' against an established government, any more than the government's systematic oppression of its people can be carried out under the doctrine of 'national security'.

While the legitimacy of revolution in some circumstances cannot be denied, just war teachings must be applied as rigorously to revolutionary—counterrevolutionary conflicts as to others. The issue of who constitutes competent authority and how such authority is exercised is essential.

When we consider in this letter the issues of conscientious objection and selective conscientious objection, the issue of competent authority will arise again.

(3) Comparative Justice Questions concerning the *means* of waging war today, particularly in view of the destructive potential of weapons, have tended to override questions concerning the comparative justice of the positions of respective adversaries or enemies. In essence: Which side is sufficiently 'right' in a dispute, and are the values at stake critical enough to override the presumption against war? The question in its most basic form is this: do the rights and values involved justify killing? For whatever the means used, war by definition involves violence, destruction, suffering and death.

The category of comparative justice is designed to emphasize the presumption against war which stands at the beginning of just war teaching. In a world of sovereign states recognizing neither a common moral authority nor a central political authority comparative justice stresses that no state should act on the basis that it has 'absolute justice' on its side. Every party to a conflict should acknowledge the limits of its 'just cause' and the consequent requirement to use *only* limited means in pursuit of its objectives. Far from legitimizing a crusade mentality, comparative justice is designed to relativize absolute claims and to restrain the use of force even in a 'justified' conflict.[36]

Given techniques of propaganda and the ease with which nations and individuals either assume or delude themselves into believing that God or right is clearly on their side, the test of comparative justice may be extremely difficult to apply. Clearly, however, this is not the case in every instance of war. Blatant aggression from without and subversion from within are often enough readily identifiable by all reasonably fair-minded people.

(4) Right Intention   Right intention is related to just cause — war can be legitimately intended only for the reasons set forth above as a just cause. During the conflict, right intention means pursuit of peace and reconciliation, including avoiding unnecessarily destructive acts or imposing unreasonable conditions (e.g., unconditional surrender).

(5) Last Resort   For resort to war to be justified, all peaceful alternatives must have been exhausted. There are formidable problems in this requirement. No international organization currently in existence has exercised sufficient internationally recognized authority to be able either to mediate effectively in most cases or to prevent conflict by the intervention of UN or other peacekeeping forces. Furthermore, there is a tendency for nations or peoples which perceive conflict between or among other nations as advantageous to themselves to attempt to prevent a peaceful settlement rather than advance it.

We regret the apparent unwillingness of some to see in the United Nations organization the potential for world order which exists and to encourage its development. Pope Paul VI called the United Nations the last hope for peace. The loss of this hope cannot be allowed to happen. Pope John Paul II is again instructive on this point:

> I wish above all to repeat my confidence in you, the leaders and members of the international organizations, and in you, the international officials! In the course of the last 10 years your organizations have too often been the object of attempts at manipulation on the part of nations wishing to exploit such bodies. However it remains true that the present multiplicity of violent clashes, divisions and blocks on which bilateral relations founder, offer the great international organizations the opportunity to engage upon the qualitative change in their activities, even to reform on certain points their own structures in order to take into account new realities and to enjoy effective power.[37]

(6) Probability of Success   This is difficult criterion to apply, but its purpose is to prevent irrational resort to force or hopeless

resistance when the outcome of either will clearly be disproportionate or futile. The determination includes a recognition that at times defense of key values, even against great odds, may be a 'proportionate' witness.

(7) Proportionality In terms of the *jus ad bellum* criteria, proportionality means that the damage to be inflicted and the costs incurred by war must be proportionate to the good expected by taking up arms. Nor should judgments concerning proportionality be limited to the temporal order without regard to a spiritual dimension in terms of 'damage', 'cost' and 'the good expected'. In today's interdependent world even a local conflict can affect people everywhere; this is particularly the case when the nuclear powers are involved. Hence a nation cannot justly go to war today without considering the effect of its action on others and on the international community.

This principle of proportionality applies throughout the conduct of the war as well as to the decision to begin warfare. During the Vietnam War our bishops' conference ultimately concluded that the conflict had reached such a level of devastation to the adversary and damage to our own society that continuing it could not be justified.[38]

Jus in Bello Even when the stringent conditions which justify resort to war are met the conduct of war (i.e., strategy, tactics and individual actions) remains subject to continuous scrutiny in light of two principles which have special significance today precisely because of the destructive capability of modern technological warfare. These principles are proportionality and discrimination. In discussing them here we shall apply them to the question of *jus ad bellum* as well as *jus in bello*; for today it becomes increasingly difficult to make a decision to use any kind of armed force, however limited initially in intention and in the destructive power of the weapons employed, without facing at least the possibility of escalation to broader, or even total, war and to the use of weapons of horrendous destructive potential. This is especially the case when adversaries are 'superpowers', as the council clearly envisioned:

'Indeed, if the kind of weapons now stocked in the arsenals of the great powers were to be employed to the fullest, the result would be the almost complete reciprocal slaughter of one side by the other, not to speak of the widespread devastation that would follow in the world and the deadly after effects resulting from the use of such weapons.'[39]

It should not be thought, of course, that massive slaughter and destruction would result only from the extensive use of nuclear weapons. We recall with horror the carpet and incendiary bombings of World War II, the deaths of hundreds of thousands in various regions of the world through 'conventional' arms, the unspeakable use of gas and other forms of chemical warfare, the destruction of homes and of crops, the utter suffering war has wrought during the centuries before and the decades since the use of the 'atom bomb'. Nevertheless, every honest person must recognize that, especially given the proliferation of modern scientific weapons, we now face possibilities which are appalling to contemplate. Today, as never before, we must ask not merely what *will* happen but what *may* happen, especially if major powers embark on war. Pope John Paul II has repeatedly pleaded that world leaders confront this reality:

> (I)n view of the difference between classical warfare and nuclear or bacteriological war — a difference so to speak of nature — and in view of the scandal of the arms race seen against the background of the needs of the Third World, this right (of defense), which is very real in principle, only underlines the urgency of world society to equip itself with effective means of negotiation. In this way the nuclear terror that haunts our time can encourage us to enrich our common heritage with a very simple discovery that is within our reach, namely that war is the most barbarous and least effective way of resolving conflicts.[40]

The Pontifical Academy of Sciences reaffirmed the Holy Father's theme in its November 1981 'Statement on the Consequences of Nuclear War'. Then, in a meeting convoked by the pontifical academy, representatives of national academies of science from throughout the world issued a 'Declaration on the Prevention of Nuclear War' which specified the meaning of Pope John Paul II's statement that modern warfare differs by nature from previous forms of war. The scientists said:

> Throughout its history humanity has been confronted with war, but since 1945 the nature of warfare has changed so profoundly that the future of the human race, of generations yet unborn, is imperiled ... For the first time it is possible to cause damage on such a catastrophic scale as to wipe out a large part of civilization and to endanger its very survival. The large-scale use of such weapons could trigger major and

irreversible ecological and genetic changes whose limits cannot be predicted.[41]

And earlier, with such thoughts plainly in mind, the council had made its own 'the condemnation of total war already pronounced by recent popes'.[42] This condemnation is demanded by the principles of proportionality and discrimination. Response to aggression must not exceed the nature of the aggression. To destroy civilization as we know it by waging a 'total war' as today it *could* be waged would be a monstrously disproportionate response to aggression on the part of any nation.

Moreover, the lives of innocent persons may never be taken directly, regardless of the purpose alleged for doing so. To wage truly 'total' war is by definition to take huge numbers of innocent lives. Just response to aggression must be discriminate; it must be directed against unjust aggressors, not against innocent people caught up in a war not of their making. The council therefore issued its memorable declaration: 'Any act of war aimed indiscriminately at the destruction of entire cities or of extensive areas along with their population is a crime against God and man himself. It merits unequivocal and unhesitating condemnation.'[43]

When confronting choices among specific military options, the question asked by proportionality is: Once we take into account not only the military advantages that will be achieved by using this means, but also all the harms reasonably expected to follow from using it, can its use still be justified? We know, of course, that no end can justify means evil in themselves, such as the executing of hostages or the targeting of non-combatants. Nonetheless, even if the means adopted is not evil in itself, it is necessary to take into account the probable harms that will result from using it and the justice of accepting those harms. It is of utmost importance in assessing harms and the justice of accepting them to think about the poor and the helpless, for they are usually the ones who have the least to gain and the most to lose when war's violence touches their lives.

In terms of the arms race, if the *real* end in view is legitimate defense against unjust aggression and the means to this end are not evil in themselves, we must still examine the question of proportionality concerning attendant evils. Do the exorbitant costs, the general climate of insecurity generated, the possibility of accidental detonation of highly destructive weapons, the danger of error and miscalculation that could provoke retaliation and war –

do such evils or others attendant upon and indirectly deriving from the arms race make the arms race itself a disproportionate response to aggression? Pope John Paul II is very clear in his insistence that the exercise of the right and duty of a people to protect their existence and freedom is contingent on the use of proportionate means.[44]

Finally, another set of questions concerns the interpretation of the principle of discrimination. The principle prohibits directly intended attacks on non-combatants and non-military targets. It raises a series of questions about the term 'intentional', the category of 'non-combatant' and the meaning of 'military'.

These questions merit the debate occurring with increasing frequency today. We encourage such debate, for concise and definitive answers still appear to be wanting. Mobilization of forces in modern war includes not only the military, but to a significant degree the political, economic and social sectors. It is not always easy to determine who is directly involved in a 'war effort' or to what degree. Plainly, though, not even by the broadest definition can one rationally consider combatants entire classes of human beings such as schoolchildren, hospital patients, the elderly, the ill, the average industrial worker producing goods not directly related to military purposes, farmers and many others. They may never be directly attacked.

Direct attacks on military targets involve similar complexities. Which targets are 'military' ones and which are not? To what degree, for instance, does the use (by either revolutionaries or regular military forces) of a village or housing in a civilian populated area invite attack? What of a munitions factory in the heart of a city? Who is directly responsible for the deaths of non-combatants should the attack be carried out? To revert to the question raised earlier, how many deaths of non-combatants are 'tolerable' as a result of indirect attacks — attacks directed against combat forces and military targets which nevertheless kill non-combatants at the same time?

These two principles in all their complexity must be applied to the range of weapons — conventional, nuclear, biological and chemical — with which nations are armed today.

The Value of Non-violence   Moved by the example of Jesus' life and by his teaching, some Christians have from the earliest days of the church committed themselves to a non-violent lifestyle.[45] Some understood the Gospel of Jesus to prohibit all killing. Some affirmed the use of prayer and other spiritual methods as means of responding to enmity and hostility.

In the middle of the second century St. Justin proclaimed to his pagan readers that Isaiah's prophecy about turning swords into ploughshares and spears into sickles had been fulfilled as a consequence of Christ's coming:

'And we who delighted in war, in the slaughter of one another, and in every other kind of inequity have in every part of the world converted our weapons into implements of peace – our swords into ploughshares, our spears into farmers' tools – and we cultivate piety, justice, brotherly charity, faith and hope, which we derive from the Father through the crucified Savior.'[46]

Writing in the third century, St Cyprian of Carthage struck a similar note when he indicated that the Christians of his day did not fight against their enemies. He himself regarded their conduct as proper:

'They do not even fight against those who are attacking since it is not granted to the innocent to kill even the aggressor, but promptly to deliver up their souls and blood that since so much malice and cruelty are rampant in the world they may more quickly withdraw from the malicious and the cruel.'[47]

Some of the early Christian opposition to military service was a response to the idolatrous practices which prevailed in the Roman army. Another powerful motive was the fact that army service involved preparation for fighting and killing. We see this in the case of St Martin of Tours during the fourth century, who renounced his soldierly profession with the explanation: 'Hitherto I have served you as a soldier. Allow me now to become a soldier of God ... I am a soldier of Christ. It is not lawful for me to fight.'[48]

In the centuries between the fourth century and our own day, the theme of Christian non-violence and Christian pacifism has echoed and re-echoed, sometimes more strongly, sometimes more faintly. One of the great non-violent figures in those centuries was St Francis of Assisi. Besides making personal efforts on behalf of reconciliation and peace, Francis stipulated that lay persons who became members of his Third Order were not 'to take up lethal weapons, or bear them about, against anybody'.

The vision of Christian non-violence is not passive about injustice and the defense of the rights of others, affirming and exemplifying what it means to resist injustice by non-violent methods.

In the twentieth century, prescinding from the non-Christian witness of a Mahatma Ghandi and its worldwide impact, the non-violent witness of such figures as Dorothy Day and Martin Luther King has had a profound impact upon the life of the church in the

United States. The witness of numerous Christians who had preceded them over the centuries was affirmed in a remarkable way at the Second Vatican Council.

Two of the passages which were included in the final version of the pastoral constitution gave particular encouragement for Catholics in all walks of life to assess their attitudes toward war and military service in the light of Christian pacifism. In Paragraph 79 the council fathers called upon governments to enact laws protecting the rights of those who adopted the position of conscientious objection to all war: 'Moreover, it seems right that laws make humane provisions for the case of those who for reasons of conscience refuse to bear arms, provided, however, that they accept some other form of service to the human community.'[49] This was the first time a call for legal protection of conscientious objection had appeared in a document of such prominence. In addition to its own profound meaning this statement took on even more significance in light of the praise that the council fathers had given in the preceding section 'to those who renounce the use of violence in the vindication of their rights'.[50] In 'Human Life in Our Day' (1968), we called for legislative provision to recognize selective conscientious objectors as well.[51]

As Catholic bishops it is incumbent upon us to stress to our own community and to the wider society the significance of this support for a pacifist option for individuals in the teaching of Vatican II and the reaffirmation that the popes have given to non-violent witness since the time of the council.

In the development of a theology of peace and the growth of the Christian pacifist position among Catholics, these words of the pastoral constitution have special significance: 'All these factors force us to undertake a completely fresh reappraisal of war.'[52] The council fathers had reference to 'the development of armaments by modern science (which) has immeasurably magnified the horrors and wickedness of war.'[53] While the just-war teaching has clearly been in possession for the past 1,500 years of Catholic thought, the 'new moment' in which we find ourselves sees the just-war teaching and non-violence as distinct but interdependent methods of evaluating warfare. They diverge on some specific conclusions, but they share a common presumption against the use of force as a means of settling disputes.

Both find their roots in the Christian theological tradition; each contributes to the full moral vision we need in pursuit of a human peace. We believe the two perspectives support and complement one another, each preserving the other from distortion. Finally, in an age of technological warfare, analysis from the viewpoint of non-violence and analysis from the viewpoint of the just war teaching often converge and agree in their opposition to methods of warfare which are in fact indistinguishable from total warfare.

WAR AND PEACE IN THE MODERN WORLD: PROBLEMS AND PRINCIPLES

Both the just-war teaching and non-violence are confronted with a unique challenge by nuclear warfare. This must be the starting point of any further moral reflection: Nuclear weapons particularly and nuclear warfare as it is planned today raise new moral questions. No previously conceived moral position escapes the fundamental confrontation posed by contemporary nuclear strategy. Many have noted the similarity of the statements made by eminent scientists and Vatican II's observation that we are forced today 'to undertake a completely fresh reappraisal of war'. The task before us is not simply to repeat what we have said before; it is first to consider anew whether and how our religious-moral tradition can assess, direct, contain and, we hope, help to eliminate the threat posed to the human family by the nuclear arsenals of the world. Pope John Paul II captured the essence of the problem during his pilgrimage to Hiroshima: 'In the past it was possible to destroy a village, a town, a region, even a country. Now it is the whole planet that has come under threat.'[54]

The Holy Father's observation illustrates why the moral problem is also a religious question of the most profound significance. In the nuclear arsenals of the United States or the Soviet Union alone there exists a capacity to do something no other age could imagine: We can threaten the entire planet.[55] For people of faith this means we read the Book of Genesis with a new awareness; the moral issue at stake in nuclear war involves the meaning of sin in its most graphic dimensions. Every sinful act is a confrontation of the creature and the Creator. Today the destructive potential of the nuclear powers threatens the human person, the civilization we have slowly constructed and even the created order itself.

We live today, therefore, in the midst of a cosmic drama; we possess a power which should never be used, but which might be used if we do not reverse our direction. We live with nuclear weapons knowing we cannot afford to make one serious mistake. This fact dramatizes the precariousness of our position, politically, morally and spiritually.

A prominent 'sign of the times' today is a sharply increased awareness of the danger of the nuclear arms race. Such awareness has produced a public discussion about nuclear policy here and in other countries which is unprecedented in its scope and depth. What has been accepted for years with almost no question is now being subjected to the sharpest criticism. What previously had been defined as a safe and stable system of deterrence is today viewed with political and moral skepticism. Many forces are at work in this new evaluation, and we believe one of the crucial elements is the gospel vision of peace which guides our work in this pastoral letter. The nuclear age has been the theater of our existence for almost four decades; today it is being evaluated with a new perspective. For many the leaven of the Gospel and the light of the Holy Spirit create the decisive dimension of this new perspective.

The New Moment

At the center of the new evaluation of the nuclear race is a recognition of two elements: the destructive potential of nuclear weapons and the stringent choices which the nuclear age poses for both politics and morals.

The fateful passage into the nuclear age as a military reality began with the bombing of Nagasaki and Hiroshima, events described by Pope Paul VI as a 'butchery of untold magnitude'.[56] Since then, in spite of efforts at control and plans for disarmament (e.g., the Baruch Plan of 1946), the nuclear arsenals have escalated, particularly in the two superpowers. The qualitative superiority of these two states, however, should not overshadow the fact that four other countries possess nuclear capacity and a score of states are only steps away from becoming 'nuclear nations'.

This nuclear escalation has been opposed sporadically and selectively, but never effectively. The race has continued in spite of carefully expressed doubts by analysts and other citizens and in the face of forcefully expressed opposition by public rallies. Today the opposition to the arms race is no longer selective or sporadic, it is widespread and sustained. The danger and destructiveness of nuclear weapons are understood and resisted with new urgency and intensity. There is in the public debate today an endorsement of the position submitted by the Holy See at the United Nations in 1976: The arms race is to be condemned as a danger, an act of aggression against the poor, and a folly which does not provide the security it promises.[57]

Papal teaching has consistently addressed the folly and danger of the arms race; but the new perception of it which is now held by the general public is due in large measure to the work of scientists and physicians who have described for citizens the concrete human consequences of a nuclear war.[58]

In a striking demonstration of his personal and pastoral concern for preventing nuclear war, Pope John Paul II commissioned a study by the Pontifical Academy of Sciences which reinforced the findings of other scientific bodies. The Holy Father had the study transmitted by personal representative to the leaders of the United States, the Soviet Union, the United Kingdom and France, and to the president of the General Assembly of the United Nations. One of its conclusions is especially pertinent to the public debate in the United States:

'Recent talk about winning or even surviving a nuclear war must reflect a failure to appreciate a medical reality: Any nuclear war would inevitably cause death, disease and suffering of pandemonic proportions and without the possibility of effective medical intervention. That reality leads to the same conclusion physicians have reached for life-threatening epidemics throughout history: Prevention is essential for control.'[59]

This medical conclusion has a moral corollary. Traditionally the church's moral teaching sought first to prevent war and then to limit its consequences if it occurred. Today the possibilities for placing political and moral limits on nuclear war are so minimal that the moral task, like the medical, is prevention: As a people, we must refuse to legitimate the idea of nuclear war. Such a refusal will require not only new ideas and new vision, but what the Gospel calls conversion of the heart.

To say no to nuclear war is both a necessary and a complex task. We are moral teachers in a tradition which has always been prepared to relate moral principles to concrete problems. Particularly in this letter we could not be content with simply restating general moral principles or repeating well-known requirements about the ethics of war. We have had to examine, with the assistance of a broad spectrum of advisers of varying persuasions, the nature of existing and proposed weapons systems, the doctrines which govern their use and the consequences of using them. We have consulted people who engage their lives in protest against the existing nuclear strategy of the United States, and we have consulted others who have held or do hold responsibility for this strategy. It has been a sobering and perplexing experience. In light of the evidence which witnesses presented and in light of our study, reflection and consultation, we must reject nuclear war. But we feel obliged to relate our judgment to the specific elements which comprise the nuclear problem.

Though certain that the dangerous and delicate nuclear relationship the superpowers now maintain should not exist, we understand how it came to exist. In a world of sovereign states devoid of central authority and possessing the knowledge to produce nuclear weapons many choices were made, some clearly objectionable, others well-intended with mixed results, which brought the world to its present dangerous situation.

We see with increasing clarity the political folly of a system which threatens mutual suicide, the psychological damage this does to ordinary people, especially the young, the economic distortion of priorities — billions readily spent for destructive instruments while pitched battles are waged daily in our legislatures over much smaller amounts for the homeless, the hungry and the helpless here and abroad. But it is much less clear how we translate a no to nuclear war into the personal and public choices which can move us in a new direction, toward a national policy and an international system which more adequately reflect the values and vision of the kingdom of God.

These tensions in our assessment of the politics and strategy of the nuclear age reflect the conflicting elements of the nuclear dilemma and the balance of terror which it has produced. We have said earlier in this letter that the fact of war reflects the existence of sin in the world. The nuclear threat and the danger it poses to human life and civilization exemplify in a qualitatively new way the perennial struggle of the political community to contain the use of force, particularly among states.

Precisely because of the destructive nature of nuclear weapons, strategies have been developed which previous generations would have found unintelligible. Today military preparations are undertaken on a vast and sophisticated scale, but the declared purpose is not to use the weapons produced. Threats are made which would be suicidal to implement. The key to security is no longer only military secrets, for in some instances security may best be served by informing one's adversary publicly what weapons one has and what plans exist for their use. The presumption of the nation-state system that sovereignty implies an ability to protect a nation's territory and population is precisely the presumption denied by the nuclear capacities of both superpowers. In a sense each is at the mercy of the other's perception of what strategy is 'rational', what kind of damage is 'unacceptable', how 'convincing' one side's threat is to the other.

The political paradox of deterrence has also strained our moral conception. May a nation threaten what it may never do? May it possess what it may never use? Who is involved in the threat each superpower makes: government officials? or military personnel? or the citizenry in whose defense the threat is made?

In brief, the danger of the situation is clear; but how to prevent the use of nuclear weapons, how to assess deterrence and how to delineate moral responsibility in the nuclear age are less clearly seen or stated. Reflecting the complexity of the nuclear problem, our arguments in this pastoral must be detailed and nuanced; but our no to nuclear war must in the end be definitive and decisive.

Religious Leadership and the Public Debate

Because prevention of nuclear war appears from several perspectives to be not only the surest but only way to limit its destructive potential, we see our role as moral teachers precisely in terms of helping to form public opinion with a clear determination to resist resort to nuclear war as an instrument of national policy. If 'prevention is the only cure', then there are diverse tasks to be performed in preventing what should never occur. As bishops we see a specific task defined for us in Pope John Paul II's 1982 World Day of Peace Message:

'Peace cannot be built by the power of rulers alone. Peace can be firmly constructed only if it corresponds to the resolute determination of all people of good will. Rulers must be supported and enlightened by a public opinion that encourages them or, where necessary, expresses disapproval.'[60]

The pope's appeal to form public opinion is not an abstract task. Especially in a democracy, public opinion can passively acquiesce in policies and strategies or it can through a series of measures indicate the limits beyond which a government should not proceed. The 'new moment' which exists in the public debate about nuclear weapons provides a creative opportunity and a moral imperative to examine the relationship between public opinion and public policy. We believe it is necessary for the sake of prevention to build a barrier against the concept of nuclear war as a viable strategy for defense. There should be a clear public resistance to the rhetoric of 'winnable' nuclear wars, or unrealistic expectations of 'surviving' nuclear exchanges and strategies of 'protracted nuclear war'. We oppose such rhetoric.

We seek to encourage a public attitude which sets stringent limits on the kind of actions our own government and other governments will take on nuclear policy. We believe religious leaders have a task in concert with public officials, analysts, private organizations and the media to set the limits beyond which our military policy should not move in word or action. Charting a moral course in a complex public policy debate involves several steps. We will address four questions, offering our reflections on them as an invitation to a public moral dialogue:

1 The use of nuclear weapons;
2 The policy of deterrence in principle and in practice;
3 Specific steps to reduce the danger of war;
4 Long-term measures of policy and diplomacy.

The Use of Nuclear Weapons

Establishing moral guidelines in the nuclear debate means addressing first the question of the use of nuclear weapons. That question has several dimensions.

It is clear that those in the church who interpret the gospel teaching as forbidding all use of violence would oppose any use of nuclear weapons under any conditions. In a sense the existence of these weapons simply confirms and reinforces one of the initial insights of the non-violent position, namely, that Christians should not use lethal force since the hope of using it selectively and restrictively is so often an illusion. Nuclear weapons seem to prove this point in a way heretofore unknown.

For the tradition which acknowledges some legitimate use of force, some important elements of contemporary nuclear strategies move beyond the limits of moral justification. A justifiable use of force must be both discriminatory and proportionate. Certain aspects of both US and Soviet strategies fail both tests as we shall discuss below. The technical literature and the personal testimony of public officials who have been closely associated with US nuclear strategy have both convinced us of the overwhelming probability that major nuclear exchange would have no limits.[61]

On the more complicated issue of 'limited' nuclear war, we are aware of the extensive literature and discussion which this topic has generated.[62] As a general statement, it seems to us that public officials would be unable to refute the following conclusion of the study made by the Pontifical Academy of Sciences:

> Even a nuclear attack directed only at military facilities would be devastating to the country as a whole. This is because military facilities are widespread rather than concentrated at only a few points. Thus, many nuclear weapons

would be exploded.

'Furthermore, the spread of radiation due to the natural winds and atmospheric mixing would kill vast numbers of people and contaminate large areas. The medical facilities of any nation would be inadequate to care for the survivors. An objective examination of the medical situation that would follow a nuclear war leads to but one conclusion: Prevention is our only recourse.'[63]

Moral Principles and Policy Choices   In light of these perspectives we address three questions more explicitly: 1) counterpopulation warfare; 2) initiation of nuclear war; and 3) limited nuclear war.

(1)   *Counterpopulation Warfare*   Under no circumstances may nuclear weapons or other instruments of mass slaughter be used for the purpose of destroying population centers or other predominantly civilian targets. Popes have repeatedly condemned 'total war', which implies such use. For example, as early as 1954 Pope Pius XII condemned nuclear warfare 'when it entirely escapes the control of man' and results in 'the pure and simple annihilation of all human life within the radius of action'.[64] The condemnation was repeated by the Second Vatican Council. 'Any act of war aimed indiscriminately at the destruction of entire cities or of extensive areas along with their population is a crime against God and man itself. It merits unequivocal and unhesitating condemnation.'[65]

Retaliatory action, whether nuclear or conventional, which would indiscriminately take many wholly innocent lives, lives of people who are in no way responsible for reckless actions of their government, must also be condemned. This condemnation, in our judgment, applies even to the retaliatory use of weapons striking enemy cities after our own have already been struck. No Christian can rightfully carry out orders or policies deliberately aimed at killing non-combatants.[66]

We make this judgment at the beginning of our treatment of nuclear strategy precisely because the defense of the principle of non-combatant immunity is so important for an ethic of war and because the nuclear age has posed such extreme problems for the principle. Later in this letter we shall discuss specific aspects of US policy in light of this principle and in light of recent US policy statements stressing the determination not to target directly or strike directly against civilian populations. Our concern about protecting the moral value of non-combatant immunity, however, requires that we make a clear reassertion of the principle our first word on this matter.

(2) *The Initiation of Nuclear War* We do not perceive any situation in which the deliberate initiation of nuclear warfare on however restricted a scale can be morally justified. Non-nuclear attacks by another state must be resisted by other than nuclear means. Therefore, a serious moral obligation exists to develop non-nuclear defensive strategies as rapidly as possible.

A serious debate is under way on this issue.[67] It is cast in political terms, but it has a significant moral dimension. Some have argued that at the very beginning of a war nuclear weapons might be used, only against military targets, perhaps in limited numbers. Indeed it has long been American and NATO policy that nuclear weapons, especially so-called tactical nuclear weapons, would likely be used if NATO forces in Europe seemed in danger of losing a conflict that until then had been restricted to conventional weapons. Large numbers of tactical nuclear weapons are now deployed in Europe by the NATO forces and about as many by the Soviet Union. Some are substantially smaller than the bomb used on Hiroshima, some are larger. Such weapons, if employed in great numbers, would totally devastate the densely populated countries of Western and Central Europe.

Whether under conditions of war in Europe, parts of Asia or the Middle East, or the exchange of strategic weapons directly between the United States and the Soviet Union, the difficulties of limiting the use of nuclear weapons are immense. A number of expert witnesses advise us that commanders operating under conditions of battle probably would not be able to exercise strict control; the number of weapons used would rapidly increase, the targets would be expanded beyond the military and the level of civilian casualties would rise enormously.[68] No one can be certain that this escalation would not occur even in the face of political efforts, to keep such an exchange 'limited'. The chances of keeping use limited seem remote, and the consequences of escalation to mass destruction would be appalling. Former public officials have testified that it is improbable that any nuclear war could actually be kept limited. Their testimony and the consequences involved in this problem lead us to conclude that the danger of escalation is so great that it would be morally unjustifiable to initiate nuclear war in any form. The danger is rooted not only in the technology of our weapons systems, but in the weakness and sinfulness of human communities. We find the moral responsibility of beginning nuclear war not justified by rational political objectives.

This judgment affirms that the willingness to initiate nuclear war entails a distinct, weighty moral responsibility; it involves transgressing a fragile barrier — political, psychological and moral — which has been constructed since 1945. We express repeatedly in this letter our extreme skepticism about the prospects for controlling a nuclear exchange, however limited the first use might be. Precisely because of this skepticism, we judge resort to nuclear weapons to counter a conventional attack to be morally unjustifiable.[69] Consequently we seek to reinforce the barrier against any use of nuclear weapons. Our support of a 'no first use' policy must be seen in this light.

At the same time we recognize the responsibility the United States has had and continues to have in assisting allied nations in their defense against either a conventional or a nuclear attack. Especially in the European theater, the deterrence of a *nuclear* attack may require nuclear weapons for a time, even though their possession and deployment must be subject to rigid restrictions.

The need to defend against a conventional attack in Europe imposes the political and moral burden of developing adequate, alternative modes of defense to present reliance on nuclear weapons. Even with the best coordinated effort — hardly likely in view of contemporary political division on this question — development of an alternative defense position will still take time.

In the interim, deterrence against a conventional attack relies upon two factors: the not inconsiderable conventional forces at the disposal of NATO and the recognition by a potential attacker that the outbreak of large-scale conventional war could escalate to the nuclear level through accident or miscalculation by either side. We are aware that NATO's refusal to adopt a 'no first use' pledge is to some extent linked to the deterrent effect of this inherent ambiguity. Nonetheless, in light of the probable effects of initiating nuclear war, we urge NATO to move rapidly toward the adoption of a 'no first use' policy, but doing so in tandem with development of an adequate alternative defense posture.

(3) *Limited Nuclear War* It should be possible to agree with our first two conclusions and still not be sure about retaliatory use of nuclear weapons in what is called a 'limited exchange'. The issue at stake is the *real* as opposed to the *theoretical* possibility of a 'limited nuclear exchange'.

We recognize that the policy debate on this question is inconclusive and that all participants are left with hypothetical projections about probable reactions in a nuclear exchange. While not trying to adjudicate the technical debate, we are aware of it and wish to raise a series of questions which challenge the actual meaning of 'limited' in this discussion.

- Would leaders have sufficient information to know what is happening in a nuclear exchange?
- Would they be able under the conditions of stress, time pressures and fragmentary information to make the extraordinarily precise decision needed to keep the exchange limited if this were technically possible?
- Would military commanders be able in the midst of the destruction and confusion of a nuclear exchange to maintain a policy of 'discriminate targeting'? Can this be done in modern warfare waged across great distances by aircraft and missiles?
- Given the accidents we know about in peacetime conditions, what assurances are there that computer errors could be avoided in the midst of a nuclear exchange?
- Would not the casualties, even in a war defined as limited by strategists, still run in the millions?
- How 'limited' would be the long-term effects of radiation, famine, social fragmentation and economic dislocation?

Unless these questions can be answered satifactorily, we will continue to be highly skeptical about the real meaning of 'limited'. One of the criteria of the just-war tradition is a reasonable hope of success in bringing about justice and peace. We must ask whether such a reasonable hope can exist once nuclear weapons have been exchanged. The burden of proof remains on those who assert that meaningful limitation is possible.

A nuclear response to either conventional or nuclear attack can cause destruction which goes far beyond 'legitimate defense'. Such use of nuclear weapons would not be justified.

In the face of this frightening and highly speculative debate on a matter involving millions of human lives, we believe the most effective contribution or moral judgment is to introduce perspectives by which we can assess the empirical debate. Moral perspective should be sensitive not only to the quantitative dimensions of a question, but to its psychological, human and religious characteristics as well. The issue of limited war is not simply the size of weapons contemplated or the strategies projected. The debate should include the psychological and political significance of crossing the boundary from the conventional to the nuclear arena in any form. To cross this divide is to enter a world where we have no experience of control, much testimony against its possibility and therefore no moral justification for submitting the human community to this risk.[70] We therefore express our view that the first imperative is to prevent any use of nuclear weapons and our hope that leaders will resist the notion that nuclear conflict can be limited, contained or won in any traditional sense.

Deterrence in Principle and Practice

The moral challenge posed by nuclear weapons is not exhausted by an analysis of their possible uses. Much of the political and moral debate of the nuclear age has concerned the strategy of deterrance. Deterrence is at the heart of the US — Soviet relationship, currently the most dangerous dimension of the nuclear arms race.

The Concept and Development of Deterrence Policy The concept of deterrence existed in military strategy long before the nuclear age, but it has taken on a new meaning and significance since 1945. Essentially deterrence means 'dissuasion of a potential adversary from initiating an attack or conflict, often by the threat of unacceptable retaliatory damage'.[71] In the nuclear age deterrence has become the centerpiece of both US and Soviet policy. Both superpowers have for many years now been able to promise a retaliatory response which can inflict 'unacceptable damage'. A situation of stable deterrence depends on the ability of each side to deploy its retaliatory forces in ways that are not vulnerable to an attack (i.e., protected against a 'first strike'); preserving stability requires a willingness by both sides to refrain from deploying weapons which appear to have a first-strike capability.

This general definition of deterrence does not explain either the elements of a deterrence strategy or the evolution of deterrence policy since 1945. A detailed description of either of these subjects would require an extensive essay using materials which can be found in abundance in the technical literature on the subject of deterrence.[72] Particularly significant is the relationship between 'declaratory policy' (the public explanation of our strategic intentions and capabilities) and 'action policy' (the actual planning and targeting policies to be followed in a nuclear attack).

The evolution of deterrence strategy has passed through several stages of declaratory policy. Using the US case as an example, there is a significant difference between 'massive retaliation' and 'flexible response', and between 'mutual assured destruction' and 'countervailing strategy'. It is also possible to distinguish between 'counterforce' and 'countervalue' targeting policies; and to contrast a posture of 'minimum deterrence' with 'extended deterrence'. These terms are well known in the technical debate on nuclear policy; they are less well known and sometimes loosely used in the wider public debate. It is important to recognize that there has been substantial continuity in US action policy in spite of real changes in declaratory policy.[73]

The recognition of these different elements in the deterrent and the evolution of policy means that moral assessment of deterrence requires a series of distinct judgments. They include: an analysis of the *factual character* of the deterrent (e.g., what is involved in targeting doctrine); analysis of the *historical development* of the policy (e.g., whether changes have occurred which are significant for moral analysis of the policy); the relationship of deterrence policy and other aspects of *US-Soviet affairs*; and determination of the key *moral questions* involved in deterrence policy.

The Moral Assessment of Deterrence   The distinctively new dimensions of nuclear deterrence were recognized by policymakers and strategists only after much reflection. Similarly, the moral challenge posed by nuclear deterrence was grasped only after careful deliberation. The moral and political paradox posed by deterrence was concisely stated by Vatican II:

> Undoubtedly, armaments are not amassed merely for use in wartime. Since the defensive strength of any nation is thought to depend on its capacity for immediate retaliation, the stockpiling of arms which grows from year to year serves, in a way hitherto unthought of, as a deterrent to potential attackers. Many people look upon this as the most effective way known at the present time for maintaining some sort of peace among nations. Whatever one may think of this form of deterrent, people are convinced that the arms race, which quite a few countries have entered, is no infallible way of maintaining real peace and that the resulting so-called balance of power is no sure genuine path to achieving it. Rather than eliminate the causes of war, the arms race serves only to aggravate the position. As long as extravagant sums of money are poured into the development of new weapons, it is imposs- ible to devote adequate aid in tackling the misery which prevails at the present day in the world. Instead of eradi- cating international conflict once and for all, the contagion is spreading to other parts of the world. New approaches, based on reformed attitudes, will have to be chosen in order

to remove this stumbling block, to free the earth from its pressing anxieties, and give back to the world a genuine peace.[74]

Without making a specific moral judgment on deterrence, the council clearly designated the elements of the arms race: the tension between 'peace of a sort' preserved by deterrence and 'genuine peace' required for a stable international life; the contradiction between what is spent for destructive capacity and what is needed for constructive development.

In the post-conciliar assessment of war and peace and specifically of deterrence, different parties to the political-moral debate within the church and in civil society have focused on one or another aspect of the problem. For some, the fact that nuclear weapons have not been used since 1945 means that deterrence has worked, and this fact satisfies the demands of both the political and the moral order. Others contest this assessment by highlighting the risk of failure involved in continued reliance on deterrence and pointing out how politically and morally catastrophic even a single failure would be. Still others note that the absence of nuclear war is not necessarily proof that the policy of deterrence has prevented it. Indeed, some would find in the policy of deterrence the driving force in the superpower arms race. Still other observers, many of them Catholic moralists, have stressed that deterrence may not morally include the intention of deliberately attacking civilian populations or non-combatants.

The statements of the NCCB-USCC over the past several years have both reflected and contributed to the wider moral debate on deterrence. In the NCCB pastoral letter 'To Live in Christ Jesus' (1976), we focused on the moral limits of declaratory policy while calling for stronger measures of arms control.[75] In 1979 Cardinal John Krol, speaking for the USCC in support of SALT II ratification, brought into focus the other element of the deterrence problem: The actual use of nuclear weapons may have been prevented (a moral good), but the risk of failure and the physical harm and moral evil resulting from possible nuclear war remained.

'This explains,' Cardinal Krol stated, 'the Catholic dissatisfaction with nuclear deterrence and the urgency of the demand that the nuclear arms race be reversed. It is of the utmost importance that negotiations proceed to meaningful and continuing reductions in nuclear stockpiles and eventually to the phasing out altogether of deterrence and the threat of mutual-assured destruction.'[76]

These two texts, along with the conciliar statement, have influenced much of Catholic opinion expressed recently on the nuclear question.

In June 1982, Pope John Paul II provided new impetus and insights to the moral analysis with his statement to the UN Second Special Session on Disarmament. The pope first situated the problem of deterrence within the context of world politics. No power, he observes, will admit to wishing to start a war, but each distrusts others and considers it necessary to mount a strong defense against attack. He then discusses the notion of deterrence:

> Many even think that such preparations constitute the way — even the only way — to safeguard peace in some fashion or at least to impede to the utmost in an efficacious way the outbreak of wars, especially major conflicts which might lead to the ultimate holocaust of humanity and the destruction of the civilization that man has constructed so laboriously over the centuries.
>
> In this approach one can see the 'philosophy of peace' which was proclaimed in the ancient Roman principle: *Si vis pacem, para bellum*. Put in modern terms, this 'philosophy' has the label of 'deterrence' and one can find it in various guises of the search for a 'balance of forces' which sometimes has been called, and not without reason, the 'balance of terror.'[77]

Having offered this analysis of the general concept of deterrence, the Holy Father introduces his considerations on disarmament, especially, but not only, nuclear disarmament. Pope John Paul II makes this statement about the morality of deterrence:

'In current conditions, 'deterrence' based on balance, certainly not as an end in itself but as a step on the way toward a progressive disarmament, may still be judged morally acceptable. Nonetheless in order to ensure peace, it is indispensable not to be satisfied with this minimum, which is always susceptible to the real danger of explosion.'[78]

In Pope John Paul II's assessment we perceive two dimensions of the contemporary dilemma of deterrence. One dimension is the danger of nuclear war with its human and moral costs. The possession of nuclear weapons, the continuing quantitative growth of the arms race and the danger of nuclear proliferation all point to the grave danger of basing 'peace of a sort' on deterrence. The other dimension is the independence and freedom of nations and entire peoples, including the need to protect smaller nations from threats to their independence and integrity. Deterrence reflects the radical distrust which marks international politics, a condition identified as a major problem by Pope John XXIII in 'Peace on Earth' and reaffirmed by Pope Paul VI and Pope John Paul II. Thus a balance of forces, preventing either side from achieving superiority, can be seen as a means of safeguarding both dimensions.

The moral duty today is to prevent nuclear war from ever occurring *and* to protect and preserve those key values of justice, freedom and independence which are necessary for personal dignity and national integrity. In reference to these issues, Pope John Paul II judges that deterrence may still be judged morally acceptable, 'certainly not as an end in itself but as a step on the way toward a progressive disarmament'.

On more than one occasion the Holy Father has demonstrated his awareness of the fragility and complexity of the deterrence relationship among nations. Speaking to UNESCO in June 1980, he said:

'Up to the present, we are told that nuclear arms are a force of dissuasion which have prevented the eruption of a major war. And that is probably true. Still, we must ask if it will always be this way.'[79]

In a more recent and more specific assessment Pope John Paul II told an international meeting of scientists Aug. 23, 1982: 'You can more easily ascertain that the logic of nuclear deterrence cannot be considered a final goal or an appropriate and secure means for safeguarding international peace.'[80]

Relating Pope John Paul's general statements to the specific policies of the US deterrent requires both judgments of fact and an application of moral principles. In preparing this letter we have tried through a number of sources to determine as precisely as possible the factual character of US deterrence strategy. Two questions have particularly concerned us: 1) the targeting doctrine and strategic plans for the use of the deterrent, particularly their impact on civilian casualties; and 2) the relationship of deterrence strategy and nuclear war-fighting capability to the likelihood that war will in fact be prevented.

Moral Principles and Policy Choices

Targeting doctrine raises significant moral questions because it is a significant determinant of what would occur if nuclear weapons were ever to be used. Although we acknowledge the need for deterrent, not all forms of deterrence are morally acceptable. There are moral limits to deterrence policy as well as to policy regarding use. Specifically, it is not morally acceptable to intend to kill the innocent as part of a strategy of deterring nuclear war. The question of whether US policy involves an intention to strike civilian centers (directly targeting civilian populations) has been one of our factual concerns.

This complex question has always produced a variety of responses, official and unofficial in character. The NCCB committee has received a series of statements of clarification of policy from US government officials.[81] Essentially these statements declare that it is not US strategic policy to target the Soviet civilian populations as such or to use nuclear weapons deliberately for the purpose of destroying population centers.

These statements respond, in principle at least, to one moral criterion for assessing deterrence policy: the immunity of non-combatants from direct attack either by conventional or nuclear weapons.

These statements do not address or resolve another very troublesome moral problem, namely, that an attack on military targets or militarily significant industrial targets could involve 'indirect' (i.e., unintended) but massive civilian casualties. We are advised, for example, that the US strategic nuclear targeting plan (SIOP — Single Integrated Operational Plan) has identified 60 'military' targets within the city of Moscow alone, and that 40,000 'military' targets for nuclear weapons have been identified in the whole of the Soviet Union.[82] It is important to recognize that Soviet policy is subject to the same moral judgment; attacks on several 'industrial targets' or politically significant targets in the United States could produce massive civilian casualties. The number of civilians who would necessarily be killed by such strikes is horrendous.[83] This problem is unavoidable because of the way modern military facilities and production centers are so thoroughly interspersed with civilian living and working areas. It is aggravated if one side deliberately positions military targets in the midst of a civilian population.

In our consultations, administration officials readily admitted that while they hoped any nuclear exchange could be kept limited, they were prepared to retaliate in a massive way if necessary. They also agreed that once any substantial numbers of weapons were used, the civilian casualty levels would quickly become truly catastrophic and that even with attacks limited to 'military' targets the number of deaths in a substantial exchange would be almost indistinguishable from what might occur if civilian centers had been deliberately and directly struck. These possibilities pose a different moral question and are to be judged by a different moral criterion: the principle of proportionality.

While any judgment of proportionality is always open to differing evaluations, there are actions which can be decisively judged to be disproportionate. A narrow adherence exclusively to the principle of non-combatant immunity as a criterion for policy is an inadequate moral posture for it ignores some evil and unacceptable consequences. Hence, we cannot be satisfied that the assertion of an intention not to strike civilians directly or even the most honest effort to implement that intention by itself constitutes a 'moral policy' for the use of nuclear weapons.

The location of industrial or militarily significant economic targets within heavily populated areas or in those areas affected by radioactive fallout could well involve such massive civilian casualties that in our judgment such a strike would be deemed morally disproportionate, even though not intentionally indiscriminate.

The problem is not simply one of producing highly accurate weapons that might minimize civilian casualties in any single explosion, but one of increasing the likelihood of escalation at a level where many, even 'discriminating,' weapons would cumulatively kill very large numbers of civilians. Those civilian deaths would occur both immediately and from the long-term effects of social and economic devastation.

A second issue of concern to us is the relationship of deterrence doctrine to war-fighting strategies. We are aware of the argument that war-fighting capabilities enhance the credibility of the deterrent, particularly the strategy of extended deterrence. But the development of such capabilities raises other strategic and moral questions. The relationship of war-fighting capabilities and targeting doctrine exemplifies the difficult choices in this area of policy. Targeting civilian populations would violate the principle of discrimination — one of the central moral principles of a Christian ethic of war. But 'counter-force targeting', while preferable from the perspective of protecting civilians, is often joined with a declaratory policy which conveys the notion that nuclear war is subject to precise rational and moral limits. We have already expressed our severe doubts about such a concept. Furthermore, a purely counter-force strategy may seem to threaten the viability of other nations' retaliatory forces, making deterrence unstable in a crisis and war more likely.

While we welcome any effort to protect civilian populations, we do not want to legitimize or encourage moves which extend deterrence beyond the specific objective of preventing the use of nuclear weapons or other actions which could lead directly to a nuclear exchange.

These considerations of concrete elements of nuclear deterrence policy, made in light of John Paul II's evaluation, but applying it through our own prudential judgments, lead us to a strictly conditioned moral acceptance of nuclear deterrence. We cannot consider it adequate as a long-term basis for peace.

This strictly conditioned judgment yields *criteria* for morally assessing the elements of deterrence strategy. Clearly, these criteria demonstrate that we cannot approve of every weapons system, strategic doctrine or policy initiative advanced in the name of strengthening deterrence. On the contrary, these criteria require continual public scrutiny of what our government proposes to do with the deterrent.

On the basis of these criteria we wish now to make some specific evaluations:

1   If nuclear deterrence exists only to prevent the *use* of nuclear weapons by others, then proposals to go beyond this to planning for prolonged periods of repeated nuclear strikes and counterstrikes or 'prevailing' in nuclear war, are not acceptable. They encourage notions that nuclear war can be engaged in with tolerable human and moral consequences. Rather, we must continually say no to the idea of nuclear war.
2   If nuclear deterrence is our goal, 'sufficiency' to deter is an adequate strategy; the quest for nuclear superiority must be rejected.
3   Nuclear deterrence should be used as a step on the way toward progressive disarmament. Each proposed addition to our strategic system or change in strategic doctrine must be assessed precisely in light of whether it will render steps toward 'progressive disarmament' more or less likely.

Moreover, these criteria provide us with the means to make some judgments and recommendations about the present direction of US strategic policy. Progress toward a world freed of dependence on nuclear deterrence must be carefully carried out. But it must not be delayed. There is an urgent moral and political responsibility to use the 'peace of a sort' we have as a framework to move toward authentic peace through nuclear arms control, reductions and disarmament. Of primary importance in this process is the need to prevent the development and deployment of destabilizing weapons systems on either side; a second requirement is to ensure that the more sophisticated command and control systems do not become mere hair triggers for automatic launch on warning; a third is the need to prevent the proliferation of nuclear weapons in the international system.

In light of these general judgments *we oppose* some specific proposals in respect to our present deterrence posture:

1 The addition of weapons which are likely to be vulnerable to attack, yet also possess a 'prompt hard-target kill' capability that threatens to make the other side's retaliatory forces vulnerable. Such weapons may seem to be useful primarily in a first strike,[84] we resist such weapons for this reason and we oppose Soviet deployment of such weapons which generate fear of a first strike against US forces.
2 The willingness to foster strategic planning which seeks a nuclear war-fighting capability that goes beyond the limited function of deterrence outlined in this letter.
3 Proposals which have the effect of lowering the nuclear threshold and blurring the difference between nuclear and conventional weapons.

In support of the concept of 'sufficiency' as an adequate deterrent and in light of the present size and composition of both the US and Soviet strategic arsenals, *we recommend:*

1 Support for immediate, bilateral, verifiable agreements to halt the testing, production and deployment of new nuclear weapons systems.[85]
2 Support for negotiated bilateral deep cuts in the arsenals of both superpowers, particularly whose weapons systems which have destabilizing characteristics; US proposals like those for START (Strategic Arms Reduction Talks) and INF (Intermediate-Range Nuclear Forces) negotiations in Geneva are said to be designed to achieve deep cuts;[86] our hope is that they will be pursued in a manner which will realize these goals.
3 Support for early and successful conclusion of negotiations of a comprehensive test ban treaty.
4 Removal by all parties of short-range nuclear weapons which multiply dangers disproportionate to their deterrent value.
5 Removal by all parties of nuclear weapons from areas where they are likely to be overrun in the early stages of war, thus forcing rapid and uncontrollable decisions on their use.

6   Strengthening of command and control over nuclear weapons
    to prevent inadvertent and unauthorized use.

These judgments are meant to exemplify how a lack of unequivocal condemnation of deterrence is meant only to be an
attempt to acknowledge the role attributed to deterrence, but not
to support its extension beyond the limited purpose discussed
above. Some have urged us to condemn all aspects of nuclear
deterrence. This urging has been based on a variety of reasons, but
has emphasized particularly the high and terrible risks that either
deliberate use or accidental detonation of nuclear weapons could
quickly escalate to something utterly disproportionate to any acceptable moral purpose. That determination requires highly technical judgments about hypothetical events. Although reasons exist
which move some to condemn reliance on nuclear weapons for
deterrence, we have not reached this conclusion for the reasons
outlined in this letter.

Nevertheless, there must be no misunderstanding of our profound
skepticism about the moral acceptability of any use of nuclear
weapons. It is obvious that the use of any weapons which violate
the principle of discrimination merits unequivocal condemnation.
We are told that some weapons are designed for purely 'counter-
force' use against military forces and targets. The moral issue,
however, is not resolved by the design of weapons or the planned
intention for use; there are also consequences which must be
assessed. It would be a perverted political policy or moral casuistry
which tried to justify using a weapon which 'indirectly' or 'unin-
tentionally' killed a million innocent people because they happened
to live near a 'military significant target'.

Even the 'indirect effects' of initiating nuclear war are sufficient
to make it an unjustifiable moral risk in any form. It is not
sufficient, for example, to contend that 'our' side has plans for
'limited' or 'discriminate' use. Modern warfare is not readily contained by good intentions or technological designs. The psychological climate of the world is such that mention of the term
'nuclear' generates uneasiness. Many contend that the use of one
tactical nuclear weapon could produce panic, with completely
unpredictable consequences. It is precisely this mix of political,
psychological and technological uncertainty which has moved us
in this letter to reinforce with moral prohibitions and prescriptions
the prevailing political barrier against resort to nuclear weapons.
Our support for enhanced command and control facilities, for
major reductions in strategic and tactical nuclear forces, and for a

'no first use' policy (as set forth in this letter) is meant to be seen as a complement to our desire to draw a moral line against nuclear war.

Any claim by any government that it is pursuing a morally acceptable policy of deterrence must be scrutinized with the greatest care. We are prepared and eager to participate in our country in the ongoing public debate on moral grounds.

The need to rethink the deterrence policy of our nation, to make the revisions necessary to reduce the possibility of nuclear war and to move toward a more stable system of national and international security will demand a substantial intellectual, political and moral effort. It also will require, we believe, the willingness to open ourselves to the providential care, power and word of God, which call us to recognize our common humanity and the bonds of mutual responsibility which exist in the international community in spite of political differences and nuclear arsenals.

Indeed, we do acknowledge that there are many strong voices within our own episcopal ranks and within the wider Catholic community in the United States which challenge the strategy of deterrence as an adequate response to the arms race today. They highlight the historical evidence that deterrence has not in fact set in motion substantial processes of disarmament.

Moreover, these voices rightly raise the concern that even the conditional acceptance of nuclear deterrence as laid out in a letter such as this might be inappropriately used by some to reinforce the policy of arms buildup. In its stead they call us to raise a prophetic challenge to the community of faith — a challenge which goes beyond nuclear deterrence, toward more resolute steps to actual bilateral disarmament and peacemaking. We recognize the intellectual ground on which the argument is built and the religious sensibility which gives it its strong force.

The dangers of the nuclear age and the enormous difficulties we face in moving toward a more adequate system of global security, stability and justice require steps beyond our present conceptions of security and defense policy. In the following section we propose a series of steps aimed at a more adequate policy for preserving peace in a nuclear world.

THE PROMOTION OF PEACE: PROPOSALS AND POLICIES

In a world which is not yet the fulfillment of God's kingdom, a world where both personal actions and social forces manifest the continuing influence of sin and disorder among us, consistent attention must be paid to preventing and limiting the violence of war. But this task, addressed extensively in the previous section of this letter, does not exhaust Catholic teaching on war and peace. A complementary theme, reflected in the scriptures and the theology of the church and significantly developed by papal teaching in this century, is the building of peace as the way to prevent war. This traditional theme was vividly reasserted by Pope John Paul in his homily at Coventry Cathedral:

'Peace is not just the absence of war. It involves mutual respect and confidence between peoples and nations. It involves collaboration and binding agreements. Like a cathedral, peace must be constructed patiently and with unshakable faith.'[87]

This positive conception of peacemaking profoundly influences many people in our time. At the beginning of this letter we affirmed the need for a more fully developed theology of peace. The basis of such a theology is found in the papal teaching of this century. In this section of our pastoral we wish to illustrate how the positive vision of peace contained in Catholic teaching provides direction for policy and personal choices.

Specific Steps to Reduce the Danger of War

The dangers of modern war are specific and visible; our teaching must be equally specific about the needs of peace. Effective arms control leading to mutual disarmament, ratification of pending treaties,[88] development of non-violent alternatives, are but some of the recommendations we would place before the Catholic community and all men and women of good will. These should be part of a foreign policy which recognizes and respects the claims of citizens of every nation to the same inalienable rights we treasure and seeks to ensure an international security based on the awareness that the Creator has provided this world and all its resources for the sustenance and benefit of the entire human family. The truth that the globe is inhabited by a single family in which all have the same basic needs and all have a right to the goods of the earth is a fundamental principle of Catholic teaching which we believe to be of increasing importance today. In an interdependent world all need to affirm their common nature and destiny; such a perspective should inform our policy vision and negotiating posture in pursuit of peace today.

Accelerated Work for Arms Control, Reduction and Disarmament

Despite serious efforts starting with the Baruch plans and continuing through SALT I and SALT II, the results have been far too limited and partial to be commensurate with the risks of nuclear war. Yet efforts for negotiated control and reduction of arms must continue. In his 1982 address to the United Nations Pope John Paul II left no doubt about the importance of these efforts: 'Today once again before you all I reaffirm my confidence in the power of true negotiations to arrive at just and equitable solutions.'[89]

In this same spirit we urge negotiations to halt the testing, production and deployment of new nuclear weapons systems. Not only should steps be taken to end development and deployment, but the numbers of existing weapons must be reduced in a manner which lessens the danger of war.

Arms control and disarmament must be a process of verifiable agreements especially between two superpowers. While we do not advocate a policy of unilateral disarmament, we believe the urgent need for control of the arms race requires a willingness for each side to take some first steps. The United States has already taken a number of important independent initiatives to reduce some of the gravest dangers and to encourage a constructive Soviet response; additional initiatives are encouraged. By independent initiatives we mean carefully chosen limited steps which the United States could take for a defined period of time, seeking to elicit a comparable step from the Soviet Union. If an appropriate response is not forthcoming, the United States would no longer be bound by steps taken. Our country has previously taken calculated risks in favor of freedom and of human values; these have included independent steps taken to reduce some of the gravest dangers of nuclear war.[90] Certain risks are required today to help free the world from bondage to nuclear deterrence and the risk of nuclear war. Both sides, for example, have an interest in avoiding deployment of destabilizing weapons systems.

There is some history of successful independent initiatives which have beneficially influenced the arms race without a formal public agreement. In 1963 President Kennedy announced that the United States would unilaterally forgo further nuclear testing; the next month (Soviet Premier Nikita) Khrushchev proposed a limited test ban which eventually became the basis of the US—Soviet partial test ban treaty. Subsequently, both superpowers removed about 10,000 troops from Central Europe and each announced a cut in production of nuclear material for weapons.

1   Negotiation on arms control agreements in isolation, without persistent and parallel efforts to reduce the political tensions which motivate the buildup of armaments, will not suffice. The United

States should therefore have a continuing policy of maximum political engagement with governments of potential adversaries, providing for repeated, systematic discussion and negotiation of areas of friction. This policy should be carried out by a system of periodic, carefully prepared meetings at several levels of government, including summit meetings at regular intervals. Such channels of discussion are too important to be regarded by either of the major powers as a concession or an event made dependent on daily shifts in international developments.

2   The Nuclear Non-Proliferation Treaty of 1968 acknowledged that the spread of nuclear weapons to hitherto non-nuclear states (horizontal proliferation) could hardly be prevented in the long run in the absence of serious efforts by the nuclear states to control and reduce their own nuclear arsenals (vertical proliferation). Article VI of the NPT pledged the super-powers to serious efforts to control and to reduce their own nuclear arsenals; unfortunately this promise has not been kept. Moreover, the multinational controls envisaged in the treaty seem to have been gradually relaxed by the states exporting fissionable materials for the production of energy. If these tendencies are not constrained, the treaty may eventually lose its symbolic and practical effectiveness. For this reason the United States should, in concert with other nuclear-exporting states, seriously re-examine its policies and programs and make clear its determination to uphold the spirit as well as the letter of the treaty.

Continued Insistence on Efforts to Minimize the Risk of Any War   While it is right and proper that priority be given to reducing and ultimately eliminating the likelihood of nuclear war, this does not of itself remove the threat of other forms of warfare. Indeed, negotiated reduction in nuclear weapons available to the super-powers could conceivably increase the danger of non-nuclear wars.

1   Because of this we strongly support negotiations aimed at reducing and limiting conventional forces and at building confidence between possible adversaries, especially in regions of potential military confrontations. We urge that prohibitions outlawing the production and use of chemical and biological weapons be re-affirmed and observed. Arms control negotiations must take account of the possibility that conventional conflict could trigger the nuclear confrontation the world must avoid.

2   Unfortunately, as is the case with nuclear proliferation, we are witnessing a relaxation of restraints in the international commerce in conventional arms. Sales of increasingly sophisticated

military aircraft, missiles, tanks, anti-tank weapons, anti-personnel bombs and other systems by the major supplying countries (especially the Soviet Union, the United States, France and Great Britain) have reached unprecedented levels.

Pope John Paul II took note of the problem in his UN address:

'The production and sale of conventional weapons throughout the world is a truly alarming and evidently growing phenomenon ... Moreover the traffic in these weapons seems to be developing at an increasing rate and seems to be directed most of all toward developing countries.'[91]

It is a tragic fact that US arms-sales policies in the last decade have contributed significantly to the trend the Holy Father deplores. We call for a reversal of this course. The United States should renew earlier efforts to develop multilateral controls on arms exports and should in this case also be willing to take carefully chosen independent initiatives to restrain the arms trade. Such steps would be particularly appropriate where the receiving government faces charges of gross and systematic human rights violations.[92]

3   Nations must accept a limited view of those interests justifying military force. True self-defense may include the protection of weaker states, but does not include seizing the possessions of others or the domination of other states or peoples. We should remember the caution of Pope John Paul II: 'In alleging the threat of a potential enemy, is it really not rather the intention to keep for itself a means of threat, in order to get the upper hand with the aid of one's own arsenal of destruction?'[93] Central to a moral theory of force is the principle that it must be a last resort taken only when *all* other means of redress have been exhausted. Equally important in the age of modern warfare is the recognition that the justifiable reasons for using force have been restricted to instances of self-defense or defense of others under attack.

The Relationship of Nuclear and Conventional Defenses The strong position we have taken against the use of nuclear weapons and particularly the stand against the initiation of nuclear war in any form calls for further clarification of our view of the requirements for conventional defense.

Nuclear threats have often come to take the place of efforts to deter or defend against non-nuclear attack with weapons that are themselves non-nuclear, particularly in the NATO—Warsaw Pact confrontation. Many analysts conclude that in the absence of nuclear deterrent threats more troops and conventional (non-nuclear) weapons would be required to protect our allies. Rejection of some forms of nuclear deterrence could therefore conceivably require a willingness to pay higher costs to develop conventional forces. Leaders and peoples of other nations might also have to accept higher costs for their own defense, particularly in Western Europe, if the threat to use nuclear weapons first were withdrawn. We cannot judge the strength of these arguments in particular cases. It may well be that some strengthening of conventional defense would be a proportionate price to pay, if this will reduce the possibility of a nuclear war. We acknowledge this reluctantly, aware as we are of the vast amount of scarce resources expended annually on instruments of defense in a world filled with other urgent, unmet human needs.

It is not for us to settle the technical debate about policy and budgets. From the perspective of a developing theology of peace, however, we feel obliged to contribute a moral dimension to the discussion. We hope that a significant reduction in numbers of conventional arms and weaponry would go hand in hand with diminishing reliance on nuclear deterrence. The history of recent wars (even so-called 'minor' or 'limited' wars) has shown that conventional war can also become indiscriminate in conduct and disproportionate to any valid purpose. We do not want in any way to give encouragement to a notion of 'making the world safe for conventional war', which introduces its own horrors.

Hence, we believe that any program directed at reducing reliance on nuclear weapons is not likely to succeed unless it includes measures to reduce tensions and to work for the balanced reduction of conventional forces. We believe that important possibilities exist which, if energetically pursued, would ensure against building up conventional forces as a concomitant of reductions in nuclear weapons. Examples are to be found in the ongoing negotiations for mutual, balanced, force reductions, the prospects for which are certainly not dim and would be enhanced by agreements on strategic weapons, and in the confidence-building measures still envisaged under the Helsinki agreement and review conference.

We must re-emphasize with all our being, nonetheless, that it is not only nuclear war that must be prevented, but war itself. Therefore, with Pope John Paul II we declare:

'Today, the scale and the horror of modern warfare — whether nuclear or not — makes it totally unacceptable as a means of settling differences between nations. War should belong to the tragic past, to history; it should find no place on humanity's agenda for the future.'[94]

Reason and experience tell us that a continuing upward spiral even in conventional arms, coupled with an unbridled increase in armed forces, instead of securing true peace will almost certainly be provocative of war.

Civil Defense Attention must be given to existing programs for civil defense against nuclear attack, including blast and fall-out shelters and relocation plans. It is unclear in the public mind whether these are intended to offer significant protection against at least some forms of nuclear attack or are being put into place to enhance the credibility of the strategic deterrent forces by demonstrating an ability to survive attack. This confusion has led to public skepticism and even ridicule of the program and casts doubt on the credibility of the government. An independent commission of scientists, engineers and weapons experts is needed to examine if these or any other plans offer a realistic prospect of survival for the nation's population or its cherished values, which a nuclear war would presumably be fought to preserve.

Efforts of Develop Non-Violent Means of Conflict Resolution We affirm a nation's right to defend itself, its citizens and its values. Security is the right of all, but that right, like everything else, must be subject to divine law and the limits defined by that law. We must find means of defending peoples that do not depend upon the threat of annihilation. Immoral means can never be justified by the end sought; no objective, however worthy of good in itself, can justify sinful acts or policies. Though our primary concern through this statement is war and the nuclear threat, these principles apply as well to all forms of violence, including insurgency, counterinsurgency, 'destabilization' and the like.

1   The Second Vatican Council praised 'those who renounce the use of violence in the vindication of their rights and who resort to methods of defense which are otherwise available to weaker parties, provided that this can be done without injury to the rights and duties of others or of the community itself'.[95] To make such renunciation effective and still defend what must be defended, the arts of diplomacy, negotiation and compromise must be developed and fully exercised. Non-violent means of resistance to evil deserve much more study and consideration than they have thus far received. There have been significant instances in which people have successfully resisted oppression without recourse to arms.[96] Non-violence is not the way of the weak, the cowardly or the impatient.

Such movements have seldom gained headlines even though they have left their mark on history. The heroic Danes who would not turn Jews over to the Nazis and the Norwegians who would not teach Nazi propaganda in schools serve as inspiring examples in the history of non-violence.

Non-violent resistance, like war, can take many forms depending upon the demands of a given situation. There is, for instance, organized popular defense instituted by government as part of its contingency planning. Citizens would be trained in the techniques of peaceable non-compliance and non-cooperation as a means of hindering an invading force or non-democratic government from imposing its will. Effective non-violent resistance requires the united will of a people and may demand as much patience and sacrifice from those who practice it as is now demanded by war and preparation for war. It may not always succeed. Nevertheless, before the possibility is dismissed as impractical or unrealistic, we urge that it be measured against the almost certain effects of a major war.

2 Non-violent resistance offers a common ground of agreement for individuals who choose the option of Christian pacifism to the point of accepting the need to die rather than to kill and those who choose the option of lethal force allowed by the theology of just war. Non-violent resistance makes clear that both are able to be committed to the same objective: defense of their country.

3 Popular defense would go beyond conflict resolution and compromise to a basic synthesis of beliefs and values. In its practice the objective is not only to avoid causing harm or injury to another creature, but, more positively, to seek the good of the other. Blunting the aggression of an adversary or oppressor would not be enough. The goal is winning the other over, making the adversary a friend.

It is useful to point out that these principles are thoroughly compatible with — and to some extent derived from — Christian teachings and must be part of any Christian theology of peace. Spiritual writers have helped trace the theory of non-violence to its roots in scripture and tradition and have illustrated its practice and success in their studies of the church fathers and the age of martyrs. Christ's own teachings and example provide a model way of life incorporating the truth and a refusal to return evil for evil.

Non-violent popular defense does not ensure that lives would not be lost. Nevertheless, once we recognize that the almost certain consequences of existing policies and strategies of war and carry with them a very real threat to the future existence of humankind itself, practical reason as well as spiritual faith demands that it be given serious consideration as an alternative course of action.

4   Once again we declare that the only true defense for the world's population is the rejection of nuclear war and the conventional wars which could escalate into nuclear war. With Pope John Paul II, we call upon educational and research institutes to take a lead in conducting peace studies: 'Scientific studies on war, its nature, causes, means, objectives and risks have much to teach us on the conditions for peace.'[97] To achieve this end, we urge that funds equivalent to a designated percentage (even one-tenth of 1 percent of current budgetary alloments for military purposes) be set aside to support such peace research.

In 1981 the Commission on Proposals for the National Academy of Peace and Conflict Resolution recommended the establishment of the US Academy of Peace, a recommendation nearly as old as this country's Constitution. The commission found that 'peace is a legitimate field of learning that encompasses rigorous, interdisciplinary research, education and training directed toward peacemaking expertise.'[98] We endorse the commission's recommendation and urge all citizens to support training in conflict resolution, nonviolent resistance, and programs devoted to service to peace and education for peace. Such an academy would not only provide a center for peace studies and activities, but also be a tangible evidence of our nation's sincerity in its often professed commitment to international peace and the abolition of war. We urge universities, particularly Catholic universities, in our country to develop programs for rigorous interdisciplinary research, education and training directed toward peacemaking expertise.

We too must be prepared to do our part to achieve these ends. We encourage churches and educational institutions, from primary schools to colleges and institutes of higher learning, to undertake similar programs at their own initiative. Every effort must be made to understand and evaluate the arms race, to encourage truly transnational perspectives on disarmament and to explore new forms of international cooperation and exchange. No greater challenge or higher priority can be imagined than the development and perfection of a theology of peace suited to a civilization poised on the brink of self-destruction. It is our prayerful hope that this document will prove to be a starting point and inspiration for that endeavor.

The Role of Conscience   A dominant characteristic of the Second Vatican Council's evaluation of modern warfare was the stress it placed on the requirement for proper formation of conscience. Moral principles are effective restraints on power only when policies reflect them and individuals practice them. The relationship of the authority of the state and the conscience of the individual on matters of war and peace takes a new urgency in the face of the destructive nature of modern war.

1 In this connection we reiterate the position we took in 1980. Catholic teaching does not question the right in principle of a government to require military service of its citizens provided the government shows it is necessary. A citizen may not casually disregard his country's conscientious decision to call its citizens to acts of 'legitimate defense'. Moreover, the role of Christian citizens in the armed forces is a service to the common good and an exercise of the virtue of patriotism, so long as they fulfill this role within defined moral norms.[99]

2 At the same time, no state may demand blind obedience. Our 1980 statement urged the government to present convincing reasons for draft registration and opposed reinstitution of conscription itself except in the case of a national defense emergency. Moreover, it reiterated our support for conscientious objection in general and for selective conscientious objection to participation in a particular war, either because of the ends being pursued or the means being used. We called selective conscientious objection a moral conclusion which can be validly derived from the classical teaching of just-war principles. We continue to insist upon respect for and legislative protection of the rights of both classes of conscientious objectors. We also approve requiring alternative service to the community — not related to military needs — by such persons.

Shaping a Peaceful World

Preventing nuclear war is a moral imperative; but the avoidance of war, nuclear or conventional, is not a sufficient conception of international relations today. Nor does it exhaust the content of Catholic teaching. Both the political needs and the moral challenge of our time require a positive conception of peace, based on a vision of a first world order. Pope Paul VI summarized classical Catholic teaching in his encyclical 'The Development of Peoples':

'Peace cannot be limited to a mere absence of war, the result of an ever precarious balance of forces. No, peace is something built up day after day, in the pursuit of an order intended by God, which implies a more perfect form of justice among men and women.'[100]

World Order in Catholic Teaching This positive conception of peace sees it as the fruit of order; order, in turn, is shaped by the values of justice, truth, freedom and love. The basis of this teaching is found in sacred scripture, St Augustine and St Thomas. It has found contemporary expression and development in papal teaching of this century. The popes of the nuclear age, from Pius XII through John Paul II have affirmed pursuit of international order as the way to banish the scourge of war from human affairs.[101]

The fundamental premise of world order in Catholic teaching is a theological truth: the unity of the human family — rooted in common creation, destined for the kingdom and united by moral bonds of rights and duties. This basic truth about the unity of the human family pervades the entire teaching on war and peace: For the pacifist position it is one of the reasons why life cannot be taken, while for the just-war position, even in a justified conflict bonds of responsibility remain in spite of the conflict.

Catholic teaching recognizes that in modern history, at least since the Peace of Westphalia (1648) the international community has been governed by nation-states. Catholic moral theology, as expressed for example in Chapters 2 and 3 of 'Peace on Earth', accords a real but relative moral value to sovereign states. The value is real because of the functions states fulfill as sources of order and authority in the political community; it is relative because boundaries of the sovereign state do not dissolve the deeper relationships of responsibility existing in the human community. Just as within nations the moral fabric of society is described in Catholic teaching in terms of reciprocal rights and duties — between individuals, and then between the individual and the state — so in the international community. 'Peace on Earth' defines the rights and duties which exist among states.[102]

In the past 20 years Catholic teaching has become increasingly specific about the content of these international rights and duties. In 1963, 'Peace on Earth' sketched the political and legal order among states. In 1967, 'The Development of Peoples' elaborated on order of economic rights and duties. In 1979, Pope John Paul articulated the human rights basis of international relations in his address to the United Nations.

These documents and others which build upon them outlined a moral order of international relations, i.e., how the international community *should* be organized. At the same time this teaching has been sensitive to the actual pattern of relations prevailing among states. While not ignoring present geopolitical realities, one of the primary functions of Catholic teaching on world order has been to point the way toward a more integrated international system.

In analyzing this path toward world order, the category increasingly used in Catholic moral teaching (and, more recently, in the social sciences also) is the interdependence of the world today. The theological principle of unity has always affirmed a human interdependence; but today this bond is complemented by the growing political and economic interdependence of the world, manifested in a whole range of international issues.[103]

An important element missing from world order today is a properly constituted political authority with the capacity to shape our material interdependence in the direction of moral interdependence. Pope John XXIII stated the case in the following way:

'Today the universal common good poses problems of worldwide dimensions, which cannot be adequately tackled or solved except by the efforts of public authority endowed with a wideness of powers, structure and means of the same proportions: that is, of public authority which is in a position to operate in an effective manner on a worldwide basis. The moral order itself, therefore, demands that such a form of public authority be established.'[104]

Just as the nation-state was a step in the evolution of government at a time when expanding trade and new weapons technologies made the feudal system inadequate to manage conflicts and provide security, so we are now entering an era of new, global interdependencies requiring global systems of governance to manage the resulting conflicts and ensure our common security. Major global problems such as worldwide inflation, trade and payments deficits, competition over scarce resources, hunger widespread unemployment, global environmental dangers, the growing power of transnational corporations and the threat of international financial collapse, as well as the danger of world war resulting from these growing tensions – cannot be remedied by a single nation-state approach. They shall require the concerted effort of the whole world community. As we shall indicate below, the United Nations should be particularly considered in this effort.

In the nuclear age it is in the regulation of interstate conflicts and ultimately the replacement of military by negotiated solutions that the supreme importance and necessity of a moral as well as a political concept of the international common good can be grasped. The absence of adequate structures for addressing these issues places even greater responsibility on the policies of individual states. By a mix of political vision and moral wisdom, states are called to interpret the national interest in light of the larger global interest.

We are living in a global age with problems and conflicts on a global scale. Either we shall learn to resolve these problems together or we shall destroy one another. Mutual security and survival require a new vision of the world as one interdependent planet. We have rights and duties not only within our diverse national communities, but within the larger world community.

The Superpowers in a Disordered World   No relationship more dramatically demonstrates the fragile nature of order in international affairs today than that of the United States and the Soviet Union. These two sovereign states have avoided open war, nuclear or conventional, but they are divided by philosophy, ideology and competing ambitions. Their competition is global in scope and involves everything from comparing nuclear arsenals to printed propaganda. Both have been criticized in international meetings because of their policies in the nuclear arms race.[105]

In our 1980 pastoral letter on Marxism we sought to portray the significant differences between Christian teaching and Marxism; at the same time we addressed the need for states with different political systems to live together in an interdependent world:

> The church recognizes the depth and dimensions of the ideological differences that divide the human race, but the urgent practical need for cooperative efforts in the human interest overrules these differences. Hence Catholic teaching seeks to avoid exacerbating the ideological opposition and to focus upon the problems requiring common efforts across the ideological divide: keeping the peace and empowering the poor.[106]

We believe this passage reflects the teaching of 'Peace on Earth', the continuing call for dialogue of Pope Paul VI and the 1979 address of Pope John Paul II at the United Nations. We continue to stress this theme even while we recognize the difficulty of realizing its objectives.

The difficulties are severe on the issue of the arms race. For most Americans the danger of war is commonly defined primarily in terms of the threat of Soviet military expansionism and the consequent need to deter or defend against a Soviet military threat.

Many assume that the existence of this threat is permanent and that nothing can be done about it except to build and maintain overwhelming or at least countervailing military power.[107]

The fact of a Soviet threat, as well as the existence of a Soviet imperial drive for hegemony, at least in regions of major strategic interest, cannot be denied. The history of the Cold War has produced varying interpretations of which side caused which conflict, but whatever the details of history illustrate, the plain fact is that the memories of Soviet policies in Eastern Europe and recent events in Afghanistan and Poland have left their mark in the American political debate. Many peoples are forcibly kept under communist domination despite their manifest wishes to be free. Soviet power is very great. Whether the Soviet Union's pursuit of military might is motivated primarily by defensive or aggressive aims might be debated, but the effect is nevertheless to leave profoundly insecure those who must live in the shadow of that might.

Americans need have no illusions about the Soviet system of repression and the lack of respect in that system for human rights or about Soviet covert operations and pro-revolutionary activities. To be sure, our own system is not without flaws. Our government has sometimes supported repressive governments in the name of preserving freedom, has carried out repugnant covert operations of its own and remains imperfect in its domestic record of ensuring equal rights for all. At the same time there is a difference. NATO is an alliance of democratic countries which have freely chosen their association; the Warsaw Pact is not.

To pretend that as a nation we have lived up to all our own ideals would be patently dishonest. To pretend that all evils in the world have been or are now being perpetrated by dictatorial regimes would be both dishonest and absurd. But having said this, and admitting our own faults, it is imperative that we confront reality. The facts simply do not support the invidious comparisons made at times even in our own society between our way of life, in which most basic human rights are at least recognized even if they are not always adequately supported, and those totalitarian and tyrannical regimes in which such rights are either denied or systematically suppressed. Insofar as this is true, however, it makes the promotion of human rights in our foreign policy, as well as our domestic policy, all the more important. It is the acid test of our commitment to our democratic values. In this light, any attempts to justify, for reasons of state, support for regimes that continue to violate human rights is all the more morally reprehensible in its hypocrisy.

A glory of the United States is the range of political freedoms its system permits us. We, as bishops, as Catholics, as citizens, exercise those freedoms in writing this letter, with its share of criticisms of our government. We have true freedom of religion, freedom of speech and access to a free press. We could not exercise the same freedoms in contemporary Eastern Europe or in the Soviet Union. Free people must always pay a proportionate price and run some risks — responsibly — to preserve their freedom.

It is one thing to recognize that the people of the world do not want war. It is quite another thing to attribute the same good motives to regimes or political systems that have consistently demonstrated precisely the opposite in their behavior. There are political philosophies with understandings of morality so radically different from ours that even negotiations proceed from different premises, although identical terminology may be used by both sides. This is no reason for not negotiating. It is a very good reason for not negotiating blindly or naively.

In this regard, Pope John Paul II offers some sober reminders concerning dialogue and peace:

> (O)ne must mention the tactical and deliberate lie, which misuses language, which has recourse to the most sophisticated techniques of propaganda, which deceives and distorts dialogue and incites to aggression . . .
>
> While certain parties are fostered by ideologies which, in spite of their declarations, are opposed to the dignity of the human person . . . ideologies which see in struggle the motive force of history, that see in force the source of rights, that see in the discernment of the enemy the ABC of politics, dialogue is fixed and sterile. Or, if it still exists, it is a superficial and falsified reality. It becomes very difficult, not to say impossible, therefore. There follows almost a complete lack of communication between countries and blocs. Even the international institutions are paralyzed. And the setback to dialogue then runs the risk of serving the arms race.
>
> However, even in what can be considered as an impasse to the extent that individuals support such ideologies, the attempt to have a lucid dialogue seems still necessary in order to unblock the situation and to work for the possible establishment of peace on particular points. This is to be done by

counting upon common sense, on the possibilities of danger for everyone and on the just aspirations to which the people themselves largely adhere.[108]

The cold realism of this text, combined with the conviction that political dialogue and negotiations must be pursued in spite of obstacles, provides solid guidance for US—Soviet relations. Acknowledging all the differences between the two philosophies and political systems, the irreducible truth is that objective mutual interests do exist between the superpowers. Proof of this concrete if limited convergence of interest can be found in some vitally important agreements on nuclear weapons which have already been negotiated in the areas of nuclear testing and nuclear explosions in space as well as the SALT I agreements.

The fact that the Soviet Union now possesses a huge arsenal of strategic weapons as threatening to us as ours may appear to them does not exclude the possibility of success in such negotiations. The conviction of many European observers that a *modus vivendi* (often summarized as 'detente') is a practical possibility in political, economic and scientific areas should not be lightly dismissed in our country.

Sensible and successful diplomacy, however, will demand that we avoid the trap of a form of anti-Sovietism which fails to grasp the central danger of a superpower rivalry in which both the United States and the Soviet Union are the players, and fails to recognize the common interest both states have in never using nuclear weapons. Some of those dangers and common interests would exist in any world where two great powers, even relatively benign ones, competed for power, influence and security. The diplomatic requirement for addressing the US—Soviet relationship is not romantic idealism about Soviet intentions and capabilities, but solid realism which recognizes that everyone will lose in a nuclear exchange.

As bishops we are concerned with issues which go beyond diplomatic requirements. It is of some value to keep raising in the realm of the political debate truths which ground our involvement in the affairs of nations and peoples. Diplomatic dialogue usually sees the other as a potential or real adversary. Soviet behavior in some cases merits the adjective reprehensible, but the Soviet people and their leaders are human beings created in the image and likeness of God. To believe we are condemned in the future only to what has been the past of US—Soviet relations is to underestimate both our human potential for creative diplomacy and God's action in our midst which can open the way to changes we could barely imagine. We do not intend to foster illusory ideas that the road ahead in superpower relations will be devoid of tension or that peace will be easily achieved. But we do warn against that 'hardness of heart' which can close us or others to the changes needed to make the future different from the past.

Interdependence: From Fact to Policy   While the nuclear arms race focuses attention on the US—Soviet relationship, it is neither politically wise nor morally justifiable to ignore the broader international context in which that relationship exists. Public attention, riveted on the big powers, often misses the plight of scores of countries and millions of people simply trying to survive. The interdependence of the world means a set of interrelated human questions. Important as keeping the peace in the nuclear age is, it does not solve or dissolve the other major problems of the day. Among these problems the preeminent issue is the continuing chasm in living standards between the industrialized world (East and West) and the developing world. To quote Pope John Paul II:

> So widespread is the phenomenon that it brings into question the financial, monetary, production and commercial mechanisms that, resting on various political pressures, support the world economy. These are proving incapable either of remedying the unjust social situations inherited from the past or of dealing with the urgent challenges and ethical demands of the present.[109]

The East—West competition, central as it is to world order and important as it is in the foreign policy debate, does not address this moral question which rivals the nuclear issue in its human significance. While the problem of the developing nations would itself require a pastoral letter, Catholic teaching has maintained an analysis of the problem which should be identified here. The analysis acknowledges internal causes of poverty, but also concentrates on the way the larger international economic structures affect the poor nations. These particularly involve trade, monetary, investment and aid policies.

Neither of the superpowers is conspicuous in these areas for initiatives designed to address 'the absolute poverty' in which millions live today.[110]

From our perspective and experience, we believe there is much greater potential for response to these questions in the mind and hearts of Americans than has been reflected in US policy. As pastors who often appeal to our congregations for funds destined for international programs, we find good will and great generosity the prevailing characteristics. The spirit of generosity which shaped the Marshall Plan is still alive in the American public.

We must discover how to translate this personal sense of generosity and compassion into support for policies which would respond to papal teaching in international economic issues. It is precisely the need to expand our conception of international charity and relief to an understanding of the need for social justice in terms of trade, aid and monetary issues which was reflected in Pope John Paul II's call to American Catholics in Yankee Stadium:

> Within the framework of your national institutions and in cooperation with all your compatriots, you will also want to seek out the structural reasons which foster or cause the different forms of poverty in the world and in your own country, so that you can apply the proper remedies. You will not allow yourselves to be intimidated or discouraged by oversimplified explanations which are more ideological than scientific — explanations which try to account for a complex evil by some single cause. But neither will you recoil before the reforms — even profound ones — of attitudes and structures that may prove necessary in order to recreate over and over again the conditions needed by the disadvantaged if they are to have a fresh chance in the hard struggle of life. The poor of the United States and of the world are your brothers and sisters in Christ.[111]

The pope's words highlight an intellectual, moral and political challenge for the United States. Intellectually there is a need to rethink the meaning of national interest in an interdependent world. Morally there is a need to build upon the spirit of generosity present in the US public, directing it toward a more systematic response to the major issues affecting the poor of the world. Politically there is a need for US policies which promote the profound structural reforms called for by recent papal teaching.

Precisely in the name of international order papal teaching has by word and deed sought to promote multilateral forms of cooperation toward the developing world. The US capacity for leadership in multilateral institutions is very great. We urge much more vigorous and creative response to the needs of the developing countries by the United States in these institutions.

The significant role the United States could play is evident in the daily agenda facing these institutions. Proposals addressing the relationship of the industrialized and developing countries on a broad spectrum of issues, all in need of 'profound reforms', are regularly discussed in the United Nations and other international organizations. Without US participation, significant reform and substantial change in the direction of addressing the needs of the poor will not occur. Meeting these needs is an essential element for a peaceful world.

Papal teaching of the last four decades has not only supported international institutions in principle, it has supported the United Nations specifically. Pope Paul VI said to the UN General Assembly:

'The edifice which you have constructed must never fail; it must be perfected and made equal to the needs which world history will present. You mark a stage in the development of mankind for which retreat must never be admitted, but from which it is necessary that advance be made.'[112]

It is entirely necessary to examine the United Nations carefully, to recognize its limitations and propose changes where needed. Nevertheless, in light of the continuing endorsement found in papal teaching, we urge that the United States adopt a stronger supportive leadership role with respect to the United Nations. The growing interdependence of the nations and peoples of the world, coupled with the extragovernmental presence of multinational corporations, requires new structures of cooperation. As one of the founders of and major financial contributors to the United Nations, the United States can and should assume a more positive and creative role in its life today.

It is in the context of the United Nations that the impact of the arms race on the prospects for economic development is highlighted. The numerous UN studies on the relationship of development and disarmament support the judgment of Vatican II cited earlier in this letter: 'The arms race is one of the greatest curses on the human race and the harm it inflicts upon the poor is more than can be endured.'[113]

We are aware that the precise relationship between disarmament and development is neither easily demonstrated nor easily reoriented. But the fact of a massive distortion of resources in the face of crying human need creates a moral question. In an interdependent world the security of one nation is related to the security of all. When we consider how and what we pay for defense today, we need a broader view than the equation of arms with security.[114] The threats to the security and stability of an interdependent world are not all contained in missiles and bombers.

If the arms race in all its dimensions is not reversed, resources will not be available for the human needs so evident in many parts of the globe and in our own country as well. But we also know that making resources available is a first step; policies of wise use would also have to follow. Part of the process of thinking about the economics of disarmament includes the possibilities of conversion of defense industries to other purposes. Many say the possibilities are great if the political will is present. We say the political will to reorient resources to human needs and redirect industrial, scientific and technological capacity to meet those needs is part of the challenge of the nuclear age. Those whose livelihood is dependent upon industries which can be reoriented should rightfully expect assistance in making the transition to new forms of employment. The economic dimension of the arms race is broader than we can assess here, but these issues we have raised are among the primary questions before the nation.[115]

An interdependent world requires an understanding that key policy questions today involve mutuality of interest. If the monetary and trading systems are not governed by sensitivity to mutual needs, they can be destroyed. If the protection of human rights and the promotion of human needs are left as orphans in the diplomatic arena, the stability we seek in increased armaments will eventually be threatened by rights denied and needs unmet in vast sectors of the globe. If future planning about conservation of and access to resources is relegated to a pure struggle of power, we shall simply guarantee conflict in the future.

The moral challenge of interdependence concerns shaping the relationships and rules of practice which will support our common need for security, welfare and safety. The challenge tests our idea of human community, our policy analysis and our political will. The need to prevent nuclear war is absolutely crucial, but even if this is achieved, there is much more to be done.

THE PASTORAL CHALLENGE AND RESPONSE

The Church: A Community of Conscience, Prayer and Penance

Pope John Paul II, in his first encyclical, recalled with gratitude the teaching of Pius XII on the church. He then went on to say:

Membership in that body has for its source a particular call, united with the saving action of grace. Therefore, if we wish to keep in mind this community of the people of God which is so vast and so differentiated, we must see first and foremost Christ saying in a way to each member of the community: 'Follow me.' It is the community of the disciples, each of whom in a different way — at times very consciously and consistently, at other times not very consciously and very consistently — is following Christ. This shows also the deeply 'personal' aspect and dimension of this society.[116]

In the following pages we should like to spell out some of the implications of being a community of Jesus' disciples in a time when our nation is so heavily armed with nuclear weapons and is engaged in a continuing development of new weapons together with strategies for their use.

It is clear today, perhaps more than in previous generations, that convinced Christians are a minority in nearly every country of the world — including nominally Christian and Catholic nations. In our own country we are coming to a fuller awareness that a response to the call of Jesus is both personal and demanding. As believers we can identify rather easily with the early church as a company of witnesses engaged in a difficult mission. To be disciples of Jesus requires that we continually go beyond where we now are. To obey the call of Jesus means separating ourselves from all attachments and affiliation that could prevent us from hearing and following our authentic vocation. To set out on the road to discipleship is to dispose oneself for a share in the cross (cf. Jn. 16:20). To be a Christian, according to the New Testament, is not simply to believe with one's mind, but also become a doer of the word, a wayfarer with and a witness to Jesus. This means, of course, that we never expect complete success within history and that we must regard as normal even the path of persecution and the possibility of martyrdom.

We readily recognize that we live in a world that is becoming increasingly estranged from Christian values. In order to remain a Christian, one must take a resolute stand against many commonly accepted axioms of the world. To become true disciples, we must undergo a demanding course of induction into the adult Christian community. We must continually equip ourselves to profess the full faith of the church in an increasingly secularized society. We must develop a sense of solidarity, cemented by relationships with mature and exemplary Christians who represent Christ and his way of life.

All of these comments about the meaning of being a disciple or a follower of Jesus today are especially relevant to the quest for genuine peace in our time.

Elements of a Pastoral Response

We recommend and endorse for the faithful some practical programs to meet the challenge to their faith in this area of grave concern.

Educational Programs and Formation of Conscience   Since war, especially the threat of nuclear war, is one of the central problems of our day, how we seek to solve it could determine the mode and even the possibility of life on earth. God made human beings stewards of the earth; we cannot escape this responsibility. Therefore we urge every diocese and parish to implement balanced and objective educational programs to help people at all age levels to undestand better the issues of war and peace. Development and implementation of such programs must receive a high priority during the next several years. They must teach the full impact of our Christian faith. To accomplish this, this pastoral letter in its entirety, including its complexity, should be used as a guide and a framework for such programs, as they lead people to make moral decisions about the problems of war and peace, keeping in mind that the applications of principles in this pastoral letter do not carry the same moral authority as our statements of universal moral principles and formal church teaching.

In developing educational programs we must keep in mind that questions of war and peace have a profoundly moral dimension which responsible Christians cannot ignore. They are questions of life and death. True, they also have a political dimension because they are embedded in public policy. But the fact that they are also political is no excuse for denying the church's obligation to provide its members with the help they need in forming their consciences. We must learn together how to make correct and responsible moral judgments. We reject, therefore, criticism of the church's concern with these issues on the ground that it 'should not become involved in politics'. We are called to move from discussion to witness and action.

At the same time we recognize that the church's teaching authority does not carry the same force when it deals with technical solutions involving particular means as it does when it speaks of principles or ends. People may agree in abhorring an injustice, for instance, yet sincerely disagree as to what practical approach will achieve justice. Religious groups are as entitled as others to their opinion in such cases, but they should not claim that their opinions are the only ones that people of good will may hold.

The church's educational programs must explain clearly those principles or teachings about which there is little question. Those teachings, which seek to make explicit the gospel call to peace and the tradition of the church, should then be applied to concrete situations. They must indicate what the possible legitimate options are and what the consequences of those options may be. While this approach should be self-evident, it needs to be emphasized. Some people who have entered the public debate on nuclear warfare, at all points on the spectrum of opinion, appear not to understand or accept some of the clear teachings of the church as contained in papal or conciliar documents. For example, some would place almost no limits on the use of nuclear weapons if they are needed for 'self-defense'. Some on the other side of the debate insist on conclusions which may be legitimate options but cannot be made obligatory on the basis of actual church teaching.

True Peace Calls for 'Reverence for Life'   All of the values we are promoting in this letter rest ultimately in the disarmament of the human heart and the conversion of the human spirit to God, who alone can give authentic peace. Indeed, to have peace in our world we must first have peace within ourselves. As Pope John Paul II reminded us in his 1982 World Day of Peace message, world peace will always elude us until peace becomes a reality for each of us personally. 'It springs from the dynamism of free wills guided by reason toward the common good that is to be attained in truth, justice and love.'[117] Interior peace becomes possible only when we have a conversion of spirit. We cannot have peace with hate in our hearts.

No society can live in peace with itself or with the world without a full awareness of the worth and dignity of every human person and of the sacredness of all human life (Jas. 4:1−2). When we accept violence in any form as commonplace, our sensitivities become dulled. When we accept violence, war itself can be taken for granted. Violence has many faces: oppression of the poor, deprivation of basic human rights, economic exploitation, sexual exploitation and pornography, neglect or abuse of the aged and the helpless and innumerable other acts of inhumanity. Abortion in particular blunts a sense of the sacredness of human life. In a society where the innocent unborn are killed wantonly, how can we expect people to feel righteous revulsion at the act or threat of killing non-combatants in war?

We are well aware of the differences involved in the taking of human life in warfare and the taking of human life through abortion. As we have discussed throughout this document, even justifiable defense against aggression may result in the indirect of unintended loss of innocent human lives. This is tragic, but may conceivably be proportionate to the values defended. Nothing, however, can justify direct attack on innocent human life in or out of warfare. Abortion is precisely such an attack.

We know that millions of men and women of good will, of all religious persuasions, join us in our commitment to try to reduce the horrors of war and particularly to assure that nuclear weapons will never again be used by any nation, anywhere, for any reason. Millions join us in our no to nuclear war in the certainty that nuclear war would inevitably result in the killing of millions of innocent human beings, directly or indirectly. Yet many part ways with us in our efforts to reduce the horror of abortion and our no to war on innocent human life in the womb, killed not indirectly, but directly.

. . .

Pope Paul VI was resolutely clear: *If you wish peace, defend life.*[118] We plead with all who would work to end the scourge of war to begin by defending life at its most defenseless, the life of the unborn.

Prayer A conversion of our hearts and minds will make it possible for us to enter into a closer communion with our Lord. We nourish that communion by personal and communal prayer, for it is in prayer that we encounter Jesus, who is our peace and learn from him the way to peace.

. . .

The practice of contemplative prayer is especially valuable for advancing harmony and peace in the world. For this prayer rises, by divine grace, where there is total disarmament of the heart, and unfolds in an experience of love which is the moving force of peace. Contemplation fosters a vision of the human family as united and interdependent in the mystery of God's love for all people. This silent interior prayer bridges temporarily the 'already' and 'not yet', this world and God's kingdom of peace.

. . .

We implore other Christians and everyone of good will to join us in this continuing prayer for peace, as we beseech God for peace within ourselves, in our families and community, in our nation and in the world.

Penance   Prayer by itself is incomplete without penance. Penance directs us toward our goal of putting on the attitudes of Jesus himself. Because we are all capable of violence, we are never totally conformed to Christ and are always in need of conversion

. . .

The present nuclear arms race has distracted us from the words of the prophets, has turned us from peacemaking and has focused our attention on a nuclear buildup leading to annihilation. We are called to turn back from this evil of total detruction and turn instead in prayer and penance toward God, toward our neighbor and toward the building of a peaceful world . . .

Challenge and Hope

The arms race presents questions of conscience we may not evade. As American Catholics we are called to express our loyalty to the deepest values we cherish: peace, justice and security for the entire human family. National goals and policies must be measured against that standard . . .

To Priests, Deacons, Religious and Pastoral Ministers   We recognize the unique role in the church which belongs to priests and deacons by reason of the sacrament of holy orders and their unique responsibility in the community of believers. We also recognize the valued and indispensable role of men and women religious. To all of them and to all other pastoral ministers we stress that the cultivation of the gospel vision of peace as a way of life for believers and as a leaven in society should be a major objective. As bishops we are aware each day of our dependence upon your efforts. We are aware too that this letter and the new obligations it could present to the faithful may create difficulties for you in dealing with those you serve. We have confidence in your capacity and ability to convert these difficulties into an opportunity to give a fuller witness to our Lord and his message. This letter will be known by the faithful only as well as you know it, preach and teach it, and use it creatively.

To Educators   We have outlined in this letter Catholic teaching on war and peace, but this framework will become a living message only through your work in the Catholic community. To teach the ways of peace is not 'to weaken the nation's will', but to be concerned for the nation's soul. We address theologians in a particular way because we know that we have only begun the journey toward a theology of peace; without your specific contributions this desperately needed dimension of our faith will not be realized. Through your help we may provide new vision and wisdom for church and state.

We are confident that all models of Catholic education, which have served the church in our country so well in so many ways, will creatively rise to the challenge of peace.

To Parents   Your role, in our eyes, is unsurpassed by any other; the foundation of society is the family. We are conscious of the continuing sacrifices you make in the efforts to nurture the full human and spiritual growth of your children. Children hear the gospel message first from your lips. Parents who consciously discuss issues of justice in the home and who strive to help children solve conflicts through non-violent methods enable their children to grow up as peacemakers. We pledge our continuing pastoral support in the common objective we share of building a peaceful world for the future of children everywhere.

To Youth   Pope John Paul II singles you out in every country where he visits as the hope of the future; we agree with him. We call you to choose your future work and professions carefully. How you spend the rest of your lives will determine in large part whether there will any longer be a world as we know it. We ask you to study carefully the teachings of the church and the demands of the Gospel about the war and peace. We encourage you to seek careful guidance as you reach conscientious decisions about your civic responsibilities in this age of nuclear military forces.

We speak to you, however, as people of faith. We share with you our deepest conviction that in the midst of the dangers and complexities of our time God is with us working through us and sustaining us all in our efforts of building a world of peace with justice for each person.

To Men and Women in Military Service   Millions of you are Catholics serving in the armed forces. We recognize that you carry special responsibilities for the issues we have considered in this letter. Our perspective on your profession is that of Vatican II: 'All those who enter the military service in loyalty to their country should look upon themselves as the custodians of the security and freedom of their fellow countrymen; and where they carry out their duty properly, they are contributing to the maintenance of peace.'[119]

It is surely not our intention in writing this letter to create problems for Catholics in the armed forces. Every profession, however, has its specific moral questions and it is clear that the teaching on war and peace developed in this letter poses a special challenge and opportunity to those in the military profession. Our pastoral contact with Catholics in military service, either through our direct experience or through our priests, impresses us with the demanding moral standards we already see observed and the commitment to Catholic faith we find. We are convinced that the challenges of this letter will be faced conscientiously. The purpose of defense policy is to defend the peace; military professionals should understand their vocation this way. We believe they do, and we support this view.

We remind all in authority and in the chain of command that their training and field manuals have long prohibited, and still do prohibit, certain actions in the conduct of war, especially those actions which inflict harm on innocent civilians. The question is not whether certain measures are unlawful or forbidden in warfare, but which measures: To refuse to take such actions is not an act of cowardice or treason but one of courage and patriotism.

We address particularly those involved in the exercise of authority over others. We are aware of your responsibilities and impressed by the standard of personal and professional duty you uphold. We feel, therefore, that we can urge you to do everything you can to assure that every peaceful alternative is exhausted before war is even remotely considered. In developing battle plans and weapons systems, we urge you to try to ensure that these are designed to reduce violence, destruction, suffering and death to a minimum, keeping in mind especially non-combatants and other innocent persons.

Those who train individuals for military duties must remember that the citizen does not lose his or her basic human rights by entrance into military service. No one, for whatever reason, can justly treat a military person with less dignity and respect than that demanded for and deserved by every human person. One of the most difficult problems of war involves defending a free society without destroying the values that give it meaning and validity. Dehumanization of a nation's military personnel by dulling their sensibilities and generating hatred toward adversaries in an effort to increase their fighting effectiveness robs them of basic human rights and freedoms, degrading them as persons.

Attention must be given to the effects on military personnel themselves of the use of even legitimate means of conducting war. While attacking legitimate targets and wounding or killing opposed combat forces may be morally justified, what happens to military persons required to carry out these actions? Are they treated merely as instruments of war, insensitive as the weapons they use? With what moral or emotional experiences do they return from war and attempt to resume normal civilian lives? How does their experience affect society? How are they treated by society?

It is not only basic human rights of adversaries that must be respected, but those of our own forces as well. We re-emphasize, therefore, the obligation of responsible authorities to ensure appropriate training and education of combat forces and to provide appropriate support for those who have experienced combat. It is unconscionable to deprive those veterans of combat whose lives have been severely disrupted or traumatized by their combat experiences of proper psychological and other appropriate treatment and support.

Finally, we are grateful for the sacrifice so many in military service must make today and for the service offered in the past by veterans. We urge that those sacrifices be mitigated so far as possible by the provision of appropriate living and working conditions and adequate financial recompense. Military persons and their families must be provided continuing opportunity for full spiritual growth, the exercise of their religious faith and a dignified mode of life.

We especially commend and encourage our priests in military service. In addition to the message already addressed to all priests and religious, we stress the special obligations and opportunities you face in direct pastoral service to the men and women of the armed forces. To complement a teaching document of this scope, we shall need the sensitive and wise pastoral guidance only you can provide. We promise our support in facing this challenge.

To Men and Women in Defense Industries   You also face specific questions because the defense industry is directly involved in the development and production of the weapons of mass destruction which have concerned us in this letter. We do not presume or pretend that clear answers exist to many of the personal, professional and financial choices facing you in your varying responsibilities. In this letter we have ruled out certain uses of nuclear weapons, while also expressing conditional moral acceptance for deterrence. All Catholics, at every level of defense industries, can and should use the moral principles of this letter to form their consciences. We realize that different judgments of conscience will face different people, and we recognize the possibility of diverse concrete judgments being made in this complex area. We seek as moral teachers and pastors to be available to all who confront these questions of personal and vocational choice. Those who in conscience decide that they should no longer be associated with defense activities should find support in the Catholic community. Those who remain in these industries or earn a profit from the weapons industry should find in the church guidance and support for the ongoing evaluation of their work.

To Men and Women of Science   At Hiroshima Pope John Paul said:

'Criticism of science and technology is sometimes so severe that it comes close to comdemning science itself. On the contrary, science and technology are a wonderful product of God-given human creativity, since they have provided us with wonderful possibilities and we all gratefully benefit from them. But we know that this potential is not a neutral one: It can be used either for man's progress or for his degradation.'[120]

We appreciate the efforts of scientists, some of whom first unlocked the secret of atomic power and others of whom have developed it in diverse ways, to turn the enormous power of science to the cause of peace.

Modern history is not lacking scientists who have looked back with deep remorse on the development of weapons to which they contributed, sometimes with the highest motivation, even believing that they were creating weapons that would render all other weapons obsolete and convince the world of the unthinkableness of war. Such efforts have ever proved illusory. Surely equivalent dedication of scientific minds to reverse current trends and to pursue concepts as bold and adventuresome in favor of peace as those which in the past have magnified the risks of war could result in dramatic benefits for all of humanity. We particularly note in this regard the extensive efforts of public education undertaken by physicians and scientists on the medical consequences of nuclear war.

We do not, however, wish to limit our remarks to the physical sciences alone. Nor do we limit our remarks to physical scientists. In his address at the United Nations University in Hiroshima, Pope John Paul II warned about misuse of 'the social sciences and the human behavioral sciences when they are utilized to manipulate people, to crush their mind, souls, dignity and freedom'.[121] The positive role of social science in overcoming the dangers of the nuclear age is evident in this letter. We have been dependent upon the research and analysis of social scientists in our effort to apply the moral principles of the Catholic tradition to the concrete problems of our day. We encourage social scientists to continue this work of relating moral wisdom and political reality. We are in continuing need of your insights.

To Men and Women of the Media We have directly felt our dependence upon you in writing this letter; all the problems we have confronted have been analyzed daily in the media. As we have grappled with these issues, we have experienced some of the responsibility you bear for interpreting them. On the quality of your efforts depends in great measure the opportunity the general public will have for understanding this letter.

To Public Officials Vatican II spoke forcefully of 'the difficult yet noble art of politics'.[122] No public issue is more difficult than avoiding war; no public task more noble than building a secure peace. Public officials in a democracy must both lead and listen; they are ultimately dependent upon a popular consensus to sustain policy. We urge you to lead with courage and to listen to the public debate with sensitivity.

Leadership in a nuclear world means examining with great care and objectivity every potential initiative toward world peace, regardless of how unpromising it might at firt appear. One specific initiative which might be taken now would be the establishment of a task force including the public sector, industry, labor, economists and scientists with the mandate to consider the problems and challenges posed by nuclear disarmament to our economic well-being and industrial output. Listening includes being particularly attentive to the consciences of those who sincerely believe that they may not morally support warfare in general, a given war of the exercise of a particular role within the armed forces. Public officials might well serve all of our fellow citizens by proposing and supporting legislation designed to give maximum protection to this precious freedom, true freedom of conscience.

In response to public officials who both lead and listen, we urge citizens to respect the vocation of public service. It is a role easily maligned, but not easily fulfilled. Neither justice nor peace can be achieved with stability in the absence of courageous and creative public servants.

To Catholics as Citizens All papal teaching on peace has stressed the crucial role of public opinion. Pope John Paul II specified the tasks before us: 'There is no justification for not raising the question of the responsibility of each nation and each individual in the face of possible wars and of the nuclear threat.'[123] In a democracy the responsibility of the nation and that of its citizens coincide. Nuclear weapons pose especially acute questions of conscience for American Catholics. As citizens we wish to affirm our loyalty to our country and its ideals, yet we are also citizens of the world who must be faithful to the universal principles proclaimed by the church. While some other countries also possess nuclear weapons, we may not forget that the United States was the first to build and to use them. Like the Soviet Union, this country now possesses so many weapons as to imperil the continuation of civilization. Americans share responsibility for the current situation and cannot evade responsibility for trying to resolve it.

The virtue of patriotism means that as citizens we respect and honor our country, but our very love and loyalty make us examine carefully and regularly its role in world affairs, asking that it live up to its full potential as an agent of peace with justice for all people.

'Citizens must cultivate a generous and loyal spirit of patriotism, but without being narrow-minded. This means that they will always direct their attention to the good of the whole human family, united by the different ties which bind together races, people and nations.'[124]

In a pluralistic democracy like the United States, the church has a unique opportunity, precisely because of the strong constitutional protection of both religious freedom and freedom of speech and the press, to help call attention to the moral dimensions of public issues. In a previous pastoral letter, 'Human Life in Our Day', we said:

'In our democratic system, the fundamental right of political dissent cannot be denied nor is rational debate on public policy decisions of government in the light of moral and political principles to be discouraged. It is the duty of the governed to analyze responsibility the concrete issues of public policy.'[125]

In fulfilling this role the church helps to create a community of conscience in the wider civil community. It does this in the first instance by teaching clearly within the church the moral principles which bind and shape the Catholic conscience. The church also fulfills a teaching role, however, in striving to share the moral wisdom of the Catholic tradition with the larger society.

In the wider public discussion we look forward in a special way to cooperating with all other Christians with whom we share common traditions. We also treasure cooperative efforts with Jewish and Islamic communities, which possess a long and abiding concern for peace as a religious and human value. Finally, we reaffirm our desire to participate in a common public effort with all men and women of good will who seek to reverse the arms race and secure the peace of the world.

CONCLUSION

As we close this lengthy letter, we try to answer two key questions as directly as we can.

Why do we address these matters fraught with such complexity, controversy and passion? We speak as pastors, not politicians. We are teachers, not technicians. We cannot avoid our responsibility to lift up the moral dimensions of the choices before our world and nation. The nuclear age is an era of moral as well as physical danger. We are the first generation since Genesis with the power to virtually destroy God's creation. We cannot remain silent in the face of such danger. Why do we address these issues? We are simply trying to live up to the call of Jesus to be peacemakers in our own time and situation.

What are we saying? Fundamentally, we are saying that the decisions about nuclear weapons are among the most pressing moral questions of our age. While these decisions have obvious military and political aspects, they involve fundamental moral choices. In simple terms, we are saying that good ends (defending one's country, protecting freedom, etc.) cannot justify immoral means (the use of weapons which kill indiscriminately and threaten whole societies). We fear that our world and nation are headed in the wrong direction. More weapons with greater destructive potential are produced every day. More and more nations are seeking to become nuclear powers. In our quest for more and more security we fear we are actually becoming less and less secure.

In the words of our Holy Father, we need a 'moral about-face'. The whole world must summon the moral courage and technical means to say no to nuclear conflict; no to weapons of mass destruction; no to an arms race which robs the poor and the vulnerable; and no to the moral danger of a nuclear age which places before humankind indefensible choices of constant terror or surrender. Peacemaking is not an optional commitment. It is a requirement of our faith. We are called to be peacemakers, not by some movement of the moment, but by our Lord Jesus. The content and context of our peacemaking is set not by some political agenda or ideological program, but by the teaching of his church.

Thus far in this pastoral letter we have made suggestions we hope will be helpful in the present world crisis. Looking ahead to the long and productive future of humanity for which we all hope, we feel that a more all-inclusive and final solution is needed. We speak here of the truly effective international authority for which Pope John XXIII ardently longed in 'Peace on Earth'[126] and of which Pope Paul VI spoke to the United Nations on his visit there in 1965.[127] The hope for such a structure is not unrealistic, because the point has been reached where public opinion sees clearly that, with the massive weaponry of the present, war is no longer viable. There *is* a substitute for war. There is negotiation under the supervision of a global body realistically fashioned to do its job. It must be given the equipment to keep constant surveillance on the entire earth. Present technology makes this possible. It must have the authority, freely conferred upon it by all the nations, to investigate what seems to be preparations for war by any one of them. It must be empowered by all the nations to enforce its commands on every nation. It must be so constituted as to pose no threat to any nation's sovereignty. Obviously the creation of such a sophisticated instrumentality is a gigantic task, but is it hoping for too much to believe that the genius of humanity, aided by the grace and guidance of God, is able to accomplish it? To create it may take decades of unrelenting daily toil by the world's best minds and most devoted hearts, but it shall never come into existence unless we make a beginning now.

As we come to the end of our pastoral letter we boldly propose the beginning of this work. The evil of the proliferation of nuclear arms becomes more evident every day to all people. No one is exempt from their danger. If ridding the world of the weapons of war could be done easily, the whole human race would do it gladly tomorrow. Shall we shrink from the task because it is hard?

We turn to our own government and we beg it to propose to the United Nations that it begin this work immediately; that it create an international task force for peace; that this task force, with membership open to every nation, meet daily through the years ahead with one sole agenda: the creation of a world that will one day be safe from war. Freed from the bondage of war that holds it captive in its threat, the world will at last be able to address its problems and to make genuine human progress so that every day there may be more freedom, more food and more opportunity for every human being who walks the face of the earth.

Let us have the courage to believe in the bright future and in a God who wills it for us — not a perfect world, but a better one. The perfect world, we Christians believe, is beyond the horizon in an endless eternity where God will be all in all. But a better world is here for human hands and hearts and minds to make.

For the community of faith the risen Christ is the beginning and end of all things. For all things were created through him and all things will return to the Father through him.

It is our belief in the risen Christ which sustains us in confronting the awesome challenge of the nuclear arms race. Present in the beginning as the word of the Father, present in history as the word incarnate and with us today in his word, sacraments and Spirit, he is the reason for our hope and faith. Respecting our freedom, he does not solve our problems, but sustains us as we take responsibility for his work of creation and try to shape it in the ways of the kingdom. We believe his grace will never fail us. We offer this letter to the church and to all who can draw strength and wisdom from it in the conviction that we must not fail him. We must subordinate the power of the nuclear age to human control and direct it to human benefit. As we do this we are conscious of God's continuing work among us, which will one day issue forth in the beautiful final kingdom prophesied by the seer of the Book of Revelation:

> Then I saw a new heaven and a new earth; for the first heaven and the first earth had passed away and the sea was no more. And I saw the holy city, new Jerusalem, coming down out of heaven from God, prepared as a bride adorned for her husband; and I heard a great voice from the throne saying, 'Behold, the dwelling of God is with men. He will dwell with them, and they shall be his people, and God himself will be with them, he will wipe away every tear from their eyes, and death shall be no more, neither shall there be mourning nor crying nor pain any more, for the former things have passed away.' And he who sat upon the throne said, 'Behold I make all things new' (Rv. 21:1—5).

NOTES

1   Vatican II, 'The Pastoral Constitution on the Church in the Modern World' (hereafter: 'Pastoral Constitution'), 77. Papal and conciliar texts will be referred to by title with paragraph number. Several collections of these texts exist although no single collection is comprehensive; see the following: *Peace and Disarmament: Documents of the World Council of Churches and the Roman Catholic Church,* (Geneva and Rome: 1982) (hereafter: Documents, with page number). J. Gremillion, *The Gospel of Peace and Justice: Catholic Social Teaching Since Pope John,* (Maryknoll, N.Y.: 1976). D. J. O'Brien and T. A. Shannon, eds, *Renewing the Earth: Catholic Documents on Peace, Justice and Liberation,* (N.Y.: 1977). A. Flannery, OP, ed., *Vatican Council II: The Conciliar and Post Conciliar Documents,* (Collegeville, Minn: 1975); W. Abbot, ed., *The Documents of Vatican II,* (N.Y.: 1966). Both the Flannery and Abbot translations of the pastoral constitution are used in this letter.

2   John Paul II, Message to the Second Special Session of the United Nations General Assembly Devoted to Disarmament, (June, 1982), 7 (hereafter: Message UN Special Session 1982).

3   John Paul II, Address to Scientists and Scholars, 4; *Origins*, 10 (1981) p. 621.

4   The pastoral constitution is made up of two parts; yet it constitutes an organic unity. By way of explanation: the constitution is called 'pastoral' because, while resting on doctrinal principles, it seeks to express the relation of the church to the world and modern mankind. The result is that, on the one hand, a pastoral slant is present in the first part and, on the other hand, a doctrinal slant is present in the second part. ('Pastoral Constitution', footnote 1).

5   Ibid.

6   Ibid., 43.

7   John Paul II, Message UN Special Session 1982, 2.

8   Pastoral Constitution, 81.

9   Ibid., 80.

10 Ibid., 16.

11 Ibid., 80.

12 The exact opposite of this vision is presented in Joel 3:10 where the foreign nations are told that their weapons will do them no good in face of God's coming wrath.

13 An omission in the New Testament is significant in this context. Scholars have made us aware of the presence of revolutionary groups in Israel during the time of Jesus. Barabbas, for example, was 'among the rebels in prison who had committed murder in the insurrection' (Mk. 15:7). Although Jesus had come to proclaim and to bring about the true reign of God which often stood in opposition to the existing order, he makes no reference to nor does he join in

any attempts such as those of the Zealots to overthrow authority by violent means. See M. Smith, 'Zealots and Sicarri, Their Origins and Relations', *Harvard Theological Review* 64 (1971) 1–19.

14 John Paul II, World Day of Peace Message, 1982, 12; *Origins*, 11 (1982) p. 477.

15 Ibid., 11, 12; pp. 477–8.

16 John Paul II, Message UN Special Session 1982, 13: Pope Paul VI, World Day of Peace Message 1973.

17 John Paul II, World Day of Peace Message 1982, 12, cited p. 478.

18 'Pastoral Constitution', 79.

19 Ibid., 71.

20 Ibid., 80.

21 Ibid., 17.

22 Ibid., 78.

23 John Paul II, World Day of Peace Message 1982, 9. The pastoral constitution stresses that peace is not only the fruit of justice, but also love, which commits us to engage in 'the studied practice of brotherhood' (78).

24 'Pastoral Constitution', 79.

25 Ibid., 82.

26 Ibid., 79.

27 Pius XII, Christmas Message 1948. The same theme is reiter ated in Pius XII's Christmas Message of 1953: 'The community of nations must reckon with unprincipled criminals who, in order to realize their ambitious plans, are not afraid to unleash total war. This is the reason why other countries if they wish to preserve their very existence and their most precious possessions, and unless they are prepared to accord free action to international criminals, have no alternative but to get ready for the day when they must defend themselves. *This right to be prepared for self-defense cannot be denied, even in these days, to any state.*'

28 'Pastoral Constitution', 80.

29 Ibid., 80.

30 John Paul II, World Day of Peace Message, 1982, 12; p. 478.

31 Augustine called it a Manichean heresy to assert that war is intrinsically evil and contrary to Christian charity, and stated: 'War and conquest are a sad necessity in the eyes of principle, yet it would be still more unfortunate if wrongdoers should dominate just men' (*The City of God*, Book IV, C. 15). Representative surveys of the history and theology of the just-war tradition include: F. H. Russell, *The Just War in the Middle Ages* (N.Y.: 1975); P. Ramsey, *War and the Christian Conscience* (Durham, N. C.: 1961), *The Just War: Force and Political Responsibility* (N.Y.: 1968); J. T. Johnson, *Ideology, Reason and the Limitation of War* (Princeton: 1975), *Just War Tradition and the Restraint of War: A Moral and Historical Inquiry* (Princeton: 1981); L. B. Walters, 'Five Classic Just-War Theories' (Ph.D. Dissertation, Yale University, 1971) W. O'Brien,

War and-or Survival (N.Y.: 1969), *The Conduct of Just and Limited War* (N.Y.: 1981). J. C. Murray, 'Remarks on the Moral Problem of War', Theological Studies 20 (1959) pp. 40–61.

32 Aquinas treats the question of war in the *Summa Theologica*, II–IIae, q. 40; also cf. II–IIae, q. 64.

33 'Pastoral Constitution', 79.

34 Pius XII, Christmas Message, 1948.

35 For an analysis of the content and relationship of these principles cf: R. Potter, 'The Moral Logic of War,' *McCormick Quarterly* 23 (1970) pp. 203–33; J. Childress in Shannon, *Renewing the Earth*, pp. 40–58.

36 Johnson, *The Just War, Ideology*, W. O'Brien, *The Conduct of Just and Limited War*, pp. 13–30; W. Vanderpol, *La doctrine scolastique du droit de guerre*, pp. 387ff; J. C. Murray, 'Theology and Modern Warfare', in W. J. Nagel, ed., *Morality and Modern Warfare*, pp. 80ff.

37 John Paul II, World Day of Peace Message 1983, 11.

38 USCC, Resolution on Southeast Asia (Washington: 1971).

39 'Pastoral Constitution', 80.

40 John Paul II, World Day of Peace Message, 1982, 12.

41 Declaration on Prevention of Nuclear War (Sept. 24, 1982).

42 'Pastoral Constitution', 80.

43 Ibid., 80.

44 John Paul II, World Day of Peace Message, 1982, 12.

45 Representative authors in the tradition of Christian pacifism and non-violence include: R. Bainton, *Christian Attitudes Toward War and Peace*, (Abington: 1960) Chs. 4, 5, 10; J. Yoder, *The Politics of Jesus*, (Grand Rapids: 1972), *Nevertheless: Varieties of Religious Pacifism*, (Scottsdale: 1971); T. Merton, *Faith and Violence: Christian Teaching and Christian Practice*, (Notre Dame: 1968); G. Zahn, *Conscience and Dissent*, (N.Y.: 1967); E. Egan, 'The Beatitudes of Works of Mercy and Pacifism', in T. Shannon, ed., *War or Peace: The Search for New Answers*, (N.Y.: 1980) p. 169–87; J. Fahey, 'The Catholic Church and the Arms Race', *Worldview*, 22 (1979) pp. 38–41; J. Douglass, *The Nonviolent Cross: A Theology of Revolution and Peace*, (N.Y.: 1966).

46 Justin, 'Dialogue With Trypho', Ch. 20; cf. also 'The First Apology', Chs. 14, 39.

47 Cyprian, 'Collected Letters'; Letters to Cornelius.

48 Suplicius Serverus, *The Life of Martin*, 4. 3.

49 'Pastoral Constitution', 79.

50 Ibid., 78.

51 'Human Life in Our Day', Ch. 2, p. 44.

52 'Pastoral Constitution', 80.

53 Ibid., 80.

54 John Paul II, Address to Scientists and Scholars, 4; cited, p. 621.

55 Cf. Declaration on Prevention of Nuclear War.

56   Paul VI, World Day of Peace Message, 1967; in Documents, p. 198.

57   Statement of the Holy See to the United Nations (1976), in *The Church and the Arms Race*; Pax Christi-USA (N.Y.: 1976) pp. 23–4.

58   R. Adams and S. Cullen, *The Final Epidemic: Physicians and Scientists on Nuclear War*, (Chicago: 1981).

59   Pontifical Academy of Sciences, 'Statement on the Consequences of the Use of Nuclear Weapons', in Documents, p. 241.

60   John Paul II, World Day of Peace Message 1982, 6, cited, p. 476.

61   The following quotations are from public officials who have served at the highest policy levels in recent administrations of our government: 'It is time to recognize that no one has ever succeeded in advancing any persuasive reason to believe that any use of nuclear weapons, even on the smallest scale, could reliably be expected to remain limited.' McG. Bundy, G. F. Kennan, R. S. McNamara and G. Smith, 'Nuclear Weapons and the Atlantic Alliance', Foreign Affairs 60 (1982) p. 757.

     'From my experience in combat there is no way that (nuclear escalation) . . . can be controlled because of the lack of information, the pressure of time and the deadly results that are taking place on both sides of the battle line.' Gen. A. S. Collins Jr. (former deputy commander in chief of US Army in Europe), 'Theatre Nuclear Warfare: The Battlefield', in J. F. Reichart and S. R. Sturn, eds, *American Defense Policy*, 5th edn, (Baltimore: 1982), pp. 359–60. None of this potential flexibility changes my view that a full-scale thermonuclear exchange would be an unprecedented disaster for the Soviet Union as well as for the United States. Nor is it at all clear that an initial use of nuclear weapons – however selectively they might be targeted – could be kept from escalating to a full-scale thermonuclear exchange, especially if command-and-control centers were brought under attack. The odds are high, whether weapons were used against tactical or strategic targets, that control would be lost on both sides and the exchange would become unconstrained.' Harold Brown, Department of Defense Annual Report FY 1979 (Washington: 1978). Cf. also: 'The Effects of Nuclear War' (Washington: 1979; US Government Printing Office).

62   For example, cf.: H. A. Kissinger, *Nuclear Weapons and Foreign Policy* (N.Y.: 1957), *The Necessity for Choice* (N.Y.: 1960); R. Osgood and R. Tucker, *Force, Order and Justice* (Baltimore: 1967); R. Aron, *The Great Debate: Theories of Nuclear Strategy* (N.Y.: 1965); D. Ball, 'Can Nuclear War Be Controlled?' Adelphi Paper No. 161 (London: 1981); M. Howard, 'On Fighting a Nuclear War', International Security 5 (1981) pp. 3–17.

63   Statement on the Consequences of the Use of Nuclear Weapons, in Documents, p. 243.

64   Pius XII, Address to the VIII Congress of the World Medical

Association, in Documents, p. 131.

65 'Pastoral Constitution', 80.

66 Ibid., 80.

67 M. Bundy, *et al.*, 'Nuclear Weapons,' cited; K. Kaiser, G. Leber, A. Mertes, F. J. Schulze, 'Nuclear Weapons and the Preservation of Peace', Foreign Affairs 60 (1982), pp. 1157–70: cf. other responses to Bundy article in the same issue of Foreign Affairs.

68 Testimony given to the NCCB Committee during preparation of this pastoral letter. The testimony is reflected in the quotes found in note 61 above.

69 Our conclusions and judgments in this area although based on careful study and reflection of the application of moral principles do not have, of course, the same force as the principles themselves and therefore allow for different opinions, as the Precis makes clear.

70 Undoubtedly aware of the long and detailed technical debate on limited war, Pope John Paul II highlighted the unacceptable moral risk of crossing the threshold to nuclear war in his 'Angelus Message' Dec. 13, 1981: 'I have in fact the deep conviction that, in the light of a nuclear war's effects, which can be scientifically foreseen as certain, the only choice that is morally and humanly valid is represented by the reduction of nuclear armaments, while waiting for their future complete elimination, carried out simultaneously by all the parties, by means of explicit agreements and with the commitment of accepting effective controls.' In Documents, p. 240.

71 W. H. Kincade and J. D. Porro, *Negotiating Security: An Arms Control Reader* (Washington: 1979).

72 Several surveys are available, for example cf: J. H. Kahin, *Security in the Nuclear Age: Developing US Strategic Policy*, (Washington: 1975); M. Mandelbaum, *The Nuclear Question: The United States and Nuclear Weapons 1946–1976*, (Cambridge, England: 1979); B. Brodie, 'Development of Nuclear Strategy'. International Security, 2 (1978) pp. 65–83.

73 The relationship of these two levels of policy is the burden of an article by D. Ball, 'US Strategic Forces: How Would They Be Used?' International Security, 7 (1982–83) pp. 31–60.

74 'Pastoral Constitution', 81.

75 USCC, 'To Live in Christ Jesus' (Washington: 1976) p. 34.

76 Cardinal John Krol, Testimony on SALT II, Origins (1979) p. 197.

77 John Paul II, Message UN Special Session, 1982; 3.

78 Ibid., 8.

79 John Paul II, Address to UNESCO, 21, 1980.

80 John Paul II, Letter to International Seminar on the World Implications of a Nuclear Conflict, Aug. 23, 1982; text in NC News Documentary, Aug. 24, 1982.

81 Particularly helpful was the letter of Jan. 15, 1983, of William Clark, national security adviser, to Cardinal Bernardin. Clark stated:

'For moral, political and military reasons, the United States does
not target the Soviet civilian population as such. There is no deliberately opaque meaning conveyed in the last two words. We do
not threaten the existence of Soviet civilization by threatening Soviet
cities. Rather, we hold at risk the war-making capability of the
Soviet Union – its armed forces, and the industrial capacity to
sustain war. It would be irresponsible for us to issue policy statements
which might suggest to the Soviets that it would be to their advantage
to establish privileged sanctuaries within heavily populated areas,
thus inducing them to locate much of their war-fighting capability
within those urban sanctuaries.' A reaffirmation of the administration's policy is also found in Secretary Weinberger's Annual
Report to the Congress (Caspar Weinberger, Annual Report to the
Congress, Feb. 1, 1983, p. 55): 'The Reagan administration's policy
is that under no circumstances may such weapons be used deliberately for the purpose of destroying populations.' Also the letter of
Weinberger to Bishop O'Connor of Feb. 9, 1983, has a similar
statement.

82 S. Zuckerman, *Nuclear Illusion and Reality*, (N.Y.: 1982); D. Ball,
    cited, p. 36; T. Powers, 'Choosing a Strategy for World War III',
    The Atlantic Monthly (November 1982) pp. 82–110.

83 Cf. The comments in Pontifical Academy of Sciences 'Statement on
    the Consequences of the Use of Nuclear Weapons', cited above.

84 Several experts in strategic theory would place both the MX missile
    and Pershing II missiles in this category.

85 In each of the successive drafts of this letter we have tried to state a
    central moral imperative: that the arms race should be stopped and
    disarmament begun. The implementation of this imperative is open
    to a wide variety of approaches. Hence we have chosen our own
    language in this paragraph, not wanting either to be identified with
    one specific political initiative or to have our words used against
    specific political measures.

86 Cf. President Reagan's Speech to the National Press Club (Nov. 18,
    1981) and Address at Eureka College (May 9, 1982). Department
    of State, 'Current Policy' 346 and 387.

87 John Paul II, Homily at Coventry Cathedral, 2; Origins, 12 (1982),
    p. 55.

88 The two treaties are the Threshold Test Ban Treaty signed July 3,
    1974, and the Treaty on Nuclear Explosions for Peaceful Purposes,
    signed May 13, 1976.

89 John Paul II, Message to UN Special Session 1982, 8.

90 Weinberger's letter to Bishop O'Connor specifies actions taken on
    command and control facilities designed to reduce the chance of
    unauthorized firing of nuclear weapons.

91 Same, 9. Cf USCC, At Issue 2: Arms Export Policies – Ethical
    Choices, (Washington: 1978) for suggestions about controlling the
    conventional arms trade.

92 The International Security Act of 1976 provides for such human rights review.

93 John Paul II, Address to the UN General Assembly, Origins, 9 (1979), p. 268.

94 John Paul II, Homily at Coventry Cathedral, cited., p. 55.

95 'Pastoral Constitution', 78.

96 G. Sharp, *The Politics of Nonviolent Action*, (Boston: 1973); R. Fisher and W. Ury, *Getting to Yes: Negotiating Agreement Without Giving In* (Boston: 1981).

97 John Paul II, World Day of Peace Message 1982, 7, cited; p. 476.

98 'To establish the US Academy of Peace: Report of the Commission on Proposals for the National Academy of Peace and Conflict Resolution', (Washington: 1981) pp. 119–120.

99 USCC, 'Statement on Registration and Conscription for Military Service' (Washington: 1980): cf. also 'Human Life in Our Day', cited, pp. 42–5.

100 Paul VI, 'The Development of Peoples' (1966), 76.

101 Cf. V. Yzermans, ed., *Major Addresses of Pius XII*, 2 vols., (St Paul: 1961) and J. Gremillion, *The Gospel of Peace and Justice*, cited.

102 Cf. John XXIII, 'Peace on Earth' (1963) esp. 80–145.

103 A sampling of the policy problems and possibilities posed by inter-dependence can be found in: R. O. Keohane and J. S. Nye Jr., *Power and Interdependence* (Boston: 1977); S. Hoffmann, *Primacy or World Order* (N.Y.: 1978); The Overseas Development Council, The US and World Development 1979; 1980; 1982, (Washington, DC).

104 John XXIII, 'Peace on Earth', 137.

105 This has particularly been the case in the two UN Special Sessions on Disarmament, 1979, 1982.

106 USCC, 'Marxist Communism' (Washington: 1980) p. 19.

107 The debate on US–Soviet relations is extensive; recent examples of it are found in: A. Ulam, 'US–Soviet Relations: Unhappy Coexistence: America and the World, 1978', Foreign Affairs 57 (1979) pp. 556–71; W. G. Hyland, 'US–Soviet Relations: The Long Road Back: America and The World, 1981', Foreign Affairs 60 (1982) pp. 525–550; R. Legvold, 'Containment Without Confrontation', Foreign Policy, 40 (1980), pp. 74–98; S. Hoffmann, 'Muscle and Brains', Foreign Policy 37 (1979–80) pp. 3–27; P. Hassner, 'Moscow and the Western Alliance', Problems of Communism, 30 (1981) pp. 37–54; S. Bialer, 'The Harsh Decade: Soviet Policies in the 1980s', Foreign Affairs 59 (1981) pp. 999–1020; G. Kennan, *The Nuclear Delusion: Soviet–American Relations in the Atomic Age* (N.Y.: 1982); N. Podhoretz, *The Present Danger* (N.Y.: 1980); P. Nitze, 'Strategy in the 1980s', Foreign Affairs 59 (1980) pp. 82–101; R. Strode and C. Gray, 'The Imperial Dimension of Soviet Military Power', Problems of Communism 30 (1981) pp. 1–15;

International Institute for Strategic Studies, 'Prospects of Soviet Power in the 1980s', Parts I and II; Adelphi Papers, 151 and 152; (London: 1979); S. S. Kaplan, ed., *Diplomacy of Power: Soviet Armed Forces as a Political Instrument* (Washington: 1981) R. Barnet, *The Giants: Russia and America* (N.Y.: 1977); M. McGwire, *Soviet Military Requirements*, the Brookings Institute (Washington: 1982); R. Tucker, 'The Purposes of American Power', Foreign Affairs 59 (1980–81) pp. 241–74. A. Geyer, *The Idea of Disarmament: Rethinking the Unthinkable* (Washington: 1982). For a review of Soviet adherence to treaties cf.: 'The SALT Syndrome Charges and Facts: Analysis of an 'Anti-SALT Documentary', Report prepared by US government agencies (State, Defense, CIA, ACDA and NSC). Reprinted in The Defense Monitor, Vol. 10; No. 8A. Center for Defense Information.

108   John Paul II, World Day of Peace Message 1983; 7.

109   John Paul II, 'The Redeemer of Man', 16, *Origins*, 8 (1980) p. 635.

110   The phrase and its description are found in R. S. McNamara, Report to the Board of Governors of the World Bank 1978; cf. also 1979; 1980 (Washington, DC).

111   John Paul II, Homily at Yankee Stadium, 4 *Origins*, 9 (1979) p. 311.

112   Paul VI, Address to the General Assembly of the United Nations (1965), 2.

113   'Pastoral Constitution', 81.

114   Cf. Hoffman, cited; *Independent Commission on Disarmament and Security Issues, Common Security* (N.Y.: 1982).

115   For an analysis of the policy problems of reallocating resources, cf: Bruce M. Russett, *The Prisoners of Insecurity*, (San Francisco: 1983). Cf: *Common Security*, cited; Russett, cited; UN Report on Disarmament and Development (N.Y.: 1982); United Nations, 'The Relationship Between Disarmament and Development: A Summary'; Fact Sheet 21; (N.Y.: 1982).

116   John Paul II, 'The Redeemer of Man', 21, cited; p. 641. Much of the following reflects the content of A. Dulles, *A Church to Believe In: Discipleship and the Dynamics of Freedom*, (N.Y.: 1982) Ch. 1.

117   John Paul II, World Day of Peace Message 1982, 4, cited; p. 475.

118   Paul VI, World Day of Peace Message, 1976.

119   'Pastoral Constitution', 79.

120   John Paul II, Address to Scientists and Scholars, 3, cited; p. 621.

121   Ibid., 3.

122   Pastoral Constitution, 75.

123   John Paul II, Address at Hiroshima, 2; *Origins*, 10 (1981) p. 620.

124   'Pastoral Constitution', 75.

125   'Human Life in Our Day', cited, p. 41.

126   John XXIII, 'Peace on Earth', 137, (1963).

127   Paul VI, Address to General Assembly of the United Nations, 2 (1965).

6

The Challenge of War: A Christian Realist Perspective

WILLIAM V. O'BRIEN

The American Catholic Bishops' 1983 Pastoral Letter on War and Peace, *The Challenge of Peace: God's Promise and Our Response*, is a flawed document.[1] Most efforts to apply Christian moral values to complex policy issues may be expected to have deficiencies and ambiguities. However, when such efforts are flawed from the outset by their approach to the empirical and moral problems addressed, the consequences of their deficiencies and ambiguities are particularly grave and pervasive. This is the case with the Pastoral Letter. Indeed, the problem with the Bishops' approach begins with the title. The subject should really be 'The Challenge of War'.

The moral issues of war are about legitimate ends and means of armed coercion employed in the defense of life, liberty, justice and peace itself. Although armed force has shaped our history and political geography and is the foundation of whatever domestic and international security we enjoy, discussion of the moral issues of its employment is unpleasant and often baffling. Thus, while the moral issues of recourse to armed force are unavoidable, they are somehow avoided, particularly by those professing the greatest interest in the moral dimensions of public affairs. The perennial fate of discussions of the morality of war is to be sidetracked into more edifying subjects such as the moral obligation to remove the supposed causes of war or to outline blueprints for a world without war. Regrettably, the American Catholic Bishops have succumbed to the temptation to change the subject of the morality of war to that of the morality of seeking a world without war, as indicated by their Pastoral Letter's title, 'The Challenge of Peace'.

Reprinted with permission from Judith Dwyer S. S. J. (ed.) *The Catholic Bishops and Nuclear War. A Critique and Analysis of the Pastoral 'The Challenge of Peace'* (Georgetown University Press, Washington, DC, 1984), pp. 39–63.

Those familiar with the 1983 Pastoral Letter may object, at this point, that the document seems to be mainly concerned with issues of nuclear deterrence and war, and that it is inaccurate and unfair to charge the Bishops with changing the subject from war to peace. However, it will be the contention of this chapter that the Bishops, having marched up to the great issues of deterrence and war, flinched at the critical moment and begged the questions that they had raised about these issues. They then beat a retreat into the more uplifting world of progress in arms control. This progress, it is thought, will lead to the elimination of the causes of war through the banishment of the arms race and the accompanying reallocation of resources and human genius to solving the economic and social problems that supposedly bar the way to the realization of true peace.

There is a need to address these problems of international economic and social justice and the Church does, indeed, address them frequently and passionately. However, there is also a need to address the problems of war and, having done so, to stick to the task until the best possible guidance has been formulated. The American Catholic Bishops' 1983 Pastoral Letter accords the problems of deterrence and war an extremely lengthy analysis, reflecting an extraordinary drafting effort, but it abandons the enterprise at the critical point. The Bishops leave the faithful and the interested public, as well as themselves, with serious unfinished business.

Surely the central point of the Bishops' inquiry was the judgment as to the moral permissibility of using nuclear weapons. While it is abundantly clear that they condemn such use on moral and practical grounds, they never reach a final, definitive, explicit statement on this question. Accordingly, they never close with the critical issue of deterrence, namely, 'Can you threaten what you would not do morally?' Instead, the Bishops leave this question, in the formulation of their principal technical adviser, Father J. Bryan Hehir, shrouded in a 'centimeter of ambiguity'.[2] 'Such an elusive and coy characterization of moral guidance on a subject of staggering import is surely extraordinary but it errs, if at all, only in the number of centimeters that are required to measure the various ambiguities of the Pastoral Letter. The analysis that follows will attempt to identify these deficiencies and ambiguities with respect to the ends and means of nuclear deterrence.

IDEALISM AND REALISM IN MORALITY AND POLITICS

Translated into the terms of the basic approaches to politics and political morality, whether domestic or international, the Bishops

in their 1983 Pastoral Letter venture out of their customary idealism, confront the moral and practical dilemmas of deterrence and
defense in the nuclear age in a manner reflecting at least some
elements of a realist approach, and then slam the door on realism,
returning to the preferred realm of idealism. This characterization
is not intended to imply that idealists are always unrealistic or
misguided any more than that realists are necessarily realistic and
wise. It is to suggest that in their latest venture into the realm of
war morality the American Catholic Bishops found themselves
suspended between their habitual idealism and an uncharacteristic
realism. The result is that realism faltered and idealism triumphed
in a way that essentially vitiated the Bishops' brief excursion into
realist analysis.

It is not necessary to reconstruct the whole classic idealist-realist
debate that dominates political and moral approaches to policy
issues. However, the present debate on the morality of nuclear
deterrence and war has been profoundly affected by the consequences of the idealist-realist dichotomy and a brief review of the
subject is in order. Idealists and realists differ on three interrelated
issues: human nature, the nature of politics, and the role of armed
force in politics. From an optimistic view of the perfectibility of
human nature, the idealist sees politics primarily as the resolution
of problems through enlightened reason and cooperation, with
little, if any, need to introduce armed coercion to assure law,
order and justice. The realist, starting with a pessimistic view of
human nature, sees politics as the balancing of competing interests
to produce a tolerable minimal consensus enforced, when necessary, by armed coercion.[3]

These are generalizations, of course, and most of us mix and
vary the elements of idealism and realism in our political views
and actions. Nevertheless, the direction of the emphases in each
approach is important, particularly in international politics where
there is no central authority to enforce law and order, much less
justice. Idealists tend to view armed force not even as a necessary
evil but as an unnecessary evil. That is to say, force may be
tolerated as a necessary evil pending the day when more progress
has been made in establishing an international political system
based on reason and cooperation. Even so, it is thought that
armed force often is far more 'evil' than 'necessary' to the point
that some idealists view it as a literally unnecessary evil.[4] This is a
critical issue that is at the heart of the failure of the American
Catholic Bishops and many morally concerned Christians and men
and women of good will to come to grips with the moral issues of
war. For them, it is not simply that war is evil and destructive.

The crowning tragedy is that war is unnecessary, *viz.* there never was a good war or a bad peace. In modern times this view has often been given the gloss of psychological and psychiatric specialists who explain confidently that war is a product of mental illness.[5] It is, of course, difficult to defend, much less promote, much less formulate the moral principles of, mental illness.

Realists, on the other hand, differ among themselves over the extent of evil to be imputed to war as an instrument of policy while agreeing generally that it is necessary. There are those who would hold that war may be more properly viewed, in some circumstances, as a good rather than an evil. In any event, realist approaches to international politics differ from idealist ones most significantly on the issue of the necessity and perennial character of recourse to armed force as a characteristic of international interaction.

The realist component in the American Catholic Bishops' 1983 Pastoral Letter is based on a reaffirmation of traditional just war doctrine. This, at least, is an achievement (not to have been lightly assumed) for which Christian realists are grateful. In the 1983 Pastoral Letter, the Bishops do not simply brush aside the problems of international security in the manner of many official Catholic pronouncements, and they do not preempt the discussion of the moral issues of deterrence and defense with an early introduction of pleas to change the international system into something different wherein war has no place.

However, the promise held out by the early reassertion of the just war doctrine as the authoritative source of guidance for analyses of the morality of war is not realized in the 1983 Pastoral Letter. This is the case because the Bishops do not follow the full just war doctrine and methodology in their analyses of nuclear deterrence and defense. They alter the sequence and the comparative weight of the elements of just war analyses so substantially as to fail to subject the subject of nuclear deterrence and war to a thorough, comprehensive just war evaluation.

Just war doctrine addresses the decision to go to war, the *jus ad bellum*, war-decision law.[6] Then it addresses the war-conduct law, the *jus in bello*. In basic terms, just war doctrine provides standards for judging the ends and means of war. In my view, the American Catholic Bishops, in their 1983 Pastoral Letter, only belatedly and inadequately mention the ends of nuclear deterrence and defense. Their discussion of war is almost exclusively an exercise in the morality of means, divorced from the ends that are the sole warrant for even considering the means in question. Inevitably, a discussion of means so portentous as nuclear deterrence and defense without a serious exploration of the putative ends for which such means are prepared is destined to be inadequate. Moreover, even within its own terms, the discussion of the means of nuclear deterrence and defense in the 1983 Pastoral Letter is deficient and ambiguous in that it does not even explicitly answer its own ultimate question of the moral permissibility of nuclear weapons.

In this chapter I will, first, explore the gap in the Pastoral Letter with regard to identification of threats to just causes that alone could justify even provisional endorsement of a means so dangerous as nuclear deterrence and defense. Second, I will show that the analysis of nuclear deterrence in the Bishops' Pastoral Letter is either incomplete and/or deliberately ambiguous to the point that it does not provide clear and helpful guidance to those who share responsibility for the defense of the free world and for their constituents. This critique will be offered from the standpoint of a Christian realist.

WHAT IS THE JUST CAUSE WARRANTING NUCLEAR DETERRENCE AND DEFENSE?

The just war-decision law requires that a number of conditions be met in order to overcome the moral presumption against recourse to armed force. These conditions are variously formulated by authorities. I incorporate them within the three conditions propounded by St Thomas Aquinas, namely competent authority, just cause and right intention, by subsuming a number of the conditions under the general category of just cause, as follows:

1 The comparative justice of the party claiming a just cause *vis-à-vis* the adversary;
2 the just cause or causes themselves in the sense of *casus belli*, in modern just war doctrine and international law almost exclusively individual and collective self-defense;
3 proportionality of the cost of defending the just cause to the good of defending it in the light of the probability of success;
4 exhaustion of peaceful alternatives to protection of the just cause by resort to armed coercion.[7]

Every element in the just war doctrine is important and, in principle, every element must be substantially satisfied in order to warrant acceptance of recourse to armed coercion as morally permissible. That is not to say that a belligerent's record of compliance with just war conditions must be perfect in order to qualify a war as just. Some failures to meet just war standards, particularly in the conduct of the war, may be overcome by an overall record of compliance with both war-decision and war-conduct requirements. However, it is clear that nothing is warranted unless the putative just cause is established. Everything done in war refers to the necessity of defending the just cause. Nothing is warranted that cannot be shown to be necessary to the defense of the just cause.[8]

It is not a matter of pedantic methodology, therefore, to insist that a just war analysis address the war-decision law issues, the just cause issues, before turning to the war-conduct issues. To be sure, one can imagine means so hopelessly evil as to be *mala in se*, e.g., genocide. But not even 'nuclear deterrence' and 'nuclear war' are self-evidently *mala in se*. Certain forms of nuclear deterrence and nuclear war may be shown to be *mala in se*. However, unless it can be shown that all forms of nuclear deterrence and war must necessarily be included in the category of means that are wrong in themselves, means that are not proper for any cause, no matter how just, then it is not possible to go very far in evaluating the moral permissibility of nuclear force without reference to the just causes in defense of which nuclear force might be used.

The concept of proportionality is central both to war-decision and war-conduct law. The very decision to engage in war requires a calculus of the proportionality of the cost of the means to the end protected in the light of the probability of success. Obviously, this calculus requires a referent, an end to which the means must be proportionate. Every decision of military necessity in war-conduct law requires proportionality to the proximate military end and, ultimately, to the just end of the war.

Accordingly, a competent just war analysis of the present moral dilemmas of nuclear deterrence and defense must begin with a statement of the just cause or causes in virtue of which states have established and maintain nuclear deterrence and defense. Such an analysis would then proceed to an estimate of the threats to those just causes. In view of the values at stake and the threats to those values, the moral permissibility of nuclear deterrence and defense would then be judged.

This was not, however, the approach of the American Catholic Bishops in their 1983 Pastoral Letter. The elements of just war doctrine are outlined in Part I.[9] But Part II, the heart of the Pastoral Letter, plunges immediately into a discussion of the morality of nuclear war that is marked from the outset by an emphasis on its extraordinary destructiveness. It is clear from the first paragraph of Part II on that nuclear war will be condemned as a practically catastrophic and morally unusable means without being considered in relation to the ends for which its use is threatened in deterrence.[10] There will be no calculus of proportionality of ends and means, only a peremptory judgment that no ends can justify such means, that nuclear deterrence and war are *mala in se*. It is clear from the first pages of Part II of the Pastoral Letter that nothing can be considered worse than the 'dead' part of the 'red or dead' dilemma that has haunted the free world since the 1940s. This is a plausible approach but it is not a just war approach. Just war judges means in relation, in proportion, to ends, not means in the abstract.

A just war approach would balance the risks of nuclear destruction with the risks of loss of freedom and fundamental rights that relinquishment of nuclear deterrence and defense would probably engender. It is not surprising that many secular humanists who oppose nuclear deterrence and war seem willing to risk the possibility, however remote it may appear to them, of loss of fundamental rights in order to preserve life. It is surprising, however, that representatives of a Church based on belief in a supernatural destiny for mankind should be inclined to place physical existence before fundamental freedoms, including the freedom to worship God. If this is an unfair criticism it is one that is invited by the fact that the American Catholic Bishops, given ample opportunity, choose not even to acknowledge the possible consequences for human freedom and rights if the protection of nuclear deterrence and defense is subverted, in part through their own efforts.

The Bishops address the issues of nuclear war with a 'morality first' approach. That is to say, they put nuclear deterrence and defense through a moral analysis without reference to the necessity of these means to the defense of freedom and human rights, and come to the conclusion that nuclear deterrence and defense do not pass the test of moral permissibility.[11] Therefore, these means must, at most, be only temporarily condoned as a necessary evil and speedily eliminated. But this 'morality first' approach is a stunted, incomplete, morality of means only approach. There is scarcely any recognition of the morality of ends and of the consequences to those ends that would be critically affected by a rigid application of the conclusions produced in the morality of means analysis.

Since the American Catholic Bishops are certainly not disposed consciously to put at risk the fundamental freedoms and values of the free world, how can one explain this failure to relate the consequences of any weakening of Western deterrence and defense to the prospects for that freedom and those values to survive? Some might suggest that the reason is that the Church, having allegedly erred on the side of excessive anti-Communism, is now seeking to alter its stand by downgrading the threat of Communist and other totalitarian aggressors to the free world. However, the more fundamental point would seem to be that suggested in the earlier discussion of idealist and realist approaches to politics.

The majority of the present generation of American Catholic Bishops appears to be committed to idealist attitudes toward recourse to armed force to the point of being doctrinaire on the subject. Their every impulse is to 'say no to nuclear war', 'say no to the arms race', 'say no to defense spending that comes at the expense of the poor' — in brief, to 'say no to war'. There are still enough Bishops with realist propensities to defend just war doctrine but the majority of American Catholic Bishops appear to differ on the issue of recourse to armed force mainly to the extent that some consider it to be a necessary evil whereas a substantial minority considers it to be an unnecessary evil. To all of them, nuclear deterrence and defense, the arms race, defense spending, are a clear and present danger. Loss of freedom and fundamental human rights as the result of intimidation and aggression are not seen as clear and present dangers. Or so it would appear.

The fact is that the American Catholic Bishops, in the 1983 Pastoral Letter, launch into an extended discussion of nuclear deterrence and defense with little if any indication as to why such military preparations ever were or are now arguably necessary. Nuclear deterrence and defense are treated from the outset as something between a deadly disease and a pernicious habit. There is no estimate of the threats that might justify maintenance of nuclear deterrence and defense systems. There is not even a judgment that there are no threats, or that the threats are distant or marginal. In effect, the Bishops find that we are in a predicament caused by our development of nuclear military capabilities and that the sole issue is how to dismantle these capabilities in order to escape the predicament. What such a dismantling might do to the security of the free world is not a subject that interested the Bishops.

Given this approach, it is surprising that the American Catholic Bishops continue the approach of Vatican II and recent popes in condoning, however reluctantly and ambiguously, the temporary continuation of nuclear deterrence on condition that all possible efforts be made to eliminate nuclear weapons, the nuclear deterrence system and the arms race through arms control.[12] It is extraordinary for the Bishops to condone the deterrent because, given their manifest horror at the risks of nuclear war incurred by the perpetuation of the nuclear deterrence system, the logical conclusion would be that they would oppose continuation of deterrence. If there is no clear and present threat to free world liberty and values worth discussing in a pastoral letter on nuclear deterrence and defense, why tolerate the continued risks of nuclear deterrence another day?

The answer appears to be that the Bishops recognize that there are some threats, hence some need for a continued deterrent until arms control progress makes possible an end to the deterrent balance of terror and the arms race. But, since the Bishops do not offer any serious estimate either of the threats to freedom and human rights from potential nuclear aggressors or of the prospects for abating those threats, the rationale for continuing the nuclear deterrence system is fuzzy and implicit rather than explicit.

The closest that the 1983 Pastoral Letter comes to identifying the main threat that engenders Western nuclear deterrence and defense is in Part II.B.2, well after the analysis of the morality of nuclear deterrence and defense has been completed in Part II.[13] A section on 'The Superpowers in a Disordered World', sandwiched in between a section on 'World Order in Catholic Teaching' and one on 'Interdependence: From Fact to Policy', touches briefly on some of the just cause issues. Obviously, it does not inform Part II very much either from the standpoint of the writing of Part II by the Bishops or the reading of the section by the faithful. Finally, however, on page twenty-five of a thirty-two-page version in *Origins*, the Pastoral Letter states:

> The fact of a Soviet threat, as well as the existence of a Soviet imperial drive for hegemony, at least in regions of major strategic interest, cannot be denied. The history of the Cold War has produced varying interpretations of which side caused the conflict, but whatever the details of history illustrate, the plain fact is that the memories of Soviet policies in Eastern Europe and recent events in Afghanistan and Poland have left their mark in the American political debate. Many people are forcibly kept under communist domination despite their manifest wishes to be free. Soviet power is very great. Whether the Soviet Union's pursuit of military might

is motivated primarily by defensive or aggressive aims might be debated, but the effect is nevertheless to leave profoundly insecure those who must live in the shadow of that might.[14]

. . .

Even supposing that the West might be as much at fault for the threat of war as the Soviet Union and its allies, or that the stakes between what is left of Christendom and the Communist world are unclear, important because 'varying interpretations' have 'left their mark in the American political debate', what is the opinion of the American Catholic Bishops, as distinct from the conventional wisdom of modern secular humanism, about the threat to free world and Christian values? Suppose, over time, the incredible happens and the Soviet Union and other Communist states take over much or all of the free world by intimidation and aggression. What would be the character of the regimes imposed? What, presumably, would be the consequences for the Christian faith? One would expect that to be a critical element in any analysis of just cause for nuclear deterrence and defense made by the episcopal leaders of the Roman Catholic Church in the United States.

The Bishops provide an answer, however brief and indirect. They observe:

> Americans need have no illusions about the Soviet system of repression and the lack of respect in that system for human rights or about Soviet covert operations and pro-revolutionary activities. To be sure, our own system is not without flaws. Our government has sometimes supported repressive governments in the name of preserving freedom, has carried out repugnant covert operations of its own and remains imperfect in its domestic record of ensuring equal rights for all. At the same time there is a difference. NATO is an alliance of democratic countries which have freely chosen their association, the Warsaw Pact is not.[15]

One can extract from this somewhat rambling paragraph one sentence recognizing that the Soviet system is repressive and lacks respect for human rights. In the following paragraph, after some further even-handed admissions of American guilt and deficiencies, the Bishops' Pastoral Letter concedes that, whatever its faults:

> The facts simply do not support the invidious comparisons made at times even in our own society between our way of

life, in which most basic human rights are at least recognized even if they are not always adequately supported, and those totalitarian and tyrannical regimes in which such rights are either denied or systematically suppressed ...[16]

This concession, however, is followed shortly by the admonition that:

Insofar as this is true, however, it makes the promotion of human rights in our foreign policy, as well as our domestic policy, all the more important. It is the acid test of our commitment to our democratic values. In this light, any attempts to justify, for reasons of state, support for regimes that continue to violate human rights is all the more morally reprehensible in its hypocrisy.[17]

These statements can be read as an admonition to avoid allies with poor human rights records. Like the Soviet Union in World War II? Unfortunately, the geopolitics of collective defense against aggression do not always lead to alliances with Jeffersonian democracies. The paragraphs from which the quotations above are derived hardly put in perspective the critical just war issue at stake in nuclear deterrence and defense, namely, 'What would the consequences be for Americans and their free world allies if they were conquered or reduced to dependencies by the Soviet Union, its allies or other totalitarian aggressors who would profit from the removal of our nuclear protection?'

Granted that the conquest of the United States and the principal free world countries is not a matter of immediate concern, particularly as long as nuclear deterrence and defense works, there are always targets for aggression at the periphery of the free world deterrence and defense systems. Each time they are threatened the issue is raised: Is their freedom worth the risks of nuclear deterrence and defense? Experience with past aggressors and the logic of collective deterrence/defense suggests that if this question is answered in the negative too many times it is likely that it will be raised with increasing frequency and closer to home. At bottom, the whole nuclear deterrence and defense system rests on the assumption that there is something so precious in the free world that its defense, even by the extreme and risky means of recourse to nuclear weapons, is morally justified.

Surely, no one reading the passages quoted above would have the remotest idea that the American Catholic Bishops consider the imposition by threat and use of armed force of Communist and other totalitarian tyrannies to be a just cause possibly warranting resistance with nuclear weapons. Put another way, the Bishops once again changed the subject. They changed the subject from the stakes in confrontations between the free and Communist worlds to the failings of what we call the free world, starting with our own and those of our allies. The moral of the story seems to be that we should worry more about human rights in South Korea, El Salvador and Egypt than about the threat to human rights in the countries that might have Gulag societies imposed upon them if US deterrence and defense faltered.

Thus, while the morality of means analysis of the 1983 Pastoral Letter is dominated from beginning to end by worst case assumptions about nuclear war,[18] the tiny and belated effort to acknowledge the just causes at stake in modern international conflict is dominated with concerns about the quality of human rights in the countries that may fall victim to Communist and other aggressors. In these circumstances, it is not surprising that the Bishops can conclude that the moral presumptions are all against those who would rely on nuclear war to defend the freedom and rights of the free world. The possibility that the presumptions might go the other way, against those who would risk a dark age of Gulag societies rather than nuclear war in any form, is not even acknowledged, much less debated.[19] It appears from the American Catholic Bishops' 1983 Pastoral Letter that, after one has brushed aside the 'centimeter of ambiguity', there is no just cause for nuclear deterrence and defense.

This means that the whole free world deterrence/defense system would collapse like a house of cards if the American Catholic Bishops' advice were followed. There patently is no serious nonnuclear defense against a nuclear aggressor unencumbered by moral scruples about using nuclear weapons. Beyond that, prospects for deterrence and defense on behalf of the free world may quickly be reduced to underground resistance, with hopes that it is more successful than in, say, the Soviet Union, Poland, Cuba, or the Peoples Republic of China. Beyond that, there is always the option of nonviolent resistance under circumstances considerably less propitious than those that confronted Mahatma Gandhi or Martin Luther King, Jr. Beyond that, there is always martyrdom. If these reflections seem melodramatic let it be recalled what Europe looked like after Hitler's successful conquests and before the United Nations rescued the peoples who did not realize the threats to their lives and liberties until it was too late.

CAN A BLUFF DETERRENT WORK UNTIL NUCLEAR WEAPONS ARE ELIMINATED?

Without having made a serious estimate of the threats to free world liberties that might possibly explain the necessity for nuclear deterrence and defense, the American Catholic Bishops undertook a morality of means analysis of nuclear deterrence and defense. The lack of a just cause referent inevitably encouraged a quality of abstractness in their analysis. This abstract quality was reinforced by the fact that pronouncements from Rome, whether of the popes or of Vatican II, on issues of war and peace have tended to be very general and clinical, seldom evidencing an awareness that among the 'nations' to which they are addressed some are on the side of the Church and its values and some are very definitely not.

Like many official Church pronouncements, including the American Catholic Bishops' 1983 Pastoral Letter, *Gaudium et Spes*, Vatican II's Pastoral Constitution on the Church in the Modern World, moves fitfully and erratically through a maze of complex issues which it often obscures through imprecision.[20] It is worth elaborating on this point since it is clear that *Gaudium et Spes* is the most influential source of official teaching on nuclear deterrence and defense in the Church today and its authority is frequently invoked in the 1983 Pastoral Letter of the American Catholic Bishops.

Gaudium et Spes is often quoted for its judgment that 'Any act of war aimed indiscriminately at the destruction of entire cities or of extensive areas along with their population is a crime against God and man himself. It merits unequivocal and unhesitating condemnation.'[21] From this condemnation it would be logical to move to a condemnation of the kind of nuclear deterrence that existed in 1965 which was predominantly tending toward so-called countervalue threats to do exactly what the Council condemned and would tend even more in that direction before the counterforce initiatives of the 1970s and 1980s.

The Second Vatican Council, however, did not take this logical step. Instead, it moved on to recognize the modern institution of nuclear deterrence, remarking that 'Many regard this state of affairs as the most effective way by which peace of a sort can be maintained between nations at the present time.' The Council objected, however, that the 'arms race' is 'not a safe way to preserve a steady peace' and that the resulting so-called balance of power is no sure path to achieving it.[22]

At the risk of seeming disrespectful, it should be observed that the treatment of deterrence in *Gaudium et Spes* is typical of the fuzzy thinking that has provided the American Catholic Bishops with a superficially impressive backdrop of authority that elicits more respect than it deserves. Typically, the strictures of *Gaudium et Spes* are addressed to 'the nations' 'the countries', without acknowledgment of the characteristics and relevance to the nuclear deterrence problems of the principal nuclear actors in the international system. Moreover, by failing to sort out the actors in the international system, Vatican II erroneously claims that nuclear deterrence has maintained 'some sort of peace', a statement valid only as between the superpowers and their allies, certainly not the hundreds of belligerents in wars fought since 1945. Thus, deterrence is described in a generalized, abstract fashion without reference to actual actors and their rationales in the nuclear deterrent system.

Gaudium et Spes then proceeds, with typical imprecision, to equate 'the arms race' with this form of deterrent'. In fact, throughout the document, the terms 'arms race' and 'deterrence' are used interchangeably.[23] The nuclear deterrence system exists at the moment when adversaries have nuclear weapons with which to threaten each other. The 'arms race' is more a buzz word than a term that is defined with any precision when it is denounced by the Church and by peace activists. Any military establishment tries to maintain and improve its capabilities. Whether such natural efforts are always part of an 'arms race' and whether arms races are inherently pernicious are controversial issues. They are not resolved by rhetorical flourishes. In any event, one may well have deterrence without an arms race. One may have deterrence while arms control is drastically diminishing nuclear capabilities. Indeed, modern arms control theory and practice emphasizes the absolute necessity of maintaining stable deterrence throughout the arms control process. Arms control experts also warn against destabilizing, dangerous asymmetries resulting from ill-considered arms reductions which leave only one party 'racing'.[24]

Finally, the proposition that the 'arms race', by which is apparently really meant the nuclear deterrence system, is 'no infallible way of maintaining real peace' is not new to those who have long wrestled with the practical and moral dilemmas of nuclear deterrence and defense. Of course, nuclear deterrence is no infallible way to real peace. It is the minimal condition for security from nuclear aggression in a world of conflict. Without the 'some sort of peace' provided by nuclear deterrence and defense, there is little prospect for 'real peace'. Once again, the idealist-realist dichotomy is strongly reflected in the differing perspectives and expectations of the authors of *Gaudium et Spes* and those of the Christian realist.[25]

Gaudium et Spes does not provide a good statement of the moral issues of nuclear deterrence. To the best of my knowledge it was not based on even as serious a research and discussion effort as that which contributed to the American Catholic Bishops' 1983 Pastoral Letter. Its handling of the issues is superficial, indeed sloppy. All of this seems to have been obscured, however, by the decision of Vatican II to emphasize escape from the 'treacherous trap for humanity' of the balance of terror instead of condemning nuclear deterrence as the logic of its position on countervalue deterrence and war would dictate.[26] In its appeal for a new approach to arms control, based on 'an entirely new attitude', Vatican II enjoined an approach to nuclear deterrence and defense that was in part sensible, in part unrealistic, but which avoided a direct confrontation with the issue of threatening to conduct countervalue war, then the basis for nuclear deterrence.[27]

The sensible component in the advice of Vatican II was the realization that it was more important to encourage efforts to decrease the dangers of nuclear war through arms control than to condemn nuclear deterrence and war as immoral, as some wished then and now. The unrealistic element in the advice of Vatican II was the suggestion that the nuclear deterrence system should be viewed as an unfortunate ephemeral phenomenon of the international system and that, in effect, the price for condoning temporarily the continuation of deterrence was the serious arms control effort necessary to eliminate, first, nuclear weapons, then, all international conflict.[28]

It makes sense to say that, because the nuclear balance of terror is precarious, every effort should be made to mitigate its risks by arms control measures. It does not make sense to say that arms control efforts must necessarily succeed in eliminating nuclear deterrence altogether and that such success is the condition for interim toleration of continued nuclear deterrence. If the purposes for nuclear deterrence continue to exist, if the need to deter nuclear aggression in a dangerous world of conflict persists, as seems overwhelmingly likely, then the need for nuclear deterrence will continue even if there is substantial success through arms control in reducing the risks of nuclear war.

One ought not to place a condition — in this case some undefined degree of progress, or at least earnestness on our side, in arms control — on the presently indispensable means of protecting the free world without understanding the necessity of that protection. Since Vatican II eschewed exploration of the threats that occasioned the deterrence system in the first place and that continue to the present, the Council was not in a position to condition nuclear deterrence on anything except compliance with just war requirements. This the Council did not do, any more than the American Catholic Bishops did in 1983. There has never been any interest in developing a morally usable nuclear deterrent in official Church pronouncements, only in eliminating nuclear deterrence, nuclear weapons and war itself, the usual Christian idealist position.[29]

A Christian realist would have wished that Vatican II had seriously considered the continuing threats to the free world and to the Church from Communist powers in the light of the perennial need of free nations for security from aggression. These would have been 'signs of the times' as pertinent as some others that were noticed. Had a Christian realist view prevailed at Vatican II, support and guidance would have been provided for those entrusted with the responsibility to provide just and limited deterrence and defense as the basis for free world security and realistic arms control. But Vatican II never reached this degree of seriousness with respect to the dilemmas of nuclear deterrence and defense.

Thus, from *Gaudium et Spes* there developed the concept of deterrence as an abstraction, a necessary evil condoned, that was to be permitted to continue provisionally, subject to the condition that all efforts would be made to eliminate nuclear deterrence through drastic arms control progress. This moral imperative was promulgated to the anonymous nations of the international community without distinction as to their comparative justice as polities or record of threatening or resisting aggression.

Eighteen years later this approach is being put to the test by the American Catholic Bishops. Building on *Gaudium et Spes*, the Bishops have been stressing two themes. One is that the kind of countervalue mutual assured destruction (MAD) deterrence system that has been the basis — at least in declaratory policy — for US and Western strategic nuclear deterrence is immoral on its face. The other is that the continuation of nuclear deterrence in some form can be condoned only in the manner of Vatican II, as a temporary posture strictly conditioned on the pursuit of arms control efforts designed to eliminate nuclear weapons and nuclear deterrence with, in effect, all deliberate speed.

By stressing these two points the American Catholic Bishops have substantially repeated the errors of *Gaudium et Spes*. First, they have concluded, admittedly after much more lengthy consideration than Vatican II, that nuclear deterrence must ultimately lead to levels of nuclear war that by any just war standard are immoral. Second, the Bishops apparently hold, behind their 'centimeter of ambiguity', that some kind of abstract deterrence can be condoned pending elimination of nuclear weapons through arms control.

Unlike the statements on nuclear deterrence by modern popes and Vatican II, the pronouncements of the American Catholic Bishops on the subject, from 1968 to the 1983 Pastoral Letter, have been progressively more informed and sophisticated regarding the various strategies and forms of nuclear deterrence and defense. It is not possible to criticize the American Catholic Bishops for condemning nuclear deterrence in sweeping, monolithic terms without having explored the possibilities of selective, flexible response deterrence and limited nuclear war. The American Bishops have explored these options to some extent and this constitutes progress.

However, the exploration of nuclear deterrence and war-fighting options short of the clearly suicidal and immoral policies such as MAD suffers from the fundamental flaw of excessive idealism discussed at the outset of this chapter. Since 1968 the American Catholic Bishops have always treated nuclear deterrence as something between a necessary evil and an unnecessary evil, with an increasing propensity toward the latter. They have consistently emphasized the horrors of nuclear war and brushed quickly by the threats to freedom and fundamental human rights that necessitate risking the horrors of nuclear war through maintenance of nuclear deterrence/defense postures. Following the lead of Vatican II, the American Catholic Bishops have treated nuclear deterrence as eminently dispensable rather than indispensable.[30]

In the absence of any serious effort to state the just causes and the threats to them that necessitate nuclear deterrence and defense, as discussed above, the American Catholic Bishops tend to treat nuclear deterrence as a monolithic instrument of defense policy that is both incredibly dangerous and ultimately unnecessary. Since it is viewed far more as an unnecessary than a necessary evil, the burden of proof is placed overwhelmingly on those who would justify continuation of nuclear deterrence in any form. Had the American Catholic Bishops, and the Fathers of Vatican II before them, considered that some kind of nuclear deterrent was a practical and moral necessity to protect the free world from nuclear intimidation and aggression by the Soviet Union and other Communist adversaries pledged to the destruction of everything that the free world and the Church stand for, they would at least have considered the task of finding a morally permissible form of nuclear deterrence to be a necessary one to which they themselves had a responsibility to offer guidance. However, since both the

Council Fathers and the American Catholic Bishops take the idealist position that nuclear deterrence and defense are not legitimate necessities but unfortunate evils that are probably unnecessary, they place a moral presumption against nuclear deterrence and defense in any form and throw the burden of overcoming that presumption upon those who claim that just and limited nuclear deterrence and defense are both necessary and feasible.

The position of *Gaudium et Spes* and the 1983 Pastoral Letter is that there is really no great moral dilemma of finding the permissible nuclear means necessary to protect the just causes of the free world. The dilemma is that 'the nations' are in a predicament that threatens the physical destruction of the world by nuclear war and that 'the nations' must all cooperate to eliminate this threat. The dilemma is not that of finding a just and limited nuclear deterrence/defense posture for the free world. It is the dilemma of dismantling a terribly dangerous and essentially unnecessary balance of terror.

From these perspectives, nuclear deterrence and war have been reduced again to the monolithic, self-evidently immoral, category of earlier Church pronouncements. The possibilities for morally permissible nuclear deterrence and defense have been investigated, found wanting, and rejected. All nuclear deterrence and war is to be judged in terms of the worst case models of nuclear deterrence and war. To be sure, no one can prove or disprove whether nuclear war can be limited and no one is anxious to conduct experiments on this subject. There are a number of technical and human vulnerabilities in any nuclear deterrence/defense system and scenario. Loss of control – through command, control and communication (C^3) and other technical failures, as well as from the inability of human beings to handle a nuclear war environment – is usually foremost in the list of problems confronting efforts to develop limited nuclear deterrence/defense options. The Bishops choose to believe that nuclear war will inevitably escalate, 'escape control', irrespective of the intentions of those who initiate it. It is believed, moreover, that proportionate and discriminate targeting may well be impossible. The argument is shut off with quotations from former high governmental officials and military commanders who admit that they have no confidence in man's ability to limit nuclear war once it has started.[31]

To the Christian realist, these difficulties present agonizing challenges that would be gladly forgone, were some form of nuclear deterrence and defense not a practical and moral necessity. Combining this conviction with commitment to just war standards, the Christian realist, with Father John Courtney Murray, sees a moral imperative to work for the realization of just and limited means of deterrence and defense, both nuclear and conventional.[32]

But what is a necessity, even a moral imperative, to the Christian realist is, for the Christian idealist, a quixotic and dangerous effort to attempt something that is probably impossible, certainly immensely risky, and, most importantly, unnecessary. There is no need, the idealist says, for nuclear deterrence and defense in any form. The task is to eliminate nuclear weapons, not to try to find morally permissible uses for them. So the idealists, and notably the American Catholic Bishops in their 1983 Pastoral Letter, conclude that unless and until it can be proven beyond question that just and limited nuclear deterrence/defense policies are feasible, they must be considered to be impossible. There is, moreover, no disposition to encourage a further search for morally usable nuclear option.[33]

The popes and Vatican II, then, were right in the first place to treat nuclear deterrence and war as an undifferentiated category that, for purposes of moral analyses, should always be viewed in its most absolute, unlimited, unthinkable form. Ironically, this has been the American Catholic Bishops' position even as the United States has moved away significantly from the extreme forms of countervalue, countercity strategic defense postures that characterized earlier policies. This fact is noted by the Bishops but they do not find reassuring the improvements in the direction of emphasis on militargeting in US policies. Rather than encourage further movement in the direction of limited nuclear options, they would counsel all-out arms control initiatives to eliminate nuclear deterrence and weapons entirely.[34]

However, even though they address the threats to the free world only belatedly, reluctantly and with considerable reflection of the view that we are as much if not more to be feared than the Communists, the Bishops do not wholly discount the need for some kind of nuclear deterrent for the immediate future. If any kind of reliance on nuclear weapons is too dangerous to countenance, how can even a temporary deterrent be maintained?

The answer is the bluff deterrent. A bluff deterrent is one in which the party has the capability of carrying out the threat of a nuclear reaction to aggression but does not have the intention and/or will to do so. If it is thought that some kind of nuclear deterrent were temporarily necessary pending arms control breakthroughs that would obviate its necessity, it would be convenient to have the appearance of a deterrent for protection without actually intending to carry out the deterrent threat.[35]

Particularly if it were thought that the most effective deterrence comes from the most immoral, 'unthinkable' threats, as in the extreme forms of MAD, it would be conceivable that one could hold out all appearances of being willing to carry out these threats without actually intending to do so. This line of thought is encouraged by the esoteric nominalism of some strategic thinking. The point is constantly made in deterrence theory that the purpose of nuclear weapons deployed in a deterrent posture is that they will never have to be used — if the deterrent works. Drawing on the free-form pop sociology and psychology of some international relations approaches, it is possible to conjure up the proposition that the whole deterrence relationship is infinitely more a matter of 'perception' than of substance. It is not what exists that counts, but what the adversary thinks exists.[36]

This kind of approach enhances an unfortunate impression that some seem to draw from the distinction between 'deterrence only' and 'deterrence plus' strategies. Deterrence only strategies, such as MAD, place such reliance on the deterrent effect of the threat of incredibly horrendous responses to aggression that it is considered to be subversive of the deterrent effect to speculate about the war-fighting strategies that would actually be followed if somehow the deterrent failed. Deterrence plus simply means that it is recognized than any deterrent can fail if it does it is necessary to have some plans for war-fighting.[37] Somehow the emphases on the psychological, perception aspect of deterrence and the concept of 'deterrence only' strategies leads to the notion that one may have nuclear deterrence without the contingency of nuclear war-fighting, something that would be true only if there were an absolute certainty that the deterrent-only deterrent would never fail.

From such concepts developed the bluff deterrent idea articulated in 1976 by Father Bryan Hehir, destined to be the American Catholic Bishops' National Security Adviser. Father Hehir, as a student of *realpolitik*, recognized the need for a nuclear deterrent. As a moralist he found the MAD deterrent morally untenable. As a student of *realpolitik* he had, on the one hand, concluded that selective, flexible response limited nuclear deterrence/defense were too problematic and risky to serve as the basis for Western deterrence. On the other hand, he had been duly impressed by the potential of the perceptions emphasis in international relations and deterrence theory and the concept of deterrence only pushed to the extreme meaning of deterrence without war-fighting. From this combination of moral and empirical expertise and insights came the bluff deterrent.[38]

The specific form that the bluff deterrent concept was to take was through the formulation of an issue of 'possession' of nuclear weapons. Father Hehir knew, as the Bishops acknowledge in their 1983 Pastoral Letter, that in order to have a deterrence system you must have the capabilities for assured retaliation against aggression, the intention and will to use those capabilities, and the means to communicate your ability and readiness to carry out your threats to the adversary.[39] In plain language, to have an effective deterrent you have to be able and willing to fight a war if the deterrent threat is defied. But if you bring yourself to believe that the whole business of deterrence is more psychological than substantive, more a matter of perception than of reality, then perhaps you can get away with a bluff deterrent based on one element, capabilities, without the others, intention and will to use the capabilities communicated to the adversary. Great reliance is placed on the ingenious proposition that the adversary will not believe you or trust you to hold to your moral scruples, an interesting reversal of the usual notion of credibility.[40]

Although the concept of bluff deterrence does not long survive serious examination (e.g., how do you simultaneously communicate an intention and will to do something you believe you cannot do morally to your adversary and to your own personnel in the deterrence/defense chain of command?), it recommended itself to Bishops anxious to condemn deterrence generally while condoning it temporarily on condition that arms control progress would be made to eliminate the problem. Hence the usage 'possession' of nuclear weapons as something separate from the other components of a nuclear deterrence deployment, e.g., facilities and arrangements to fire the weapons, and the other components of deterrence, e.g., intention, will and their communication to the adversary.

The period 1968–79 saw a succession of statements by the US Catholic Bishops obviously reflecting the bluff deterrent concept. Nuclear deterrence was condemned even more explicitly than it had been in *Gaudium et Spes* but the effect of the condemnations was mitigated by the concession that a kind of deterrence could be maintained based on possession of nuclear weapons until the moment when arms control progress made possible their elimination.[41] Early in the elaborate drafting process of the 1983 Pastoral Letter, the issue of possession of nuclear weapons was still raised. By the time that the final version was voted on by the Bishops in May 1983, the possession issue as such had been removed, perhaps as a result of Christian realist criticism.[42]

Nevertheless, the bluff deterrent lives on in the 1983 Pastoral

Letter. If one re-reads the letter often enough, one comes away with the impression that the Bishops intended to admit that some kind of nuclear deterrent must be accepted for the time being. It clearly cannot be anything like a basic MAD countervalue deterrent based on an actual intention to carry out the MAD countervalue threats if the deterrent failed. On the other hand, every effort to develop alternative, counterforce-emphasis limited nuclear deterrence based on just and limited war-fighting strategies is rejected as too risky. The result is a kind of 'none of the above' treatment of nuclear options. The Bishops can think of no morally permissible nuclear option. The burden of proof is on those who claim that there might be some. However, the Bishops discourage any attempt to overcome the moral presumption against just and limited nuclear options by trying to develop the capabilities to carry them out.[43]

In these circumstances, of what does the existing nuclear deterrent that is being condoned consist? If no available form of nuclear war-fighting is morally permissible, as the Bishops all but declare, then the bluff deterrent is all that is left. This bluff deterrent is based solely on the possession of nuclear weapons. This possession is accompanied, if we are to take the Bishops seriously, not simply by a negative lack of intention and will to use nuclear weapons against an aggressor but by a positive public commitment never to use nuclear weapons. If this is not a fair reading of the 1983 Pastoral Letter, let the Bishops emerge from behind their centimeter of ambiguity and set the record straight.

The bluff deterrent concept is reinforced in the 1983 Pastoral Letter by enthusiastic espousal of an abstract 'deterrence only' position. The Bishops quote the authority of Pope John Paul's view that deterrence can only be condoned, 'not as an end in itself but as a step on the way toward progressive disarmamen'.[44] But deterrence is not an end in itself. It is, first, the indispensable basis for free world security and, second, but only second, the indispensable basis for any lasting arms control progress.

Deterrence is not an abstraction. It is a real world system based on the credible capability, intention and willingness, communicated to an adversary to resist aggression, particularly nuclear aggression, by a defensive nuclear war. It is not an end in itself but a means to an end, just defense. There is, in the real world, no "deterrence only" option in the literal sense that one may have nuclear deterrence without the distinct possibility of having to fight a nuclear war if deterrence fails. The 1983 Pastoral Letter apparently will condone nuclear deterrence that 'exists only to prevent the *use* of nuclear weapons' (original emphasis).[45] However, it opposes 'planning for prolonged periods of repeated nuclear strikes and counterstrikes, or "prevailing" in nuclear war,' as 'not acceptable'.[46] The Bishops conclude that such efforts' encourage notions that nuclear war can be engaged in with tolerable human and moral consequences. Rather, we must continually say no to the idea of nuclear war.'[47]

If deterrence can fail, and it can, and if a victim of aggression had to choose between surrender and resistance against a nuclear aggressor, is there any alternative to planning and preparing for that dread eventuality and trying to find ways to mitigate its horrors and to terminate it on some basis that would preserve freedom? The question does not arise if one takes an extreme 'deterrence only' view and simply refuses to imagine deterrence failing. It does not arise if one is prepared to surrender if the deterrence fails.

There is a third alternative. Perhaps we will be saved the red or dead choice by the overwhelming sweep and pace of arms control agreements which will eliminate nuclear weapons, nuclear deterrence and, ultimately, war itself. A truly Christian idealist solution. But even granting for the sake of argument the remote possibility of some of these achievements, what happens to the nuclear deterrence system while all of these unprecedented breakthroughs are taking place? How many years will it take to obviate the necessity for nuclear deterrence? Will a bluff deterrent hold indefinitely while arms control proceeds? These are questions that the Bishops preferred not to address. They preferred to say no to nuclear war but the Christian realist finds that a simplistic, question-begging, escapist response to the dilemmas of deterrence and defense in an age of conflict wherein the basic freedom and human rights that the Church holds so dear are endangered.

The Christian realist sees a perennial need for armed coercion, within polities and between them. Since nuclear weapons cannot be uninvented, this need will include nuclear coercion. That being the case, the Christian realist sees the problem of nuclear war as one of mitigation and control, not elimination. No arms control 'progress' will change this fundamental fact and certainly no reliance on a bluff deterrent that cannot be backed up by effective just and limited defense against aggression will be responsive to the challenges of war.

Whether such a just and limited nuclear deterrence/defense posture is feasible today is very much in question but the prospects are not hopeless.[48] For the Christian realist, the challenge of war is not to eliminate it but to make limited war, the foundation of a morally acceptable deterrent, possible. In a nuclear age this means just and limited nuclear deterrence and defense, the sole realistic basis for the security of the free world and for arms control.

NOTES

1 National Conference of Catholic Bishops, *The Challenge of Peace: God's Promise and Our Response* (Washington, DC: United States Catholic Conference, 1983).

2 '"Only a centimeter of doubt" has prevented the US Catholic Conference of Bishops from declaring their support of an all-out ban on nuclear weapons, Rev. J. Bryan Hehir, director of the Office of International Justice and Peace of the US Catholic Conference, told a meeting of the World Affairs Council in Boston last night.' Judy Foreman, '"Centimeter of Doubt" for Bishops on N-ban,' Boston *Globe* (March 1, 1983). Father Hehir used the same expression on the NBC special, 'The Bishops and the Bomb', shown on May 15, 1983. In a panel discussion at St. Peter's Church in Washington, DC in May 1983, Father Hehir was reported as saying: 'If you ask me does it rule out any use of nuclear weaponry under any circumstances, the Letter never says that. There is a centimeter of ambiguity. And on that centimeter of ambiguity the deterrence ...' Tom Bethell, 'The Bishops' Brain', *The American Spectator* (July 1983), p. 3.

3 For idealists' approaches to international relations, see Kenneth E. Boulding, *Conflict and Defense, A General Theory* (New York: Harper & Row, 1962); Grenville Clark and Louis B. Sohn, *World Peace through World Law* (3rd edn, Cambridge, Mass.: Harvard University Press, 1966); John Herz, *Political Realism and Political Idealism* (Chicago: Chicago University Press, 1953); Louis Henkin, *How Nations Behave* (2nd edn, New York: Council on Foreign Relations/Columbia University Press, 1979).

   An extraordinary example of an idealist approach is John XXIII, *Pacem in Terris: Peace on Earth* (Washington, DC: NCWC, 1963).

   For realist approaches to international relations, see E. H. Carr, *International Relations between the Two World Wars* (London: Macmillan, 1947); Hans A. Morgenthau, *Politics among Nations* (New York: Knopf, 1948); Kenneth W. Thompson, *Political Realism and the Crisis of World Politics* (Princeton, NJ: Princeton University Press, 1960); Reinhold Niebuhr, *Christianity and Power Politics* (New York: Charles Scribner's Sons, 1940); William V. O'Brien, *War and/or Survival* (Garden City, NY: Doubleday, 1969).

   A classic critique of idealism and realism is Inis Claude, Jr., *Power and International Relations* (New York: Random House, 1962).

4 See Robert W. Tucker, *The Just War* (Baltimore, Md.: The Johns Hopkins University Press, 1960).

5 See James E. Dougherty and Robert L. Pfaltzgraf, Jr., *Contending Theories of International Relations* (Philadelphia: J. B. Lippincott, 1971), Chapter 7, pp. 251–300; on psychological factors in deterrence, pp. 375–8.

6 On just war doctrine, see John Courtney Murray, S. J., *We Hold These Truths* (New York: Sheed & Ward, 1960), Chapters 10 and 11, pp. 221–72; Paul Ramsey, *The Just War: Force and Political Responsibility* (New York: Charles Scribner's Sons, 1968); James T. Johnson, *Ideology, Reason and Limitation of War* (Princeton, NJ: Princeton University Press, 1975) and *Just War Tradition and the Restraint of War* (Princeton, NJ: Princeton University Press, 1981); William V. O'Brien, *The Conduct of Just and Limited War* (New York: Praeger, 1981); David Hollenbach, S. J. *Nuclear Ethics* (New York: Paulist Press, 1983).

For a thorough and fair compendium and analysis of American Catholic writing on nuclear war and morality, see Judith A. Dwyer, SSJ, 'An Analysis of Nuclear Warfare in Light of the Traditional Just War Theory: An American Roman Catholic Perspective (1945–1981'. (PhD dissertation, The Catholic University of America, 1983.)

7 See O'Brien *Conduct of Just and Limited War*, Chapter 2, pp. 13–38.

8 Ibid, pp. 35–36; William V. O'Brien, 'Just-War Doctrine in a Nuclear Context', *Theological Studies* 44 (June 1983), p. 197.

9 NCCB, *Challenge of Peace*, I, C3, 80–110.

10 Ibid, II, 122.

11 O'Brien, *War and/or Survival*, pp. 112–14.

12 NCCB, *Challenge of Peace*, II, D2, 167–99.

13 Ibid., III, B2, 245–50.

14 *Origins* 13 (May 19, 1983). NCCB, *Challenge of Peace*, III, B2, 249.

15 NCCB, *Challenge of Peace*, B2, 250.

16 Ibid., 251.

17 Ibid.

18 Ibid., Introduction, 1–4; I, 5; II, A, 130.

19 See the critical view of the Bishops' emphasis on the most catastrophic scenarios for nuclear war and their down-grading of the consequences of failure to protect free world security in Albert Wohlstetter, 'Bishops, Statesmen, and Other Strategists on the Bombing of Innocents', *Commentary* 75 (June 1983), pp. 15–35.

20 Vatican II, *Pastoral Constitution on the Church in the Modern World (Gaudium et Spes)*, Walter M. Abbott, SJ, *The Documents of Vatican II* (New York: Guild/America/Association, 1966), pp. 199–308.

21 Ibid., no. 80, p. 294.

22 Ibid., no. 81, pp. 294–5.

23 Ibid., nos. 80–82, pp. 293–7.

24 On deterrence, see generally Roger D. Speed, *Strategic Deterrence in the 1980s* (Stanford, Calif.: Hoover Institute, 1979); Patrick M. Morgan, *Deterrence: A Conceptual Analysis* (Beverly Hills, Calif.:

Sage, 1977); Donald M. Snow, *Nuclear Deterrence in a Dynamic World* (University, Ala.: University of Alabama Press, 1981); Dougherty and Pfaltzgraf, *Contending Theories of International Relations*, Chapter 9, pp. 368–416.

25 See O'Brien, *War and/or Survival*, pp. 1–68, 112–14.

26 *Gaudium et Spes*, no. 81, p. 295.

27 'All these considerations compel us to undertake an evaluation of war with an entirely new attitude.' Ibid., no. 80, p. 293.

28 Ibid., no. 82, pp. 295–7.

29 Ibid.

30 See *Human Life in Our Day*, Pastoral Letter of the American Hierarchy, November 15, 1968, *Pastoral Letters of the American Hierarchy*, 1792–1970, nos. 93–132, pp. 694–701; *To Live in Christ Jesus*, A Pastoral Reflection on the Moral Life, November 11, 1976 (Washington, DC; United States Catholic Conference, 1976), pp. 30–9; *The Gospel of Peace and the Danger of War*, Statement, USCC Administrative Board, February 15, 1978 (Washington, DC: United States Catholic Conference, 1978); Testimony of John Cardinal Krol, representing the US Catholic Conference before the Senate Foreign Relations Committee, September 6, 1979, in *The Nuclear Threat: Reading the Signs of the Times*, Patricia L. Rengel, ed. (Washington, DC: Office of International Justice and Peace/USCC, October 1979).

31 It should be observed that the definition of the war-conduct principles of proportion and discrimination is scarcely a matter for debate in *The Challenge of Peace*, since it is assumed that nuclear war will almost certainly escalate and/or escape control to a point where it is disproportionate and indiscriminate by any standard. See NCCB, *Challenge of Peace*, II, C, 144–5, 152–3; D, 179–80.

32 See Murray, *We Hold These Truths*, pp. 270–1.

33 NCCB, *Challenge of Peace*, II, D2, 178–99.

34 Ibid.

35 On bluff deterrents, see Ramsey, *Just War*, pp. 249–58 and his disavowal of the idea in Paul Ramsey, 'A Political Ethics Context for Strategic Thinking', in Morton A. Kaplan, ed., *Strategic Thinking and its Moral Implications* (Chicago: University of Chicago Center for Policy Study, 1973), p. 142.

The central source of the Bishops' bluff deterrent position appears to be Father Hehir's parts of Robert A. Gessert and J. Bryan Hehir, *The New Nuclear Debate* (New York: Council on Religion and International Affairs, 1976), pp. 44, 47–53, 66–9.

For critical reactions to the bluff deterrent concept, see Wohlstetter, 'Bishops, Statesmen and Other Strategists on the Bombing of Innocents', pp. 16, 30–1; O'Brien, 'Just-War Doctrine in a Nuclear Context', pp. 214–16.

36 See, generally, Wohlstetter, 'Bishops, Statesmen, and Other Strategists on the Bombing of Innocents'. A useful survey is Robert Jervis,

'Deterrence Theory Revisited', *World Politics* 31 (January 1979),
pp. 289–324.

37 On the 'deterrence only' – 'deterrence plus' dichotomy, see
Wohlstetter's authoritative critique in 'Bishops, Statesmen, and Other
Strategists on the Bombing of Innocents' especially pp. 30–5. See,
generally, Snow, *Nuclear Deterrence in a Dynamic World*, pp. 5–6,
44, 69–73, 79.

See the treatment of deterrence, with emphasis on discouraging
deterrence plus planning and policies, NCCB, *Challenge of Peace*, II
D2, 178–99.

38 See Hehir in Gessert and Hehir, *New Nuclear Debate*, pp. 44,
47–53, 66–9.

39 NCCB, *Challenge of Peace*, II, D1, 162–6.

40 See Hehir in Gessert and Hehir, *New Nuclear Debate*, pp. 44, 47–
53, 66–9.

41 See the treatment of the issue of possession of nuclear weapons as a
discrete subject in *Human Life in Our Day* (1968), no, 106, p. 697,
wherein *Gaudium et Spes*, no. 81 is cited as authority for the
distinction.

In his testimony before the Senate Foreign Relations Committee
Cardinal Krol stated:

The moral judgment of this statement ['To Live in Christ
Jesus', 1976] is that not only the *use* of strategic nuclear
weapons, but also the *declared intent* to use them involved
in our deterrence policy is wrong. This explains the Catholic
dissatisfaction with nuclear deterrence and the urgency of
the Catholic demand that the nuclear arms race be reversed.
It is of the utmost importance that negotiations proceed to
meaningful and continuing reductions in nuclear stockpiles,
and eventually, to the phasing out altogether of nuclear
deterrence and the threat of mutual-assured destruction.

As long as there is hope of this occurring, Catholic moral
teaching is willing, while negotiations proceed, to tolerate
the possession of nuclear weapons for deterrence as the
lesser of two evils. If that hope were to disappear, the moral
attitude of the Catholic Church would almost certainly have
to shift to one of uncompromising condemnation of both
use *and* possession of such weapons.

[original emphasis]

42 In the First Draft Pastoral Letter on Peace and War, then entitled
God's Hope in a Time of Fear, June 11, 1982, the issue is raised: 'If
we were to reject any conceivable use of nuclear weapons, we would
face the very difficult question *whether it is permissible even to
continue to possess nuclear weapons*.' (Working Text, p. 31) [original
emphasis]

In the Second Draft Proposed Pastoral Letter, *The Challenge of Peace: God's Promise and Our Response*, General Meeting, November 15–18, 1982, it is contented that 'The moral questions about deterrence focus on five issues: (1) the *possession* of weapons of mass destruction . . .' (Working Text, p. 50) [original emphasis]

In the Third Draft of the Pastoral Letter, May 1983, the discrete issue of possession of nuclear weapons is no longer raised. Instead, emphasis is placed on the necessity that violation of the principles of noncombatant immunity and proportionality not be intended in a strategy of deterrence and that 'Deterrence is not an adequate strategy as a long-term basis for peace; it is a transitional strategy justifiable only in conjunction with resolute determination to pursue arms control and disarmament.' (Working Text, p. v) The four key issues listed for discussion on p. 66 of the working text do not include possession of nuclear weapons.

The 1983 Pastoral Letter does not distinguish possession of nuclear weapons as a separate subject. It is instructive to observe that quotations from Cardinal Krol's 1979 Senate Foreign Relations Committee statement do not include his separate observations on possession, cited *supra*, note 41. See NCCB, *Challenge of Peace*, II, D2, 170.

43 Ibid., II, C, 157–61; D, 178–99.
44 John Paul II, Message, UN Special Session, 1982, cited in NCCB, *Challenge of Peace*, II, D2, 173.
45 Ibid., 188.
46 Ibid.
47 Ibid.
48 I survey the problem of just and limited deterrence and defense in *Conduct of Just and Limited War*, pp. 127–44; 'Just-War Doctrine in a Nuclear Context', pp. 214–20.

7

Can War Be Morally Justified? The Just War Theory

ROBERT L. HOLMES

[There are] men who assert that the contradiction between the striving and love for peace and the necessity of war is terrible, but that such is the fate of men. These for the most part sensitive, gifted men see and comprehend the whole terror and the whole madness and cruelty of war, but by some strange turn of mind do not see and do not look for any issue from this condition.

Leo Tolstoy

Augustine makes a powerful case for the justifiability of war. Grant just a few of his premises, and all the rest follows, enveloped in a theological − metaphysical − eschatalogical wrapping that renders it impervious to countervailing evidence and argument. Virtually every major just war theorist in the Western tradition builds upon his work.

This is not to say there is not other important work on morality and war outside of the Western tradition. Both Judaism and Islam give attention to the issue, particularly to the question of how war should be conducted, as does some Eastern thought. It is clear, for example, from the Old Testament that wars commanded by God are considered righteous and that definite rules have been laid down for the conduct of war. These two considerations − the conditions under which one may have recourse to war and the manner in which war may be conducted − are components of any complete just war doctrine. And Islam, in the concept of *Jihād*, has a clearly developed just war doctrine that represents the war of Islam against the non-Moslem world as a permanent condition (at least until the establishment of a Moslem world). The war need

Reprinted with permission from Robert L. Holmes *On War and Morality* (Princeton University Press, Princeton, New Jersey, 1989), pp. 146−82.

not be, or at least need not be exclusively, military, and Moslems may participate in the *Jihād* 'by the heart, the tongue, or the hands, as well as by the sword'[1] But it is seen as enjoined by Allah, giving it much the same justification that Augustine saw in wars commanded by God, and it has as its mission the establishment of a universal Islamic state.

My concern, however, is with the just war doctrine in the Western tradition, where it has been heavily influenced by Christianity, and in particular with some of its more recent formulations. I shall not present a history of the evolution of the tradition; that has been done by others and would be beside the point of our present concerns. My aim, rather, is to examine those aspects of the tradition that bear most directly upon my central argument concerning the morality of war and to assess the just war theory as an approach to the morality of war.

Two principal objections have been brought against the just war approach to war, neither of which, in my judgment, is successful, but one of which helps to focus a third objection that I think is decisive.

The first concerns alleged consequences of the prevalence of just war theorizing in certain historical periods. It is sometimes said that the most terrible wars in history occurred during the ascendancy of the just war theory and that the longest periods of relative tranquillity occurred when the theory was in eclipse. This is sometimes taken, without further argument, to constitute a refutation of the theory. It is true that the sixteenth and seventeenth centuries, when the just war theory was extensively discussed among theologians and jurists, was a time of some of the most vicious wars in history, a fact that provided much of the impetus to try to humanize the conduct of war. It is also true that but for the Napoleonic wars and the American Civil War, both of which caused widespread devastation but were for the most part professionally conducted, much of the period from that time to the twentieth century (a time during which, contrary to the just war theory, it was generally held that nations could justifiably go to war for virtually any reason) was relatively free of the worst excesses of war.

But as tempting as it may be to dismiss the just war approach on these grounds, claims of the preceding sort are difficult to substantiate. We have seen this to be true with the related claim by political realists in their critique of US policy during World War I. They argued that to allow morality to govern foreign policy leads in time of war to a crusading mentality that stands in the way of the cool, dispassionate assessment of self-interest that can limit war's excesses. They were not talking about the just war theory specifically, but in the sense in which that approach embraces any attempt to provide a moral justification of war, their arguments apply to it. Such claims require disentangling complex religious and moral elements in the thinking about war from other cultural, technological, and military developments that shape its character. This is a difficult task at best. Even if it could be accomplished, it would be hard to be certain that any resultant correlation between the acceptance of the just war theory in a given period and the documentable horrors of war in that same period represented a causal connection. To my knowledge, this has never been convincingly shown.

The second objection bears upon the changing character of war in the nuclear age. It holds that the nuclear age, with the threat of annihilation in the case of an all-out war between the superpowers, has rendered the just war theory obsolete. Michael Walzer, for example, speaks of the 'monstrous immorality that our policy contemplates, an immorality we can never hope to square with our understanding of justice in war,' adding that 'nuclear weapons explode the theory of just war'.[2] Various just war theorists, including James Turner Johnson, William V. O'Brien, and Robert L. Phillips,[3] defend the theory and argue that it is relevant to the contemporary age and, indeed, represents the only defensible way of thinking about the problem of morality and war.

I want to examine this second objection in greater detail. Before that, however, it is important to consider certain aspects of the evolution of the just war doctrine, since there are developments there that are important to understanding the newer forms of the theory as well as to understanding my own argument concerning the morality of war.

I

The second main stage in the development of the just war theory following Augustine comes with St. Thomas Aquinas in the thirteenth century, who takes over Augustine's requirements that a war be declared by a legitimate authority and be for a just cause but adds to them a third requirement his own.

What this is can best be appreciated by recalling Augustine's subjectivistic understanding of the morality of warfare. The real evils of war, he said, are 'love of violence, revengeful cruelty, fierce and implacable enmity and the like'. This, as we have seen, was part of the interiorization of Christian ethics, emphasizing purity of soul and motivation, and it is taken over by Aquinas. But he emphasizes something that is only implicit in Augustine, which is that any action may have bad consequences, whatever the intentions of the agent performing it. And this seems correct. Most actions have *some* bad consequences, particularly in the area of social and political affairs; the best of policies impose demands upon some persons or ask sacrifices of them. The relevant question is not whether those policies would benefit some individual or group but rather whether their benefits outweigh their costs — whether the good produced would outweigh the bad. In more general terms ... the question for conduct is: How can one lead a fully moral life if he cannot help doing some bad in the ordinary course of things?

Aquinas proposes a solution in the third condition he adds to Augustine's requirements, which occurs in the context of an argument to show that one may sometimes justifiably kill another person in self-defense.

> Nothing hinders one act from having two effects, only one of which is intended, while the other is beside the intention ... Accordingly the act of self-defence may have two effects, one is the saving of one's life, the other is the slaying of the aggressor. Therefore this act, since one's intention is to save one's own life, is not unlawful, seeing that it is natural to everything to keep itself in *being*, as far as possible.[4]

... Here, more explicitly than Augustine, Aquinas calls attention to the further distinction between our intention — that which it is our purpose to bring about through an action — and what we merely foresee or expect as the outcome, and maintains that we may sometimes justifiably kill another person provided the killing is 'beside the intention' — that is, merely foreseen and not intended (he also requires that one have public authority for the act, use no more violence than necessary, and act for the common good).

In the case of the resort to war, it is expressly required that one have a right intention. This means that one must intend to promote the good and avoid evil; merely having a just cause and legitimate authority is insufficient. What constitutes a right intention during the conduct of war is less clear. It has been taken by subsequent writers to require that one not 'directly' intend the killing of persons as persons but only intend the killing of them as combatants, or that one pursue peace and avoid unnecessary destruction, or that one protect rights.[5] In any event, the emphasis is subjectivistic, dependent upon inner purity. (There is a similar emphasis in Islam in the requirement that the *jihadist* fight with a good intention, specifically to promote Islam rather than, say, to achieve personal gain.)

II

The troublesome question of whether both sides can be just in a war arises here, however. For the first and third of the preceding conditions — legitimate authority and right intention — could easily be met by both sides. Even Hitler arguably had the legitimate authority to declare war in World War II. And it might just as easily be the case that both sides have a right intention in the required sense; good Christians and good Moslems will have no less, as the crusades attest. The crucial question concerns whether both sides could have a just cause, and this issue engaged just war theorists for years and led to some of the most significant developments in the evolution of the theory, particularly in its relationship to international law.

Vitoria in the sixteenth century came close to making explicit a distinction that has its origins in Augustine. He denied that war could be just on both sides, saying that 'if the right and justice of each side be certain, it is unlawful to fight against it, either in offence or denfence.' But he qualified this by adding: 'Assuming a demonstrable ignorance either of fact or of law, it may be that on the side where true justice is the war is just of itself, while on the other side the war is just in the sense of being excused from sin by reason of good faith, because invincible ignorance is a complete excuse.'[6] He said further, in the spirit of Augustine, that although a prince may knowingly carry on an unjust war, his subjects may not know that the war is unjust and 'in this way the subjects on both sides may be doing what is lawful when they fight'.

Two senses of justice emerge here: an objective sense designating the actual moral status of a war, which is unaffected by whether people *think* the war is just; and a subjective sense, according to which a war is just if it is believed through invincible ignorance to be just, even if in fact it is objectively unjust. In this way a war might be subjectively just on both sides but it could never be objectively just on both sides.[7]

This is a useful and important distinction, and it is elaborated by more recent ethical theorists. But an even more sophisticated handling of this problem is found in the eighteenth century in the writings of E. Vattel, whose influential analysis becomes the prevailing view into the twentieth century. Central to it is the distinction between legality and morality. While Hugo Grotius had clearly recognized the distinction in the seventeenth century, and some awareness of it can be found in Vitoria and possibly even in Augustine, Vattel brings it to bear upon international problems in a way that sheds important light on the interrelationships between law and morality in connection with war.

Let us consider first the nature of international law, after which we will be in a better position to appreciate Vattel's argument.

III

Philosophers and jurists are not fully agreed as to precisely what international law is, but they largely agree that its modern origins lie in the rise of the nation-state in the sixteenth and seventeenth centuries. It was at that time that diverse and often tenuous loyalties to monarchs, princes, and feudal lords began to congeal around larger, politically and territorially definable units having a monopoly of force. The command of such a monopoly came to be a defining characteristic of the state in later writers like Weber. Not only did this process establish nation-states as the principal actors in the interrelationships among peoples but it also added new fuel to the furnace of war. For by the time of the Napoleonic wars between 1792 and 1815 patriotism became an added ingredient in the mixture of emotion, fear, hope, and courage that was to impel peoples to fight and die for the state, a factor that, combined with the advance in weaponry brought by the industrial revolution, made possible the unprecedented capacity for warfare possessed by the industrial nations of the twentieth century.

Both the emergence of states and the increased destructiveness of war contributed to the development of modern international law, but they did so in different ways. The emergence of states altered the character of the entities, or 'juristic persons', who are subject to that law. In antiquity the subjects of such rudimentary international law as there was were peoples: the Athenians, the Corinthians, the Romans, the Vandals, and so forth. Today they are states, and it is their conduct that international law seeks to regulate. It is also their rights and obligations that are largely at issue in disputes over international law. I say largely because the Nuremberg trials challenged that view and attempted to extend international law to the conduct of individual persons as well as to states. This raises questions about what sorts of entities states are what it is for a state to 'act,' how they can have rights and obligations, and what those rights and obligations are — questions that underlie many of the problems of contemporary international law as it bears upon the problem of war.

The destructiveness of war, on the other hand, contributed to the development of international law by creating a perceived need to mitigate war's horrors. We saw in the preceding chapter the warlike footing Christianity was put on by Augustine. By the seventeenth century the militarization of Christianity had progressed to the point where Grotius, in explaining his reasons for writing his major study on the laws of war and peace, lamented:

> Throughout the Christian world I observed a lack of restraint in relation to war, such as even barbarous races should be ashamed of; I observed that men rush to arms for slight causes, or no cause at all, and that when arms have once been taken up there is no longer any respect for law, divine or human; it is as if, in accordance with a general decree, frenzy had openly been let loose for the committing of all crimes.[8]

The concern for the most part was not to do away with war; it was rather to civilize it and bring it into line with humanitarian ideals. This led to efforts to formulate so-called 'laws of war'.

Early discussions of the laws of war had two concerns. One, dealing with *jus in bello*, was to establish rules for the conduct of war once it had begun. It dealt with such issues as the legitimacy of killing noncombatants, the treatment of prisoners, the use of poisons, appropriation of property, and the use of especially terrible weapons. The other, dealing with *jus ad bellum*, which in its moral dimension was the primary concern of Augustine, was to establish rules governing the resort to war in the first place and to lay down conditions under which war could justifiably be waged at all. On this view war, no matter how scrupulously waged, could be unjust depending upon how and why it began. The distinction between these concerns is central to Vattel's analysis.

I have been speaking of international law as though there were a clearly specified body of rules comprising such law. But there is not. There is an International Court of Justice (World Court) but no world legislature that enacts legislation and sets penalties for its violation. Nor has there ever been. International law has other origins. What these are is a matter of disagreement among scholars, but three alleged sources stand out: natural law, custom, and convention.

Natural law dates back at least as far as the Stoics, and perhaps to Anaximander. The Stoics conceived of nature as a rational manifestation of God and took rightness and duty to be determined by what accords with it. 'This, then, ... has been the decision of the wisest philosophers,' Cicero wrote in one of the clearest classical statements of this idea, 'that law was neither a thing contrived by the genius of man, nor established by any decree of the people, but a certain eternal principle, which governs the entire universe, wisely commanding what is right and prohibiting what is wrong.'[3] Natural law so conceived contains the criteria for judging moral rightness and wrongness. It in unchangeable and transcends man-made laws. It provides a natural standard by which to judge human, or 'positive', law as well as the conduct of peoples of different countries who may not be bound together by positive laws. Sometimes such law is represented as taking the form of precepts impressed by common sense upon the minds of all persons, sometimes as taking the form of natural inclinations that are a part of human nature. Aquinas, who Christianized the concept, represents it in both ways. In his view natural law is part of eternal law, God's plan for the governance of the whole of creation, and as such it perfects man unto well-being and happiness in his relation to the natural world and his fellow men.

This sets natural law theory in a metaphysical or theological framework concerning the nature of man and his relationship to the cosmos. The theory varies according to the underlying philosophies of those giving accounts of it. In a more general sense, however, natural law theory is simply the view that moral considerations are or should be the governing considerations behind positive law. In this sense it need not have the implications associated with the formulations of Cicero and Aquinas, and may simply represent an appeal to morality in the formulation and assessment of laws.

Custom, or customary law, on the other hand, designates practices that develop of their own accord without benefit of design or legislation. It represents a kind of international common law, which in turn represents legal norms for the conduct of states. Needless to say it is always an open question whether the practices of people and states are right from a moral standpoint, which means that what is prescribed by natural law and what is dictated by customary law may diverge. Grotius in effect recognized both sorts. Natural law provided the foundation of his account, but the better part of his discussion concerns the practices and customs surrounding warfare. In fact, he takes the law of nations, which along with municipal law is part of human law, to be rooted in 'unbroken custom and the testimony of those who are skilled in it'.[10]

Conventional law, finally, refers to enactments by treaty and convention. Although binding only upon states that are a party to the particular treaty or convention, they play a role in the establishment and acceptance of the rules that states recognize and must take account of in their dealings with one another.

Any one of these might be claimed to be the prime source of international law. The philosophy underlying international law has undergone change depending upon which has been emphasized. Natural law gradually gave way after Grotius and his followers to customary law, which is widely regarded today as the major source of international law, as it is in this statement by Hans Kelsen:

> [T]he general norm which obligates states to behave in conformity with the treaties they have concluded . . . is a norm of general international law, and general international law is created by custom constituted by acts of states. The basic norm of international law, therefore, must be a norm which countenances custom as a norm-creating fact, and might be formulated as follows: The states ought to behave as they have customarily behaved.[11]

This view takes customary law to be more basic than conventional law, since it represents the latter as merely codifying what is contained in the former. It leaves natural law out of the picture altogether. It also conflates the 'is' and the 'ought' of international conduct by taking custom to be prescriptive.

Despite the preeminence of customary law, natural law can be seen to underlie the Nuremberg Charter and the Human Rights Declaration of the United Nations. In connection with warfare natural law was implicit in a statement by the prosecution at Nuremberg: 'The law of war is to be found not only in treaties, but in the customs and practices of states which gradually obtained universal recognition, and from the general principles of justice applied by jurists and practiced by military courts. This law is not static, but by continual adaptation follows the needs of a changing world.'[12] If 'principles of justice' is taken to refer to moral principles rather than merely to the conceptions of justice held by jurists and military courts, this formulation blends all three of the preceding sources. Along with explicit references to natural law by the prosecution during the trials, this suggests a reemergence of natural law in the thinking about international affairs. Crimes against peace were taken by the tribunal to pertain to the initiation of war, hence to belong to that aspect of international law dealing with recourse to war. Crimes of war, or simply war crimes, were taken to pertain to the conduct of war. Crimes against humanity were defined as consisting of various inhumane acts against 'any civilian population, before or during the war, or persecutions on political, racial or religious grounds in execution of or in connec-tion with any crime within the jurisdiction of the Tribunal'. (In its judgment the tribunal issued guilty verdicts on this score only in connection with inhumane acts committed after the outbreak of the war, and insofar as those acts were not also war crimes, issued them on the ground that they were committed in connection with an aggressive war. The implication is, though the tribunal did not draw it, that virtually all mistreatment of civilians in the course of an aggressive war is a crime against humanity.)

Lest it be thought that the foregoing distinctions and the question of.what priority to assign to the various sources of international law are of merely theoretical interest, it should be noted that men have been put to death as a result of differences over the nature, scope, and authority of international law. The defendants at Nuremberg were charged with crimes against humanity as well as with war crimes and crimes against peace. In addition they were charged with conspiracy to commit such crimes. The principal basis for the charges was the London Charter, officially known as the Agreement for the Establishment of an International Military Tribunal, concluded at London, August 8, 1945, which specifically identified the aforementioned as crimes. This fact gave rise to one of the central issues in the trial, namely, whether the London Charter constituted retroactive law, inasmuch as the acts for which the defendants were indicted occurred before that charter existed. The prosecution seemed at times to concede that new law had been created, or at least that existing law had been supplemented, but for the most part it argued that all the charter did was to codify existing law. Here it appealed to the League of Nations Covenant, the Kellogg-Briand Pact, and the Hague Conventions. Germany, of course, had withdrawn from the League of Nations in 1930 and had renounced the Kellogg-Briand Pact.

The defense argued that even if the relevant laws had been in effect, they would not apply to individuals but only to states. They called attention to the fact that only states had customarily been considered the subjects of international law. The reasoning was that, even though it was true, as the prosecution pointed out, that acts of states are acts of men, nonetheless individuals are not personally responsible for such acts and should not be punished for them. They pointed out that at the conclusion of World War I the United States had argued against punishing the Kaiser on the ground that such punishment would imply a limitation upon the sovereignty of the state to punish its citizens for acts performed by them in their capacity as its agents.

The defendants argued that they had been under orders with regard to at least certain of the alleged crimes. The orders were embodied in the *Führerprinzip*, according to which Hitler's orders were binding upon the citizens of Germany. These defenses were repudiated by the prosecution. While the tribunal did not accept the plea of having acted under superior orders as exculpatory, it did allow that it might mitigate punishment in some cases. Nearly all of the major figures among the accused were found guilty, and most were executed.

IV

Vattel recognizes each of the preceding sources of international law. In addition, following Christian Wolff, he recognizes voluntary law, which along with conventional and customary law makes up what he calls positive law. According to natural law, a war cannot be just on both sides. In this he agrees with Vitoria. But he holds that natural law dictates a number of more specific rules to govern the conduct of nations in light of their nature and the circumstances in which they act. The particularly relevant circumstance is that they are free, independent, and sovereign moral persons, and in a state of nature such as exists among nations none can dictate morally to others. These rules make up what he calls the voluntary law of nations. And thus it is that 'the necessary [or natural] law prescribes what is of absolute necessity for Nations and what tends naturally to their advancement and their common happiness; the voluntary law tolerates what it is impossible to forbid without causing greater evils.'[13] Nations are presumed to consent to voluntary law whether they do so in fact or not because otherwise they would be violating the liberties of all.

One of the rules of voluntary law holds '*that regular war, as regards its effects, must be accounted just on both sides*'.[14] A regular war is one that is authorized on both sides by the sovereigns and is accompanied by appropriate formalities. This does not mean that from the standpoint of natural law both sides *are* in the right; only that from the standpoint of legality they should both be accounted in the right. It is the consequences of failing to do this that concern Vattel: 'If an unjust war can give rise to no legal rights, no certain possession can be obtained of any property captured in war until a recognized judge, and there is none such between Nations, shall have passed definitely upon the justice of the war; and such property will always be subject to a claim for recovery, as in the case of goods stolen by robbers.'[15] This suggests that territorial acquisitions through war, even if the war is unjust, should be regarded as legitimate lest there be continuing claims for recovery. Because such acquisitions cannot effectively be prohibited, tolerating them will have better consequences than denying their legitimacy.

This would seem to give carte blanche to nations to take what they want whenever they can get away with it. But this, in fact, is the way most nations have conducted themselves throughout history, including the period of European colonialism and the appropriation of North America from the Indians. They have done so to such an extent that if existing territorial boundaries, not to mention the ownership of various kinds of national treasure, were to be subjected to review from the standpoint of historical justice, few claims to legitimacy would survive. Except perhaps in the Middle East, where memories are longer than elsewhere, time generally legitimizes the results of war — at least from the standpoint of legality — if the acquiring nation consolidates its position and is able of achieve stability. For better or worse, this tends to be accepted principle of international affairs.

Thus, paradoxically, in Vattel's view the very law of nature according to which at least one side in a war must be acting unjustly dictates that for the good of all peoples it is best from a legal standpoint that both sides be considered just. This marks a clear separation of the conditions for a morally just war from those for a legally just war. It establishes that nations may wage war for any reason without violating international law. This view prevailed into the twentieth century when, following World War I, with the League of Nations Covenant and the Kellogg-Briand Pact, international law was taken once again to govern recourse to war as well as the conduct of war, a conception reaffirmed at Nuremberg and built into the United Nations Charter.

V

Renewed attention to *jus ad bellum*, the justice of going to war, has, however, brought some changes in the thinking about war.

Classical just war theorists, as we saw in the case of Augustine, believed it was sometimes just to initiate war. The question of who initiates a war was not in itself of particular concern to them. However, in the League of Nations Covenant, the Kellogg-Briand Pact, and the London Charter (Charter of the International Military Tribunal), the emphasis is upon aggression. The crimes against peace for which the defendants at Nuremberg were tried covered 'planning, preparation, initiation or waging of a war of aggression.' And it is the notions of aggressive and defensive wars that have come to dominate the discussions of war throughout much of the twentieth century. Whenever hostilities break out, each side accuses the other of aggression and proclaims that it, on the other hand, acts only in self-defense. Aggression is commonly regarded as a criterion of the illegality of war as well as the immorality of war.

This means there have emerged two sets of distinctions: one between just and unjust war, the other between defensive and aggressive war. Their interrelations are complex in light of the fact that both are subject to different interpretations.

If aggression is understood in a neutral sense (let us call it aggression$_1$), as standing simply for the initiation of hostilities without regard for the rights or wrongs of so doing, then it is clear that a just war in the traditional sense can be either aggressive or defensive. Who initiates a war is irrelevant. What is relevant is whether he has a just cause, is acting from legitimate authority, and so forth. This, however, is at odds with the more recent use of these notions according to which an aggressive war is unjust virtually by definition. In this normative sense (call it aggression$_2$) aggression stands not simply for the initiation of hostilities but for the *unjustified* initiation of hostilities. To call something a war of aggression is not only to classify it; it is to judge it as well.[16]

But even a third use of the notion can be discerned. In Michael Walzer's *Just and Unjust Wars*, it is used in a way that does not even require the initiation of hostilities. Walzer contends that

> aggression can be made out not only in the absence of a military attack or invasion but in the (probable) absence of any immediate intention to launch such an attack or invasion. The general formula must go something like this: states may use military force in the face of threats of war, whenever the failure to do so would seriously risk their territorial integrity or political independence. Under such circumstances it can fairly be said that they have been forced to fight and that they are the victims of aggression.[17]

Such an implicit definition as this (let us call it aggression$_3$) enables one to render just and unjust wars virtually coextensive with defensive and aggressive wars. It expands the notion of aggression to cover cases of mere threats, provided the threats are serious enough. If one assumes further that such threats provide a just cause for going to war in self-defense, this would enable one to hold that it is possible to initiate a just war. In this way, the apparent proscription of the initiation of war in the League of Nation's Covenant, the Kellogg-Briand Pact, the London Charter, and the United Nations Charter is overridden in favor of an approach more in keeping with the traditional just war theory.

This is at some cost, however. For as one moves from aggression$_1$ to aggression$_2$ to aggression$_3$, the conceptual content of the notion changes. In aggression$_1$ there is an objective and neutral criterion for deciding when aggression has occurred, namely, when someone fires the first shot. It may not always be easy to apply in practice, but it is simple and clear. In aggression$_2$ the idea of initiating hostilities is retained, but whether aggression has occurred requires showing that the initiation of hostilities was unjustified. Reference to the initiation of hostilities drops out altogether in aggression$_3$ and is replaced by reference to a 'threat of war' where this does not even require an immediate intention to attack. Aggression$_1$ has the shortcoming that many people, including heads of state, some just war theorists, and experts in international law, feel there are circumstances in which one is justified in initiating war; in other words, that aggression$_1$ is sometimes justified. Israel's attack upon Egypt initiating the 1967 Arab—Israeli War is a case in point. This means that to incorporate this sense of the concept in laws defining criminal action in the resort to war is to render illegal some wars widely held to be just. Aggression$_2$ and aggression$_3$, on the other hand, leave discretion to potential initiators of war to determine when hostilities are warranted. Since virtually every nation that starts a war believes it does so justifiably, this enables nations to go to war pretty much when they want and for whatever reasons they want and to call it a response to aggression. Since, furthermore, to respond to aggression by force is understood by all to be self-defense, and to wage war in self-defense is recognized by all except pacifists to be legitimate, this provides a rationale for virtually every war.

Some of these difficulties figured in the protracted effort by the United Nations to define aggression. If to call something an act of aggression is to imply that it is wrong, no nation will settle for a definition according to which its past or future actions are rendered aggressive. This made agreement on a definition by the United Nations difficult to achieve. The one finally adopted affirms that '[a]ggression is the use of armed force by a State against the sovereignty, territorial integrity or political independence of another State, or in any other way inconsistent with the Charter of the United Nations, as set out in this definition.' However, the second of eight Articles following the definition asserts:

> The first use of armed force by a State in contravention of the Charter shall constitute *prima facie* evidence of an act of aggression although the Security Council may, in conformity with the Charter, conclude that a determination that an act of aggression has been committed would not be justified in the light of other relevant circumstances including the fact that the acts concerned or their consequences are not of sufficient gravity.[18]

This qualification so dilutes the definition as to render it of questionable value. But it does make clear that aggression$_1$ is not the sense the UN Special Committee proposing the definition had in mind, since the first use of force is taken to represent only prima facie evidence of aggression. Defensive wars, once begun, are often directed against the 'sovereignty, territorial integrity or political independence of another State'. The situation is less clear regarding aggression$_2$. But then Article 4 states that 'the acts enumerated above are not exhaustive and the Security Council may determine that other acts constitute aggression under the provisions of the Charter.' This opens up still further the possibility that acts which do not involve the imminent or actual first use of force might nonetheless constitute aggression, which is the essential idea contained in aggression$_3$. It also suggests that the UN attempt to define aggression is hopelessly muddled.

The legality of war is, as we have seen, but one concern of *jus ad bellum*; the main concern is with the morality of war, and parallel problems arise here. Does one, for example, treat the concept of aggression as neutral for purposes of moral judgment, implying nothing one way or the other about the justifiably of the use of force it represents, or does one require as part of the definition that the use of force in question be unjustified? And does one allow that aggression may be committed without the use of force, as allowed by aggression$_3$? In the absence of the resolution of these and related issues, neither the legal nor the moral dimensions of the just war theory can provide adequate criteria for *jus ad bellum*.

VI

Most modern theorists, however, devote little attention to the question of *whether* war is justified; they assume that it is and ask only under what conditions it is justified and how it is to be conducted justly. Their actual prescriptions, in fact, differ little from those of political realists, and apart from the underlying rationales they provide for them it would be difficult to tell them apart. If anything, the just war theorists may be more hardline than political realists, which suggests that adopting a moral perspective does not per se make it less likely that one will be militaristic. They tend to be strongly anticommunist, particularly anti-Soviet, to be pro nuclear deterrence, and to feel that one is sometimes justified in initiating a war. All of them agree, however, that *jus in bello* requires that the conduct of war be limited, and most of them favor a counterforce as opposed to a countervalue (or countercities) policy with respect to the targeting of nuclear weapons.

No single statement of the conditions of just war would do justice to all of the just war theorists, since the number of conditions vary from writer to writer, ranging from about five to ten for both *jus ad bellum* and *jus in bello* combined, and their interpretation often varies as well. But they all include just cause for *jus ad bellum* and principles of proportion and discrimination for *jus in bello*.

A fairly representative statement is that of the National Conference of Catholic Bishops in their pastoral letter on war and peace. For one to be justified in resorting to war, they say, the following conditions must be met:

1 Just Cause: 'War is permissible only to confront "a real and certain danger" i.e., to protect innocent life, to preserve conditions necessary for decent human existence, and to secure basic human rights.'
2 Competent Authority: '[W]ar must be declared by those with responsibility for public order, not by private groups or individuals.'
3 Comparative Justice: In recognition of the fact that there may be some justice on each side, '[e]very party to a conflict should acknowledge the limits of its "just cause" and the consequent requirement to use *only* limited means in pursuit of its objectives.'
4 Right Intention: '[W]ar can be legitimately intended only for the reasons set forth above as a just cause.'

5 Last Resort: 'For resort to war to be justified, all peaceful alternatives must have been exhausted.'

6 Probability of Success: This criterion is not precisely stated, but the bishops affirm that 'its purpose it to prevent irrational resort to force or hopeless resistance when the outcome of either will clearly be disproportionate or futile.'

7 Proportionality: '[T]he damage to be inflicted and the costs incurred by war must be proportionate to the good expected by taking up arms ... This principle of proportionality applies throughout the conduct of the war as well as to the decision to begin warfare.'

Two principles, finally, govern the conduct of war, even when justifiably resorted to:

8 Proportionality: as above.

9 Discrimination: '[T]he lives of innocent persons may never be taken directly, regardless of the purpose alleged for doing so ... Just response to aggression must be ... directed against unjust aggressors, not against innocent people caught up in a war not of their making.'[19]

We find here an elaboration of the conditions set forth by Augustine, with explicit recognition that justification must be given both for the resort to war as well as for the manner of conducting it. There is also recognition here of the problem of whether there can be justice on both sides during a war. The bishops imply there may at least be degrees of justice, that these must be compared, and that war must be kept limited in light of this possibility. Finally, it is notable that the notion of innocent life plays an important role in both areas of *justum bellum*, its protection being a central element in the constitution of a just cause and the prohibition against taking it being a central condition of the just conduct of war. In this, modern just war theorists depart from Augustine, for whom the importance of protecting innocent life is at best implied in the notion of a just cause and virtually absent in the few things he says about the conduct of war. In fact, the idea of protecting innocent life has today become one of the chief justifications for resorting to violence in general. By extension it has come to play an important role in most accounts of *jus ad bellum*. What it is for innocent lives to be 'directly' taken, however, is crucial to understanding *jus in bello*, for in most accounts it is only the direct taking of innocent life (and of the lives of non-combatants, as it is about equally as often put) that is prohibited.

Although just war theorizing has been closely identified with the Catholic tradition, there has been wide interest in it among Protestant and secular writers as well in more recent thought, with Paul Ramsey leading the way among Protestants.[20] He is one of the relatively few to devote much attention to the origins of the just war tradition, and we have considered ... his analysis of Augustine on the matter of noncombatant immunity. We may add here that he breaks with tradition on the issue just considered and reads Augustine as allowing that there may be justice on both sides in war. However, he seems to regard the sense of justice involved in this claim as a subjective one, representing the good will and intentions of a people bound together by agreement on common aims, this constituting a form of political justise. In this he is more in the tradition of Vitoria and Gentili. But he is skeptical about the possibility of discerning true or 'universal' justice in war, and in this his orientation is strongly Augustinian, as the distinction between true and temporal justice was central for Augustine. This leads Ramsey to give limited attention to *jus ad bellum* and to concentrate almost exclusively upon *jus in bello*. His thought also marks a return to another important feature of the classical just war theory in that he allows that sometimes an aggressive (or offensive) war can be just or, at the very least, that a fast adherence to the distinction between aggressive and defensive war is unreasonable. Finally, he virtually identifies just war in the modern age with counterforce war (that is, war targeting only military forces and installations) as opposed to countercities or countervalue war. But although he attaches great importance to noncombatant immunity, he does not see this as precluding the use of nuclear weapons or the destruction of homes that may be used as sanctuaries by the enemy. ...

James Turner Johnson likewise focuses almost exclusively on the question of the conduct of war, saying that his concern is with the *jus in bello* of the just war tradition, the broad cultural consensus on the appropriate limits to force that has developed over Western history'.[21] The problem as he sees it is how to limit the violence of war. The assumption is that certain values are so important that their defense sometimes requires going to war; as he says, '[I]t is sometimes necessary to oppose evil by force unless evil is to triumph.'[22] The just war tradition, he contends, has full relevance to the contemporary situation, and he examines the applicability of *jus in bello* criteria both to nuclear deterrence and to such conventional conflicts as the Falklands War and the Israeli invasion of Lebanon. Indeed, he claims that the ideas contained in the just war tradition represent the 'only way actually open for persons in our culture to think about morality and war'.[23] Although he thinks an all-out nuclear war between the super-powers would strain the limits of a just war conception of proportionality, he believes there are sufficient restraints operating in the international situation to make such an outcome unlikely.[24] Nonetheless he favors the strengthening of conventional forces and the development of weapons that can be used effectively with minimum risk to noncombatants. 'In this regard,' he says, 'the continued existence and enhancement of nuclear deterrent forces, including the progressive development of less massively destructive means of deterrence and alongside the provision of effective means of defense and warfighting capability, is the lesser evil not only politically and militarily, but also morally.'[25]

VII

This issue is important for the just war theory. For however justifiable war is taken to be, one cannot help but wonder whether waging it all-out with nuclear weapons can ever be justified. And if it cannot, can the just war theory remain relevant in the nuclear age?

William V. O'Brien, like Johnson, believes it can, arguing that limited nuclear war need not necessarily escalate into all-out war. But the deeper issue is whether the conditions that make for justice in the recourse to war, whether it be conventional or nuclear, can justify violations of moral constraints in the conduct of war; that is, whether *jus ad bellum* can override *jus in bello* in circumstances in which they conflict. Michael Walzer maintains there may be such violations in the case of what, following Churchill, he calls supreme emergencies, such as was represented by the Nazi threat in World War II. If this should be correct, it would at least open the way (though Walzer does not argue this) to justifying such violations in the case of nuclear war as well. And that is crucial to showing that the just war theory can demonstrate the permissibility of war in the nuclear age, since it is virtually certain ... that one cannot wage modern war of any sort, much less nuclear war, without killing innocent persons.

Walzer's appeal to supreme emergencies has been taken by O'Brien to represent an alternative to the just war theory, and O'Brien argues that the just war approach is the more defensible of the two.[26] I believe it can be shown, however, that there is no significant difference between the ethics of supreme emergency, as O'Brien characterizes it, and the just war theory as he conceives it. This requires taking a closer look at Walzer's theory.

Walzer devotes rather more attention to *jus ad bellum* than do most recent writers, but he also assumes with little argument that war is justified. Although he sometimes speaks as though aggression only creates a presumption in favor of armed resistance, he usually affirms that aggression suffices to justify the resort to war. He says, for example, that '[a]ll aggressive acts have one thing in common; they justify forceful resistance'; and again that '[a]ggression is a singular and undifferentiated crime because, in all its forms, it challenges rights that are worth dying for.'[27] He states unequivocally, however, that *only* the defense of rights can justify war.

His analysis of aggression centers about the legalist paradigm. He analogizes the international order to the civil order, except that the international order 'is unlike domestic society in that every conflict threatens the structure as a whole with collapse. Aggression challenges it directly and is much more dangerous than domestic crime, because there are no policemen.'[28] Because of the gravity of aggressive violations of the international order, the violation of those rights must be vindicated; the members of international society have not done enough if they 'merely contain the aggression or bring it to a speedy end'.

The theory of aggression as he construes it consists of six points: 1 that '[t]here exists an international society of independent states'; 2 that this society has a law establishing the rights of individual members, above all to territorial integrity and political sovereignty; 3 that '[a]ny use of force or imminent threat of force by one state against the political sovereignty or territorial integrity of another constitutes aggression and is a criminal act'. 4 Aggression justifies a war of self-defense by the victim and a 'war of law enforcement' by the victim and any other member of society; 5 'Nothing but aggression can justify war'; and 6 'Once the aggressor state has been militarily repulsed, it can also be punished.'[29]

Walzer then proposes revisions to take account of the disanalogies between domestic and international society. I shall mention only the one of these that bears most directly upon our preceding discussion. It is the revision of 3 above, to count as aggression certain acts that fall short of the first use of force or even an immediate intention to initiate hostilities. It is this which commits him to the concept of aggression$_3$. He finds this revision justified by the 1967 Arab–Israeli War. Though the Israelis launched the initial attack, he believes that circumstances justified the attack because of Egypt's threat to Israel's security. This he believes effectively made Israel a victim of aggression.

Although his emphasis upon aggression has a modern ring, and his insistence that only aggression justifies resort to war seems to place him in the legalist tradition developed since World War I, in certain respects Walzer's position actually lies closer to that of the traditional just war theorists. With Augustine, he emphasizes that resort to war is justified only to vindicate the violation of rights, and his expanded conception of aggression enables him to justify the initiation of war, as Augustine did. In these respects his position is a restatement in modern dress of a basically traditional theory. But in certain other respects, as I shall point out, particularly in what he says about supreme emergencies, it resembles political realism.

It is in his exploration of the relationship between *jus ad bellum* and *jus in bello* that he appeals to supreme emergencies. He contends that justice in these two domains may sometimes conflict. When it does, rules governing the conduct of war may in some circumstances be violated in the promotion of a just cause. Thus he holds that Nazism was such a menace that one could have done anything to defeat it,[30] including violating the rights of the innocent. But he stops short of saying that one is justified in doing this. Rather, he says that the rights violated remain in effect even as one violates them.[31] Johnson, it should be noted, takes this issue to be so important that he says: 'The problem of just warfare in the contemporary age is not the problem of warfare in this age as such; rather, it is the problem of how to avoid what Michael Walzer terms "supreme emergency" situations.'[32]

Walzer's last contention is as important as it is puzzling. There are two ways of reading it. According to the first, individual rights sometimes have to be overridden in the interests of a just cause, namely, in circumstances of supreme emergency. The rights remain 'in effect' only in the sense that they remain prima facie claims to certain sorts of treatment. According to the second interpretation, the rights remain fully in effect, and their violation is wrong even though it is morally justified by the supreme emergency. This, however, would seem to render some actions both right and wrong at the same time, and as this is incoherent, I shall assume that Walzer intends the first interpretation. The first, in any event, is consistent with the few remarks he makes about the moral theory underlying his position.

That theory is a morality of human rights, with considerations of utility secondary.[33] But when it comes to justifying the violation of the rights of the innocent — apparently to the point of being willing to kill them[34] — the situation is reversed. In a tantalizingly equivocal passage, Walzer says first that the rights of innocent people 'cannot simply be set aside, nor can they be balanced, in utilitarian fashion, against this or that desirable outcome,' and then:

> And yet the case for breaking the rules and violating those rights is made sufficiently often, and by soldiers and statesmen who cannot always be called wicked, so that we have to assume that it isn't pointless. Anyway, we know its point all too well. We know how high the stakes sometimes are in war and how urgent victory can be ... The very existence of a community may be at stake, and then how can we fail to consider possible outcomes in judging the course of the fighting? At this point if at no other, the restraint on utilitarian calculation must be lifted.[35]

As though unable to let stand a decision on the dilemma he has posed between collective security and individual rights, he then adds: 'Even if we are inclined to lift it [the restraint on utilitarian calculation], however, we cannot forget that the rights violated for the sake of victory are genuine rights, deeply founded and in principle inviolable.'[36]

He seems, in the last analysis, then, to say that utilitarian considerations sometimes override rights. But whatever the justification, the appeal in the above passage is to the survival of the 'community', presumably meaning the nation or state; which suggests that national survival, or more basically, national egoism, is the governing norm. He does not always speak this way; sometimes he speaks of opposing 'immeasurable evil' and the like. But repeatedly it is the survival and well-being of the state that is his ultimate appeal, which means that reason of state begins to show itself in the guise of the just war theory. The survival of the state becomes the ultimate end (with no clear underlying moral justification of that end), and one is willing to do anything to promote that end.

O'Brien contends that Walzer's position, though resembling that of the German doctrine of *Kriegsraison* during World War I (basically, an unqualified principle of military necessity), differs from that position in that Walzer allows that measures warranted by supreme emergencies are justified only so long as the emergency lasts.[37] When they are no longer necessary one must conform once again to moral constraints in the conduct of war. The allies during World War II failed to recognize this limitation, O'Brien argues, in their bombing of cities; hence although their policies differed from those of the German proponents of *Kriegsraison* of World War I in that their justification was much more plausible, 'they resembled the Germans in their propensity to use exceptional and morally impermissible means beyond the point where they could be justified by even a bona fide argument of necessity.'[38]

Whatever the actual practice of the Germans in World War I and the allies in World War II, there is nothing in the notion of military necessity to authorize killing and destruction beyond what is militarily necessary; while it does not preclude going beyond that, military necessity provides no authorization for doing so. And in circumstances of supreme emergency, exceptional measures are called for precisely *because* they are militarily necessary; there would be no warrant in Walzer's view for violating the rights of innocent persons were that not the only way to preserve the community or to combat 'immeasurable evils'. As circumstances change, those measures may no longer be justified. But that is because they are no longer *necessary*. By the same token, measures that are militarily necessary in one set of circumstances may cease to be so in others. Their justification on grounds of military necessity then likewise ceases. So whatever the end for which one is fighting, and however justified the resort to war in the first place, Walzer's supreme emergency provisions justify the same measures as military necessity. For this reason, *if* Walzer believes that it is the preservation of the state that justifies the resort to war and the resort, when in war, to the extraordinary measures called for by supreme emergencies, his position begins to look indistiguishable in practical import from that of political realism.

O'Brien points out that *Kriegsraison* as advanced by Germany during World War I held that 'the German state possessed superior worth and had the right to greater latitude in self-preservation and self-advancement than other states.'[39] He discounts this claim, saying that 'Germany would be eligible for a supreme-emergency claim if its very existence and its fundamental values were at stake, but no more eligible than any other state.' This is an important observation. It reflects the fact that if a principle is to have any claim to being moral it must extend equally to all and be equally usable by them in the same sorts of circumstances. But would one be willing to acknowledge the right of Nazi Germany to make such a claim? Few even consider the kind of justification the Nazis gave for their policies; as O'Brien says, 'I take it that it is unnecessary to discuss justification for the conduct of the Third Reich in World War II.'[40]

But *Mein Kampf* represents the German nation (meaning the German people, not the state) as confronting the very kind of threat to its survival and values that Walzer takes to justify supreme emergencies and that just war theorists almost universally take to constitute a just cause. Hitler saw the German nation as threatened by a Marxist—Jewish conspiracy of diabolical proportions, sapping its life, poisoning its blood, and dragging it down from its prior heights of cultural achievement. Reason of state demanded strong measures. This led to the Nuremberg Laws of 1935, to increasing persecutions of Jews and Communists (and others considered undesirable for other reasons), and eventually to exterminations of both as war broke out. That many more Jews were exterminated than non-Jews should not obscure the fact that in Hitler's mind Jews and Communists were part of the same threat. That he was mistaken in these views is beside the point. One acts necessarily upon what he *believes*. People can only apply principles that seem to them relevant. And this allows for error. So, if one lays down such requirements for a just war as that one have a just cause, what this means in practice is that nations may resort to war when they *believe* they have a just cause. By the same token, to justify the killing of innocent persons when necessitated by a supreme emergency is to say, in effect, that nations may resort to such measures when they *believe* they confront such an emergency. And in Walzer's account, as well as those of just war theorists, it is always the nation proposing to resort to war that is the judge of whether it has justice on its side or whether a given emergency is supreme. There is no correcting mechanism by which to detect errors. (Augustine had a better sense of this than some contemporary theorists because he recognized that one can never know when true justice is present.) It also does little to argue that Hitler did not really believe these things. The evidence is that he did. To imply otherwise is to underestimate the seriousness of the threat he posed and the sense of conviction he imparted to followers. And in any event one *could* believe equally vile things and convince himself that equally severe measures were justified for the survival of the state or of a particular people. If claims of supreme emergency, or appeals to military necessity, are to have even a prima facie warrant to being moral, they must be available equally to all to use.

Do Walzer and O'Brien differ sufficiently on these issues to warrant saying that their analyses represent different approaches to the morality of war? I suggest they do not. Their accounts will likely justify precisely the same sorts of acts and in the same sorts of circumstances, with only the rationales differing in certain points of detail.

Walzer contends that in supreme emergencies one may override the rights of innocent persons. And O'Brien says repeatedly that violations of the principles of proportionality and discrimination by the allies during World War II and by the United States in Korea and Vietnam did not prevent those wars from being just.[41] The violations were *wrong*; unlike Walzer, he is unequivocal about this. It is just that they were offset by the overwhelmingly just causes for which the United States was fighting. But to say that a war can be just *overall* despite violations of *jus in bello* criteria differs little from saying that a war can be just even though supreme emergencies justify violating these criteria. It is just that in the one case the rights of the innocent are violated, in the others they are 'overriden'. The overwhelmingly just cause and the supreme emergency become practically equivalent. Both Walzer and O'Brien think war may be a justifiable response to aggression, and both think that response may necessitate violating the moral constraints upon the conduct of war (with O'Brien holding further that such a war may be just even if such violations occur but are not necessitated). That is, both believe that there may be conflicts between *jus ad bellum* and *jus in bello* and that when they occur *jus ad bellum* may override *jus in bello*.

If now we return to the second of the objections considered at the outset of this chapter, concerning the relevance of the just war approach to the nuclear age, we may observe that for all of this O'Brien may nonetheless be correct in saying in response to that objection that a limited use of nuclear weapons would not necessarily escalate into an all-out war. No one can know for certain. If *that* is what is meant by saying that the just war theory is relevant to the nuclear age, the point can be granted and the second objection considered met.

But there is another reply to the objection that is more telling. It is that even if O'Brien and others should be wrong about the possibility of keeping a limited nuclear war limited, all that would follow is that by just war criteria themselves an all-out war would be unjust. The fact that a certain type of war turns out to be unjust does not show that the just war theory is inapplicable to it; it shows only that it yields a certain outcome when applied to that type of war.[42] So if the question is whether the nuclear age has rendered the just war theory obsolete in the sense of showing that its criteria are no longer appropriate for the assessment of war, the answer is that it has not. Whether some, or all, or no nuclear wars turn out to be just by just war criteria is immaterial. That those assessments can be made shows the relevance of the theory to nuclear war in the sense its advocates intend.

The preceding discussion suggests a third and more serious objection to the just war doctrine. We have seen that there are serious problems in reconciling the claims of *jus ad bellum* with those of *jus in bello* with regard to whether a just cause sometimes warrants, or at least excuses, violations of moral constraints in the conduct of war. A more fundamental question is whether even a war that is just according to both *jus ad bellum* and *jus in bello* criteria will still unavoidably involve the violation of moral constraints; whether, that is, there is something in the very nature of war that renders it wrong and that is not dealt with directly by the just war theory. The just war theory says that if certain conditions are met, it is permissible to go to war; and it says further that if certain other conditions are met, one's manner of conducting the war is moral. What it does not do is to ask whether there are things that one unavoidably does even when *all* of these conditions are met which cannot be justified morally. If there are, then the just war theory is defective in a far more serious way than suggested by either of the first two objections.

I believe that there are, and that is what I shall argue. ... But the issue is complex and requires an examination of the relationship between *jus ad bellum* and *jus in bello*.

VIII

A war, once again, is justified if it is characterized by *jus ad bellum*: if, that is, the conditions constituting justice in the resort to war are met. These include but are not limited to a just cause. Traditionally, as we have seen, one had to have legitimate authority and a right intention as well, with various other requirements often added, such as that the war be a last resort, have a likelihood of success, that the use of force be restrained, and that there be proportionality in the resultant good and evil.

A justified war, however, is not necessarily a just war. To be fully just a war must be characterized by both *jus ad bellum* and *jus in bello*. A war obviously cannot be just if one is unjustified in entering upon it in the first place, but neither can it be just, however just the cause and right the intention, if it utilizes indefensible means.[43] Even those like Walzer who think that normally indefensible means may sometimes be used affirm this. Though the earliest just war theorists gave insufficient attention to this issue, there must be rules or principles governing the conduct of war as well as governing the decision to enter into it.

Notice that I am concerned here with what is morally justified in the conduct of war, not with what is legally justified. There exist certain rules, known as the laws of war, generally accepted as governing the conduct of warfare on all sides. These, as we have seen, are part of international law. Individual soldiers, whether fighting for a just cause or not, are not considered accountable for their participation in a war so long as they observe these rules. This, however, is not my concern at the moment. My concern is with what is morally justified in warfare, whether or not it coincides with what is legally permissible. The laws of war, as Grotius recognized,[44] might as a matter of fact allow many things that in the last analysis cannot be justified morally.

In the eighteenth century William Paley proposed a principle to govern the conduct of war in his *Principles of Moral and Political Philosophy*, writing that 'if the cause and end of war be justifiable; all the means that appear necessary to the end, are justifiable also.'[45] Súarez before him had written even more simply that 'if the end is permissible, the necessary means to that end are also permissible.'[46] Except that they are intended to apply only to just wars, and that Súarez expressly added a prohibition against the killing of innocents, these formulations resemble the principle of military necessity. If one is justified in going to war, they say, he is justified in doing whatever is necessary to win. Moderation in the prosecution of a just war, in the sense of refraining from doing what is necessary to achieve your objectives, would be no less an absurdity on this reasoning than Clausewitz thought it to be in the prosecution of any war.

Let us call the principle that one may do whatever is necessary to prosecute a just war a principle of just necessity. Though only occasionally expressly formulated, it probably has many adherents. One often hears that it is wrong to send men to fight and be killed unless you are willing to fight to win. If one adds to this the qualification that it applies only to justified wars, as often seems the intent, one has just necessity.

According to this view, then, whatever justifies resorting to war in the first place justifies the means necessary to winning it (or achieving one's objectives, if they fall short of victory). There are no independent moral constraints upon the conduct of war. This represents what may be called an internalist view of the relationship between *jus ad bellum* and *jus in bello*, in the sense that the standards for judging *jus in bello* are already, as it were, contained in the standards for judging *jus ad bellum*.

Distinguished from this, however, is an externalist view, which holds that there are independent standards for judging *jus in bello* — independent, that is, of *jus ad bellum*. Whatever the justice of one's resort to war, there are in this view limits to what one may do in conducting it. The most prominent of these concerns the treatment of innocent persons, with writers like Ramsey, Phillips, and Anscombe maintaining that there is an absolute prohibition against the intentional killing of such persons.[47]

The issue between internalism and externalism in the theory of *jus in bello* is important because whatever undesirable consequences follow from the principle of military necessity also follow from the principle of just necessity in a justified war. Any action that one principle legitimizes the other will also.

It is easily imaginable that the only way to win an otherwise just war (assuming there may be such) would be to demoralize the civilian population by terror bombing. This, indeed, was much the rationale for the saturation bombing of German cities during World War II, except there the bombing was probably thought necessary only to hasten victory, not to achieve it. But if World War II was a just war on the side of the allies, and if such bombing *had been* necessary to win, just necessity no less than military necessity or supreme emergency would have dictated it. If, moreover, Elihu Root was correct that adherence to military necessity would spell the end of international law, then one should expect the same to be true of adherence to just necessity; or at least that it would have a strong tendency to that end (unlike military necessity it will be implementable only by the side acting justly, and hence its bad effects may reasonably be thought to be less than in the case of military necessity). Circumstances can bring military necessity into conflict with international law. These may have nothing to do with the justice of the war and can arise as easily in a just war (meaning for the side that is warring justly) as in an unjust one.

To justify the pursuit of victory in war requires showing that the necessary means to that end are justified. The permissibility of going to war provides no assurance they will be. One may not even know fully what those means are until the war has progressed, perhaps nearly to its conclusion. Yet, according to the usual thinking in just war theory, one may know in advance of going to war whether or not he is justified in so doing. If that is true, then the standards for *jus ad bellum* cannot by themselves, determine the standards for *jus in bello*.

This means that the internalist position, and with it the principle of just necessity, must be rejected. It is not the end that justifies the means but the means (among other things) that justify the end.[48]

This has even more far-reaching implications. Both the internalist and the externalist assume that war may be just; they differ only over the criteria for *jus in bello*. But if the impermissibility of the means necessary to win a war means that one may not justly pursue victory in that war, then the impermissibility of the acts necessary to the very *waging* of war mean that one may not justly wage war, whatever one's objectives. Waging war requires justifying the means of so doing as much as winning a war requires justifying the means to that end.[49]

To justify going to war, then, that is, to establish *jus ad bellum* in the first place, requires showing that what one would be doing by waging it is justified. If a war is justified, then the necessary means to waging it will indeed *be* justified — but not because they are legitimated by the justice of the war assessed independently of those means. They will be justified because to be justified in going to war requires establishing antecedently that those means are permissible. Again, it is not the end that justifies the means but the permissibility of the means (including the killing and destroying that are part of the nature of warfare) that, along with satisfaction of the other requirements of *jus ad bellum*, justifies the end.

The point is that killing and destruction are inherent in warfare, and unless they can be justified, war cannot be justified. It will by its very nature be wrong.

Two conclusions follow from this. First, the issue of a possible conflict between *jus ad bellum* and *jus in bello* is more complicated than it first appears. There cannot be a conflict between the two on the internalist view because the standards for the former constitute the standards for the latter. Satisfaction of the conditions of *jus ad bellum* (just cause, right intention, and the like) in the light of the principle of just necessity entails satisfaction of the conditions of *jus in bello* as well — at least so long as one does only what is necessary to achieving one's objectives and does not engage in gratuitous violence. But there can be a conflict on the externalist view if one assumes, as much of the just war tradition does, that it is possible to justify the resort to war independently of consideration of the constraints upon its conduct. For then one might adopt unjustifiable means to the attainment of otherwise justifiable ends. But there are compelling reasons for dropping this latter assumption. One does not just go to war. One goes to war for certain reasons, to achieve certain ends or objectives. The very act of embarking upon war presupposes them, as does the selection of certain means by which to try to achieve them. This means that to justify going to war requires justifying the selection of means from the outset. There are not two separate acts here, the embarking upon war and the implementing of chosen means. To embark upon war *is* to implement chosen means. What one justifies doing, in applying the standards of *jus ad bellum*, is inseparable from the conduct of war. Not that there cannot still be a conflict between *jus ad bellum* and *jus in bello*; as I have said, one may not always know in advance precisely what means the successful prosecution of a war will require. As events unfold, to prevail in a war may require the resort to morally impermissible tactics that could not have been foreseen at its outset. This notwithstanding, one can never justify the resort to war without justifying the means by which one proposes to fight the war.

On the other hand, there is no presumption at all that a war that meets the conditions of *jus in bello*, as these are usually conceived, will meet those of *jus ad bellum*. I am speaking here of the usual conditions that comprise the rules of war (regarding noncombatant immunity, treatment of prisoners, and the like). War is not a game. Following the rules is not exculpatory if you should not be involved in the enterprise in the first place. Even when the conditions are intended to be moral, like those of proportionality and discrimination, they do not ensure the justifiability of resorting to war. It would be different if they included *all* of the morally relevant considerations pertaining to the treatment of persons. For then, if those conditions were met, a war could hardly fail to be just, since everything one did in the course of fighting it would be permissible. To say one might still be acting wrongly by fighting it would then be vacuous. So, if *jus in bello* were understood in this way (which it is not by just war theorists), the satisfaction of its standards would virtually guarantee the satisfaction of those of *jus ad bellum* as well.

The relevant question, then, is whether all of what one does in the course of fighting a war can be morally justified (by which I mean, all of what one does that is associated with the nature of war; obviously one can do many gratuitously barbarous things that are unessential to the aims of war and that are morally prohibited). This is why I say that in addition to justifying the *means* of conducting war as part of justifying the resort to war, one must also justify those acts which are *constitutive* of the waging of war by whatever means. War by its nature is organized violence, the deliberate, systematic causing of death and destruction. This is true whether the means employed are nuclear bombs or bows and arrows. Often it is the doing of psychological violence as well ... So given that one can know to a virtual certainty that he commits himself to doing these things in going to war, fully to justify going to war requires justifying these acts as well. A necessary condition of the justifiable pursuit of *any objectives* in war, by *any means* whatever (hence a necessary condition of the satisfaction of the criteria of both *jus ad bellum* and *jus in bello*), is that one be justified in engaging in such killing and violence in the first place.

Second, and relatedly, this means that most attempts to justify war from the early just war theorists to the present day are inadequate. For they do not meet this necessary condition.

Discussions of *jus in bello*, if they deal with the conduct of war in moral rather than just legal terms at all, talk mainly about whom one may kill and in what proportions one may cause destruction, not about whether that which they seek to regulate should be taking place at all. That is supposedly the province of *jus ad bellum*. But discussions of *jus ad bellum* mainly require both certification that an appropriate wrong has been committed, that is, that one has a just cause, and satisfaction of other conditions (like legitimate authority, right intention, probability of success, etc.) which are appropriate if one assumes *in advance* that killing and violence are justifiable responses to wrongdoing but which do not establish that. It is as though the only question were what violence is acceptable and the only issue were to specify when it is acceptable – with little recognition of the fact that, to establish that wrongdoing has occurred does not suffice to establish what one's response to it should be, that the response is a separate act and needs justifying in its own right. Most just war theorists proceed, in short, as though they assume that one can justify the resort to war independently of, and antecedently to, justifying both the necessary means to conducting it and the acts constitutive of waging it.[50]

If this is correct, it means that attention in *jus ad bellum* must be shifted away from the almost exclusive concern with the offenses and ancillary conditions commonly thought to justify war to a consideration of the precise nature of what one is doing in the waging of it; not, as in traditional accounts of *jus in bello*, starting from the assumption that war is justified and needs only to be waged humanely, but rather starting with an open mind about whether it is ever justified in the first place. *Unless one can justify the actions necessary to waging war, he cannot justify the conduct of war and the pursuit of its objectives; and if he cannot do this, he cannot justify going to war.*

So what we might call justice in the waging of war (by which I mean the justifiability of the violence and killing and destruction that are part of the nature of warfare) is a necessary condition of both justice in the conduct of war (*jus in bello*) and justice in the resort to war (*jus ad bellum*).[51] This means further that as interesting and important as many of the historical and contemporary issues are in the just war tradition — issues concerning what constitutes a just cause, what constitutes aggression, whether nuclear war can ever be justified, and so forth — their satisfactory resolution can never by itself justify the resort to war. In short, the just war theory in its historical and contemporary forms fails to do justice to the central moral problems in war's justification.

NOTES

1 Ali Raza Navqvi, 'Laws of War in Islam', *Islamic Studies* 13, no 1 (Mar. 1974): 25.
2 Michael Walzer, *Just and Unjust Wars* (New York: Basic Books, 1977), p. 282.
3 See James Turner Johnson, *Can Modern War Be Just?* (New Haven, Conn.: Yale University Press, 1984); William V. O'Brien, *The Conduct of a Just and Limited War* (New York: Praeger, 1981); William V. O'Brien and John Lagan, eds, *The Nuclear Dilemma and The Just War Tradition* (Lexington, MA: Lexington Books, 1986); and Robert L. Phillips, *War and Justice* (Norman: University of Oklahoma Press, 1984).
4 *The Summa Theologica of Saint Thomas Aquinas*, Dominican trans. (London: Burns Oates & Washbourne, Ltd., 1929), II–II, q. 64, art. 7. See also q. 40, art. 1. Aquinas is sometimes thought to have added a fourth condition, that there be a right use of means as well. See Austin Fagothy, *Right and reason: Ethics in Theory and Practice* (St Louis: The C. V. Mosby Company, 1953), p. 516.
5 See, for example, The Pastoral Letter on War and Peace of the National Conference of Catholic Bishops, *The Challenge of Peace: Promise and Our Response* (Washington, DC: United States Catholic Conference, 1983), p. 30; Phillips, *War and Justice*, chap. 2; Paul

Ramsey, 'Vietnam and Just War', *Dialog* 6 (Winter 1967): 19–29, reprinted in *The Just War: Force and Political Responsibility* (New York: Charles Scribner & Sons, 1986), pp. 497–512.

6 *The Spanish Origins of International Law: Francisco De Vitoria and His Law of Nations*, pt. 1, app. B, *De Jure Belli*, in *The Classics of International Law*, ed. James Brown Scott (Oxford: Clarendon Press, 1934), pp. lx–lxi.

7 A war that is truly just in the Augustinian sense would be objectively just in this sense, and vice versa. But a war that is subjectively just in this sense, that is, which is merely *believed* to be just, might or might not be temporally just in the Augustinian sense. The sixteenth century writer A. Gentili is sometimes thought to have maintained that justice can reside on both sides in war. But despite some misleading statements, his position is not far from Vitoria's. He maintains, for example, that the Israelites, led by the voice of God, justly made war against the Canaanite and that the later nonetheless justly resisted in self-defense, through ignorance of divine law. But even he distinguishes between 'that purest and truest form of justice, which cannot conceive of both parties to a dispute being in the right' and justice as it appears from man's standpoint, and asserts that 'therefore we aim at justice as it appears from man's standpoint'. As undeveloped as the point is, he tacitly invoked a similar – though not identical – distinction to that made by Vitoria. He hedges still further by adverting to his normative definition of war as 'a just and public contest of arms' and claims that if one side is contending 'without any adequate reason, that party is surely practicing brigandage and not waging war'; and thus he says that 'if it is doubtful on which side justice is, and if each side aims at justice, neither can be called unjust.' For quoted material see Alberico Gentili, *De Jure Belli: Libri Tres*, in *The Classics of International Law*, ed. James Brown Scott, trans. John D. Rolfe (Oxford: Clarendon Press, 1933) pp. 31–2. Hugo Grotius, sometimes thought of as the father of international law, clearly recognizes different senses of justice in his treatment of this topic in the seventeenth century. See Hugo Grotius, *De Jure Belli ac Pacis Libri Tres*, in *The Classics of International Law*, ed. James Brown Scott, trans. Francis W. Kelsey (Oxford: Clarendon Press, 1925), pp. 565–6.

8 Prolegomena, *De Jure Belli ac Pacis Libri Tres*, p. 20.

9 *The Treatises of M. T. Cicero*, Trans. C. D. Yonge (London: George Bell and Sons, York St., Covent Garden, 1876), p. 431.

10 Grotius, *De Jure Belli ac Pacis Libri Tres*, p. 44.

11 *Principles of International Law* (Berkeley: University of California Press, 1952), p. 417, as cited in William W. Bishop Jr., ed., *International Law: Cases and Materials*, 3rd. edn (Boston: Little, Brown and Company, 1962), p. 9.

12 *International Military Tribunal, Trial of Major War Criminals, Proceedings* (Nuremberg, Germany, 1948), 22:464.

13 E. de Vattel, *The Law of Nations or the Principles of National Law: Applied to the Conduct and to the Affairs of Nations and of Sovereigns*, in *Classics of International Law*, ed. James Brown Scott, trans. Charles G. Fenwick (Washington: The Carnegie Institute of Washington, 1916), 3:306.

14 Ibid., p. 305. Cf. Hugo Grotius, *De Jure Belli ac Pacis Libri Tres*, p. 644.

15 E. de Vattel, *The Law of Nations*, p. 304.

16 For a somewhat different way of drawing the distinction among kinds of aggression, see Yehuda Melzer, *Concepts of Just War* (Leyden: A. W. Sijthoff, 1975), pp. 86−7. Aggression, I have suggested, is the sense found most often in discussions. A theoretical basis for a somewhat similar account is provided by David Luban in his essay 'Just War and Human Rights', *Public Affairs* 9, no. 2 (Winter 1980): 160−81. He argues that aggression should be regarded as a crime against individuals, not states. States, he reasons, have a right against aggression only insofar as they enjoy legitimacy, where legitimacy must be understood in terms of the honoring of human rights. Thus he believes that unjust war can be defined as war subversive of human rights. Aggression, though it does not figure explicitly in the characterization of a just war, is then understood in terms of the subversion of human rights. This makes it an evaluative notion, though not one that entails the initiation of hostilities. In any event, his characterization of a just war as '(i) a war of defense of socially basic human rights (subject to proportionality); or (ii) a war of self-defense against an unjust war' (p. 175) enables him to say, in keeping with classical theorists, that aggression is not the sole crime of war.

The Pastoral Letter of the National Conference of Catholic Bishops similarly characterizes just war in terms of human rights. In setting down the requirements for a just cause it says: 'War is permissible only to confront 'a real and certain danger', i.e., to protect innocent life, to preserve conditions necessary for decent human existence, and to secure basic human rights' (*The Challenge of Peace: God's Promise and Our Response*, p. 28). Though the bishops seem not to recognize this, such a characterization leaves open the possibility that a just war could be an aggressive war, that is, one in which the just side initiates hostilities. It is easily conceivable that protection of innocent life and the security of human rights might require initiating hostilities; this, after all was among the rationales given for the US invasion of Grenada in 1983. 'The present-day conception of "aggression",' Elizabeth Anscombe says on this issue, referring pretty clearly to aggression, 'like so many strongly influential conceptions, is a bad one. Why *must* it be wrong to strike the first blow in a struggle? The only question is, who is in the right.' See 'War and Murder', in *War and Morality*, ed. Richard Wasserstrom (Belmont, CA: Wadsworth Publishing Company, Inc., 1970), pp. 43−4. In a similar vein, Paul Ramsey observes, 'There is really no reason to be found in the justice of war itself for forbidding aggressive war and allowing only the right of self-defense or for forbidding the use of certain weapons systems as such.' See 'Tucker's Bellum Contra Bellum Justum', in *Just War and Vatican II: A Critique*, by Robert W. Tucker, with commentary by Paul Ramsey et al. (New York: The Council on Religion and International Affairs, 1966), p. 100; reprinted in Ramsey, *The Just War*, chap. 17. See also Johnson, *Can Modern War Be Just?* pp. 177–8, and Tucker, *The Just War: A Study in Contemporary American Doctrine*, p. 15.

17 Page 85.

18 This and the above definition are cited in Melzer, *Concepts of Just War*, pp. 29–30. Melzer's book contains an excellent discussion of these and related issues. See further, Julius Stone, *Conflict Through Consensus: United Nations Approaches to Aggression* (Baltimore: The Johns Hopkins University Press, 1977).

19 See the Pastoral Letter of the National Conference of Catholic Bishops, *The Challenge of Peace: God's Promise and Our Response*, pp. 28–34.

20 See his *War and the Christian Conscience: How Shall Modern War be Conducted Justly?* (Durham, NC: Duke University Press, 1961) and *The Just War*.

21 Johnson, *Can Modern War Be Just?*, p. 3.

22 Ibid., pp. 31, 94.

23 Ibid., p. 29.

24 Ibid., p. 186.

25 Ibid., p. 104.

26 See his 'The Future of the Nuclear Debate', in O'Brien and Langan, eds, *The Nuclear Dilemma and the Just War Tradition*, pp. 223–48.

27 Walzer, *Just and Unjust Wars*, pp. 52–3.

28 Ibid., p. 59.

29 Ibid., pp. 61–2.

30 Ibid., pp. 248–9.

31 Ibid., p. 231.

32 Johnson, *Can Modern War Be Just?*, p. 185.

33 Walzer, *Just and Unjust Wars*, p. xvi.

34 Ibid., pp. 259–60.

35 Ibid., p. 228.

36 Ibid.

37 In, 'The Future of the Nuclear Debate', in O'Brien and Langan, eds, *The Nuclear Dilemma and the Just War Tradition*, p. 235.

38 Ibid., p. 233.

39 Ibid., p. 231.

40 Ibid.

41 See his *The Conduct of a Just and Limited War*, chaps 4 and 5.

42 This point is well made by Phillips in *War and Justice*, p. xi.

43 On the issue of the relationship between *jus ad bellum* and *jus in bello*, see Melzer, *Concepts of Just War*, esp. chap. 2.

44 *De Jure Belli ac Pacis Libri Tres*, bk. 3, chap. 10.

45 *The Principles of Moral and Political Philosophy* (London: J. Faulder, 1814), 2: 425.

46 *Selections for the Three Works of Francisco Suarez*, specifically *On the Three Theological Virtues: On Charity* (disputation 13: On War, sec. 7, p. 840), in *The Classics of International Law*, ed. James Brown Scott (Oxford: Clarendon Press, 1944). See also Hugo Grotius, *De Jure Belli ac Pacis Libri Tres*, p. 599. In a more recent approximation, Robert W. Tucker says that 'the ethics of war may justify the use of almost any weapons and the employment of any methods of which realize the ends or purposes of the just war' (*The Just War: A Study in Contemporary American Doctrine*, p. 75). Walzer considers much this same principle in responding to possible criticisms of his own view of combat equality (see *Just and Unjust Wars*, p. 230).

47 See Anscombe, 'War and Murder', in Wasserstrom ed., *War and Morality*, pp. 42–53; Phillips, *War and Justice*, Chap. 2; and Ramsey, *The Just War*, especially chap. 7.

48 One is justified in performing any act only if he is justified both in employing the means necessary to its performance and in performing any subsidiary acts constitutive of it. I cannot be justified in watering my garden unless I am justified in attaching the hose and turning on the water; or in mowing my lawn unless I am justified in cutting the grass. The justification of the act is not one thing and the justification of the means another. What one justifies in the first place *are* those means; to justify the act *is* to justify the means (and/or the constitutive acts). This is the truth in the saying that the end does not justify the means.

Some, of course, would argue that if the end is justified, then so must be the means. And this is true, if properly understood. But it does not follow from it that the end justifies the means. For there is an asymmetry here. One must justify the necessary means before one can justify pursuing the end, whereas the reverse is not the case. I do not need to justify watering my garden before I justify hooking up the hose and turning on the water; I may do these things as means to a different end, such as washing the car. If the end is justified, the means will in fact *be* justified. But that is because one must justify them in course of justifying the end, not because the justification of the end in isolation somehow justifies them.

49 I am, for the sake of simplicity, speaking here as though what one must do in order to wage war constitutes the means of waging war. In actuality, those acts are constitutive of waging war. There are two related but distinguishable relationships here. One is that of means to end. It figures in the argument to show that the internalist position is incorrect. It involves showing that the means to victory in war must be justified in their own right; their permissibility does not follow automatically from the fact that the resort to war may be justified. The other is that of constituent to whole; it is central to the present argument regarding the justification of the resort to war,

which involves pointing out that to be justified in resorting to what one must be justified in doing all those things that make up the waging of war.

50   This is not, I should say, true of all just war theorists. Among classical theorists, Grotius is notable for trying to specify with some precision the conditions under which an individual person's life may be taken. See *De Jure Belli ac Pacis Libri Tres*, bk. 13, chap. 11. And both he and Augustine, as well as others, deem it important to try to rebut interpretations of the New Testament that would seem to block the way to justifying the violence of war.

51   The American Catholic bishops show an awareness of this when they acknowledge the presumption against war and ask: '[D]o the rights and values involved justify killing? For whatever the means used, war, by definition, involves violence, destruction, suffering, and death.' (*The Challenge of Peace: God's Promise and Our Response*, p. 29).

8

Morality and Survival in the Nuclear Age

SUSAN KHIN ZAW

I

Most people feel that the existence of nuclear weapons confronts us with some kind of moral difficulty or dilemma, or that their advent on the scene has somehow made a moral difference. I believe that this feeling is right, that nuclear weapons have changed our moral world, but that we do not yet have a very clear perception of this change. Consequently attempts to grapple with the moral issues raised by nuclear weapons often misidentify the issues and thus seem academic and unsatisfying. This paper attempts to redescribe the change in our moral world in a way which will allow moral concerns to take their proper place and have their proper weight in the political and strategic debate.

What then are the current areas of moral disagreement about nuclear weapons, and in what way is the discussion in these areas unsatisfying? The first thing to note is that there is at least some *agreement*: most seem to agree that total nuclear war would be a moral catastrophe, i.e. it would certainly be a terrible moral wrong if both superpowers actually did fire off all their existing nuclear weapons. However there is considerable debate about the morality of:

1 deterrence, i.e. *threatening* and/or *intending* to launch a full-scale nuclear attack;
2 *limited* nuclear war between the super-powers, as envisaged in 'flexible response' scenarios;

Reprinted with permission from Nigel Blake and Kay Pole (eds) *Objections to Nuclear Defense Philosophies on Deterrence* (Routledge & Kegan Paul, London, 1984), pp. 115–43.

3   use of nuclear weapons on a small (virtually 'one-off') scale by small powers in the settlement of local differences.

Even in relation to these areas of debate, though, there is some measure of agreement. It is generally agreed that discussing 1 and 2 in isolation is somewhat academic, since both cases carry a high risk of escalation to all-out world nuclear war. Still, are there any special moral problems associated with 'flexible response' itself? Well, the point of flexible response must be to make limited nuclear war at least *possible*; and given that a state of limited war exists, it would clearly be right for the superpowers to seek to avoid escalation rather than to invite it. Now, if the best chance of this lay in making sure in advance that no limited nuclear exchange took place on the nuclear superpowers' own territories, then the moral obligation of doing one's best to avert the moral catastrophe of *total* holocaust might seem to make it a moral requirement that they should find somewhere other than their own territories to fight the limited nuclear wars which flexible response make possible. But clearly a nuclear war 'limited' to say, the European theatre would almost certainly end up as a 'total' war as far as Europe was concerned (that is, Europe could expect to be totally destroyed as a human habitat), and if the superpowers actually did thus destroy some other part of the world in pursuit of their own policy objectives, few would deny that they would be doing a terrible moral wrong. Yet it seems that accepting the possibility of doing this terrible wrong, and indeed intending to do it and threatening to do it if the need arose, would be part of a flexible response capability which took the risk of escalation seriously, and might even be morally required of it. This version of flexible response thus raises the same moral problem as deterrence: namely, can it be right to threaten or intend to do something acknowledged to be terribly wrong, even for the sake of avoiding actually having to do it? Europeans may feel themselves caught in a special moral dilemma, however. Concern for the welfare of humanity at large plus acceptance of the theory of 'flexible response' strategy might lead them to wonder if they should, perhaps, accept the sacrificial role for which geography as much as anything else nominates them; yet it is impossible for any European to avoid feeling that if the superpowers wish to dice with death, it should be with their own death in their own backyard, not with anybody else's. How does this claim – which seems transparently just – bear on the strategic issue? Does or should it bear on the strategic issue at all? Does justice *matter* in the face of strategy for world survival?

Though case 3, the case of small-scale nuclear strikes between minor powers, is somewhat different, it too raises this last question. The risks of escalation there come from the major powers getting in on the act, and are therefore, while perhaps foreseeable by the minor powers, largely beyond any possibility of their control. Let us suppose that for one small country to drop one small nuclear bomb is in certain circumstances morally justifiable, and that secure in this knowledge it does so, but that the actual consequence of its doing so is Armageddon. Arguing along familiar moral lines, one might say that since the bombing country neither intended Armageddon, nor used the risk of it as an instrument of policy, nor had any control over its eruption, it could not be held morally responsible for it, nor would it be obliged to take the possible consequences of its action into account when considering the morality of its various options. One might even argue that it would be *wrong* for the government of that country to forego its nuclear option and thereby virtually commit national suicide for the sake of avoiding the risk of the general holocaust: for the duty of governments is to mind their own country's business first and foremost.

It seems to me that arguments like the ones I have just sketched invite scepticism about the relevance of morality in discussions of nuclear policy. What does it matter if threatening and intending the destruction of half the world is morally wrong, if doing so is the only way to avoid actually destroying the whole, or even half, the world? What does it matter if dropping one small bomb is morally justified if the foreseeable, though unintended, result of it is that the whole world is destroyed? There is of course a practical debate over whether deterrence is, in fact, the most likely way of preventing total destruction, but let us leave that aside for the moment and assume that it is. The movements like the Campaign for Nuclear Disarmament (CND) which seek to alert citizens to the realities of nuclear war and inspire fear and moral horror at the prospect will be positively dangerous; for if the fear and moral horror became widespread, this might in democratic countries bring about irresistible political pressure for some policy which undermined deterrence and thus made nuclear war more rather than less likely. But then urging the immorality of nuclear war for the sake of avoiding it is irrational: since it makes *more* likely the outcome which the moralists seek to avoid. Concern with morality of nuclear policy is thus associated with irrationality. This is often also linked with a further charge that moral claims are themselves essentially irrational, being merely expressions of personal predilections or emotional commitment which cannot in the end be rationally justified. Those who urge the changing of current nuclear stances on moral grounds are thus often represented as well-meaning but irrational or anti-rational naïfs, out of touch or out of sympathy with the harsh realities of the modern world and borne along by their emotions to urge unreasoned and dangerous policies. Alternatively, attempts may be made to demonstrate the irrationality of the objectionable moral claims by philosophical argument. This variant of the defence of the *status quo* concedes that moral claims *can* to some extent be rationally supported, but denies that the claim that deterrence is immoral is proved.

That accusations of this kind should be made seem unsurprising when one surveys the literature. For there certainly is a style of *committed* moral argument, usually urging the immorality of current nuclear policy and the need therefore for radical changes of policy, which seems to make its case in a way visibly unlike the normal style of academic argument about morality; but it is arguments in the academic style which are usually assumed to be the prime candidate for rationality in this sphere. No wonder, then, that the committed style is suspected of irrationality, and that attempts are made to discredit its assertions. These attempts to discredit betray more anxiety than perhaps one might have expected. I suspect they are responses to, and hence an acknowledgment of, a persuasiveness the committed anti-nuclear style has which the austere calculations of the military strategists and administrators lack. Its appeal to morality gestures towards a dimension which the strategists leave out, but whose power to persuade they perhaps feel though they cannot correctly identify or approve it. I am interested in identifying and describing this persuasive extra element. Its detractors tend to stigmatize it as unrealistic idealism or emotional, subjective and excessive concern with morality, and to assume that such writing must be persuasive *not* because of its content, but because of its form — its literary qualities, its rhetoric, its aptitude to arouse emotion. But this seems too facile an analysis; I doubt if content can be so neatly divided from form. So I want to explore the possibility that the persuasiveness has as much to do with *what* is said as with *how* it is said. In that case it may be that to understand what is going on in these debates we need to rethink our view of what moral writing (writing about morality) *is*. That is what I attempt to do in this paper.

I have already suggested that there appear to be two distinct going styles of moral argument. (This volume contains examples of both.) The first task must be a more careful descriptions of the two styles. For convenience I shall call proponents of an exhortatory or 'emotional' style *crusaders* and proponents of a philosophical or 'rational' style *casuists*. Crusaders and casuists do on occasion make use of each other's style; the label indicates which style predominates.

Crusaders want to change the world; they argue for the sake of making people do things. This style of moral writing typically attempts to awaken moral revulsion from some aspect of things as they are and to communicate both some vision of a better state of things and a belief in its possibility. It is the stuff of which reforming campaigns and revolutions are made; in both of these, political action is allied with and justified by changed and even seemingly paradoxical moral perceptions (property is theft; women are not angels but the slaves of men). This sort of moral argument is directed toward not the settlement of difficult, complex or borderline moral cases but at changed, or awakened, moral perceptions. It measures its success not by agreements reached over specific cases but by how widely its influence is diffused over a person's judgments and actions. This leaves a great deal of scope for disagreement over particular actions or policies among adherents of the same cause; what unites them is at least some central shared moral perceptions, some shared vision of the moral organization of the world, or of a fragment of the world. In CND, for instance, a core of shared ideas unites people more strongly than detailed differences of opinion divide them.

Since attacks on one's perceptions are threatening, moral on-slaughts of this kind, if they do not produce enthusiasm, are liable instead to provoke angry and impatient rejection; for they seem to say things which obviously are not so (property is *not* theft — if there were no property, there could not be any theft; women are not the slaves of men, since they freely accept their condition). It is, of course, possible for crusaders to counter these responses by producing resemblances between property and theft, or women and slaves; it is indeed normal for crusaders to back up their claims with argument, and if they are philosophers with casuistical argument, which has even been known to convince. (Or so many converts to religion claim.) Nevertheless crusading activities tend to make professional philosophers nervous. For crusading seems inimical to the detachment with which a professional intellectual ought to pursue truth. A crusader *cannot* be detached about the cause for which he is crusading, since he has already made up his mind about it. And since he wants to change the world, it is in his interest to awaken enthusiasm — faith being reputed to move mountains. But is there not something dangerous to reason, and to truth, in the awakening of enthusiasm? Does not the crusader use reason, if he does, in the service of enthusiasm? Should not intellectually respectable moral argument be of a quite different kind: And contemporary academic philosophy offers copious examples of this different kind: the moral arguments of the casuist.

The casuist, as the name suggests, typically argues difficult or disputed cases. The standard way to do this is by patient and often subtle analysis of paradigms and disputed cases whose object is to show that the disputed cases do or do not resemble some undisputed case sufficiently to be assigned the same moral standing. Thus ... Bernard Williams seeks to show that nuclear deterrence is objectively quite unlike accident control by tying babies to car bumpers.[1] ...

Do these descriptions suggest anything about the basis of the charge of emotionalism? In the case of nuclear policy, the object of anti-nuclear crusaders is to awaken us to the moral enormity of aspects of our nuclear stance which we may not have noticed or may prefer to forget, in the hope that perception of the enormity will induce us to work to change the policy. Casuistical rebuttals reject the blanket charge of enormity and try to show that though it attaches to some possible and perhaps to some actual pro-nuclear stances, it certainly does not attach to all. The object is presumably to neutralize the *moral* revulsion that crusaders might otherwise induce in relation to these arguably acceptable stances and thus remove a possible obstacle to their adoption. Now, if moral revulsion counts as an emotion — or even if it does not, but is normally or frequently associated with an emotion — then in a very obvious sense, crusaders in such debates appeal to emotion and casuists do not: for crusaders seek to arouse revulsion while casuists seek to get rid of it. But that they seek to arouse moral revulsion cannot in itself be an objection against the *moral* claims of the crusaders; and if in the process they *also* arouse emotion, this will merely be the result of the crusaders disagreeing with casuists in thinking a nuclear stance morally wrong, and of psychological facts about moral revulsion. In the context of moral argument, that crusaders try to arouse revulsion only justifies a charge of anti-rational emotionalism if supported by a theory of morality which says that moral judgment is essentially a matter for calm rational calculation which *any* influx of emotion is likely to distort, including the emotion often associated with moral revulsion; so that when seeking to show that moral revulsion is what is called for in some particular case, the philosopher should take special pains *not* to arouse emotion.

This, however, is only an unproven philosophical view, and moreover a highly controversial one. Certainly no philosopher has come up with an indisputed rational decision-procedure for settling doubtful cases in morality (other than the casuistical one); nor is there any reason to suppose that philosophers will or can. If the charge of irrational emotionalism in moral argument is to be more than expression of philosophical prejudice, it must reduce to the objection that the crusader does not use, or does not use properly, the only generally accepted method of moral argument — the rational methods of the casuist. In that case the claim would be that the crusader is irrational to the extent that he is not a casuist.

But to what extent is the crusader not a casuist? Does not he also at important points use exactly the casuistical method of comparison of the disputed case with a paradigm and the pointing out of similarities or differences? Property is *like* theft in that it deprives another of enjoyment of something to which he has a right; it is therefore bad for the same reason that makes theft bad. Wives are *like* slaves in that they suffer loss of autonomy, and labour for another without recompense or recognition of the real value of their labour. Or, using our illustrative example from this volume, nuclear deterrence is *like* putting babies on car bumpers. The crusader's method of argument is procedurally identical to the casuist's; the difference is in his striking examples, novel filing system (e.g. classifying property as theft, or wives as slaves) and his lack of interest in borderline cases. And *that* his filing should surprise is inevitable, given that he is trying to *change* moral perceptions. For his object is precisely to get us to see similarities which we did not see before. True, in order to make them visible he may have to supply a new context or perspective. But changing perspectives is the business he is in. It is not the business of the typical casuist, who uses the same method to file new cases along familiar lines.

Now, I would claim that it is a fact of human nature that changing perspectives runs a high risk of being an emotional business, both in that one whose perspective is changed is unlikely to remain entirely unmoved, and in that in order to produce a change in perspective it may be necessary to deliver an emotional jolt in the form of, say, a highly-charged example. (Like, for instance, babies on bumpers.) In other words, when attempts are being made to change perspectives, there is likely to be emotion around. This is another source of the charge of emotionalism. If a casuist interlocutor does not recognize or does not accept the revolutionary strand in the crusader's endeavour, then his (the crusader's) filing will seem quixotic and irrational and his use of highly-charged examples irresponsible and misleading. For of course a casuist staying within the old perspective will always be able to point out *dis*similarities between the cases the crusader is trying to assimilate (if they were not in some respects dissimilar, there would be no need for the crusader to try to assimilate them – and, from his point of view, no point in trying to either). In this situation a casuist will claim the crusader is saying things which are not true, and playing on the emotions of his readers to put over something which he could not put over by rational means. But the crusader cannot avoid giving the impression of wildness and irrationality, because the novelty of his filing system generates at least surface implausibility and possibly even paradox. He *may* perhaps avoid the appearance of emotionalism (by avoiding highly-charged examples). But then he may fail in his object (for instance his reader may not bother to look beyond his surface implausibility). So what can he do? Only protest that the casuist has missed the point.

Is it, however, *rational* to seek to change perspectives? That must depend on whether the situation calls for such a change. Paradoxes certainly *look* irrational; but crusading paradoxes are frequently devices for breaking down old perspectives. When is this appropriate? This is a large question to which I will return. Here I will only note that deterrence itself generates paradox – for instance, in the moral sphere, the paradoxes I sketched at the beginning of this paper; and in the practical, the paradox of making total disaster ever more possible and probable in order to prevent it happening. When paradox appears, something has to give somewhere. Rationality itself suggests that if we have arrived at this paradoxical solution, we must have got something badly wrong in the parameters of the problem, so that a change in perspective may not be quixotic but necessary for a rational solution. Even pro-nuclear casuists cannot avoid responding to this aspect of the problem, and in so doing becoming technically crusaders: for instance when they suggest it is not wrong to intend to do something wrong, they are in fact proposing a change in the existing moral filing system. What distinguishes them from overt anti-nuclear crusaders is not that one side avoids while the other embraces paradox (i.e. irrationality), but that the two sides differ over *what* has to give in order to avoid the nuclear paradox. How is one to decide which side has the better solution? Again this raises large questions to which I will return. But first I want to examine another attempt to substantiate the charge of emotionalism against crusaders.

It may now appear that in admitting that crusaders may need to deliver emotional jolts, I have conceded the main point against them. Could not casuists argue that whatever one's views on the philosophy of morals, nevertheless there surely is such a thing as morally and rationally reprehensible rabble-rousing — the provocation of one's audience to action by appeal to the non-rational elements in human nature, rather than to the rational elements? And is not the crusader delivering an emotional jolt doing exactly that? Take the example of babies on bumpers. An anti-crusading casuist might say: of course if we imagine babies really placed in this situation, it works powerfully on our emotions, and we recoil in horror. And that is exactly why the crusader chooses it: what else can be the *point* of such a bizarre example? But what should matter is not the violence of our recoil but exactly what it is about the example that makes us recoil at all. The crusader, however, is not interested in this. All he wants is to select some feature which the example shares with the disputed case, paying insufficient attention to whether it is indeed *that* feature from which recoil, and thus by a kind of sleight of hand transferring the recoil from babies on bumpers to deterrence. But the transfer is illegitimate, for the two cases are simply not alike. In this particular example the feature selected is the placing of innocents in the firing-line: preventing accidents by putting babies on car-bumpers is wrong *because* it places innocents in the firing-line, and as deterrence does this too, we should recoil from it just as much as we do from babies on bumpers, according to the crusader. But, says the casuist, this is a case of illegitimate transfer. Thus, Williams suggests that the reason why we recoil from babies on bumpers is, roughly, that travelling around on bumpers is no life for a baby. It just so happens that in this particular case materially altering the babies' quality of life is *also* the placing of innocents in the firing-line. This is not so in the case of deterrence, which indeed places innocents in the firing-line but does not at all otherwise alter their quality of life. Our recoil, in the case of babies on bumpers, is our response to the sort of life babies are likely to lead on bumpers, *not* to their being, in that situation, innocents in the firing-line. Therefore it is a mistake to suppose that because we recoil from babies on bumpers, we ought to recoil from nuclear deterrence.

Certainly if what is said above of the crusader is true, he is guilty of mistaken analysis and misuse of the example. And it is certainly *possible* for him to do this out of excessive emotionalism: it is *possible* he made the mistake because he was too worked up, or that he misused the example because his motives were suspect. But his mistake could also just be a mistake, which had nothing to do with either his emotions or his motives. To find the source of a particular mistake one would have to look carefully at the particular crusader who made it. The casuist has not yet shown anything in crusading *procedure* as such which makes it more likely to produce mistakes than casuistry; he has simply offered a competing analysis of the example. Moreover, *has* he yet shown that the crusader really has made a mistake, and if so, how has he done it? He has shown that there is a difference between babies on bumpers and nuclear deterrence. But he has produced nothing to support his assumption that this difference is relevant to the disputed moral issue. And it is already perfectly obvious that accident prevention by babies on bumpers differs from nuclear deterrence in all sorts of ways. What needs to be shown is that the differences and similarities assumed to be relevant to the morality of deterrence really are so. (Williams himself does not explicitly make the relevance claim; though presumably he intends it, he certainly does not argue it.) If a casuist neglects to argue that the disregarded difference *is* morally relevant, he has no rational edge over a crusader assuming the opposite; both sides are simply making conflicting assumptions about moral relevance, and if this unsupported assertion of moral claims is supposed to indicate emotion and irrationality, each side is as emotional and irrational as the other. It is easy to miss this, because so much of the casuist's effort will have gone into detailing the differences, and we are so used to regarding the distinguishing of cases and analysis as rational philosophical procedure *par excellence*. But of course the crusader had done just the same sort of thing in finding a similarity. And *both* are in fact *looking to the moral intuitions of their audience* to support their relevance claim. In that respect they are both like, for instance, someone who tries to convince his audience that nuclear warfare is obscenely immoral by graphically describing its likely effects. All three offer their audience something as a candidate for test by moral recoil, in effect saying: in your heart do you believe it is morally right to do this? The opponent of nuclear weapons confronts them with the horrors of nuclear war. The crusader against deterrence in our example confronts them with a striking case of innocents in the firing-line. The pro-deterrence casuist might draw their attention to the misery of babies on bumpers.

If either the casuist or the crusader is to have the rational edge in this case (in the analysis of what is wrong about babies on bumpers), they must show not only that their own moral and relevance claims are supported by intuition, but also that their opponent's are not. But it seems to me that I recoil morally from babies on bumpers *both* because it is no life for a baby on a bumper *and* because it is putting innocents in the firing-line. Suppose, then, it is granted that both features are morally wrong and that nuclear deterrence is like babies on bumpers in that it is putting innocents in the firing-line, unlike it in that being in the nuclear firing-line leads to no accrual of misery. If putting innocents in the firing-line was a reason for moral objection to babies on bumpers, it is presumably still a reason for moral objection to nuclear deterrence, in the absence of arguments to the contrary. True, in the deterrence case we do not have the *additional* reason (accrual of misery) which is present in the case of babies on bumpers. But this does not show that there is *no* ground of moral objection or even that there is less ground for objection to deterrence than to babies on bumpers. (There may be all sorts of *other* grounds of moral objection peculiar to nuclear deterrence.) At this point it appears to be the crusader, *qua* opponent of deterrence rather than *qua* crusader, who must seem to have the rational edge, at any rate to those who share my moral intuitions about the example.

But now someone may want to say: 'Surely this means that the so-called rational method of moral argument, what has been described as the casuistical method, isn't really rational at all, since in the end it relies on intuition. Doesn't that make it just subjective and unreliable? What do you do if you get a conflict of intuitions? There doesn't seem to be any way the method could resolve that, so what use is it? Can't philosophers come up with something better than this?' The short answer to this is: 'No they can't. This is the best method of moral argument we've got, and we're stuck with it; so rather than throwing it away in disgust, I'd advocate understanding what it can and can't do. It can't resolve a conflict between unshakeable opposing intuitions, when the method is used against a background of other, *shared* intuitions, and when the contenders both subscribe to rational values like consistency. This is its use, and it also means that though in a sense it *is* a subjective method, in that it presupposes some degree of subjectivity in moral judgment, it does not allow its users to be rampantly sub-jective: for its use implies membership of a moral community defined by shared intuitions.' In other words, the method relies on there being some degree of *agreement* in subjective moral judgments. However, not even a set of universally shared moral intuitions will get rid of all conflict, if these relate to general *kinds* of thing (as most widely shared intuitions seem to). For intuitions about general kinds may conflict with each other in particular cases, when these are simultaneously instances of different kinds (e.g. when joining the resistance is abandoning your family). The conflict may then be within the individual, and the casuistical method may be incapable of resolving it. In such a case all the individual can do is *choose*. It is the relevance problem again. This is not to say his action becomes totally arbitrary. There will still be reasons for the *action* chosen. But the reasons need not be compelling as reasons for the *choice* (hence the possibility of irresolvable conflict). This state of affairs is recognized by the importance we attach to the notion of moral autonomy. In a world with an objective, quasi-mechanical decision-procedure for settling moral questions, there would be no room for values such as freedom of conscience (not necessarily religious, but embodied in such things as, for instance, the right to conscientious objection to military service).

If this is how things are in relation to moral argument, however, crusading may now seem problematical. Can it in fact be in any way a rational activity? For if, as has been suggested, the crusader's primary purpose is to *change* moral perceptions, is he not in fact trying to disrupt the moral community? And if it is only *within* a moral community that moral argument can take place, must not moral argument be impossible for a crusader, who is operating from somewhere outside it? Does this not suggest that he is in fact *obliged* to use shock tactics, if he is to have any hope of success? And is not an obscure awareness of this the reason why charges of irrationality and emotionalism tend to be levelled against him? For if this is right then there *is* a structural reason for the shock tactics.

These questions call for some reconsideration of the description of crusading. First, is the crusader trying to disrupt the moral community? Well, he need not be trying to disrupt all of it, and when we consider what his 'shock tactics' consist in, he does not seem to be doing this. For the only 'shock tactic' yet mentioned is the use of examples which evoke a powerful moral and emotional response, i.e. the appeal to shared intuitions again. And to the extent that the crusader still shares intuitions, he remains *within* the moral community. But he can still try to change it piecemeal from within.

Consider from this point of view a crusader who thinks deterrence is morally objectionable, but does not think most people realize this. He will thus be trying to *change* the existing consensus of moral judgment. How he proceeds will depend on his diagnosis of why people currently judge wrongly, but one thing he will *not* be inclined to do is make a direct appeal to intuitions about deterrence: for the consensus being what it is, the appeal to intuition may go against him. This in itself puts pressure on him, as a member of a moral community, to think about why *he* thinks deterrence is immoral, i.e. he will look for that feature of deterrence which elicits his moral response. This will probably consist in trying to think of some other clearly immoral thing which deterrence is *like*: the casuistical method. Once he has found it, or thinks he has found it (it is possible for him to make a mistake), it will seem to him that the reason why others do not perceive the immorality of deterrence must be that they simply have not noticed this feature, or have not given it enough importance. It will seem, then, that the best thing for him to do to bring others round to his way of thinking is to point up this feature of deterrence in as dramatic and striking a way as possible, a way which gives it the salience he feels it deserves. For in deciding relative importance he may be exercising choice, i.e. going beyond argument. If others are to understand this choice they must see the world as he sees it. And to achieve this he may need to *light* deterrence in a particular way (hence 'seeing things in the same light'), a way which will throw into high relief that feature of deterrence in which he is interested (thereby inevitably obscuring other features which he regards as less relevant), and capture the attention of people who if left to themselves will not see anything here that particularly needs to be attended to. He may do this by, for example, likening deterrence to babies on bumpers. Hence his selective focus and use of powerful examples. These manoeuvres thus *are* dictated by the nature of the crusader's enterprise. But they are dictated *also* by the nature of moral argument, as we have it. I cannot see anything intrinsically reprehensible or irrational in these proceedings, though no doubt they can on occasion be reprehensibly and irrationally conducted. But that will be the fault of the individual crusader, not of crusading as such. Nevertheless to those who are not brought round to the crusader's way of thinking the proceedings are likely to appear both inept and reprehensible. But they should remember (as indeed should he) their own proceedings are going to appear just so to him. Their differences are going to appear irreconcilable as long as both sides fail to acknowledge that what is required for understanding the other position is an effort not just of rationality but also of imagination. To do them justice such arguments must be entered into before being fought. One may do one's best at this and still fail to see the world as the other sees it: it may still seem that deterrence just is not like, or not enough like, babies on bumpers. But it is idle to think that, given the current state of our understanding, this can be objectively proved. For 'like' here means 'like in all morally relevant respects'. And moral relevance cannot in the end be proved without recourse to intuition, gut feeling, or prior conviction, at any rate in the current state of the art.

Intuition, however, though it may be our last resort, may yet not take us all the way to our destination. Thus, everyone seems to share the intuition that nuclear war is a moral horror, but there is very little agreement over what follows from that – i.e. what are the implications for action of this judgment, and what *else* is a moral horror because nuclear was is (deterrence? flexible response? unilateralism? stasis?)? The casuistical method has been deployed on a grand scale to try to answer these questions, but with disappointing results. Let me now try to suggest why this might be, and to envisage some different way of proceeding.

II

So far I have been considering relatively marginal forms of crusading, involving not so much radical changes of moral perception as the activation and rearrangement of existing perceptions in which the casuistical method still plays a central role. But I think there may be changes of perception in which the casuistical method misleads more than it enlightens. It is possible for the conditions of life to change so drastically that the values with which one is already equipped are simply inadequate for dealing with the world. I am thinking of examples such as Colin Turnbull's description of the Ik in his book *The Mountain People*.[2] The Ik were a tribe for whom food became so scarce that the amount available could not support the existing numbers. What happened was that some individuals ate and others starved and died; those who ate ceased to have any concern for those who starved, regarding their misfortunes as matters for hilarity (as when an old woman fell down a ravine). What struck Turnbull was that the old woman laughed too: the weak seemed not to expect help but to acquiesce in their fate. When compassionate observers rushed to help, though, the weak sometimes broke down, and admitted remembering and longing for a time when things were different and people helped each other. Experiencing compassion again when, for very obvious reasons, it had disappeared from their world, made the present unbearable to them: they were no longer capable of the miracles of altruism which had hitherto sustained them.

One can view what was happening here as the emergence of a new morality suited to the exigencies of the time: the Ik could only bear the world as it was by thinking that (given the food situation) it was right that it should be as it was, that people should not help each other and that the weak should starve. Maybe what they did was literally make a virtue of necessity; which is one way of living with necessity. The new virtue was, however, initially incomprehensible to the compassionate observers who at first were taken up by their horror at the absence of the virtues (such as compassion) with which they were familiar. They found, though, that practice of those virtues did not *work* in this world: it simply made necessity harder to bear (for the observers could not supply enough food to feed all the people: they could not change the prevailing necessity). Their conviction of the universal validity of their own virtues, among *these* people and in *these* conditions, began to slacken: they began to find it possible to see the world as the Ik saw it, without a virtue of compassion. This was achieved not by crusading but by looking at the world of the Ik and imagining what it must be like to live in it.

Now, it is possible to look at the world and see accumulating changes in it whose *future* effects make new virtues necessary *now* (an analogue of the Ik's situation) without those virtues coming into being because the future effects are not certain or are not generally known or are too far off. Such a perception may give rise to radical crusading: the attempted creation of new virtues, which are what they are because of changes in the world, and are justified by these changes, not by making them out to be one of the old virtues in disguise. (Similarly old virtues can become obsolete. Thus most modern readers find some of the virtues listed by Aristotle in his *Nicomachean Ethics* incomprehensible *as virtues*.) I suspect that we are now in such a time of virtue-generating change, not just because of the existence of nuclear weapons but given the vast effect that individual human activity can now have, through technological advance, on the whole of the rest of the world. The individual action of relatively small numbers of people (those controlling governments and multinationals) can within the span of an ordinary life radically affect vast numbers of others and the natural world itself which supports us; nuclear war is only the most dramatic example of this. Another example is the diminishing of plant and animal species by land development and new methods of farming. Conversely, *large* numbers of people feel impotent to alter courses of action set by the few whose effects radically alter or threaten their own lives. All this, and nuclear weaponry in particular — not to mention other features of the modern world (such as its economic organization) — places us in the position of the Ik: plausibly, if we go on as we are we shall not survive.

This is a new situation and calls for new thoughts. We are confused about the implications of the immorality of nuclear war, confused about the morality of deterrence, because the immorality we *can* perceive is actually *new*. New crimes are now possible, as are new virtues. Of course these will bear *some* relation to familiar moral values; thus a possible new virtue such as concern for the preservation of species may be seen as related to the old virtue of thrift (which incidentally seems to have vanished from a world in which credit-card advertisers urge us to take the waiting out of wanting). And yet it is not *quite* like thrift, because (a) it is a virtue which institutions rather than individuals exercise, (b) more is involved in it than simply prudent provision for the future. Most conservationists would I think see more that is good in species conservation than just the biological prudence of keeping the gene-pool as large as possible; some seem to feel a sense that other species have a *right* to exist too; others that the richness and variety of the world is an intrinsic good. Because the new organizational structure of the world endows us with new capacities for good and evil, it demands new virtues of us, and in conjunction with our old viciousness, creates new vices. Because we do not clearly realize this we do not know how to handle the new moral situation even intellectually, let alone practically.

This may be granted, but now it may be said: why should the new thoughts which are called for be thoughts about *morality*? In the case of nuclear weapons at any rate, given the danger and the size of the mess, is not the first priority just getting out of the mess, i.e. averting the threat of universal destruction — never mind the morality of the mess itself or of features of it or of the means necessary to get out of it? Is not the most urgent problem one of *survival* — finding the most effective means of averting destruction — and not one of morality at all? The Ik, after all, adjusted their morality to the necessities of survival; but they settled on a means of survival first, the means being the crude biological one of the fittest surviving. Is not *that* the right parallel with our situation? Thus, suppose deterrence is the best means to survival. Then moral objections to it are irrelevant, just as compassion was irrelevant to the Ik's efforts to survive.

I would say to this: we have more time than the Ik (though perhaps not much). This creates problems. I cannot see the ditching of morality over nuclear matters as a workable solution, because, *having* more time, a lot has meanwhile to go on as before. The Ik could not tolerate the simultaneous existence of the old and the new virtues; the old compassion and the new altruism could not coexist. *We* cannot tolerate the simultaneous maintenance (for the purposes of ordinary life) and abandonment (for the purposes of nuclear policy) of moral values. Attempts might be made to justify this (the exclusion of morality from the nuclear sphere because survival is at stake) on familiar models, such as the justification of normally prohibited actions, e.g. deliberate killing of another person, is self-defence. But this seems to involve a view of morality as a system of prohibitions which lapse when survival is at stake — an unsatisfactory view on at least two counts: first, it suggests that the very same action can be wrong or not wrong depending on the circumstances. But killing in self-defence is held not to be wrong because it differs internally (in its motivation) from murder; it is a different kind of action. Second, morality comprises not just the rejection of wrong things but the furtherance of right ones; to ignore this and view it as a system of prohibitions leads to impatience with morality at just the point where one would have expected it to have most to say — in the context of describing, not just what is *wrong* with the world, but how the world ought to be. Whether or not it is true, it is nevertheless *intelligible* that among the Ik the acceptance of death by the weak was experienced as a virtue (i.e. the way you ought to be if you were weak); and this should remind us that morality is not just a system of prohibitions for the restraint of anti-social impulses, but a *coherent* way of living in the world and enduring necessity.

This dimension is, I think, the extra element which informs the writing of crusaders and is conspicuously lacking from the calculations of military strategists and planners. Their projections of the future horrify us, not just because of the frightful suffering and killing anticipated, but because the future they anticipate, the suffering included, *makes no sense*. The deaths and suffering seem *pointless*. In a way it is unfair of us to be horrified; their brief does not include *making sense* of what may happen. They are supposed only to work out what to do if it does happen. But this is an absurd brief, for how can they determine, how could anyone determine, what should be done in a world which makes no sense? They can *obviously* only fulfil their brief within the framework of the way they make sense of the world as it now is. The paradox is, of course, that the state of affairs they anticipate is precisely the one in which so much havoc has been wreaked on the world as it now is that it *no longer has* the sense it has now. So when the decisions they make now become effective, the sense will have been removed from them.

The current British plans for civil defence against nuclear attack are a nice example of this: the plan seems to be to preserve a government structure by preserving the lives of key local government officers. In the state of affairs envisaged, this is the best that can be done to preserve Britain. But to preserve government structure will constitute perserving Britain only if there is enough left of what Britain is *now* after a nuclear attack for that structure to function recognizably as it does now. But this seems most unlikely. And if there is no functioning *social* structure, the 'government structure' will *then* be no such thing, but a selection of favoured individual survivors with means of force against other less favoured survivors. What sense is there in a government *now* taking care to bring about *that* state of affairs? Such a situation lacks human sense because it offends against justice, and it lacks even biological sense because it offends against function. There seems no reason why good local government officers should make good post-nuclear survivors or leaders. Thus those who urge that we exclude morality from our nuclear planning *now* seem to me to have become so hypnotized by the vision of this possible senseless future that they seek to bring forward some of its horrors to *now*, as if planning for a senseless future must itself be senseless. The senseless future infects the present and draws the present towards it. But to accept this is to forget that *that* future is only a *possible* future. Maybe the way not to make it actual is to try all the harder to envisage a possible future which *does* make sense and can be made actual, and aim for that. This is bound to seem unrealistic, for the world as it now really is seems to be headed for the senseless future. If so, then if we want to avoid it we must change the world.

Moralities, systems of values placed on actions and attitudes, are a central part of the enterprise of making sense of the world, and are thus part of what gives life meaning and hence survival its *point*. (Job despaired of the world when it no longer seemed to embody the moral order.) To urge those with functioning moralities to forget about morality in order to survive is thus like urging them, for the duration of the concern with survival, to concern themselves exclusively with survival while making survival itself pointless. (What is the point of surviving if *that* is what I have to do in order to survive?) This is surely the core of the controversy about the morality of deterrence. It seems to me undeniable that intending or threatening to fire off all the weapons *is not* as bad as it would be actually to fire them. But so what? That hardly justifies the policy or exhausts the moral unease it arouses. Now, the point of the debate about the morality or immorality of deterrence is usually seen as being this: if we decide it is immoral, we ought not to go in for it, whatever the consequences; but if we decide it is not immoral, it is all right to go in for it. But this question seems to fall short of the scale of the problem involved in deterrence, because it *ignores* the question of survival. I think the trouble is a false separation between morality and survival. The question we really want an answer to, the question which the nature of deterrence forces on us, is *not* the relatively restricted one about its morality (which as sometimes interpreted excludes questions about survival), but the wider and vaguer question about sense, to which morality is relevant but does not entirely determine: does deterrence make sense? *Does it* make sense to intend or threaten to do something terrible which makes no sense? What I claim for morality is that it is of its nature *relevant* to this question. But so is survival. Morality helps us to make sense of the present, but the present makes sense only if there is a (meaningful) future. If we have to exclude morality and sense from our contemplation of the future, or the possibility of the future from our morality, the present itself begins to lose *its* sense.

My suggestion, then, is that it is not useful to recommend the abandonment of morality with regard to nuclear policy in the interests of survival, because morality cannot be abandoned here without abandoning sense, and abandoning sense is not a possible way to live. We cannot simultaneously take and not take our morality seriously. Someone may now object: but people live like that all the time, by the simple device of selective blindness. Thus treatment of another that is not tolerated among the members of a particular group is regarded as wholly appropriate for those outside the group. The difference of treatment is not regarded as problematic because it is held, as a rule, to be justified by some actual difference between the two groups. This blinds those involved to any similarities there may also actually be which would tend to render the difference of treatment paradoxical. In answer to this, I would point out that the *need* for an aid to blindness shows that those involved feel themselves constrained by *rationality* — in the form of consistency in the application of their moral categories. Thus, in saying 'this is not a possible way to live', I mean not a possible way to live a *rational* life. One familiar form of crusading has been to seek to remove this selective blindness, and thus to bring under the protection of the moral community groups which had previously been excluded from it. Thus slavery and racism, for instance, have been attacked by insistence on justice and the brotherhood of man. Crusading nuclear moralists are often attempting something similar. And in so far as their efforts are motivated by a desire for greater consistency in practical judgment, it is motivated by rational values (i.e. valuing the rational). This is why anti-nuclear crusaders often, in their turn, accuse their opponents of irrationality.

A similar thing applies to another arm of the attack on current policy. Defenders of deterrence on the whole do admit that even though it may be the best available option for avoiding war, nevertheless its own dynamic has brought and still brings a continual and increasing risk of war. They claim, however, that things being as they are, realism still requires us to recognize deterrence as the best hope, even though a world that has to rely on deterrence may be a doomed world. Such 'realism' does seem to require us to embrace a contradiction: for a chance of survival for the world which itself dooms the world is not a chance of survival. The more rational course would surely be to recognize that one of the assumptions which generate the contradiction must be false: either there is *no* very good chance of survival for the world, or deterrence is not that chance. This is a familiar enough crusading theme: since deterrence brings such great dangers, it is *not* realistic to treat it as the best chance of survival for the world, for the chance it offers is unacceptably small. It only appears to be the best chance because other (usually political) features of our world are regarded as fixed. Changing these may be difficult, but one of the things that makes it difficult is our belief that we cannot change them. Since deterrence offers such a poor chance of survival, changing these supposedly immutable features of the world *must* offer a better chance — and so, to improve our chances, we *must* believe we can. It is rather like Pascal's bet on the existence of God: if we lose the bet, we only lose something we never had. But if we win, we win everything. So *it is rational* to bet — on God, or on our ability to change things. Thus the attack on current policy can again be seen as a demand for *greater* rationality in practical matters, not less.

Obviously to gamble rationally one must assess the probabilities as accurately as possible; but in this case (though of course one must take account of as many relevant *facts* as one can) still assessing the probabilities is inescapably a matter of judgment. For judging what can be changed depends on judging probabilities of human behaviour, and there is no science of that sufficiently detailed and established to yield the sort of reliable predictions which would make assessment of probabilities a matter of calculation rather than judgment.

I want now to deal with another possible objection to the very idea of changed moral perceptions. I have been suggesting that the pressure for a new morality can come from the necessities of survival. But, it may be said, this begs the crucial question of the relation between morality and prudence (survival being the most urgent task of prudence). The so-called 'necessities' of survival are necessities only if survival itself is regarded as a necessity. But it is not, and morality has never regarded it as such. Take the Ik. Maybe they did as a group effectively, even if not consciously, choose that the fittest of them should survive, and adjust their morality to suit. But they did not have to choose that. They *could* have chosen to maintain their old system of values governing human relationships and accept the collective death which would have been the price of it. Would not this, in fact, have been the *truly* moral alternative, as acknowledging the supremacy of moral over prudential values? It is, after all, possible for us to prefer death to dishonour, and we regard those who do as morally admirable. In deciding what we think of the Ik we should compare them to, say, someone living under a corrupt regime which makes right living inconsistent with survival. We consider the morally right (though difficult) course for such a person to be to continue to live rightly and accept the death which will be the consequence, rather than to betray his values in order to survive. Just so the Ik should have accepted death rather than betray their original values. Otherwise we end up with the conclusion that whatever is, is right — the antithesis of all morality. For an individual in some regimes is just as impotent, the conditions of life laid by the regime are just as much a necessity for him/her, as the conditions of life laid down for the Ik by their position in the natural and political world. It is sophistry to distinguish between the abandonment of morality and the change of moral values when confronted with the issue of survival in the nuclear age. Our situation may indeed be that, like the Ik, we have to *choose* between morality and survival.

I accept that the relation between morality and survival is crucial here, but I think the analogy with the Ik fails at this very point. For *whose* survival is at stake? In the case of the Ik, normal values seem to have been abandoned for the sake of the survival of some individuals, either *qua* individuals or *qua* members of the tribe, by whom the tribe could perhaps be regenerated in some possibly better future time. The parallel case to this in the case of nuclear war seems to be that of the individual nation: discussing nuclear policy and deterrence purely from the point of view of whether *Britain*, say, or at least some of the people in it, was going to survive. Now, individual Britons might well feel an overriding concern with this which was essentially prudential in origin. The survival at stake for a Briton thinking in these terms is in a sense always *my* survival — either *my own individual* survival or the survival of *my people*. Similarly with the Ik. It is not, however, in these contexts conceived as a moral necessity *that I or my people should survive*. On the other hand, it is when we try to think about the problem as a whole and not from an individual or national point of view that the imperative of survival in the context of nuclear war seems most compelling. I suggest that this is precisely because the question of survival is then *not* considered from an individual point of view and is therefore felt at least partly as a *moral* rather than a prudential imperative. For those threatened by an all-out nuclear war are not particular people or classes or nations, but an indefinitely large proportion of the whole of humanity (not to mention an indefinitely large slice of non-human nature which currently sustains it). Nuclear threat forms a *de facto* collective whose membership is unknowable and which is represented by no existing political or cultural or social group with which one might now as an individual feel identified. The collective is bonded together by nothing more than their common humanity (and if we include threatened nature, not even that) and their common danger. This gives a new, dark meaning to the idea of the brotherhood of man and the human (or natural) community: we are now indeed all members of one another, because very many of us are threatened by the same man-made death, and any one of us — impossible to tell which — may belong to that many. It is the survival of the collective that we feel it imperative to ensure, and *not* just because each of us may be a member of it (or otherwise why not just dig our own fully-equipped hole in the ground?). That at least must be what is implied by the generally accepted view that nuclear war is a moral horror. It is so because in waging nuclear war, far from ensuring survival of the collective, we kill it off; we fail in a *moral* duty to something other than and more important than ourselves. *This* imperative of survival is thus a *moral* imperative. And I think it is also a *new* moral imperative, because it enjoins concern for a new entity, for something other than individuals or existing social entities. The old duties of compassion and benevolence no doubt enjoin concern for the fate of the members of the collective as *individuals*, but I do not think nuclear war seems unquestionably a moral horror just because it will cause a very large number of individuals to perish horribly. For much more than that will be destroyed; not just the individuals but most of the structures which support them and the achievements which have given their life meaning. The crime is not just killing people but causing chaos to come again, or rather *creating* chaos out of order. If this were actually to happen I cannot believe it is not part of human nature to see it as other than a transition from a better to a worse state, not just for a particular person undergoing it but *in itself*. (I should add that I regard aversion to pain as likewise part of human nature, despite the existence of both masochists and neurological variation. 'Human nature', as I use it, is a normative concept.) If moving from order to chaos is thus a human disaster, then failure to prevent it is a moral failure − indeed the failure of morality itself. Similarly, I think we feel a moral requirement to prevent the destruction of the collective over and above the requirement to concern ourselves with the fate of its members as individuals. We thus feel a moral requirement of concern for a *new entity*, which I would therefore call a new moral requirement.

I have no designation for this entity other than vague expressions like 'humanity as we know it'; or perhaps the new concern is for the collective plus what sustains it, in which case the entity might be 'human society and nature as we know it'. (Finding a better designation than this is a task for moral philosophy.) The entity has in a sense been created by the fact that there is now a way to express *lack* of concern for it: nuclear war. Military technology has made this entity thinkable in concrete terms, and we have tried to rise *morally* to the occasion by confusedly seeing destruction of the new entity as a crime, and overriding concern for its survival as a duty. In this respect, concern for survival in the case of nuclear war is different from the concern for survival of the Ik, who were concerned with their own survival in a very familiar sense. The cases become more like each other if we think of the new, nuclear-threatened collective as a tribe to which we *all* belong;

but this seems a purely intellectual manoeuvre in the absence of anything binding the members of the collective together at all analogous to the sorts of things which bind the members of a tribe together in such a way as to *make* them all members of one tribe. That is precisely the problem: there is no tribe to look after the members of this collective. Another way of seeing the efforts of the crusaders is as the start of an attempt to *create* such a sustaining tribe, by at least getting the members of the collective to think of themselves as a tribe, and thus have some hope of creating the social and political structures necessary to bring the tribe concretely into being and protect its interests. It will, however, be a tribe quite unlike any others, if only in that ideally it includes *everybody*.

I have been suggesting that the imperative of averting nuclear holocaust is a moral as much as a prudential imperative. Someone may now say: 'Of course it is a moral imperative, and what your argument shows is that it is moral precisely because it *isn't* prudential. That is what is wrong with your interpretation of the Ik: their abandonment of compassion was immoral precisely because it *was* prudential. You still haven't answered the claim that the Ik *ought* to have chosen death rather than callousness. What about the analogy suggested between the case of the Ik and that of the individual living under a corrupt regime?'

I think there is a difference between the choices facing the Ik and the choices facing such an individual which affects their moral perceptions and hence what can be said to be morally required of them. It is a question of how their choice appears to them, of what it is they seem to themselves to be choosing. We regard the heroic dissident's choice of death as obviously right because we see his acts and choice as taking place within the context of ongoing societies (his and our own) for which his choice is *significant*. His choice of death is a comment on the regime. Since societies continue even though the individual does not, his death seems worthwhile both to us and to him because there is always the possibility, perhaps the hope, that *someone* will see its significance, will read correctly what it says (even if it is only his killers). Belief in its significance is what makes it worth doing. One may think here of Auden's poem 'In Memory of W. B. Yeats':

> Time that is intolerant
> Of the brave and innocent ...
>
> Worships language and forgives
> Everyone by whom it lives.

This might suggest that we value such acts because though men die, the word lives. It is true that words, and significant acts, last longer than those who make them; but even the word lives only as long as it is heard. Signifiers must signify *to someone*. Suppose now that the Ik do choose collective death rather than the abandonment of compassion: when they have died their death for sake of virtue as they conceive it, for whom will this supreme sacrifice be *significant*? Awareness of a significance-conferring context makes the heroic dissident's sacrifice seem good by allowing him to see it as having a point beyond his own personal concerns, and hence a point he can die for: for though he loses *his* future, there is still a future — the future of the context which gives his death significance. The difference with the Ik is that they stand to lose, not just a personal future, but *the* future: in their situation, choosing compassion means choosing the death not just of individuals but of the tribe. The act itself destroys the context which gives it significance, and thus in its accomplishment becomes merely a meaningless suicide. Perhaps the significance-conferring context need not be human: religion may supply a view of the world as a society or ordered set of beings of which human society is only a part. If the Ik have such a religion it is conceivable that collective death could appear to them, in the context of the world supplied by religion, as morally required. But *without* a context, I do not think such a collective death can appear as other than pointless suicide. And I do not think morality can require such a suicide: *that* is the link, in such cases, between morality and survival.

If the above fails to convince, consider the following case. Suppose that in the nuclear aftermath two small social groups are the last people left on earth. The groups are normally in contact with each other. Leaving a religious justification aside, what would be the morally right thing to do in the following circumstances: one group falls sick of a coñagious disease and becomes helpless. All will die without help. There is a good chance that some will survive if helped, but a near certainty that the other group will catch the disease too and also die if they approach and help the sick ones. If they help, there is a near certainty that human life on earth will cease; if they do not, there is a chance that it will continue. Without a religious or other-wordly justification, who will say that the right thing for them to do is obviously to help the sick? Can not we imagine the sick accepting their death and not asking for or expecting help, so that humanity might live? Would that not be virtue, and the forgoing of compassion by the other group, wisdom? Would maintenance of compassion, in these circumstances, not be senseless suicide? And would that not seem just not to be an option, as in normal cicumstances suicide is regarded as not an option? There is a reason why suicide has seemed both irrational and a crime, and I think the reason is that there is a self-evidence in the assertion that something is better than nothing. Survival of some thus just is better than survival of none, and so it is a moral requirement to ensure it (our duty is to prefer the good). For by that survival even those that do not survive retain awareness of a possible future in which their death has significance, and so moral worth. There is perhaps another lesson to be drawn from this. Maybe governments should now remember not just their duty to those they govern, but also their duty to the threatened nuclear collective. Maybe on occasion the interests of this override the interests of the governed, and make national suicide obligatory if the alternative really is *total* loss of the future (i.e. loss of *everyone's* future). Maybe this is a closer analogy to the man under the corrupt regime.

To conclude with a summary: some crusading is an imperfectly understood struggle to create the new values we need not only to survive but to live endurably in the world we have made, that is, to continue to find meaning in our lives in it. Because we have more time than the Ik there is time for rival moral creations to emerge (typically in the form of proposed political solutions: but political solutions always carry strong moral implications within them). How are we to assess them? I cannot offer anything more helpful than this: *not* by harking back always to old models, but by measuring them against the world (are things like this? Is this what is needed to ensure survival?) and against ourselves (is this liveable? Does it speak to our condition?). If the answer to all these questions is 'yes', then what is proposed *must be* (however impossible current circumstances may make it look). That is the true, and rational, imperative of survival.

NOTES

1 Editor's note: Zaw refers to a piece by Bernard Williams, 'Morality, Scepticism and the Nuclear Arms Race', in Nigel Blake and Kay Pole (eds) *Objections to Nuclear Defence: Philosophers on Deterrence* (Routledge, Kegan Paul, London, 1984), pp. 99–114. Zaw makes use of this example throughout her essay.
2 See Colin Turnbull, *The Mountain People* (Simon & Schuster, New York, 1972).

9

Reflections on War and Political Discourse: Realism, Just War, and Feminism in a Nuclear Age

JEAN BETHKE ELSHTAIN

HOW DID WE get from Machiavelli to MAD, to Mutual Assured Destruction? The tradition of realism that dominates our thinking about international relations not only presumes but requires a move 'from ... to' in ways I shall take up in the first part of this article as I examine realism's givens in light of feminist questions. In part two, I assay the most important historic contender against realism's discursive hegemony, just war theory, with similar questions in mind. Because the central markers of realist and just war thinking are well-known to most readers, I shall concentrate on rethinking the too-thinkable — exposing the presumptions that get wheeled into place when the matter at hand is collective violence. As the argument in parts one and two unfolds, feminism as a critical lever gives way to contemporary feminisms as articulated positions. I note the ways in which feminist thinking on war and politics may get stuck within received discursive forms, reproducing presumptions that deepen rather than challenge the present order.[1] I conclude with an interpretation of Hannah Arendt's *On Violence*, a text with animating symbols and images that suggest an alternative discourse.

WHAT MAKES REALISM RUN

Realism's bracing promise is to spring politics free from the constraints of moral judgment and limitation, thereby assuring its autonomy as historic force and discursive subject-matter, and to offer a picture of the world of people and states as they really are rather than as we might yearn for them to be. We have all marked

Reprinted with permission from *Political Theory*, Vol. 13, No. 1, February 1985 pp. 39–57. Copyright 1985 Sage Publications Inc.

this story and its designated prototypical events and spokespersons. The genealogy of realism as international relations, although acknowledging antecedents, gets down to serious business with Machiavelli, moving on to theorists of sovereignty and apologists for *raison d'état*, and culminating, in its early modern forms, with Hobbes's *Leviathan* before continuing the trek into the present. The contemporary realist locates himself inside a potent, well-honed tradition. Realist thinkers exude the confidence of those whose narrative long ago 'won the war'. Realism's hegemony means that alternatives to realism are evaluated from the stand-point of realism, cast into a bin labeled idealism that, for the realist, is more or less synonymous with dangerous if well-intentioned naiveté.[2]

But is the realist throne that secure? We are familiar with what modern realism presumes: a world of sovereign states as preposited ontological entities, each seeking either to enhance or to secure its own power. State sovereignty is the motor that moves the realist system as well as its (nearly) immutable object. Struggle is endemic to the system and force is the court of last resort. It cannot be otherwise, for states exist in a condition of anarchy in relation to one another. Wars will and must occur because there is nothing to prevent them. On one level, then, realism is a theory pitched to structural imperatives that are said to bear on all actors in the international arena. No state, argues the realist, can reasonably or responsibly entertain the hope that through actions it takes, or refrains from taking, it may transform the wider context. Given that context, conflict is inevitable. There is nothing to prevent wars. The only logical solution to this unhappy state of affairs is a unitary international order to remedy international chaos.[3] Alas, what is logically unassailable is practically unattainable given the realist refrain: a world of sovereign and suspicious states.

Historic realism involves a way of thinking — a set of presump-tions about the human condition that secretes images of men and women and the parts they play in the human drama; and, as well, a potent rhetoric. Whether in its uncompromising Hobbesian version or the less remorseless Machiavellian narrative, realism exaggerates certain features of the human condition and down-grades or ignores others.[4] Interpreting foundational realist texts from a vantage point informed by feminist concerns, one is struck by the suppression and denial of female images and female-linked imperatives, hence alert to the restricted and oversimplifying terms through which realism constitutes symbolism and narrative roles more generally.

For example, Hobbes describes a world of hostile monads whose relations are dominated by fear, force, and instrumental calculation. Yet (and almost simple-mindedly) we know this to be anthropologically false. From the simplest tribal beginnings to the most complex social forms, women have had to tend to infants – no matter what the men were up to – if life was to go on in any sustained manner. That important features of the human condition are expunged from Hobbes's universe suggests that his realism is a dramatic distortion rather than a scientific depiction of the human condition at rock bottom. To acknowledge this by insisting that the state of nature is an analytic fiction fails to address the concerns I raise here. Fictions are also truths and what gets left out is often as important as what is put in and assumed.

To be sure, the contemporary realist is unlikely to endorse a full constellation of Hobbesian presumptions. He might reject Hobbes's vision of the state of nature, and his depiction of social relations, as dire and excessive. It is likely, however, that he would continue to affirm the wider conclusions Hobbes drew by analogy from the miserable condition of human beings in the state of nature to the unrelenting fears and suspicions of states in their relations to one another. Yet it seems plausible that if Hobbes omitted central features of human existence internal to civil societies and families, perhaps he is guilty of similar one-sidedness in his characterization of the world of states. To take up this latter possibility is to treat Hobbes's realism as problematic, not paradigmatic.

Machiavelli goes down more smoothly in large part because we have internalized so much of his legacy already. We all know the story. Human beings are inconstant and trustworthy only in their untrustworthiness. Political action cannot be judged by the standards of Christian morality. Civic virtue requires troops 'well disciplined and trained' in times of peace in order to prepare for war: This is a 'necessity', a law of history.[5] *Si vis pacem, para bellum*, a lesson successive generations (or so the story goes) must learn, though some tragically learn it too late, others in the nick of time.

Machiavelli's narrative revolves around a public–private split in and through which women are constituted, variously, as mirrors to male war-making (a kind of civic cheerleader) or as a collective 'other', embodying the softer values and virtues out of place within, and subversive of, *realpolitik*.[6] Immunized from political action, the realist female may honor the Penates but she cannot embark on a project to bring her values to bear on the civic life of her society. J. G. A. Pocock calls Machiavelli's 'militarization of citizenship' a potent legacy that subverts (even for some feminists, as I argue below) consideration of alternatives that do not bind civic and martial virtue together. Military preparedness, in this narrative, becomes the sine qua non of a viable polity. Although women cannot embody armed civic virtue, a task for the man, they are sometimes drawn into the realist picture more sharply as occasions for war (we must fight to protect her), as goads to action, as designated weepers over the tragedies war trails in its wake, or, in our own time, as male prototypes mobilized to meet dwindling 'manpower' needs for the armed forces.[7]

Rethinking realism using feminist questions defamiliarizes its central categories: the male *homme de guerre* retains his preeminent role, to be sure, but we recognize explicitly the ways in which his soldierly virilization is linked to the realist woman's privatization, and so on. But matters are never quite so simple. There are variants of modern feminist argumentation indebted to realist discourse in its Hobbesian and Machiavellian modes respectively.[8]

Hardline feminist realists, for example, endorse a Hobbesian social ontology and construe politics as a battleground, the continuation of war by war-like means. They advise women to learn to 'fight dirty'. Making generous use of military metaphors (Who is the Enemy? Where is he located?), Hobbesian feminists declare politics and political theory inevitably a 'paradigm case of the Oppressor and the Oppressed'.[9] There is tough talk about sex-war, shock troops, and the need for women to be integrated into the extant power structure construed as the aggregate of all those who defend law and order, wear uniforms, or carry guns for a living — 'the national guard ... state troopers ... sheriffs'. Women are enjoined to prepare for combat as the only way to end their 'colonization'.[10]

Such feminist realists share with their Hobbesian forefather a self-reproducing discourse of fear, suspicion, anticipated violence, and force to check-mate force. Their discussions are peppered with worst-case scenarios and proclamations of supreme emergency that reaffirm the bleakest images of 'the enemy' and pump up the will to power of combatants. Possibilities for reciprocity between men and women, or for a politics not reducible to who controls or coerces whom, are denied in much the same way Hobbes eliminates space for any noninstrumental human relations.

This hard-line position is less important, however, than the modified realism, more Machiavellian in its claims and categories, expressed in a 1981 legal brief filed by the National Organization for Women (NOW) as part of a challenge to all-male military registration.[11] Beginning with the claim that compulsory, universal military service is central to the concept of citizenship in a democracy, NOW buttresses an ideal of armed civic virtue. If women are to gain 'first-class citizenship' they, too, must have the right to fight. Laws excluding women from draft registration and combat duty perpetuate 'archaic notions' of women's capabilities; moreover, 'devastating long-term psychological and political repercussions' are visited upon women given their exclusion from the military of their country.[12]

NOW's brand of equal opportunity or integrationist feminism here loses a critical edge, functioning instead to reinforce 'the military as an institution and militarism as an ideology' by perpetuating 'the notion that the military is so central to the entire social order that it is only when women gain access to its core that they can hope to fulfill their hopes and aspirations'.[13] In its deep structure, NOW's legal narrative is a leap out of the female/ private side of the public/private divide basic to Machiavellian realism and straight into the arms of the hegemonic male whose sex-linked activities are valorized thereby. Paradoxically, NOW's repudiation of 'archaic notions of women's role' becomes a tribute to 'archaic notions of men's role'. Because of the indebtedness of their discourse to presumptions geared historically against women and the values to which they are symbolically if problematically linked, feminist realism, whether in its Hobbesian or less extreme 'armed civic virtue' forms, fails to provide a sustained challenge to the Western narrative of war and politics. Ironically, female-linked symbolism is once again suppressed or depreciated this time under a feminist imprimatur as a male-dominant ideal — the 'heroic fighter' or the 'citizen-warrior' is urged on everyone.

JUST WARS AS MODIFIED REALISM

In a world organized along the lines of the realist narrative, there are no easy ways out. There is, however, an alternative tradition to which we in the West have sometimes repaired either to challenge or to chasten the imperatives realism claims merely to describe and denies having in any sense wrought.

Just war theory grows out of a complex genealogy, beginning with the pacifism and withdrawal from the world of early Christian communities through later compromises with the world as Christianity took institutional form. The Christian saviour was a 'prince of peace' and the New Testament Jesus deconstructs the powerful metaphor of the warrior central to Old Testament narrative. He enjoins Peter to sheath his sword; he devirilizes the image of manhood; he tells his followers to go as sheep among wolves and to offer their lives, if need be, but never to take the life of another in violence. From the beginning, Christian narrative presents a pacific ontology, finding in the 'paths of peace' the most natural as well as the most desirable way of being. Violence must justify itself before the court of nonviolence.

Classic just war doctrine, however, is by no means a pacifist discourse.[14] St Augustine's *The City of God*, for example, distinguishes between legitimate and illegitimate use of collective violence. Augustine denounces the *Pax Romana* as a false peace kept in place by evil means and indicts Roman imperialist wars as paradigmatic instances of unjust war. But he defends, with regret, the possibility that a war may be just if it is waged in defense of a common good and to protect the innocent from certain destruction. As eleborated over the centuries, non-combatant immunity gained a secure niche as the most important of *jus in bello* rules, responding to unjust aggression is the central *jus ad bellum*. Just war thinking requires that moral considerations enter into all determinations of collective violence, not as a post hoc gloss but as a serious ground for making political judgments.

In common with realism, just war argument secretes a broader world-view, including a vision of domestic politics. Augustine, for example sees human beings as innately social. It follows that all ways of life are laced through with moral rules and restrictions that provide a web of social order not wholly dependent on external force to keep itself intact. Augustine's household, unlike Machiavelli's private sphere, is 'the beginning or element of the city' and domestic peace bears a relation to 'civic peace'.[15] The sexes are viewed as playing complementary roles rather than as segregated into two separate normative systems governed by wholly different standards of judgment depending upon whether one is a public man or a private woman.

Just war discourse, like realism, has a long and continuing history; it is a gerrymandered edifice scarred by social transformation and moral crisis. A specific strength embedded in its ontology of peace is the vantage point it affords with reference to social arrangements, one from which its adherents frequently assess what the world calls peace and find it wanting. From Augustine's thunderings against the *Pax Romana* to John Paul II's characterization of our present armed-to-the-teeth peace as the continuation of war by other means — not war's opposite but one of the forms war takes in the modern world — just war thinking has, from time to time, offered a critical discursive edge.[16]

My criticisms of just war are directed to two central concerns: One flows directly from just war teaching; the other involves less explicit filiations. I begin with the latter, with cultural images of males and females rooted, at least in part, in just war discourse. Over time, Augustine's moral householders (with husbands cast as just, meaning neither absolute nor arbitrary heads) gave way to a discourse that more sharply divided males and females, their honored activities, and their symbolic force. Men were constituted as just Christian warriors, fighters, and defenders of righteous causes. Women, unevenly and variously depending upon social location, got solidified into a culturally sanctioned vision of virtuous, nonviolent womanhood that I call the 'beautiful soul', drawing upon Hegel's *Phenomenology*.

The tale is by no means simple but, by the late eighteenth century 'absolute distinctions between men and women in regard to violence' had come to prevail.[17] The female beautiful soul is pictured as frugal, self-sacrificing, and, at times, delicate. Although many women empowered themselves to think and to act on the basis of this ideal of female virtue, the symbol easily slides into sentimentalism. To 'preserve the purity of its heart', writes Hegel, the beautiful soul must flee 'from contact with the actual world'.[18] In matters of war and peace, the female beautiful soul cannot put a stop to suffering, cannot effectively fight the mortal wounding of sons, brothers, husbands, fathers. She continues the long tradition of women as weepers, occasions for war, and keepers of the flame of non-warlike values.

The just warrior is a complex construction, an amalgam of Old Testament, chivalric, and civic republican traditions. He is a character we recognize in all the statues on all those commons and greens of small New England towns: the citizen-warrior who died to preserve the union and to free the slaves. Natalie Zemon Davis shows that the image of warlike manliness in the later Middle Ages and through the seventeenth century, was but one male ideal among many, having to compete, for example, with the priest and other religious who foreswore use of their 'sexual instrument' and were forbidden to shed blood. However, 'male physical force could sometimes be moralized' and 'thus could provide the foundation for an ideal of warlike manliness'.[19] This moralization of collective male violence held sway and continues to exert a powerful fascination and to inspire respect.

But the times have outstripped beautiful souls and just warriors alike; the beautiful soul can no longer be protected in her virtuous privacy. Her world, and her children, are vulnerable in the face of nuclear realities. Similarly, the just warrior, fighting fair and square by the rules of the game, is a vision enveloped in the heady mist of an earlier time. War is more and more a matter of remote control. The contemporary face of battle is anomic and impersonal, a technological nightmare, as weapons technology obliterates any distinction between night and day, between the 'front' and the 'rear'. Decades before laser weapons, however, the reality of battle had undermined the ideal of the warrior. World War I constituted the foot-soldier as cannon-fodder. In the first day of the Battle of the Somme, July 1, 1916, 110,000 British men got out of the trenches and began to walk forward along a thirteen-mile front. They had no visible enemy to fight; they wore number tags hung around their necks; 60,000 were dead by the end of the day.

A just war requires agents to carry out its purposes. But if the warrior no longer serves as an avatar of justice, how is war itself to claim this imprimatur? If the present human condition can be described as the continuation of war by other means, a false peace, how can human agents legitimate their aims in the waging of a real war rather than the maintenance of a bogus peace? Does it make sense any longer to construe war as a coherent entity at all? These questions take me to my criticisms of just war argument in our time.

Just war discourse from its inception recognized the rights of political entities to self-defense. The moral requirements for waging war have also remained essentially unchanged from the fourth century to the present. Over time, of course, much has changed including the nature of political bodies, the context of international life, and the totalistic deadliness of weapons. Faced with historic transformations of such awesome magnitude, just war thinkers seek valiantly to apply the appropriate rules to cover increasingly horrific situations. All agree that violence is regrettable, tragic, and to be avoided devoutly. But much slips through the cracks when one gets down to hard cases.

For example, in Michael Walzer's *Just and Unjust Wars*, the most lucid modern treatment of the topic by a nontheologian, queries concerning past practice (the British decision to engage in saturation bombing of German cities during World War II) and present policy (nuclear deterrence theory) are assessed on consequentialist criteria that frequently override the deontological formulae of classic just war teaching (though it, too, required projections of consequence in certain situations). For example,

Walzer justifies, with regret, British saturation bombing of German cities in light of the Nazi threat and given the predictable outcome should Britain fall to Germany. Present threat and future danger override *jus in bello* rules.[20] By declaring Nazism an 'immeasurable evil', Walzer foreordains his judgments: 'Immeasureable' is an absolute and the 'determinate crime' of terror bombing is clearly a lesser evil — it must be the way the issues get framed.

By continually adjusting to the realities of total war, just war discourse is hard to distinguish from modified realism. I noted the example from World War II above in part because Walzer proclaims the present moment one of continuing 'supreme emergency', analogous to the Nazi peril. If what we've got is supreme emergency, what we need — nuclear deterrence — is inexorable. Once again, Walzer regrets his own conclusion. Deterrence is a 'bad way' of 'coping' with supreme emergency but 'there may well be no other that is practical in a world of sovereign and suspicious states. We threaten evil in order not to do it.'[21]

Despite the impressive and determined efforts of Walzer, the US Catholic Bishops, and others, the just war frame is stretched to the breaking point as it can no longer provide a coherent picture of its discursive object — war in any conventional sense. Take, for example, Walzer's discussion of American use of the atomic bombs on Hiroshima and Nagasaki, unjustifiable, he argues, within a just war frame. He goes on to ask: 'How did the people of Hiroshima forfeit their rights?'[22] The language of rights and their forfeiture is impoverished in this context, inadequate to describe what happened on those dreadful days. The shakiness of just war discourse, then, is forced upon us by 'the nature of the modern state combined with the nature of modern total war'.[23] In a twilight zone of false peace, with war deeply rooted inside the infrastructure of the modern state, the discourses of just war and realism link up to confront jointly the seemingly intractable present. I return to this matter in part three.

Few feminist writers on war and peace take up just war discourse explicitly. There is, however, feminist theorizing that may aptly be situated inside the broader frames of beautiful souls and just warriors as features of inherited discourse. The strongest contemporary feminist statement of a beautiful soul position involves celebrations of a 'female principle' as ontologically given and superior to its dark opposite, masculinism. (The male 'other' in this vision is not a just warrior but a dangerous beast.) The evils of the social world are traced in a free-flowing conduit from masculinism to environmental destruction nuclear energy, wars, militarism, and states. In utopian evocations of 'cultural feminism', women are enjoined to create separate communities to free themselves from the male surround and to create a 'space' based on the values they embrace. An essentially Manichean vision, the discourse of feminism's beautiful souls contrasts images of 'caring' and 'connected' females in opposition to 'callous' and 'disconnected' males. Deepening sex segregation, the separatist branch of cultural feminism draws upon, yet much exaggerates received understandings of the beautiful soul.[24]

A second feminist vision indebted implicitly to the wider discursive universe of which just war thinking is a part features a down-to-earth female subject, a soul less beautiful than virtuous in ways that locate her as a social actor. She shares just war's insistence that politics must come under moral scrutiny. Rejecting the hard-line gendered epistemology and metaphysic of an absolute beautiful soul, she nonetheless insists that ways of knowing flow from ways of being in the world and that hers have vitality and validity in ways private and public. The professed ends of feminists in this loosely fitting frame locate the woman as a moral educator and a political actor. She is concerned with 'mothering', whether or not she is a biological mother, in the sense of protecting society's most vulnerable members without patronizing them. She thinks in terms of human dignity, as well as social justice and fairness. She also forges links between 'maternal thinking' and pacifist or non-violent theories of conflict without presuming that it is possible to translate easily particular maternal imperatives into a public good.[25]

The pitfalls of this feminism are linked to its intrinsic strengths. By insisting that women are in and of the social world, its framers draw explicit attention to the context within which their constituted subjects act. But this wider surround not only derogates maternal women, it bombards them with simplistic formulae that equate 'being nice' with 'doing good'. Even as stereotypic maternalisms exert pressure to sentimentalize, competing feminisms are often sharply repudiating, finding in any evocation of 'maternal thinking' a trap and a delusion. A more robust concept of the just (female) as citizen is needed to shore up this disclosure, a matter I take up below.

RESCUING POLITICS FROM WAR: HANNAH ARENDT'S HOPE

Hannah Arendt's attempt to rescue politics from war deepens an important insight of just war theory — underdeveloped in the theory itself — by insisting that the problem lies not only in the compulsions of international relations but in that ordering of modern, technological society just war thinkers call a 'false' or 'armed' peace. Dulled by the accretion of tropes, truths, necessities, and concepts that help us talk ourselves into war, situated inside a world of armed peace, Norman Mailer's claim in 1948 that 'the ultimate purpose' of modern society is continuation of the army by other means seems exaggerated but not altogether far-fetched.[26] Michel Foucault, too, argues that 'politics' (the single quotes are his) 'has been conceived as a continuation, if not exactly and directly of war, at least of the military model as a fundamental means of preventing civil disorder. Politics . . . sought to implement the mechanism of the perfect army, of the disciplined mass, of the docile, useful troop,' and so on.[27]

In an over-coordinated social world, violence may promise a release from inner emptiness or a temporary escape from over-planned pointlessness. Paradoxically, on this view, the routinization of everyday life, much at odds with a heroic or warrior society, nevertheless feeds rather than sates a deeper will to warfare as the prospect of escape from 'impersonality, monotony, standardization', the chance to take and to share risks, to act rather than to persist in predetermined behavior.[28] That promise, however, is itself a victim of our armed peace. War technology devirilizes war fighting. The fighter exists for, and is eclipsed by, his weapons and an awesome nuclear arsenal.

More problematic than the inadequacies of just war doctrine in light of social mimesis of military order, however, is the discourse of 'disassociation' evident in contemporary rationalist, scientized realism. Such realists portray themselves as clear-sighted, unsentimental analysts describing the world as it is. At present, hundreds of think tanks, universities, and government bureaucracies support the efforts of 'scientifically minded brain trusters' who should be criticized, argues Arendt, not because they are thinking the unthinkable, but rather because 'they do not *think* at all'.[29] The danger is this: a world of self-confirming theorems invites fantasies of control over events that we do not have. The scientization of rationalist realism eclipses the strengths classical realists could claim, including awareness of the intractability of events and a recognition that relations between and among states are necessarily alienated. Through abstracted models and logic, hyper-rationalism reduces states and their relations to games that can be stimulated. Consider the following depiction of Western Europe by a strategic analyst: 'Western Europe amounts geographically to a peninsula projecting out from the Eurasian land mass from which large continents of military force can emerge on relatively short notice to invade the peninsula.?[30] Western Europe, reduced to an undifferentiated, manageable piece of territory, becomes (theoretically) expendable or indiscriminately usable for our strategic planning.

Modern thinkers of the abstracted unthinkable are not alone in doing violence to complex realities. 'If truth is the main casualty in war, ambiguity is another,' notes Paul Fussell, and one of the legacies of war is a 'habit of simple distinction, simplification, and opposition'.[31] Mobilized language, wartime's rhetoric of 'binary deadlock', may persist and do much of our thinking for us. The absorption of politics by the language and imperatives of war becomes a permanent rhetorical condition.[32] J. Glenn Gray reminds us that one basic task of a state at war is to portray the enemy in terms as absolute and abstract as possible in order to distinguish as sharply as possible the act of killing from the act of murder. It is always '*the enemy*', a 'pseudo-concrete universal'. This moral absolutism is constituted through language: there is no other way to do it. We are invited to hate without limit and told we are good citizens for doing so.

At one time war fighting often served, paradoxically, to deconstruct war rhetoric as soldiers rediscovered concreteness and particularity in tragic and terrifying ways. For example, Eric Maria Remarque's protagonist in *All Quiet on the Western Front*, bayonets a frightened French soldier who, seeking refuge, has leapt into the trench beside him. Four agonizing hours later the Frenchman dies and when he has died, Remarque's hero, his capacity to perceive and to judge concretely restored, speaks to the man he has killed: 'Comrade, I did not want to kill you ... But you were only an idea to me before, an abstraction that lived in my mind and called forth its appropriate response. It was that abstraction I stabbed.'[33] Gray, similarly, observes that the abstract bloodthirstiness expressed by civilians furthest removed from war fighting was often in contrast to the thinking of front-line soldiers whose moral absolutism dissolved once they met 'the enemy' face to face.[34] Because it is now possible for us to destroy the enemy without ever seeing him or her, abstract hatreds are less likely to rub against concrete friction.

If realism's modern offspring invites dangerous disassociations, an alternative discourse should be one less available for such purposes even as it offers a compelling orientation to the systemic imperatives at work in a world of 'sovereign and suspicious states'. Too often alternatives to 'thinking war' reproduce problematic

features of the discourse they oppose, for example, by insisting
that we love (rather than hate) abstract collectives. But 'the human
race' is a pseudoconcrete universal much like 'the enemy'. Pitched
at a level of abstract universals, the discourse of 'the victims' falls
apart if one moves to specify connections between its grand vision
and political exigencies. Also, an alternative discourse must
problematize war narratives with their teleological assurance of
triumphant endings and their prototypical figurations of fighting
men and weeping women, even as it acknowledges the attraction
of the narrative.[35] Admitting rather than denying what Gray calls
'the communal enthusiasm and ecstasies of war', we are invited to
ask if we might not enlist our energies in some other way. Peace
discourse that denies the violent undercurrents and possibilities in
everyday life and in each one of us, perhaps by projecting that
violence outward into others ('masculinism') is but the opposite
side of the hard-line realist coin.

Hannah Arendt's *On Violence* responds to these concerns by
exposing our acceptance of politics as war by other means. Arendt
asks what historic transformations and discursive practices
made possible a consensus 'among political theorists from Left to
Right ... that violence is nothing more than the most flagrant
manifestation of power?'[36] (The violence Arendt has in mind is
that of groups or collectives, not individual outrage culminating in
a single violent act; Melville's *Billy Budd* is her example.) Her
answer is multiple: teleological constructions of historic inevitability
(known to us as Progress); theories of absolute power tied to the
emergence of the nation-state; the Old Testament tradition of
God's Commandments that fed command-obedience conceptions
of law in Judaeo—Christian discourse; the infusion of biologism
into political discourse, particularly the notion that destruction is
a law of nature and violence a 'life promoting force' through
which men purge the old and rotten. All these 'time-honored
opinions have become dangerous'. Locked into dangerously self-
confirming ways of thinking, embracing 'progress' as a standard
of evaluation, we manage to convince ourselves that good will
come out of horrendous things; that somehow, in history, the end
does justify the means. Both classical liberals and their Marxist
adversaries share this discursive terrain, Arendt argues, though she
is especially critical of 'great trust in the dialectical "power of
negation"' that soothes its adherents into believing that evil 'is but
a temporary manifestation of a still-hidden good'.

By conflating the crude instrumentalism of violence with power,
defined by Arendt as the human ability to act in concert and to

begin anew, we guarantee further loss of space within which authentic empowerment is possible. In this way violence nullifies power and stymies political being. One important step away from the instrumentalism of violence and toward the possibility of politics is to resist the reduction of politics to domination. Arendt evokes no image of isolated heroism here; rather, she underscores the ways in which centralized orders dry up power and political possibility. If we recognize the terms through and means by which this happens, we are less susceptible to unreflective mobilization and more open to finding and creating public space in the current order. As citizens through their actions break repetitive cycles of behavior, power as the 'true opposite' of violence reveals itself.

Arendt's discourse constitutes its subjects as citizens: neither victims nor warriors. She paints no rosy picture of her rescue effort. Just as Gray argues that the will to war is deepened by the emptiness of a false peace, Arendt believes that the greater a society's bureaucratization, the greater will be secret fantasies of destruction. She repudiates grandiose aims and claims, refusing to dictate what politics should do or accomplish instrumentally, for that would undermine her exposé of the future oriented teleologies on which violence and progress feed. To the extent that we see what she is doing and let it work on us, her symbolic alternative for political being offers a plenary jolt to our reigning political metaphors and categories — state of nature, sovereignty, statism, bureaucratization, contractualism, nationalist triumphalism, and so on. If we remain entrapped in this cluster of potent typifications, each of them suffused with violent evocations or built on fears of violence, we will face only more, and deadlier, of what we've already got. Contrastingly, Arendt locates as central a powerful but pacific image that engenders hope, the human capacity that sustains political being.

Evidence of hopelessness is all around us. The majority of young people say they do not believe there will be a future of any sort. We shake our heads in dismay, failing to see that our social arrangements produce hopelessness and require it to hold themselves intact. But the ontological possibility for hope is always present, rooted, ultimately, in 'the fact of natality'. Arendt's metaphor, most fully elaborated in the following passage from *The Human Condition*, is worth quoting in full:

The miracle that saves the world, the realm of human affairs, from its normal, 'natural' ruin is ultimately the fact of natality, in which the faculty of action is ontologically rooted. It is , in other words, the birth of new human beings and the new beginning, the action they are capable of by being born. *Only the full experience of this capacity can bestow upon human affairs faith and hope, those two essential characteristics of human existence ...* that found perhaps their most glorious and most succinct expression in the new words with which the Gospels accounted their 'glad tiding': 'A child has been born unto us.'[37]

The infant, like all beginnings is vulnerable. We must nurture that beginning, not knowing and not being able to control the 'end' of the story.

Arendt's evocation of natal imagery through its most dramatic ur-narrative is not offered as an abstraction to be endorsed abstractly. Rather, she invites us to restore long atrophied dispositions of commemoration and awe; birth, she declares, is a 'miracle', a beginning that renews and irreversibly alters the world. Hers is a fragile yet haunting figuration that stirs recognition of our own vulnerable beginnings and our necessary dependency on others. Placed alongside the reality of human beginnings, many accounts of political beginnings construed as the actions of male hordes or contractualists seem parodic in part because of the massive denial (of 'the female') on which they depend. A 'full experience' of the 'capacity' rooted in birth helps us to keep before our mind's eye the living reality of singularities, differences, and individualities rather than a human mass as objects of possible control or manipulation.[38]

By offering an alternative genealogy that problematizes collective violence and visions of triumph, Arendt devirilizes discourse, not in favor of feminization (for the feminized and masculinized emerged in tandem and both embody dangerous distortions), but politicalization, constituting her male and female objects as citizens who share alike the 'faculty of action'.[39] At this juncture, Arendt's discourse makes contact with that feminism I characterized as a modified vision of the beautiful soul. Her bracing ideal of the citizen adds political robustness to a feminist picture of women drawn to action from their sense of being and their epistemic and social location. Arendt's citizen, for example, may act from her maternal thinking but not as a mother – an important distinction that could help to chasten sentimentalism or claims of moral superiority.

But war is the central concern of this essay. Does Arendt's

discourse offer a specifiable orientation toward international relations? Her discourse shifts the ground on which we stand when we think about states and their relations. We become skeptical about the forms and the claims of the sovereign state; we deflate fantasies of control inspired by the reigning teleology of progress; we recognize the (phony) parity painted by a picture of equally 'sovereign states' and are thereby alert to the many forms hegemony can take. Additionally, Arendt grants 'forgiveness' a central political role as the only way human beings have to break remorseless cycles of vengeance. She embraces an 'ascesis', a refraining or withholding that allows refusal to bring one's force to bear to surface as a strength not a weakness.

Take the dilemma of the nuclear arms race that seems to have a life and dynamic of its own. From an Arendtian perspective, we see current arms control efforts for what they are — the arms race under another name negotiated by a bevy of experts with a vested interest in keeping the race alive so they can 'control' it. On the other hand, her recognition of the limiting conditions internal to the international political order precludes a leap into utopian fantasies of world order or total disarmament. For neither the arms control option (as currently defined) nor calls for immediate disarmament are bold — the first because it is a way of doing business as usual; the second because it covertly sustains business as usual by proclaiming 'solutions' that lie outside the reach of possibility.

Instead, Arendt's perspective invites us — as a strong and dominant nation of awesome potential force — to take unilateral initiatives in order to break symbolically the cycle of vengeance and fear signified by our nuclear arsenals. Just as action from an individual or group may disrupt the automisms of everyday life, action from a single state may send shock waves that reverberate throughout the system. Arendt cannot be pegged as either a 'systems dominance' nor 'sub-systems dominance' thinker — a form of argumentation with which she has no patience in any case. She recognizes systemic imperatives yet sees space for potentially effective change from 'individual (state) action'. The war system is so deeply rooted that to begin to dismantle it in its current and highly dangerous form requires bold strokes.

At this juncture, intimations of an alternative genealogy emerge. Freeman Dyson suggests the *Odyssey* or the theme of homecoming rather than the *Iliad* or the theme of remorseless force as a dominant up-political myth if we are to break the deadlock of victims versus warriors. Socrates, Jesus of Nazareth, and Nietzsche, in some of his teachings, emerge as articulators of the prototypical virtues of restraint and refusal to bring all one's power to bear. For it was Nietzsche, from his disillusionment, who proclaimed the only way out of 'armed peace' to be a people, distinguished by their wars and victories who, from strength, not weakness, 'break the sword' thereby giving peace a chance. 'Rather perish than hate and fear,' he wrote, 'and twice rather perish than make onself hated and feared.'[40] Historic feminist thinkers and movements who rejected politics as force take center stage rather than being relegated to the periphery in this alternative story.

To take up war-as-discourse compels us to recognize the powerful sway of received narratives and reminds us that the concepts through which we think about war, peace, and politics get repeated endlessly, shaping debates, constraining consideration of alternatives, often reassuring us that things cannot really be much different than they are. As we nod an automatic yes when we hear the truism (though we may despair of the truth it tells) that 'there have always been wars', we acknowledge tacitly that 'there have always been war stories', for wars are deeded to us as texts. We cannot identify 'war itself' as an entity apart from a powerful literary tradition that includes poems, epics, myths, official histories, first-person accounts, as well as the articulated theories I have discussed. War and the discourse of war are imbricated, part and parcel of political reality. Contesting the discursive terrain that identifies and gives meaning to what we take these realities to be does not mean one grants a self-subsisting, unwarranted autonomy to discourse; rather, it implies a recognition of the ways in which received doctrines, 'war stories', may lull our critical faculties to sleep, blinding us to possibilities that lie within our reach.

NOTES

1   Although MAD no longer dominates as strategic doctrine, the central theme here elaborated retains vitality. A full elaboration of the major theoretical frames of contemporary feminism as political discourse appears in Jean Bethke Elshtain, *Public Man, Private Women: Women in Social and Political Thought* (Princeton, N.J., Princeton University Press, 1981), Chap. 5.

2   This was one of the things I learned in graduate school.

3   Interestingly, Hannah A rendt, in *On Violence*, seems to endorse this view. Yet she qualifies it and, as I argue in the final section of this article, finally undermines the ground on which such claims are based.

4 I am drawing on portions of *Public Man, Private Woman* for this discussion.

5 Niccolo Machiavelli, *The Prince and the Discourses* (New York: Modern Library, 1950), p. 61

6 Ibid., p. 503. My views on Machiavelli are not widely shared, especially by those theorists who evoke his name as a father of civic republicanism. Nevertheless, I believe there is textual warrant for my claims. Women, or woman, also gets cast as a symbolic nemesis in portions of Machiavelli's discourse, but I do not take up that theme here.

7 Nancy Huston, 'Tales of War and Tears of Women', *Women's Studies International Forum*, 5 no. 3/4 (1982), pp. 271–82, wonderfully evokes women's supporting roles in war narrative.

8 It should be noted that many realists of the 'old school' express skepticism concerning the modern hyperrationalized realism I discuss later on.

9 Ti-Grace Atkinson, 'Theories of Radical Feminism', *Notes from the Second Year: Women's Liberation*, ed. Shulamith Firestone (n.p., 1970), p. 37.

10 Susan Brownmiller, *Against Our Will: Men, Women and Rape* (New York: Simon and Schuster, 1975), p. 388.

11 My point here is not to argue either the fairness or the constitutionality of the all-male draft but to examine the kinds of arguments NOW brought to bear in the case. It should also be noted that there was division inside NOW on this matter.

12 The brief is available from the NOW Legal Defense and Educational Fund, 132 West 42nd Street, New York, NY 10036.

13 Cynthia Enloe, *Does Khaki Become YOU? The Militarisation of Women's Lives* (London: Pluto Press, 1983), pp. 16–17.

14 The 1983 Pastoral Letter of the US Bishops on War and Peace restored the pacifist tradition to a place of importance, however. The pastoral is printed in full in *Origins* (May 19, 1983), pp. 1–32.

15 Henry Paolucci, ed., *The Political Writings of St Augustine* (Chicago: Henry Regnery, 1967), p. 151.

16 John Paul II, 'On Pilgrimage: The UN Address' *Origins* 9, no. 42, pp. 675–80.

17 Natalie Zemon Davis, 'Men, Women, and Violence: Some Reflections on Equality, *Smith Alumnae Quarterly* (April, 1972), p. 15.

18 G. W. F. Hegel, *The Phenomenology of Spirit*, trans. A. V. Miller (Oxford: Clarendon Press, 1977), pp. 399–400.

19 Davis, 'Men, Women and Violence', p. 13.

20 Michael Walzer, *Just and Unjust Wars* (New York: Basic Books, 1977), pp. 251–63. A different view of the process is found in Freeman Dyson's *Disturbing the Universe* (New York: Harper Colophon, 1979). Dyson served in the 'Operational Research Section' of British Bomber Command during the war, calculating probabilities for bombing raids without much of a 'feeling of personal responsibility.'

278   Jean Bethke Elshtain

None of us ever saw the people we killed. None of us particularly cared' (p. 30). But his reflections after the fact are mordant. He writes: 'I began to look backward and to ask myself how it happened that I got involved in this crazy game of murder. Since the beginning of the war I had been retreating step by step from one moral position to another, until at the end I had no moral position at all' (pp. 30–1).

21 Walzer, *Just and Unjust Wars*, p. 274.
22 Ibid., p. 264.
23 Gordon Zahn, *Another Part of the War. The Camp Simon Story* (Amherst, MA: University of Massachusetts Press, 1979), p. 251.
24 The separatist literature is vast but the strongest statement of its theory remains Mary Daly's works, including *Gyn/Ecology: The Metaethics of Radical Feminism* (Boston: Beacon Press, 1979). A softer version in which men may be redeemable is Helen Caldicott, *Missile Envy* (New York: William Morrow, 1984).
25 This perspective has past and present elaborations. See, for example, Jane Addams, *The Long Road of Women's Memory* (New York: Macmillan, 1916) and Sara Ruddick, 'Maternal Thinking', which appears most recently in Joyce Trebilcot, ed., *Mothering: Essays in Feminist Theory* (Totowa, NJ: Rowman and Allanheld, 1984), p. 213–30. I have evoked Ruddick'a formulation in several of my essays. The strengths and weaknesses of 'maternal thinking' as a basis for political actionn are described in historic depth by Amy Swerdlow in her forthcoming work on the Mothers Strike for Peace.
26 Cited in Paul Fussell, *The Great War and Modern Memory* (Oxford: Oxford University Press, 1975): p. 320.
27 Michel Foucault, *Discipline and Punish* (New York: Vintage Books, 1979), pp. 168–9.
28 J. Glenn Gray, *The Warriors. Reflections on Men in Battle* (New York: Harper Colophon, 1970), p. 224.
29 Arendt, *On Violence*, p. 12.
30 Cited in E. P. Thompson, *Beyond the Cold War* (New York: Pantheon, 1982), p. 10.
31 Fussell, *Great War and Modern Memory*, p. 79.
32 See Fussell's discussion in *Great War and Modern Memory*. p. 108.
33 Eric Maria Remarque, *All Quiet on the Western Front* (New York: Fawcett, 1975), p. 195.
34 Gray, *The Warriors*, p. 135.
35 Huston's 'Tales of War, Tears of Women' reminds us of the antiquity and pervasiveness of this narrative in Western history.
36 Arendt, *On Violence*, p. 35.
37 Hannah Arendt, *The Human Condition* (Chicago: University of Chicago Press, 1958), p. 247.
38 Arendt, *On Violence*, p. 81.
39 Arendt makes no gender-based distinction in this faculty though some commentators have argued – I am one of them – that the way

she construes social arrangements contains its own built-in, unacceptable restrictions on action for particular groups and classes. I am not as persuaded of the thorough soundness of this criticism as I once was. The most complete treatment of a strategic doctrine based on neither 'warrior' nor 'victim' thinking, but drawing from each, is Freeman Dyson's recent *Weapons and Hope* (New York: Basic Books, 1984).

40   Gray cites in full the paragraph from Nietzsche's *The Wanderer and His Shadow* in which he repudiates the corruptions that flow from being hated and feared, pp. 225–6. To be sure, one could count twenty declarations by Nietzsche in praise of war for every one condemning it but even in such passages an ironic ambivalence may be at work. A genealogy that locates Jesus and Nietzsche on the 'same side' is provocative and I cannot make a full argument here. But see René Girard, 'The Extinction of Social Order', *Salmagundi* (Spring-Summer, 1984), pp. 204–37 for a discussion of the Gospel deconstruction of mimetic (violent) rivalries and the mechanism of the scapegoat on which rests the 'false transcendence' of violent systems.

10

The Limits of Allegiance in a Nuclear Age

STEPHEN TOULMIN

In recent years, the traditional debate about 'the just war' – i.e., about the special conditions on which a resort to war, or its subsequent conduct, can be morally justified – has won fresh attention. Up to now, Michael Walzer's *Just and Unjust Wars* is the most striking academic product of this revival, but it is only the tip of an iceberg. Meanwhile, in the public arena, the US Catholic Bishops' pastoral letter on War and Nuclear Weapons is firmly rooted in earlier traditions of 'case reasoning' about moral matters.

Either way, the outlines of the just-war analysis are, by now, once again familiar; so, instead of spending needless time on historical exposition, I will state a few commonplaces, and then move to the specific issues raised by the development and use of nuclear weapons. To state certain traditional conclusions concisely:

- The use of violence against the person is in itself immoral, injurious or unjust, and can be justified only when it can be shown that the situation in question is exceptional: e.g., if the violence is the only available means to preserve one's life against attack, and so is the lesser evil. That much is true of state action, quite as much as it is of the actions of individuals.
- War is the use of violence by one sovereign or state against another, as a means of achieving the political goals of that sovereign or state.
- If legitimate and necessary goals of a sovereign or state (e.g., self-defense) can be gained without war, then war ought to be avoided; if this is not so, then at least the resulting war ought to be conducted in a just rather than an unjust manner.

Reprinted with permission from Steven Lee and Avner Cohen (eds) *Nuclear Weapons and the Future of Humanity* (Rowman & Allanheld, Totowa, NJ, 1986), pp. 359–72.

- A war is conducted justly if and only if the violence used is a necessary means of achieving legitimate goals, its use is discriminating, and no more violence is used than is proportionate to the situation: i.e., if and only if it is the only way to achieve those goals, it is aimed exclusively at targets that obstruct this, and its scale is not disproportionate to their value.

- Citizens who owe allegiance to a sovereign state are morally bound to take part in its properly declared wars to the extent — but only to the extent — that the wars are conducted in a just manner.

- If the authorities of a sovereign state wage unjust wars persistently, or as a matter of policy, the moral claims of allegiance binding the citizens to the state are loosened, and may be overridden by other loyalties.

- In extreme cases, citizens may even have the moral duty to resist the state authorities, and restrain them from continuing to wage an unjust war.

Calling these statements 'commonplaces' registers the fact that the traditional debate accepts them as beyond question. Serious argument begins only beyond that point, when one seeks to apply them to ambiguous practical situations: asking (e.g.) what room the claims of allegiance to the modern nation-state leave for the distinction between 'combatants' and 'non-combatants', or on what conditions a 'liberation organization' (say) is morally entitled to act as a state authority.

Some contemporary writers assume that the very existence of nuclear weapons renders the just-war analysis of the morality of warfare irrelevant to our situation. That assumption is hasty and unhelpful. The traditional analysis was, of course, formulated in another age, and its terms apply unambiguously only to the situation at that time. Still, even now it remains one of the few available starting points from which to survey our own moral territory; and, despite all the military innovations and horrors that face us today, we can find some important continuities between 'then' and 'now'. So, the older analysis has not become flatly irrelevant. We need only take special care in extending its conclusions to our own problems, and in identifying the special difficulties that arise in bringing its application up to date.

Three terms particularly need to be exemplified: (a) that 'disproportionate' force, (b) that of a 'sovereign' state, and (c) that of 'allegiance' to the nation-state. The just-war analysis was formulated long before the development of modern explosives, to say nothing of military aircraft, in an age of crossbows, swords, and simple cannon. The doctrine of necessary, proportionate, and discriminating force was first addressed to such questions as, 'How violently may artillery be used to bombard a besieged city?' It was also a time when the locus of sovereign authority was not hard to identify: an age of monarchs, whose rights and powers were defined and understood. Conversely, the claims of allegiance, too, were well-defined, and limited in the well-understood ways. The claims that a monarch could make on the life, time, or property of his subjects — or on those of his 'lieges', which was not the same thing — was limited. At the stage, the romantic totalitarian claims of twentieth century nation-states and superpowers had not yet been conceived.

The definitive statement of the just-war analysis evolved during the sixteenth and seventeenth centuries, because they were a time of turmoil. Both the overseas expansion of the European powers, and the wars of religion between Catholics and Protestants nearer home, posed new and serious moral problems: 'Do the traditional rules of war apply in fighting pagans or barbarians? What about heretics? Still, up to the year 1800, one could still wage war in the spirit of Mozart's aria, 'Non piu andrai'. The first step backward toward the *dis*proportionate, *un*necessary and *un*discriminating violence characteristic of our own century seems to have been taken only as a result of the *professionalization* of warfare initiated by Napoleon Bonaparte.

Living as we do in a time of nuclear weapons and heedless nationalism, we cannot help seeing our ethical problems as vastly graver than those of the 18th century or even the Napoleonic Era. Still, it will be helpful here to consider them in traditional terms. Indeed (I shall argue) the novel difficulties posed by nuclear weapons can be stated with real precision *only* in those terms: viz., as questions about proportionality, sovereignty, and allegiance. Specifically, then, let us address the following questions:

1 Given the destructiveness of nuclear weapons, could their use ever be proportionate to a legitimate goal of state action? If it could not, will not any war in which nuclear weapons are actually used become, *ipso facto*, an unjust war?

2 Given the unlimited violence of nuclear weapons, can their use ever be presented as a legitimate means of self-defense? If not, has not the development of nuclear weapons made the standard assumptions about national sovereignty obsolete?

3 If nuclear warfare makes injustice unavoidable, and renders the claims of national sovereignty hard to sustain, does it not

also make a citizen's allegiance to a nuclear power of superpower equally qualified and ambiguous?

4   When we take all these considerations together, how does the existence of nuclear weapons oblige us to reevaluate our loyalties, as between (say) the claims of sovereign nations, our professions, and humanity at large? And what new institutional restraints should we consider setting in place, to reflect the changing pattern of loyalties and allegiances?

PROPORTIONALITY, NECESSITY AND DISCRIMINATION

Technically speaking, the effects of nuclear bombardment exceed anything known from the use of conventional weapons. But, morally speaking, the objections to using nuclear weapons are not without conventional parallels. One may compare them, for example, with the objections raised against the obliteration bombing campaign, using high explosives and fire bombs, against the cities of Germany and Japan (notably Dresden, Hamburg, and Tokyo) executed by the Allies during the closing phase of World War II.

At the time, some people on the Allied side, who knew with some accuracy what was being done in their names, had scruples about this policy, and those scruples are worth recalling. They were of two kinds. They sprang immediately from the fact that the bombardment was *indiscriminate* — most of the victims were civilians, not soldiers — and from a conviction that, even during so-called 'total war' the distinction between combatants and noncombatants ought not to be wholly ignored. More generally, however, they also had to do with the lack of restraint (i.e., *proportionality*) characteristic of the campaign: the fact that no serious attempt was made to limit damage from the bombardment to 'what was unavoidable to bring about the legitimate goals of State action'. Even at the time, it was not clear that the mass destruction of civilian housing promoted any legitimate goal of state action; and, in retrospect, this is even less arguable. While the Allies may have been justified in pursuing the war against Nazi Germany with resolution, and with all legitimate technical means, calling the resulting conflict 'total war' did not justify removing all traditional moral restraints from the ways in which it was conducted; and 40 years later, some of us are still ashamed to recall how little we actively challenged the obliteration bombing, while it was still going on.

Is that sense of shame merely personal, idiosyncratic, and over-scrupulous? Not at all. Once the indiscriminate character of the bombing was more widely understood, there was a widespread revulsion against it, not least in Britain, which had itself been on the receiving end of mass air attacks, on a smaller scale. Thus, Air Chief Marshall Sir Arthur Harris, the commander-in-chief of RAF Bomber Command responsible for carrying out this obliteration policy, was one of the few major British commanders who did not receive a peerage after the war. Why was he discriminated against? That is a matter for historical debate. But, certainly, with the passage of time — and especially after Hiroshima — there was a general sentiment among people in Britain that the mass bombing policy had not been 'their finest hour'; and Sir Arthur Harris himself emigrated to Rhodesia, to become one of the more eminent supporters of Mr Ian Smith and his white-separatist 'unilateral declaration of independence'.

Physically and medically, the damage and casualties produced by a single nuclear weapon may be unique in horror and scale, but the line between defensible and indefensible ways of conducting warfare was already crossed, long before the issue of nuclear warfare arose. Indeed, the fact that the obliteration bombing of Germany and Japan in 1943–5 was already open to strong, though conditional, moral objection adds force to the argument that the use of nuclear weapons is *un*conditionally immoral. Given that the material damage and civilian suffering at Hamburg or Dresden were already disproportionate to any legitimate goals of state action, how much more clearly will this be the case about any use of nuclear weapons?

By setting the effects of nuclear weapons alongside those of conventional weapons, we make it clear that the burden of proof — already in doubt at the end of World War II with the growing violence of modern total war — has by now shifted decisively. Whether the casualties and damage produced in the bombing of Dresden, Hamburg, and Tokyo were excusable is a matter about which disagreement is still possible. Given its historical context, residual doubt is also possible about President Truman's decision, to drop nuclear bombs on Hiroshima and Nagasaki without a prior 'demonstration' of the new weapons. But, with all that we know now, any serious analysis of the issue must surely lead to the same conclusion as that of the US Catholic Bishops.

To put the point concisely:

- No one has yet formulated *any* legitimate goal of state action that can be gained *only* by the actual use of nuclear weapons. So the moral presumption against such undiscriminating and disproportionate violence remains in place.

This is not the place to pursue the vexing question of whether the possession of nuclear weapons, as instruments of deterrence, is either morally acceptable in itself, or practically compatible with the acknowledgment that it would be morally *un*acceptable to put those instruments to actual use. There is no satisfactory way of dealing with that question briefly, and the discussion in the Catholic Bishops' letter is a useful starting point for any fuller discussion. But we must here consider one possible objection to the present argument: namely, that, in conceivable circumstances, it might be necessary and legitimate to use tactical nuclear weapons against a large-scale attack in Central Europe by conventional forces of the Warsaw Pact.

As to that, one may reply that those who advance this objection in full seriousness need to spell out for themselves, in specific and concrete detail, what the immediate character and likely effects of their actions would be, keeping in mind the nature of the actual terrain of Central Europe, the distribution of population in the region, and the long-term sterilization of the land that would follow from that use. If we reflect once again on the indiscriminate and disproportionate nature of the violence that this suggestion proposes, we shall see that its plausibility is similar to that of the World War II obliteration bombing policy. It looks like a neat way of solving an undoubted military problem; but it is a technique whose actual employment — even if it apparently 'worked' in the short term — would become the object of retrospective shame and regret, in a similar way and for similar reasons to those which have, in retrospect, discredited the obliteration bombing policy of World War II.

Why are people so ready to contemplate this possibility, as a matter to be considered coolly, in a spirit of moral equanimity and political realism? If we study the rhetoric of this argument carefully, to see how the balance is tilted, we cannot wholly overlook the continuing influence of cold war demonology. The rivalry of the superpowers remains a major obstacle to any moral critique of contemporary political issues: on either side of this great divide, it is sufficient to hold up the possible victory of evil over good, i.e., of them over us, in order to give the color of justification to even the most inexcusable of policies. On both sides, fanaticism distorts political perception, both of the intrinsic character of the policies discussed and of their long-term consequences and implications: notably, what kinds of policies they will be seen to have been, and what their broader consequences will be perceived as having been (pardon the phrase) 'once the dust has settled'.

The issue is not a new one. In their passion for conquest, the sixteenth century European invaders of the Americas resented the pope's insistence that the Native Americans were human beings, and so entitled to the same consideration as other human beings. Enthusiastic participants in the sixteenth and seventeenth century wars of religion likewise saw their victims' heresies as excusing any brutality toward them. At the present time, some people are equally tempted to banish communists (or terrorists, or counter-revolutionaries, or imperialists, as the case may be) outside the moral pale, and beyond the reach of all human consideration. So, when holders of public office talk like Alexander Haig, as though we may legitimately use nuclear weapons against the foes of righteousness, we must beg them to consult their consciences, and consider whether they are not yielding to fanaticism.

To put the issue in these terms is not to attribute motives to Alexander Haig or anyone else. (Who can imagine what morally serious state of mind people are in, when they accept the idea of a 'limited nuclear exchange'?) It is merely to reformulate the central point that, as matters stand, the presumption (or moral burden of proof) against any use of nuclear weapons is vastly too high to be surmounted by any of the excuses advanced up to now. Many of us, indeed, are unable to think of any considerations that could excuse, or even palliate, the pain and destruction that would unavoidably result from any future use of nuclear violence, and are confident that the moral presumption against the use of nuclear weapons will remain unrebutted. From this point of view, it would even be morally inexcusable to repeat the obliteration bombing of 1943–45 if none but conventional weapons were employed; and that is *a fortiori* the case of nuclear weapons, with their vastly greater power to destroy, injure, and poison living things of all kinds.

Putting the point as moderately as the gravity of the issues permits, let me summarize it as follows: *In the absence of fresh rebuttals ('excuses') far more powerful than any offered up to now, there is at present no reason to believe that any future use of nuclear weapons will be anything but gravely immoral.*

SOVEREIGNTY

At this point, we may step back. The just-war analysis was first addressed to a situation in which political relations, as much as military technology, were much simpler than they now are. In the Middle Ages, local lords made war against their neighbors using military forces that comprised both horse-riding knights, who were their feudal dependents and sworn 'liegemen' and paid mercenaries, who volunteered to 'die for a living'. The damage these forces were capable of doing was quite limited, and there was no stronger power that could prevent them fighting at all. So a comprehensive moral injunction against all wars would have had no effect: it was more urgent and more realistic to regulate and moderate the wars, by drawing some first lines (e.g.) between those people who were, and those who were not, justly at risk in the associated violence. In legal terms, the knights were justly open to injury and loss, because their feudal oaths implied an assumption of risk: the mercenaries accepted the same risks voluntarily, as explicit or implied terms of their contracts of employment. (Hence the moral weight that was initially attached to distinguishing military or 'combatant' from civilian or 'noncombatant' personnel.)

With this first context in mind, we can see why the just-war account emphasized the kinds of considerations it did; and also, in consequence, why social and political changes since the eighteenth century (no less than changes in military technology) oblige us to reconsider the terms of that analysis, before we apply it to our own times and problems. These social and political changes affect all the parties to military violence: the 'sovereign' authorities at whose instance the war is carried on, the military or combatant forces who are the actual agents of violence, and the civilians, or noncombatants, who are the nonviolent contributors to, onlookers at, and/or victims of warfare.

As to the notion of 'sovereignty': absent effective limits or institutional constraints on the actions of sovereign nations, international relations are organized as relations between nation-states. At least *de jure*, each of these states is accepted as having unabridged liberty to manage its internal affairs. True, it is understood that these states generally agree to conform to a range of agreements governing many of their interactions, the exchange of mail (say), or the regulation of deep-sea fishing. Such agreements are, treated, however, not as formal abridgments on their 'national sovereignty' but as voluntary restraints on their *exercise* of that sovereignty. Even the provisions to which member-nations of the European Economic Community are subject, with the associated sanctions, are no exception to that general statement. They were all accepted voluntarily, as a consequence of each nation's adhesion to the Treaty of Rome; and they can be legally avoided, by a free decision to secede from the community. (In the American sense, that is, there as yet exists no 'United States of Europe'.)

It was all very well to leave the claims of national sovereignty unabridged for so long as the exercise of sovereign rights had (and could have) only limited, controlled, and well-directed effects. In our own time, that is less and less the case, not merely because of the introduction of new military technologies, but more widely. The degree of interdependence between nation-states is generally increasing in the areas of ecology, agriculture, medicine, and elsewhere. To an increasing extent, for instance, any state that ignores responsibility for (say) the flow of industrial effluents from its factories, or the movement of smallpox carriers across its frontiers, risks finding itself an outlaw in the community of nations. *De facto*, if not yet *de jure*, such a state increasingly exposes itself to sanctions at the hands of other nations.

As yet, of course, the 'supranational' republic of nations lacks formal institutions capable of imposing sanctions on outlaw nations. To that extent, the powers by which the nations jointly restrain such outlaws rest at most on agreements to pool their forces and institutions in the service of common interests. But, just, as state power did not always begin as centralized power, so too 'supranational' power may first take shape, not through the deliberate creation of a world state, but through the tacit acceptance of decentralized modes of supranational collaboration. Long before it is abandoned *de jure*, which will be a long time happening, the hitherto unrestricted 'sovereignty' of the nation-state will be hedged in by voluntary limits and restrictions, to such an extent that it loses, at least *de facto*, most of the probability of its being gravely misused.

This general statement calls for qualifications. It assumes that on the international level, as within particular states, greater interdependence makes it increasingly disadvantageous for states to act as 'outlaws', even in advance of formal machinery for the enforcement of international law. On certain occasions, of course, certain states still tend to calculate that the potential gains from the outlawry are worth their price; to that extent, the risks to humanity at large from the survival of 'national sovereignty' will remain grave for many years. But, as Vico and the Epicureans both foresaw, the pragmatic demands of the actual situation may nonetheless lead to the progressive crystallization of supranational institutions and constraints, without any prior need for the sovereign nations involved to agree explicitly on any formal treaty or contract.

What is the relevance of this general argument to nuclear weapons and warfare? It reminds us that in form, if not degree, the problem of developing institutions for the control of new and threatening technologies is one that humanity has successfully dealt with before. One legacy of that victory is the myth of Prometheus. Many people wonder why Prometheus, the benefactor of humanity, was sentenced in folk memory to be crucified and disemboweled. The answer is not hard to guess. Those who saw what power Prometheus had put into the hands of malefactors — e.g., how they could use fire to burn down their neighbors' crops and houses — found the very name of fire as alarming as the word 'atom' is to some people today. In their eyes, the destructive threat of fire outweighed all the blessings of controllable heat; and all the good that Prometheus had thought to bring the human race was apparently canceled out by the risks to which his discovery had exposed them.

What brought the technology of fire under human control was a *legal* invention: the concept of 'arson'. The use of fire was safely naturalized into human life through the development of new institutions and public attitudes, by which the *mis*use of fire was stigmatized as antihuman and punished as a crime. And, if effective ways of controlling nuclear power have so far eluded us, that represents a failure of our institutional imaginations. Lacking the means to police, arraign, and restrain the governments of nation-states, we risk the worst arson ever perpetrated, with neither police protection nor judicial process.

In these circumstances, the intensification and spread in *all* nations of public sentiment about the threat from nuclear weapons, about lack of care in the siting, construction, and management of nuclear power plants, and about the disposal of nuclear wastes are probably the best instruments immediately available to prepare for the emergence of the novel institutions we need. As Henry Maine observed on the national level, the *fiat* of a sovereign can be fully effective as law only where its execution recruits the support and sentiment of the subjects. So here, the breadth and intensity of general public sentiment about nuclear issues, as about environmental ones, will in the long run force the hands of the authorities of nation-states, by creating constraints that will limit *de facto* the practical exercise of powers which those states, as 'sovereigns', technically (*de jure*) still possess.

Is that hope realistic? Or are there special reason why developments that were effective in earlier cases cannot work in the nuclear case? As to that, we should not underrate the beneficent effects of historical obsolescence. The Holy Roman Empire existed in theory, long after it lost any practical role in European politics. This fact was no doubt very *untidy*, but any attempt to abolish the empire formally, with the agreement of all parties concerned, would have done more harm than good: it was better to let it sink into irreversible impotence. Under its fading umbrella, there grew up the smaller, individual nations that eventually took over the powers that Charlemagne's successors (like those of Alexander before him) retained only in name, not in effect.

During the 1970s, there were similar hopeful signs that the so-called 'superpowers' were losing their dominance over world affairs, as smaller regional groupings began to tackle local problems in their own ways, over which America and Russia no longer had a controlling influence. In the 1980s, this hopeful tendency has (it is true) been checked, but that check could well be transient. In time, the diseconomies of scale that now hamper the dinosaurs of the industrial world may well make political superpowerdom, also, irrelevant to the everyday conduct of international affairs. In that case, smaller powers will see that the nuclear strength of both superpowers rests on an element of bluff, and they may develop the courage to call that bluff.

ALLEGIANCE

Once we move beyond this point, the argument becomes more radical. A just-war analysis obliged subjects to take part in a sovereign's wars only *conditionally*. If the sovereign were in grave or repeated breach of those conditions, their duty became to resist, restrain, or depose him. Persistent violation of the moral restraints on military operations, *ipso facto*, made a war an unjust war; and a sovereign who persistently involved his subjects in unjust wars dissolved those bonds of allegiance that required his subjects to obey his commands.

Thus, feudal allegiance was conditional. Knights were open to injury and loss because of their feudal oaths, mercenaries because they were under contract; in both cases there was a *quid pro quo*. The sovereign owed mercenaries whatever was due under their contracts and, although such contracts were usually verbal, they were nonetheless binding on men of honor. To his knights and liegemen, the sovereign owed something more: his support, his

protection, and a share in the fortunes of his realm, on account of
their obedient collaboration. Still, subjects of neither kind were
bound to obey unjust commands. The relations of liege and liege-
man, sovereign and subject, mercenary and lord were two-way
relations, and the obligations so created could be breached by the
sovereign as much as by his subjects. So, quite apart from all
matters of prudence, a medieval monarch (like a pirate chief) had
a standing obligation to keep 'in' with his subjects and to 'deliver
the goods'. Embroiling his subjects in unjust wars was just one
way in which the sovereign could fail in his duties, and put his
subjects' 'allegiance' at risk.

What protection did this situation provide to the civilians or
noncombatants who were not direct parties to the contracts or
oaths of obedience? The answer to that question survives to this
day in the traditions of 'common law', which coincided with those
of current 'common morality'. Both oaths and contracts have an
effect only within broader limits set by morality. Neither the
consequences of an oath nor the provisions of a contract can —
even now — be insisted upon or enforced where they violate those
moral limits. (Gambling debts are matters of honor, and neither
morally binding nor recoverable by law; prostitutes are under
neither a moral nor a contractual obligation to provide sexual
services, etc.) When attempts are made to extend the scope of
contracts or promises beyond morally acceptable limits, courts
will refuse to enforce them, on the ground that their effects will
be 'unconscionable', i.e., against conscience.

No doubt, in actual practice, this doctrine gave medieval civilians
little protection and left them highly vulnerable — especially since
they were under pressure to place themselves, too, in a subject
position, and accept obligations within the larger social hierarchy.
But the moral position was quite clear: it was never a knight's (or
a mercenary's) moral duty to rape or pillage, even if his lord
ordered him to do so. At that point, the lord's orders overreached
their standing limits, and must be set aside as unconscionable.

How does the traditional notion of 'allegiance' apply to the
citizens of a modern nation-state? And how can we apply to those
citizens the aspects of a just-war analysis that hang on this notion?
Those questions do not have clear or obvious answers. In the
United States, the political education of schoolchildren, is confused
by the ceremony of pledging allegiance to the flag. (That phrase is
at best a romantic figure of speech: there is no intelligible sense in
which a flag can undertake to perform the obligations of a 'liege
lord'.) In any other respect, the term 'allegiance' figures rarely in

modern life and thought. Instead, romantic communal enthusiasms are permitted to conceal the fact that the moral obligations that arise from the bonds of loyalty to any state are conditional on the conduct of its officials, and can quite easily be forfeited by them.

Still, despite all the changes in social organization since the Middle Ages, a citizen's obligations do remain conditional. By itself, the mere fact that the officials who exercise a state's sovereign powers were dramatically elected, and not imposed on the state by an hereditary ruling group, by a single dominant party, or by naked force, does nothing to exempt them from the traditional obligations of a sovereign to his subjects. Nor are those officials free to demand that subjects obey any and all of their orders, just and unjust alike. That much will be familiar to all readers of Thoreau's essay *Civil Disobedience*: here, we may just pursue the special implications of the point for the issues raised by nuclear weapons and war.

In discussing 'proportionality' and 'discrimination', we saw that a just-war analysis leads to three conclusions:

1 No legitimate goal of state action which is urgent and important enough to excuse the suffering produced by the use of nuclear weapons could be achieved *only* by the use of those weapons.
2 In no foreseeable circumstances can nuclear weapons be the necessary means to any legitimate goals of military action; and
3 A war in which nuclear weapons are actually used will thus, *ipso facto*, be an unjust war.

We can now add the fourth conclusion:

4 Any actual use of nuclear weapons by a state will at once dissolve the bonds of loyalty and call into question the duty of obedience otherwise binding on the citizens of that state.

In short: as matters stand, *one immediate effect of any actual use of nuclear weapons by the governing authorities of a modern state will be to justify its citizens in disobedience.*

Taken in an isolated and general form, that conclusion is too weak and theoretical to be of use. Once a nuclear exchange between two states has actually begun, what good will it do for a few citizens on either or both sides to declare themselves in a state of disobedience? Still, if we carry our analysis a stage further, two practical suggestions are worth considering:

1 The threat of widespread, morally based disobedience in the event of actual nuclear war will be a healthy check on the

military planning of any Nuclear Power. (We may refer to this as the doctrine of counter-deterrence.)

2   A redirection of people's loyalties, away from the nation-state and toward other independent moral claims, can provide a parallel check on the reckless or irresponsible conduct of governments. (We may refer to this as the doctrine of multiple loyalties.)

The Doctrine of Counter-Deterrence

Imagine that the citizens of the nuclear powers unambiguously require the state's officials to acknowledge the moral situation. In future, they insist, any use of nuclear weapons must put the organs of the state irretrievably in the wrong. Once this has happened, the citizens will declare the bonds of national loyalty dissolved; they will be released from the moral claims of allegiance to their former nation-states; and, as they rebuild their towns and their lives, they will be free to organize themselves into fresh political entities from the ground up. Under a just-war analysis, the nation-state will have forfeited its authority and abdicated its sovereignty. That being so, its citizens may take public affairs into their own hands and order them according to their own decisions.

Surely, that declaration will have little practical effect: even the effect of threatening it will be little greater than the effect of the current state policy of nuclear deterrence. But neither nuclear deterrence nor counter-deterrence (which is its mirror image) addresses the actual situation: both resort to hypothetical scenarios to make points of political rhetoric.

When, for instance, representatives of the nuclear powers present their policies, either in diplomatic contexts or as exercises in public relations, they always take care to add pious disclaimers. They do not really foresee using those weapons: they retain them only because they are in danger from the nuclear weapons of their adversaries. Under the theory of deterrence, rival powers are held back from nuclear war by a fear that springs from the threat of actions that, at the same time, both sides disclaim as unthinkable. Unfortunately, their disclaimers are no more self-interpreting than a broad wink. No hearer can be entirely sure which to take seriously: the threat to use nuclear weapons in hypothetical circumstances, or the disclaimers that accompany this threat. Nor can onlookers ever be fully confident that the officials who formulate these policies are clear about them in their own minds. The US nuclear freeze movement, in fact, got a major boost from things that Alexander Haig said as secretary of state. These provoked the reasonable fear that he himself no longer knew when he was winking and when he was serious. He had apparently talked himself beyond mere deterrence, and now thought of nuclear weapons as morally tolerable instruments of war.

If the state doctrine of deterrence is based on governmental posturing, therefore, it is no objection to a citizens' doctrine of counterdeterrence that it, too, rests on histrionics. In the world of political rhetoric, the sham of deterrence can only be answered by an equally striking countergesture. If the state authorities build up nuclear arsenals that they plan to use only on 'hypothetical' conditions, their citizens are entitled to insist in reply that one further consequence of that hypothetical scenario will be the moral suicide of the state concerned.

At this point, an historical sidelight can be helpful. The medieval balance of church and state placed a check on willful and impetuous monarchs or barons; but, from the sixteenth century on, that check was lost. Fragmentation of spiritual authority and secularization of the state brought into being a new world of absolute sovereigns, who were viewed as God's political agents. Soon enough, of course, the claim of these individual monarchs to unrestricted sovereign power was challenged by their subjects; but that challenge merely shifted the same unrestricted sovereign power from the individual autocrat to other larger, oligarchic or democratic parties and assemblies. From 1650 on, the locus of sovereignty moved from the king to other estates of the realm, but its moral exercise remained effectively unchecked by any countervailing institutions.

True, the new institutions of representative government were supposed (*inter alia*) to speak as the moral voice of the people's conscience. But it was not easy to combine this task with that of being the political voice of larger constituencies: in actual practice, parliaments and congresses have been more effective in their political functions than in their moral ones. Instead of standing aside and serving as moral critics of the sovereign authorities, they have competed for a share of sovereign power. As a result, the political operation of modern nation-states has no more been restricted by institutionalized moral criticism than were the decisions of seventeenth century absolute monarchs; and the resulting state of affairs has persisted for some 300 years, punctuated only by a series of revolutions, in the British North American colonies, France, Russia, and elsewhere, whose spokesman always chose to justify the resulting shifts in political power as fulfilling, also, important *moral* goals.

Once again, however, the compromise on which this 300-year interregnum rested is undercut by the development of nuclear weapons. In their roles as the moral critics of nation-states, parliaments, congresses and supreme Soviets alike share a common failing: they, too, are committed to a belief in unqualified national sovereignty. Yet the claims of morality cannot be kept within the frontiers of any single state; and the voice of moral criticism can be — and often has been — raised across national boundaries. That is why, for lack of a better forum, we so often see the organs of the United Nations used as a locus for moral declarations and denunciations.

The Doctrine of Multiple Loyalties

So far, the kernel of our argument has been that twentieth century nations, states and communities are laying claim to rights and loyalties as unlimited as those of absolute monarchs: meanwhile, the facts of life, death, and power in a nuclear age make it morally proper and vitally necessary to find a way of restricting the scope of those claims.

Given the moral authority of the medieval church, monarchs and barons were open to external criticism, and could no longer claim to be in the right when they acted unconscionably. It was no doubt annoying for a monarch to find his authority challenged: in this respect, the conflict of wills between King Henry II and Thomas Becket, represented in T. S. Eliot's *Murder in the Cathedral*, was merely typical. Nowadays, when the conduct of affairs falls into the hands of unscrupulous or willful generals, presidents, and party leaders, we have no such defense. In our pluralistic society, there is neither a generally accepted source of moral criticism, nor a common standard against which their conduct can be measured; as a result, the state authorities can defend their claims to authority against external criticism by appealing to nationalistic passions — i.e., by 'wrapping themselves in the flag'.

Historically, then, the current reaction against the claims of nationalism, and the rise of morally based pressure groups, have a longer-term importance. Taken together, they can even be seen as first steps toward a renewed system of civil religion. Sometimes alongside, and sometimes in alliance with, the churches, a coalition of 'movements' (devoted to enviromental protection, nuclear freeze, consumer's rights, and similar issues) is engaged in restating that consensus about the human interests underlying moral arguments, which, ever since Aquinas, has been seen to carry conviction with 'the natural reason' of all humans alike. And when industrialists and politicians find these pressure groups irritating, the reasons are once again familiar: recall King Henry II's heartfelt cry, 'Who will rid me of this meddlesome priest?'

There is no occasion to relax this pressure. Whoever is its current occupant, the White House can never be a bed of roses; nor can major political decisions be exempt from moral appraisal and criticism. When, for instance, Richard Nixon spoke neither of the people, nor of the Constitution, but of *himself* as 'the Sovereign' his hearers well understood that, in his fantasies, the powers of the president were those of an absolute monarch. If the authorities of nation-states have been able to elevate themselves above criticism, as the sole judges and guardians of 'the national interest', that is because, in the countries of the industrialized world, the earlier consensus has fallen into disorder. So the central question becomes: *In the name of whom, or what, can this external criticism of the modern nation-states — its governors, officials and functionaries — be conducted? In a largely secular society, what other loyalties can counterbalance the unqualified claims of nation, community, or state?*

This is where the issue of multiple loyalties is crucial. The medieval church spoke in the name of a God whose authority no one, however great his temporal power, was ready to challenge. Faced with the exaggerated claims of the modern nation-state, individual citizens need other foci of loyalty and interest, in order to counter those claims. The issue is both complex and delicate, and we can land ourselves in trouble by tackling it on too abstract a level. The French revolutionaries, for instance, saw the problem clearly; but their counterreligion of reason and humanity quickly degenerated into authoritarian idolization. Rival groups of Marxist, Leninist, and Maoist ideologues today speak, with passionate intensity, about the interests of the workers, and the policies that will (in their views) promote those interests. At once, however, moral conflicts arise: by some preestablished harmony, those policies are always ones that guarantee the ideologues themselves positions of great political power. So, we need to find foci of loyalty that are as powerful as those of nationalism, but also less abstract, more familiar, and associated with values that are less easily corrupted.

One such focus is the loyalties and values we encounter in professional life. Commonly, these loyalties and values have a transnational, or even international, scope and institutional expression. (The USSR views that World Psychiatric Association with the same jaundiced eye that Henry II turned on Becket.) In the history of the nuclear freeze movement, one supranational forum within which the antinuclear case has made real progress has been the professions, most notably the medical profession. Physicians, preeminently, have special reason to recognize other moral claims besides those of nation-states; and, to a lesser extent, the same is true of all professionals. So, if groups like Physicians for Social Responsibility have had a major role in the public advocacy of a nuclear freeze, that is no accident, owing (say) to the charismatic personalities of some individual speakers. Rather, it reflects the multiple loyalties to which physicians are essentially subject, as being not merely citizens, but also humans and professionals.

Professionals of many kinds — physicians most of all — can understand the consequences of a nuclear exchange and explain to their fellow citizens the catastrophic implications of current policies in all the nuclear powers. If any alternative focus of loyalty can serve today as an immediate check on the unqualified claims of the idolatously 'sovereign' nation, it is the duties that are well known to all professionals: duties toward clients, patients, and fellow-humans in general, whose scope carries across the boundaries between different nations and states. An American physician or Russian psychiatrist, an Israeli lawyer or Danish mathematician faces his own built-in ethical conflicts. Between purely national duties to a state and (say) the supranational duties of a physician to all sick human beings, such conflicts are to be expected. So there is special room for professional people to band together and use their shared commitment to the values of their disciplines as a ground to question authority and 'think otherwise'.

To sum up: The claims of the nation-state over the citizen have increased, are increasing, and ought to be diminished. As professional people, for instance, we are not merely entitled to weigh our loyalties as professionals against our loyalties as (say) Russians or Americans; we are morally obliged to do so. If we find these professional obligations overriding those of national affiliation, so be it. *It is in fact a professional duty for people to measure their national loyalties against their human and professional consciences, and to question the judgment of politicians and other spokesmen for 'the national interest', whenever their factual knowledge or their moral perceptiveness requires.*

In both of these directions — both counter-deterrence and multiple loyalties — critics of current nuclear weapons policy in the nation-state are already following, intuitively, the route that a just-war analysis legitimates. A world in which people still act on the maxim 'My country, right or wrong' is a world headed for self-destruction; for any worship of the nation can blind us to the conditional claims which are all that sovereign power — even, that of a beloved country — can justly make on us.

We can win back our souls, and have a reasonable chance of preserving our bodies, only by fighting against the idolatry of the nation; since, in the last resort, the claims of human survival must override the claims of sovereignty and nationhood. As human beings and professionals, we must oppose the unjust act — above all, the unjust wars and threats of war — conducted by our own nation-states. And, if this means threatening disobedience, then, once again, so be it. Along that road, we shall at least be traveling in excellent company.

11

On Surviving Justly:
Ethics and Nuclear Disarmament

STANLEY HAUERWAS

BEGINNING WITH THE END

I am going to begin by telling you how the analysis that constitutes the main portion of this chapter comes out — that is, I am going to begin with the end. My conclusion is that culturally we lack a coherent morality to sustain the current antinuclear enthusiasm on the part of many. By typifying and analyzing what I take to be the four main moral positions underlying the antinuclear move-ment — that is, the pacifist, just war, survivalist, and sovereign-states deterrence — I will try to support this conclusion.

In another, more substantive sense, I am going to begin with the end. For I want to show that the challenge of nuclear weapons involves theological issues that require a theological response — a response, however, that our culture lacks the resources to develop. In particular I will contend that the ethical confusion underlying the proposals for nuclear disarmament is at least partly due to false eschatologies. Put differently, the peace sought by many is too often equivalent to order while lacking a sufficient sense of what a just peace entails.[1] For a peace based on insufficient eschatology cannot help but be an abstract ideal that lacks concrete embodiment in the lives and habits of an actual community. Moreover without such a community our strategies for nuclear disarmament as well as the moral resources on which they draw cannot help but offer short term solutions and false consolation.

Before I begin analyzing the four moral positions, I need to make two general points. The first is to remind you that they are types — that is, they are ideal characterizations that may fail to depict accurately the complexity of any actual position. For example, my last two types — the survivalist and sovereign-state

Reprinted with permission from Stanley Hauerwas *Against the Nations* (Winston Press, Minneapolis, Minnesota, 1985), pp. 132–59.

deterrence – can both be interpreted as forms of just war logic since each is a way to work out the criteria of proportionality. The differences I locate between these types are more a matter of classifying different kinds of rhetorical appeal than strict logic.[2] Yet I hope to show that such differences are illuminating as they represent significant moral and strategic alternatives.

Second, the analysis I offer necessarily involves moral and strategic considerations not easily separated. Any one moral position may have several strategic alternatives, but it is just as likely that agreement on strategic alternatives may mask deep moral differences. That such is the case means that the analysis I provide oversimplifies at some points. However, I hope the attempt to locate the complex relation between moral and strategic considerations will compensate for this obvious problem.

There is a more profound problem with the task I have set for myself in this chapter. Why bother trying to make explicit the various ethical positions underwriting the antinuclear movement since no more is claimed by the participants in that movement than that they are a political coalition? They do not presuppose that they share a common moral position nor do they need one to sustain the movement. But I think such a response is insufficient since the diverse ethical commitments are by no means compatible. Unless our differences are uncovered, moreover, the movement risks losing its power once it is no longer able to command the attention of the media.

But this puts me in a rather odd position, especially since I am a pacifist. For it almost seems immoral to do what I propose as it may have the result of making the political task of disarmament more difficult. My only defense is to retreat to the questionable assumption that the unexamined life is not worth living. But let us not forget the classical words of Peter Devries, 'The unexamined life may not be worth living, but the examined life is no bowl of cherries either.'

PACIFISM

I will not discuss the pacifist responses to nuclear disarmament at any length since pacifism, at least in principle, does not make any particular claims about nuclear war that it does not make about any war – except that if war is bad, nuclear war is worse. Pacifism needs to be discussed briefly, however, as a necessary backdrop for helping us understand the logic of the just war position and how the latter differs from survivalism. By pacifism, which obviously has many different forms and types, I mean any position that involves the disavowal of violence as a means to secure otherwise legitimate ends.

The pacifist claims the issue raised by nuclear weapons is not one of being killed but of unjust killing. For example, as Ed Laarman has suggested:

> For Christians, the first issue raised by nuclear or any other kind of war should not be, 'Am I ready to die?' but 'Am I ready to kill?' Christians in the United States should be more troubled by American missiles pointed at the Soviet Union than by Soviet missiles pointed at them. While this may be existentially hard to achieve, it is clearly required by our confession. As Christians, we believe that it is more important for us to be faithful to God the Father and our Lord Jesus Christ than it is simply to survive. The central question for Christian citizens in this instance is whether the use and possession of nuclear weapons is consistent with our Christian commitment.[3]

Though pacifist and just war positions are often seen as opposites, they share the assumption that the first question about violence is whether or how I should be ready to kill. Moreover the just war perspective, like that of the pacifist, places the burden of proof on those who would take up violence, rather than those who would refrain from it. As a result, the pacifist and just war positions have a 'moralistic' cast that the other two positions lack. Both the pacifist and just war advocate approach these issues already armed with certain moral presuppositions that challenge the resort to violence. The question of the legitimacy and use of nuclear weapons is thus answered by determining the degree to which they conform to pre-determined moral presuppositions. The significance of this will be most clearly seen once the just war position is contrasted with that of sovereign-state deterrence.

Before leaving the pacifist option, however, I need to qualify my claim that the pacifists have nothing particular to say about nuclear warfare that they do not also say about any warfare. There are some pacifists who justify their position in consequential terms, calling attention to the bad results of violence. Undoubtedly they could make their case more strongly with reference to nuclear war. Pacifists of this sort might share presuppositions with the survivalist inasmuch as the latter has a stake in showing that nuclear warfare, unlike other forms of war, threatens the very existence of the human species. Viewed in this way war becomes the ultimate form of irrationality.

A pacifism of a more theological sort — for example, a pacifism based on the conviction that any resort to violence betrays one's relation to God even if it otherwise might have good results — makes no particular judgment against nuclear warfare that is not an extension of the general negative judgment about all violence. That such is the case, moreover, reminds us that it makes a difference how and what kind of religious convictions are used to inform the various typological positions I have isolated. For example, while they share a certain approach to the question, the pacifist is more likely to make more direct theological appeals than the advocates of just war positions. In the hopes of commanding the conscience of many, the latter has a stake in justifying his or her position in terms of appeal to some account of natural law. In contrast, the survivalist tends toward apocalyptic appeals though such appeals do not necessarily require theological presuppositions. The sovereign-states deterrent advocates, as we shall see, share a natural affinity with various forms of Augustinianism and/or realism.

JUST WAR AND THE LIMITS OF NUCLEAR WAR

My partial treatment of the just war position in relation to pacifism already suggests its complexity. Contrary to the assumed or asserted clarity of the just war criteria, complex questions concerning the status and content of the just war position remain outstanding. On the surface the just war position appears straightforward enough. For example, we have become used to characterizing the criteria of the just war as: (1) declared by a legitimate authority; (2) has a just cause; (3) that there be a reasonable hope of success; (4) proportionally more good than evil comes from the war; (5) the war be fought with a just intention; (6) non-combatant immunity; (7) the object is not to kill the enemy but to incapacitate them, therefore prisoners of war are treated respectfully; and (8) unnecessary suffering is avoided.[4]

But this simple list is deceptive as each of these 'criteria' is ambiguous. What is legitimate authority? What does it mean to 'declare' war and how do we distinguish 'defensive' from 'offensive' wars? Who are non-combatants in the age of democracies? Do all the criteria have to be met to make a war just or only some of them? If the latter, which ones? Is there a lexical order among the criteria and if so what is its basis? And why these criteria and not others? Where did these come from and from what paradigm of legitimate violence do they draw their justification? For example, is the just war position developed from a paradigm of self-defense or from one of defense of the innocent?[5] (Interestingly this also has implications for the theological appeals required since the latter paradigm is more likely to require special theological assumptions not thought necessary for self-defense. But then the latter may well involve assumptions about the status of survival not easily reconciled with some of Jesus' teaching concerning the secondary status of regard for self.)

Even more important than these questions is the status given to the just war position. The questions raised in the last paragraph are overly formal if the just war position is interpreted not as a deductive set of rules, but rather as an ongoing discussion of a civilization which limits the extent of the destruction caused by wars. From this latter perspective, the just war is more appropriately described as a tradition that can be expressed only as a theory if, as James Johnson insists, 'care is taken to express this theory generally and with a degree of open-endedness. That is, room must be left for particular interpretations of the general provisions of the theory and for development of its ideas to cope with new experiences of reality.'[6]

When just war is understood in this fashion nuclear weapons are not automatically ruled out simply because they seem to violate the principle of noncombatant immunity. Since the purpose of just war thinking is not to determine in a legalistic manner what is or what is not a just war, but rather to make war as nearly just as it can be, there is no clear distinction that can be drawn between just and unjust weapons. Again, as Johnson reminds us:

> Moral values are perceived by individuals and cultures in the encounter with history, and persistence of the ideas of non-combatant immunity and the authority to initiate war over so long a time argues as strongly as possible that these represent deeply held values in Western culture. The weakness of weapons limitation is that it does not draw directly on some such deeply held value, but rather proceeds indirectly from others; for example one way to protect noncombatants is by restricting weapons used in the presence of non-combatants to those most capable of being used discriminatingly against combatants. Weapons limits represent a means,

not an end; the categories of noncombatant immunity and right authority instead point to ends perceived as valuable by Western culture generally.[7]

Thus the often made, but seldom analyzed, claim that nuclear weapons have made just war thinking irrelevant fails adequately to understand the purpose of just war thought. On the contrary, it has made such thinking all the more relevant. By drawing on the just war tradition we are forced to find and develop ways to conduct even nuclear warfare less unjustly – e.g., the development of the neutron bomb.[8] For again, as Johnson reminds us:

> There is a kind of implicit impetus in the just war tradition to conceive of strategies and tactics, to invent and deploy weapons that are less massively destructive of persons and their values than those already at hand. It is thus, for example, an implication of just war tradition that an alternative should be found to tactical nuclear weapons intended for use against land forces. Use of such weapons, besides risking escalation to a general nuclear interchange, would cause immediate and long-term damage to noncombatants that is hard or impossible to justify.[9]

Interesting as these issues are for an interpretation of the just war position, for my purposes it is more important to locate the moral logic underlying the just war tradition. As I have already noted, just war thinking necessarily draws on pacifist presuppositions for its rationale – that those who resort to violence bear the burden of proof. Equally important is how that proof is supplied, for it is not prima facie evident that the justification for the resort to violence does or should draw on the alleged 'right to self-defense'. Indeed, there is evidence that the strongest accounts of just war thinking are based on the duty to aid the innocent. From this perspective it can be seen that morally the just war tradition is first of all much more a matter of social theory about legitimate authority than simply a casuistical attempt to justify the use of violence to protect one's own person.

Thus Paul Ramsey calls attention to the fact that Augustine refused to justify Christian participation in war on grounds of self-defense. Since it is better to suffer evil than to do it, Christians must be personally ready to die rather than defend themselves if such defense requires that the aggressor be killed. Here the rationale for the just war is not self-defense, but defense of the innocent.

Consistently Ramsey argues that such a defense of the innocent must be made impersonal through the office of the state.[10] Such impersonality is exactly what allows the limited form of response since the state has reason, and indeed is required, to use no more force than is necessary to prevent the attacker from destroying the innocent. Indeed it may be one of the most important insights of the just war position to limit the right to make war to but a few 'sovereigns', for otherwise we have no way to limit the individual's destructive capacity. This distinction between individual and state makes it possible, at least in principle, for one to be personally a pacifist and yet, in the interest of limiting the violence necessary to protect the innocent, support a state policy of just war.[11]

So one might well offer a defense of certain forms of nuclear strategies on the grounds that the state has a duty to those it is pledged to defend when threatened by the nuclear weapons of the other side. Of course such a defense would require these strategies be shaped as much as possible by a commitment in accordance with just war thinking. However, when such a commitment significantly affects policy making, it often encounters new difficulties. For example, a discriminating nuclear strategy might well require that our nuclear weapons be counter-force targeted rather than counter-city. The problem with that strategy, however, is it increases the likelihood of nuclear war since it tempts the other side to think that they might be able to wage nuclear war in which they might be a relative 'winner'.

But perhaps such difficulties, and the objections they encourage to just war theories, fail to do justice to the moral integrity of the just war position. For remember that just war logic, at least as I have depicted it, does not draw on survival as an overriding value to justify its logic. It assumes neither the survival of the individual nor the nation as an end in itself. Survival must be subordinated to the moral obligation to protect the innocent, of which the nation is only the means. Thus it might be possible to develop a just war nuclear strategy — for example, a counter-force targeting — that increases the danger of nuclear war, but that is not in itself a decisive moral consideration for those committed to a just war tradition. For it is inherent in their position that war must be subject to political ends beyond survival. As we shall see, therefore, just war thinkers share the concern with sovereign-state deterrence advocates to subject the nuclear buildup to rational political objectives.[12]

The integrity of the moral logic of the just war position in this respect seems to me unassailable. What must be asked, however, is whether it is capable of commanding the necessary political support. For in an interesting way once the implications of the just war position are spelled out the possibility of a society sustaining the moral ethos necessary to support such a war seems as unlikely and utopian as a nation taking a pacifist stance. For example, are the American people ready to support a nuclear policy that is more nearly just if that means destabilizing a system of mutually assured destruction in a manner that increases the likelihood of nuclear war? The commitment necessary for a nation to sustain a just war strategy is almost as demanding as that necessary to sustain a consistent pacifism.

Returning to those who interpret the just war position in a more formal manner, they are not without resources when it comes to the issue of nuclear war. Even if they judge that nuclear weapons are inherently indiscriminate, they might still argue that such arms can be possessed as a bluff and thus serve as a deterrent. The bluff position assumes it is immoral to use nuclear weapons; yet it allows us to possess those weapons as a threat against the enemy provided we have no intention of ever carrying it out. Indeed, even if we are attacked, we must resolve not to return in kind. The only proviso is that the enemy must remain uncertain whether we are bluffing or not.

One problem with such a strategy is that the enemy must be unsure whether you are really so moral you would not return in kind. Indeed the resolution not to use our weapons requires the leader of a just war nation to act as if he or she is not bluffing. But such a position confuses our professed commitment to democratic polity since citizens cannot know if their leaders are or are not willing to refrain from using these weapons. Thus such a strategy by its very nature excludes the possibility of public debate necessary to sustain a just war strategy.[13]

The final problem with the bluff position, or the possession-but-no-use strategy, is it does nothing to help stabilize, and may even make more unstable, our current weapons balance. In order to sustain a peace based on the existence of our ability to annihilate one another, we are constantly forced to counter the supposed strength of the other side. But since we are never sure how the strength of the other side should compare to ours, we are in the position of having to add to the nuclear arsenal in the hope of finding a position from which we can begin to disarm ourselves. But if we ever approached such a position (e.g., if we knew how to develop an unfailing laser defense system), it would only contribute to the danger since the other side could never let such a system be deployed. And so it goes ...

THE SURVIVALIST

In contrast to pacifists and the just war advocates, the survivalists do not begin with an established theory about if and when life can be taken justly. Rather survivalists are so impressed with the destructive power of nuclear weapons and a sense of horror with the prospect of their use they conclude nuclear war must excluded at all costs. Their concern is not whether nuclear weapons can be used in a discriminating manner, but whether the very existence of such weapons does not threaten the existence of the human species. It is extremely important that we understand why the issue of human survival is so central for them.

The survivalists do not begin with any commitment to pacifism. They, at least in principle, assume and accept the possibility of conventional war (though as we shall see they think nuclear war has now made that impossible). But if one accepts war as a possible means to settle disputes among nations, then why single out nuclear weapons as particularly wrong? Are they not but another stage, admittedly an extraordinary stage, in mankind's attempt to secure weapons of war that are effective? Hence survivalists must show the essential discontinuity between conventional and nuclear weapons. They do so by condemning nuclear weapons not because they cannot be used in a discriminating manner but because they threaten the existence of the globe. So survivalists have an interest in maintaining that nuclear war will be total war since otherwise they would have no basis for singling out nuclear weapons as deserving particular condemnation.

Jonathan Schell has developed this position well in his *The Fate of the Earth*. After a painstaking analysis of the unimaginable destructive power of nuclear weapons, he concludes:

Bearing in mind that the possible consequences of the detonations of thousands of megatons of nuclear explosives include the blinding of insects, birds, and beasts all over the world; the extinction of many ocean species, among them some at the base of the food chain; the temporary or permanent alteration of the climate of the globe, with the outside chance of 'dramatic' and 'major' alteration in the structure of the atmosphere; the pollution of the whole ecosphere with oxides of nitrogen; the incapacitation in ten minutes of unprotected people who go out into the sunlight; the blinding of people who go out into the sunlight; a significant decrease in photosynthesis in plants around the world; the scalding and killing of many crops; the increase in rates of cancer and mutation around the world, but especially in targeted zones, and the attendant risk of global epidemics; the possible poisoning of all vertebrates by sharply increased levels of Vitamin D in their skin as a result of increased ultraviolet light; and the outright slaughter on all targeted continents of most human beings and other living things by the initial nuclear radiation, the fireballs, the thermal pulses, the blast waves, the mass fires, and the fallout from the explosions; and considering that these consequences will all interact with one another in unguessable ways and, furthermore, are in all likelihood an incomplete list, which will be added to as our knowledge of the earth increases, one must conclude that a full-scale nuclear holocaust could lead to the extinction of mankind.[14]

Of course this is the worst-possible-case scenario, but Schell argues that we have no reason to think that a nuclear exchange once begun would lead to any other results. And in the absence of any knowledge to the contrary it is immoral to continue to possess such weapons.

But why is it immoral? According to Schell it is because 'we have no right to place the possibility of this limitless, eternal defeat on the same footing as risks that we run in the ordinary conduct of our affairs in our particular transient moments of human history.'[15] We have no right to prevent the possibility of a common world which encompasses our past, present, and future. And it is just that world which is the source of all value. The creation of 'a common world is the use that we human beings, and we alone among the earth's creatures, have made of the biological circumstances that, while each of us is mortal, our species is biologically immortal. In fact, it is only because humanity has built up a common world that we can fear our destruction as a species.'[16] And such destruction in unthinkable for 'there are no ethics apart from service to the human community, and therefore no ethical commandments that can justify the extinction of humanity.'[17] Therefore the question the peril of extinction puts before the living is: 'Who would miss human life if they extinguished it? To which the only honest answer is: Nobody.'[18] That very fact is enough to sustain the judgment that nuclear weapons must be eliminated because anything that threatens the very value of value itself is inherently immoral.

But it is not sufficient to eliminate nuclear weapons, according to Schell, for their existence has in fact brought an end to war itself. With 'the invention of nuclear weapons, it became impossible for violence to be fashioned into war, or to achieve what war used to achieve. Violence can no longer break down the opposition of the adversary; it can no longer produce a victory and defeat; it can no longer attain its ends. It can no longer be war.'[19] As if this were not enough, Schell argues further that nuclear weapons have not only ended the possibility of war, but war's necessary correlative, the nation-state. For there is an insoluble connection between war and sovereignty, and the price we pay for our insistence on dividing ourselves into sovereign states is the peril of extinction.[20]

Thus, those who tell us that we must have nuclear weapons to prevent their use are deceiving themselves and us. We deploy them not for protection, but to protect national sovereignty and, 'if this aim were not present, they would be quickly dismantled.' Yet to call into question the status of national sovereignty has a further implication, for it means that there is no way we can disarm nuclear weapons without disarming conventionally. Conventional arms continue to insure for some nations the ability to employ the science, which cannot be destroyed, to build nuclear weapons. Through this chain of reasoning Schell reaches the extraordinary conclusion that has become the most quoted passage of this important and widely read book:

> But if we accept both nuclear and conventional disarmament, then we are speaking of revolutionizing the politics of the earth. The task we face is to find a means of political action that will permit human beings to pursue any end for the rest of time. We are asked to replace the mechanism by which political decisions, whatever they may be, are reached. In sum, the task is nothing less than to reinvent politics: to reinvent the world.[21]

As we approach the year 2000 we must expect a good deal of apocalypticism; yet it is a bit surprising when it comes in the pages of the *New Yorker*[22] and in the rhetoric of nuclear terror. For Schell's depiction of our situation certainly has an apocalyptic tone and his solution, if it can be called that, utopian. But neither his description nor his solution are to be belittled for that. After all, Christians are a people who follow a savior who was clearly apocalyptic and made utopian appeals. Rather the problem with Schell's position is not its apocalyptic tone, but our inability to assess his claims. For his argument against nuclear weapons is valid only if his empirical claim is valid — namely, that the use of nuclear weapons will lead to the destruction of the human species. He may well be right about this, and he certainly provides us with some graphic illustrations of the power of nuclear weapons, but we have no way of knowing whether in fact he is right — at least we can have no way of knowing until it is too late. The moral significance of this point cannot be ignored, for it illustrates what happens when the moral issue raised by nuclear weapons shifts from the problem of discrimination to that of the survival of the human species. (Moreover there is the further problem of knowing whether *all* humans must be destroyed for Schell's case to be made good. One feels a bit like Abraham bargaining with God over Sodom — what about a hundred, ten, etc.)

However, a more profound problem with Schell's apocalyptic account is not that it is apocalyptic, but that it is apocalyptic humanism. It can properly be asked if human survival is the ultimate good, or whether, without humanity, there will be nothing left to value. Certainly there are religious traditions that can respond with a resounding yes when asked if there will be anyone to value anything if mankind is destroyed. Moreover the survival of the human species as an end in itself has moral implications about the relation of humanity to the animal world that certainly needs to be analyzed if not questioned. Schell simply does not tell us why we should make morally normative the philosophically questionable, but scientifically useful, designation of 'species'.

Schell's reliance on the status of the human species as the determinative moral factor reveals the deep gulf between himself and pacifism and the just war position. The latter assume that, even if it threatens the very survival of the human species, one must not do evil that good may come — for example, murder another human being. Such an assumption draws on profound theological convictions about how God would have us care for this creation that constitutes a theocentrism quite different from that of Schell.[23]

It is interesting to note that Schell does appeal to the example of Christ in support of his views. He tells us Christ stated that

> religious faith that is divorced from the love of human beings is empty and dangerous. For example, He said, 'If thou bring thy gift to the altar, and there rememberest that thy brother has aught against thee; leave there thy gift before the altar, and go thy way; first be reconciled to thy brother, and then come and offer thy gift.' We who have planned out the

deaths of hundreds of millions of our brothers plainly have a great deal of work to do before we return to the altar. Certainly, the corpse of mankind would be the least acceptable of all conceivable offerings on the altar of this God.[24]

But would it? It is surely correct to say the murder of the human species would hardly please God, but that is not to say that our death, indeed the death of the human species itself, would deny his ultimate love for us. Schell's humane concerns can cause us to ignore that he subordinates to survival all other values that we think make our living and our dying worthwhile.

The significance of this point is nicely displayed by Paul Ramsey's argument in *War and the Christian Conscience* against Arnold Toynbee and others who had suggested it would be better to negotiate with the Soviets from a position of weakness than to continue to risk nuclear annihilation. In response Ramsey reminds us that as Christians we always know the world will end, and 'knowledge of an end by nuclear destruction in twenty-four hours has no more inherent power to render present life meaningless than does an end for natural cosmic reasons two billion years from now. Liberty and justice can only be preserved by forces which today can be used only at the risk of vastly destructive nuclear war.'[25] Moreover, we must take that risk, for, according to Ramsey, 'On their way to the heavenly city, the children of God make use of *pax-ordo* of the earthly city and acknowledge their share in responsibility for its preservation.'[26] Because Christians have their hope in the heavenly city they need not adopt a nuclear pacifism based on fear or death, even the death of the human species. In his *Just War* Ramsey further suggests that because our secular age no longer has the confidence that we have an ultimate destiny, wars have become more dangerous. We spiritualize our politics; that is, we make absurd claims that wars can be fought for peace, and as a result increase the terror of war. Indeed we must recognize that coercion is the mother's milk of this earthly order and that any justice achieved will not eliminate but depend on this fact. Thus we will be more able to discipline our warfare once we recognize that wars can only be pursued to secure a relative balance of violence that allows for some justice.[27]

Finally Schell's position has been criticized because of his utopianism. Theodore Draper says:

This [Schell's book] is a travesty on thinking about nuclear war. It is also the most depressing and defeatest cure-all that has ever been offered. If we have to 'reinvent the world' to control nuclear war, the chances of saving the human race must be somewhere near the vanishing point. Deterrence is child's play compared with what Schell demands of us. His prescription is a disguised counsel of despair. It gives up the struggle against nuclear war in the world as it is in favor of chanting and shouting for a world that does not exist. Utopians are like that: they hold out the vision of a feast to starving people who are never permitted to eat any of it.[28]

Schell, in *The Fate of the Earth*, is certainly utopian, but that does not mean he is wrong. At the very least it seems to me he has helped us to locate some of the fundamental ethical issues entailed by calls for nuclear disarmament. The morality of nuclear deterrence does raise profound theological issues concerning the status of humanity and the status of our moral commitments that cannot, as Schell has shown, be avoided. If we are to disarm, and disarm justly, it may well mean that we will have to take larger risks than Schell is willing to envision. The peace we pursue must not be any peace, but a peace based on truth and justice. The problem with Schell's utopianism is not that it is utopian but that the peace he envisions may not be just.

SOVEREIGN-STATES DETERRENCE

The position I here call sovereign-states deterrence seems at first to be the exact opposite of Schell's. It has little or no use for his moral fervor. Indeed many of the advocates of this position deny all moral commitments. They disavow all moral claims since they assume that we must begin thinking about the nuclear situation not as it should be but as it is. They thus pride themselves on being 'realistic' rather than allowing their thinking to be clouded with legalistic distinctions between killing and murder, or sentimental concerns about the 'fate of the earth.'[29]

What is often overlooked both by advocates and critics of sovereign-states deterrence is that their disavowal of morality involves substantial moral conviction. For their 'realism' is based on the assumption that we do better to face limits and try with humility and imagination to do the best we can within those limits. For them, the fundamental limit that we must accept for thinking about war, and in particular nuclear war, is the nation-state system. For all its obvious failures, the nation-state system provides the best means we have for securing a relatively just international order. Advocates of this type do not assume that individual nations themselves are just, but rather that the nation-state system is the best means we have to secure what justice and peace are possible in this world. Such justice and peace no doubt will always be less than the idealist desires; nevertheless it is better than the violence legitimated by those who would have us kill in the illusion of eradicating war from our lives.

Fundamental to the sovereign-states deterrence position is the rejection of what Michael Howard, in his brilliant book, *War and the Liberal Conscience*, had described as the liberal theory for wars.[30] According to Howard, the liberal conscience, which began as early as Erasmus, simply refused to accept war as a rational endeavor. Impressed by the horror of war, the liberals assume that war was the result of some hidden conspiracy or intellectual or moral failure that could be corrected. Interestingly the various reasons the liberals gave for the existence of war and the strategies they suggested for its elimination are employed by those currently call for the reduction, if not elimination, of nuclear weapons.

For example, Howard suggest that liberals allege wars 'occurred because they were a way of life among a militarized aristocratic ruling class and would die out when this was replaced by what St. Simon called *les industrieux*.'[31] Hence, war could only be eliminated when republican and democratic principles were extended to all the nations, or at least to the nations of Europe. But exactly the opposite took place, for the rise of democracy went hand in hand with the rise of the violence in war. Ironically, authoritarian regimes have greater freedom to fight limited wars since they do not need to use ideals to convince a reluctant populace that they should support and fight for something from which they would receive little personal benefit. The modern scale of war, and perhaps the modern scale of weaponry, are correlative to our democratic convictions and institutions.

Another liberal theory was that if wars did not result from aristocratic habit, they must be the result of vested interests, the distorted perceptions of a governing class and their capitalist interest — particularly arms manufacturers. But this theory seems not to hold up when twentieth-century war is considered. It remains a matter of debate to what extent it may be the case with regard to the advanced weapons systems of today. Yet as we shall see, one of the main interests of advocates of sovereign-states deterrence is to subject economic and technological interest in weapon development to political control.[32]

Finally, liberals blamed the diplomats and their manipulation of the balance of power for the existence of war. Now certainly it is the case that clumsy diplomacy and ruthless power-politics can result in wars, but what the liberal has ignored, according to Howard, is that power-politics are the politics of not being over-powered. Indeed, many liberals were prepared to fight wars of self-defense, but it is the business of the diplomat to make it unnecessary to fight such wars, or to insure that:

> ... if they do come, their country should not be confronted by a coalition so overwhelming, and be left so bereft of help, that it fights in a hopeless cause. To transcend this necessity and create a genuine world system of collective security has been the aim of liberal statesmen throughout this century. But such a system demands a degree of mutual confidence, a homogeneity of values and a coincidence of perceived interests such as did not exist even in the limited society of inner-war Europe. We are a long way from creating it in the culturally heterogeneous world we inhabit today.[33]

Underlying the liberal search for the cause of war from the perspective of sovereign-state advocates is a fundamentally mistaken assumption — that war is irrational. According to Howard, what the liberal has failed to see, and I take this to be the essential assumption of the sovereign-states deterrence advocates, is that

> War is an inherent element in a system of sovereign states which lacks any supreme and acknowledged arbiter; and the more genuinely those states by reason of their democratic structure embody indigenous and peculiar cultural values and perceptions, the less likely are they to sacrifice that element of sovereignty which carries with it the decision, if necessary to use force to protect their interest. To this extent surely Mazzini was right: in order to have internationalism, one must first create nations: and those peoples who have already achieved cultural self-consciousness and political independence can all too easily forget the claims of those who have not. Where Mazzini and his imitators were at fault was in assuming that, because the creation of nation states was a necessary condition for peace, it would also be a sufficient one.[34]

At the root of the liberal thinkers' confusion about war, Howard argues, lies the habit of seeing war as a distinct and abstract entity. 'War is simply the generic term for the use of armed force by states or aspirants to statehood for the attainment of their political objectives.'[35] Thus from the perspective of sovereign-states deterrence, war is not something we should seek to eliminate, but rather is part and parcel of our way of life. The only concern is how it can best be used.

Contrary to Schell, sovereign states advocates hold that nuclear weapons are but one development among others in the continued state of war that exists between nations. Like all weapons, they are created to serve the purpose of advancing our particular nation's ends. Such weapons do exist to preserve a peace of sorts, but it is a 'peace' that is the name for the accommodations that at any one time benefit all parties to a lesser and greater extent. In so far as nuclear weapons serve that end they are not inherently immoral.

From the perspective of the sovereign-states deterrence advocate, we must be smart in our violence. As a result they tend to side with those who would have us subject our nuclear weapons and policies to political ends — that is, we must make them serve purposes and interests. In particular they are concerned that technology is now determining the politics rather than being under the control of a rational foreign policy. This point of view was classically stated by Henry Kissinger in 1974 (although subsequently disavowed) when he said, 'What in the name of God is strategic superiority? What is the significance of it politically, militarily, operationally at these levels of numbers? What do you do with it?'[36]

Indeed what bothers advocates of sovereign-states deterrence about the current talk of a policy of a 'winnable' nuclear war is that because it has no political purpose, it is extremely dangerous. Winnability, according to Theodore Draper, 'presupposes that a nuclear war could go on "over a protracted period" without unacceptable and uncontrollable destruction of the countries waging it. It assumes that "favorable terms" would have some human meaning after such a nuclear conflict.'[37] For Draper such a scheme has only one saving grace: 'it is so grotesque and mindless that it is inconceivable that the American people will not rebel against it and make Congress refuse to accept it.'[38]

But then what should be our strategy? According to Draper we must make mutually assured destruction the object of our nuclear policy. Having accepted that we must quit asking, 'How much is enough?' Likewise we must stop relying on negotiations to produce reductions.

Negotiations tend to register the progress of the arms race rather than to put an end to it. Any numerical change that leaves intact the ability of each nuclear superpower to destroy the other cannot change the fundamental strategic balance between them; the excess of the nuclear weapons is so great that a ceiling or reduction which does not get below the level of redundancy cannot significantly change the basic character of the problem. Anyone who expects a great power to give up an advantage in negotiations or not to get the best trade possible for it, is already living in Jonathan Schell's reinvented world. Unfortunately, we have only one real world, and it is not hospitable to illusions or fantasies. This way of thinking about nuclear war is a trap for the innocent and a boon to nuclear warriors.[39]

So Draper realistically advocates a policy of deterrence which seeks not to abolish nuclear weapons in the hope we will never have to use them. The crucial point for a deterrence policy is that any level of 'nuclear weapons over and above what is necessary to have a devastating effect on the other side is no more than an exercise in redundancy'.[40] The question of 'Who is ahead' is simply meaningless or, worse, stupid. We do not need more; all we need is enough. The arsenal of nuclear arms should be fixed at some rational level by a calculation of needs of deterrence rather than by competition and rivalry. Such a procedure would free the United States to set its own foreign policy rather than react constantly to the Soviets. Therefore some form of unilateral actions makes all the sense in the world.

As I have already pointed out, while sovereign-states deterrence advocates make no exaggerated moral claims, they are clearly morally motivated. Their attempt to make nuclear policy serve political ends is a moral policy because politics always entails moral assumptions. While sharing some strategies with certain just war positions, sovereign-states deterrence fundamentally differs from them since it sets its nuclear strategy not by prior criteria which determine legitimate violence but by what is good for the sovereign-states system. Thus a sovereign-states deterrence position does not in principle deny the right to have nuclear weapons on grounds of the principle of discrimination; nor does it prevent us from aiming our weapons at civilian populations if this would result in a more stable relation between the two superpowers; nor would the sovereign-state deterrence position require the moral gymnastics of the bluff position for it is certainly committed to the use of the weapons. We threaten, and our threat is real. Indeed, people in charge of our government would be immoral not to use the weapons to prevent an attack or retaliate.

But I suspect at this point we also encounter some of the deepest difficulties in the sovereign-states deterrence position. It is not clear that we are morally prepared as a population to sustain the realism it demands. Put differently, the ability to sustain a just-nation deterrence policy requires the citizens of a nation to view themselves as individuals who must be willing to use nuclear weapons for limited moral ends and purposes, such as preserving the values inherent to the nationstate system. Such a position is certainly coherent, but what the sovereign-states deterrence advocates have failed to do is show us how it can be lived as an ongoing project − that is, as a position requiring the killing of millions − without its destroying any sense of what makes life a morally worthy enterprise.

On a more practical level, the problem with the sovereign-nations deterrence position is that, like the just war position, it is beset with instability. Calculating 'deterrence' turns out to be an extraodinarily difficult matter. It certainly helps to ask 'What is enough?', but determining that is not simple.[41] For the issue is not simply the destructive weapon itself, but how and where it is to go. Thus we are in the ironical position that weapons and delivery systems that may promise us more security threaten instability and a greater likelihood of nuclear war. What could be more utopian than Draper's assumption that the Pentagon will be open to a signficant reduction in nuclear weapons?.

Finally, there is the problem of nuclear proliferation. It is one of the virtues of the sovereign-state deterrence system that it attributes no special moral status to one nation more than to another. But just to the extent that it legitimates each nation pursuing its en-lightened self-interest, it has little reason to deny to other nations the possession of nuclear weapons. Thus it appears, to employ Garrett Hardin's image of the commons, that what is good for each nation might well result in our having no commons at all and in which the more fortunate cows would be killed outright rather than left to starve to death.

ENDING WITH A BEGINNING

At the risk of ending with a whimper rather than a bang I must now ask where this has analysis gotten us. In some ways it seems

to have made our situation worse for it seems we lack, as I
suggested at the beginning, a coherent moral response that unambiguously requires nuclear disarmament. Or in other words those
positions that entail such disarmament are based on questionable
moral convictions that we would be hesitant to apply in other
aspects of our lives. We thus seem left with our nuclear arsenals
not knowing how to live with them and not knowing how to rid
ourselves of them.

Moreover we fear this situation may be profoundly pathological.
As Schell suggests:

> When one tries to face the nuclear predicament one feels
> sick; whereas when one pushes it out of mind, as apparently
> one must do most of the time in order to carry on with life,
> one feels well again. But this feeling of well-being is based on
> a denial of the most important reality of our time, and
> therefore is a kind of sickness. A society that systematically
> shuts its eyes to an urgent peril to its physical survival and
> fails to take steps to save itself cannot be called psychologically
> well. In effect whether we think about nuclear weapons or
> avoid thinking about them, their presence among us makes
> us sick, and there seems to be little of purely mental or
> emotional nature we can do about it.[42]

I think Schell is right about this — nuclear weapons do make us
sich but not just in a psychological sense; they make us morally
sick. More accurately, however, these weapons manifest that the
moralities that form our existence are insufficient insofar as they
presuppose survival as the overriding good. Ironically there is a
deep kinship between Schell and the sovereign-states deterrence
advocates as both draw deeply on our fear of death as individuals,
nations, and species for support of their position. But it is exactly
such fear that is the basis of our creation and possession of the
bomb.[43]

It is the peculiar wisdom of the just war tradition to relativize
the value of survival and to ask us to die and, more importantly,
kill for the limited moral good embodied by the sovereigns that
currently take the form of the nation state. Thus the advocates of
just war, at least in principle, acknowledge the finite status of our
values for which we should be willing to die. Such a view obviously
draws on profound eschatological assumptions concerning how
we are to live in this time between the times.

That just war advocates presuppose such an eschatology, moreover, reveals a still more profound commonality between them and the pacifist. For the Christian pacifist agrees that life cannot be an end in and of itself – there are many things for which we should be willing to die rather than lose these goods. For example, we should be willing to sacrifice much, perhaps even our lives, rather than abandon the innocent to violent destruction. Such protection after all is not simply a formula for achieving a safe society but essential for the achievement of justice.

Where the pacifist differs with the just war advocate is whether killing can ever be compatible with the achievement of genuine justice. Indeed just to the extent that just war theory can provide a rationale for the possession and perhaps use of nuclear weapons, it may be a sign of the questionable nature of all justice based on violence. Or put differently, it may reveal the profound unreality of the kind of realism that results from a just war perspective. For what values, however significant, could ever legitimate the use of these weapons which seem to offer no promise of being subjected to moral limits or purpose? Of course that same question, I think, finally challenges the possibility of war itself.

It has not been my intention in ending in this fashion to suggest our situation is hopeless unless we have a return to God and/or accept a pacifist stance. No one should believe in God as a means to challenge nuclear way any more than anyone should become a pacifist as a strategy for preventing war. Rather we should only believe in God if God in truth is the beginning and end of our existence; we should only take up the way of nonviolence if we believe that is the way of God with the world.[44] Neither a massive return to belief in God nor nonviolence would solve the nuclear dilemma. All I have tried to show is how the absence of each illumines why we have come under the power of our own creation.

NOTES

1   For a fuller development of this point see my essay, 'An Eschatological Perspective on Nuclear Disarmament' in *Against The Nations* (Minneapolis, MN. Winston Press, 1986), pp. 160–168.

2   I am grateful to James Childress and John Howard Yoder for helping me see this point.

3   Edward Laarman, 'Nuclear Deterrence and the Bluff', *The Reformation Journal* (June, 1982), 15.

4   I draw this list from James Childress' fine essay, 'Just War Theories: The Bases, Interrelations, Priorities and Functions of Their Criteria', *Theological Studies*, 39 (September, 1978), 435–41.

5 See, for example, Paul Ramsey's still very important discussion of this in *War and the Christian Conscience* (Durham: Duke University Press, 1961), 34–59.

6 James Johnson, *Just War Tradition and the Restraint of War* (Princeton: Princeton University Press, 1981), XXII.

7 Johnson, 167.

8 John Connery has recently argued along these lines in his 'The Morality of Nuclear Warpower', *America* (July 17, 1982), 25–8. He quotes John Courtney Murray's claim that 'since nuclear war may be a necessity, it must be made a moral possibility. The possibilty must be created. To say that the possibility of nuclear war cannot be created by human intelligence and energy, under the direction of a moral imperative is to succumb to some sort of determinism in human affairs.' However the bishops of the American Catholic Church in their recent Pastoral are increasingly inclined to deny any moral legitimacy for the planning or possessing of nuclear weapons.

9 Johnson, XXXV.

10 Ramsey's important discussion of Augustine in *War and the Christian Conscience* has often failed to be appreciated in this respect. For Ramsey saw quite clearly that just war is as much a theory of state craft as it is an instrument for casuistry. This is perhaps clearer in his *The Just War* (New York: Scribners, 1968).

11 Johnson, 47–9.

12 Thus Ramsey argued in *War and the Christian Conscience*: 'The Great Deterrent leaves us without a link between force and purpose. We needed then and need now some substitute for the kind of warfare that can in no sense be an extension of national policy; and this can mean the creation of the possibility of limited application of power. The more this is understood, the better. The risks involved in this are the risks of walking the earth as men who do not deny that they know the difference between murder and war or between warfare that is justified and that which exceeds all limits. The risks are the risks of seeing to it that war, if it comes, will have some minimal national purpose connected with it' (166).

13 I owe this point to Laarman, 15–19.

14 Jonathan Schell, *The Fate of the Earth* (New York: Alfred Knopf, 1982), 93.

15 Ibid., 95.

16 Ibid., 118–19.

17 Ibid., 132.

18 Ibid., 171.

19 Ibid., 191. It is interesting to note that Schell accepts a presupposition of the 'realist' who insists that war must serve political purpose.

20 Ibid., 187.

21 Ibid., 226. In his most recent book Schell provides a more 'realistic' account of how the world might move from deterrence to an abolition agreement. It is interesting however, that his account

clearly continues to presuppose the existence of the nation state system. See his *The Abolition* (New York: Alfred Knopf, 1984).

22   Schell's book was originally published as a three-part essay in the *New Yorker*.

23   It is interesting to compare Schell's position with that of James Gustafson in his recent *Ethics in a Theocentric Perspective*. Vol. I (Chicago: University of Chicago Press, 1982).

24   Schell, 134.

25   Ramsey, *War and the Christian Conscience*, 193.

26   Ramsey, 205. While I am sympathetic with Ramsey's basic point that our thinking about the morality of war cannot be based on survival and fear one can still maintain as a Christian that the how of survival is not unimportant. It may be true that God intends to kill us all in the end, but that does not mean how we live in between the time is unimportant.

27   Paul Ramsey, *The Just War: Force and Political Responsibility* (New York: Charles Scribner's Sons, 1968), 42–69.

28   Theodore Draper, 'How Not to Think About Nuclear War', *New York Review of Books*, XXIX, 12 (July 1982), 38.

29   Systematic statements and developments of this position are not easily found but I associate it with people like McGeorge Bundy, George Kennan, and Solly Zuckerman. I have used the thought of Michael Howard below even though his book does not explicitly deal with the nuclear question because it states more candidly the essential moral presuppositions behind this position.

30   Michael Howard, *War and the Liberal Conscience* (New Brunswick: Rutgers University Press, 1978).

31   Ibid., 130.

32   Interestingly Solly Zuckerman, who is otherwise a realist, continues to lay the blame for the nuclear arms race on the scientist. Thus he says, 'The basic reason for the irrationality of the whole process is the fact that ideas for a new weapon system derive in the first place, not from the military, but from different groups of scientists and technologists who are concerned to replace or improve old weapons systems – for example by miniaturising components – or by reducing weight/yield ratios of nuclear warheads so that they can be carried further by a ballistic missile. At base, the momentum of the arms race is undoubtedly fueled by the technicians in governmental laboratories and in the industries which produce the armaments.' *Nuclear Illusion and Reality* (New York: Viking Press, 1982), 103. On the basis of such an analysis it would seem that perhaps the best thing we could do would be to kill the scientists who are working at these projects. On a more serious level, however, I suspect that Zuckerman is right at least to the extent that the issue becomes one of the imagination – for it is not simply new weapons systems that lure us deeper into suicide but our failure to envisage peace as a genuine alternative.

33 Howard, 132.
34 Ibid., 133.
35 Ibid., 134.
36 Quoted by Alan Geyer in his *The Idea of Disarmament: Rethinking and Unthinkable* (Elgin, Illinois: The Brethren Press, 1982), 71. Geyer's book is an eloquent and well-argued position for the possibility of disarmament.
37 Draper, 40.
38 Ibid., 40. Where Draper gets this rather touching faith in the American people is not revealed. In this respect he seems to be as utopian as Schell.
39 Ibid., 41–2. Draper is generally in agreement with the proposals advanced by Zuckerman.
40 Ibid., 42.
41 Again see Geyer for some very useful suggestions in this respect.
42 Schell, 8.
43 David Novak, in a yet unpublished paper, 'The Threat of Nuclear War: Jewish Perspective', suggests that the idolatry embodied in nuclear weapons is first of all revealed by our assumption that we now have the power to destroy ourselves. Novak rightly reminds us that God alone reserves that power for himself.
44 For the best analysis of the nuclear dilemma from this perspective see Dale Aukerman, *Darkening Valley: A Biblical Perspective on Nuclear War* (New York: The Seabury Press, 1981). Aukerman says: 'Humanly considered, there seems so little prospect of stopping the rush toward nuclear annihilation. But communities of disciples will not, because of this, be immobilized or impelled into frantic activism. World War III is not inevitable. The God of Scripture continues to make His offer of rescue in utter seriousness and His is a sovereignty of surprises. A group of disciples, listening together in prayer, will be able to discern forms and acts of witness God wants of them' (205).

12

Epilogue: Continuing Implications of the Just War Tradition

JEAN BETHKE ELSHTAIN

> Christians, even as they strive to resist and prevent every form of warfare, have no hesitation in recalling that, in the name of an elementary requirement of justice, peoples have a right and even a duty to protect their existence and freedom by proportionate means against an unjust aggressor.
>
> — *Gaudium et Spes* (the Pastoral Constitution on the Church in the Modern World, a Vatican II document)

> Given the view of Nazism that I am assuming, the issue takes this form: should I wager this determinate crime (the killing of innocent people against that immeasurable evil (a Nazi triumph)?
>
> — MICHAEL WALZER, *Just and Unjust Wars*

One way to tell the story of just-war discourse is to treat it as an authoritative tradition dotted with its own sacred texts, offering a canonical alternative to realism as received truth. Rather than beginning with Machiavelli (or, reaching further back, Thucydides), just war as continuous narrative starts with Augustine; takes up a smattering of medieval canonists; plunges into the sixteenth century with Luther as the key figure; draws in a few natural/international-law thinkers (Francisco Suarez, Francisco de Vitoria, Hugo Grotius), then leapfrogs into the era of modern nation-states — and wars. At that historic juncture, with religious and philosophic discourse severed, just war becomes a partial preserve of theologians. Catholic thinkers predominate, but Protestants also figure. The professionalization of moral and ethical discourse, similar in this sense to that of international relations, spawns

Reprinted with permission from Jean Bethke Elshtain *Women and War* (Basic Books, New York 1987), pp. 149–59.

essays and monographs on the moral philosophies of deontology versus consequentialism as applied, for example, to such questions as the rule of proportionality and weighing problems of collateral damage, which are primarily accessible to other professionals: this has been a partial fate of just-war thinking.[1]

Canalized as just-war *doctrine* historically and *theory* currently, just-war teaching is sometimes presented as a cluster of 'Thou shalts' and 'Thou shalt nots', Augustine's rich ruminations giving way to a list of seven (or more or less) requirements presumed operative on states, statesmen and women and war fighters. These are: (1) that a war be the last resort to be used only after all other means have been exhausted; (2) that a war be clearly an act of redress of rights actually violated or defense against unjust demands backed by the threat of force; (3) that war be openly and legally declared by properly constituted governments; (4) that there be a reasonable prospect for victory; (5) that the means be proportionate to the ends; (6) that a war be waged in such a way as to distinguish between combatants and noncombatants; (7) that the victorious nation not require the utter humiliation of the vanquished.[2]

Just-war thinkers as layers-down-of-the-law insist that they are not propounding immutable rules so much as clarifying the circumstances that should — and actually, if imperfectly, do — justify a state in going to war (*jus ad bellum*), and what is and is not allowable in fighting the wars to which a state has committed itself (*jus in bello*). Cast in this form, modern just-war discourse downplays some features of the human condition and the Western tradition and brings others into sharp and prominent focus.

With their aims of constraining collective violence, chastening *realpolitik*, and forging human identities, the current heirs of this way of thinking assume (1) the existence of universal moral dispositions, if not convictions — hence, the possibility of a nonrelativist ethic; (2) the need for moral judgments of who/what is aggressor/victim, just/unjust, acceptable/unacceptable, and so on; (3) the potential efficacy of moral appeals and arguments to stay the hand of force. This adds up to a vision of civic virtue, not in the classical armed sense but in a way that is equally if differently demanding.

One brief example: the American Catholic bishops, in common with all Christian just-war thinkers, do not locate survival as an absolute, hence do not accept retaliation as an acceptable way of 'fighting back'. It follows that the use of nuclear weapons for the purpose of destroying population centers is to be condemned *under all circumstances*, even if one's own cities have been the target for a first strike. The capacity to *refrain* from violence when one has been the victim of it is central to pacifism, of course, but it also lies at the heart of just-war thinking which shares with pacifism the insistence that violence, not nonviolence, must bear the burden of proof. Although combat soldiers learn the harsh lesson of *restraint* in the vagaries of actual fighting, noncombatants do not experience the need to refrain in the same way.

One can imagine two scenarios: in the first, survivors of a first-wave assault on key American cities thirsting for revenge, demand that the perpetrators be 'punished' — indeed, 'wiped out'.[3] In the second, survivors, having been apprised in the most horrendous and visible way of the horrors of nuclear war, call for forbearance, not retaliation: they become peace witnesses like the survivors of Hiroshima or Nagasaki. That there is historic warrant for this alternative scenario comes from two recognitions, one abstract, the other concrete: first, that just-war thinking as popular morality cuts across the West, offering the possibility for sober reflection by ordinary men and women on questions of violence; and, second, that opinion polling in Great Britain in 1941 showed that 'the most determined demand for [reprisal raids against Germany] came from ... rural areas barely touched by bombing, where some three-quarters of the population wanted them. In central London, conversely, the proportion was only 45 percent.' Michael Walzer concludes that 'men and women who had experienced terror bombing were less likely to support Churchill's policy than those who had not — a heartening statistic.'[4] I agree.

Just-war thinking as a form of civic virtue cannot endorse the unleashing of aggressivity sanctioned by armed civic virtue in a time of total war. Indeed, what is demanded instead is *deep reflection* by Everyman and Everywoman on what his or her government is up to. This, in turn, *presupposes* a 'self' of a certain kind, one attuned to moral reasoning and capable of it; one strong enough to resist the lure of seductive, violent enthusiasms; one bounded by and laced through with a sense of responsibility and accountability. In other words, a *morally formed civic character* is a precondition for just-war thinking as a civic virtue. Determining whether and to what extent this possibility *really* exists is not my task at the moment; rather, I shall look briefly at current ferment from persons religious and theoretical working within a just-war frame.

CATHOLIC CONTROVERSIES: THE BISHOPS' 1983 PASTORAL LETTER

On one end, the Catholic just-war tradition makes contact with pacifism; on the other, it elides into holy wars against infidels. If medieval Catholicism gave us the Crusades, contemporary Catholicism edges nearer the pacifist pole, sanctioning pacifism as personal identity and collective witness without embracing it wholesale, and rejecting unequivocally crusading enthusiasms. All modern popes — from Pius XII who condemned total war *during* total war, repudiating the terror bombing of German and Japanese cities with the means of conventional war; to John Paul II, who has been outspoken on nuclear arms, the arms race, and the distortion of science given its complicity in building up 'arsenals of destruction'[5] — have situated themselves as spokesmen for peace, as nuclear but not absolute pacifists. Thus, they find no moral justification any time anywhere for the *use* of nuclear weapons, no matter what the alleged provocation, danger to oneself, or wounding by another.

War is still 'permissible' if all peaceful alternatives have been exhausted in serious efforts; if the war is waged under *jus in bello* rules which prohibit making war on noncombatants, hence rule out much of the panoply of modern war; and if war is a response to aggression or the only way to protect the innocent from 'certain' harm. These statements add up to a powerful construction proffered as an occasion for reflection *and* as prohibitive moral rules: 'Thou shalt not ...' Papal pronouncements also affirm Gospel injunctions against punishing one's foes once you have beat them: there shall be no postwar retaliation nor vengeance against the defeated. After war, those who have prevailed must show the face of mercy and forgiveness rather than bare the talons of retribution.[6]

Nor are Catholic bishops latecomers to just-war reflection and teaching. The 1983 pastoral letter issued by the American bishops is the latest in a long train, reiterating the nuclear pacifist position, condemning total war, instructing statesmen and citizens on war and peace within a just-war frame. The strategic debate of recent years has focused in part on deterrence. The bishops insist that the United State's current strategic doctrine is unacceptable on moral grounds, as it targets civilian populations; and, as well, that deterrence is structured in such a way that arms buildups are its automatic outgrowth given the 'worst case scenarios' that guide and feed it. The proposition *Si vis pacem, para bellum* ('To have peace, you must prepare for war'), always debatable, now lacks any credibility (we have seen and know too much), functioning instead as a whitewash of one's own moves to gain the upper hand.

The enormous flap created by the bishops' pastoral letter arose in part from the widespread insistence that it is not the bishops' job to pronounce on such hefty matters as nuclear strategy — but is, instead, a task for the experts. The bishops listened to hours of expert testimony, only to be blasted, by some critics, for not being themselves strategic-deterrence professionals. By what right, then, did they speak? The need to shore up the epistemological privilege of professional elites comes through loud and clear in such criticisms, showing just how defensive the defensive establishment has become. Telling the bishops to shut up and stay inside their churches signifies the continued simplistic insistence that religion and politics must not mix.

Politics as policy formulation and implementation is not for amateurs. Women, too, are well advised to keep their noses out of this complex business *unless* they have learned not to think and speak 'like women' — that is, like human beings picturing decimated homes and mangled bodies when strategies for nuclear or other war fighting are discussed. The worlds of 'victims' — overwhelmingly one of women and children — and of 'warriors', as Freeman Dyson characterizes them,[7] have become nearly incommensurable universes to one another. Contemporary rationalist realism freezes this division. Although images of male fighters and female noncombatants have been the usual expectation, just-war discourse at present tends to see both soldiers and civilians as likely *victims* of future wars and places men and women in all walks of life under the purview of its teaching as practical morality. Thus the pastoral letter addresses: Educators, Parents, Youth, Men and Women in Military Service, Defense Industry, Science, Media, Public Officials as well as Citizens.

JUST WAR AS POLITICAL PHILOSOPHY: MICHAEL WALZER

Michael Walzer's *Just and Unjust Wars* (1977), a reformulation and justification of just-war thinking that shares some but not all of the ontological and moral commitments just discussed, consists of sets of presumptions and arguments that require consequentialist assessments. Walzer rejects pacifism outright, being far less open to its message than the bishops, for example, and leaves a crack that opens onto the door to crusading enthusiasms that theologians have tried to slam shut. Walzer goes this route because he locates the survival and freedom of political communities – states – as the highest value. For Catholic thinkers, contrastingly, the rights of states to an ongoing existence is a pre-eminent but not a penultimate good. As a 'book of practical morality', in his words, Walzer's text offers complex cases involving often fine distinctions.[8] The insistence that violence is always regretable and devoutly to be avoided holds. But many horrors slip through for Walzer that do not for other just-war thinkers: for example, his treatment of British decisions to bomb German cities during the Second World War, and nuclear deterrence theory, revolve around means – ends calculations in tension with classic just-war prohibitions on targeting civilians.

Thus he justifies the saturation bombing of German cities – Dresden excepted – given the *nature of the Nazi* threat and the predictable out-come should Britain fall to Germany. Present threat and future danger fuse to override *jus in bello* rules. The British made total war on the most densely populated areas of major German cities, some of them not 'military' targets in any compelling meaning of the term. By constructing Nazism as an *immeasurable* evil, not just *an* evil, Walzer must put his question concerning terror bombing this way: Should I wager a determinate crime against an immeasurable evil? A condition of 'supreme emergency' – the Second World War – erodes the force of just-war restrictions in his argument. By adjusting to the exigencies of total war, Walzer slides into conclusions a 'modified realist' would probably be able to live with. Concluding that our present circumstance is one of continuing 'supreme emergency', Walzer, in a schematic discussion, finds nuclear deterrence criminal but 'unavoidable': not a very good way 'to cope' but cope we must 'in a world of sovereign and suspicious states.'

Because Walzer owes so much to modern constructions of 'rights' engrafted from one tradition – liberal, rationalist, litigious – his language is sometimes inadequate to his task. Opposing American use of atomic bombs on Hiroshima and Nagasaki, for example – finding them unjustifiable within his frame – Walzer goes on to ask: 'How did the people of Hiroshima forfeit their rights?'[10] The language of rights is impoverished in this context, inadequate to capture what happened on those dreadful days. Pope Paul VI got closer to the mark when he spoke of a 'butchery of untold magnitude', and drew upon prophetic language, which Walzer avoids just as he eschews vivid descriptions of wartime carnage, making no attempt to evoke actual war experience. Walzer's 'practical morality' seems a bit too abstract, too finely tuned, to guide most of us, bleaching out the texture of historic experience as it does.[11]

THE MODERN DILEMMA

The great strength of all this moral stock taking is the fact that it begins with presumptions that challenge the use of force — hence, all acts of collective and individual violence. Constituting men and women as *concerned citizens*, just-war thinkers enjoin them, whatever their respective vocations, to get serious about matters of war and peace. But how does this 'play in Boston'? Brought down to parish and popular levels, the resurgence of just-war thinking offers moral dilemmas and provides clear-cut or provisional answers that are urged upon others.[12]

In actual wartime, it seems likely that many of these stipulations will go unheeded. They *may* have sufficient force to give warmakers a bad conscience, and they offer men and women a 'voice' in and through which to register their objections and their moral distress. That just-war teaching *has* made a difference in concrete situations and reactions is clear. *Commonweal*, a Catholic lay journal, condemned terror bombing in 1942, as did other Catholic journals of opinion. Reinhold Niebuhr, cohabiting at times with just-war views, called the total-war mentality 'nauseous self-righteousness'. The atomic bombings were an occasion for sorrow and criticism on the part of many leading Protestant and Catholic journals of any note. For example: in its 24 August 1945 issue, *Commonweal* concluded its editorial condemning the atomic bombs in these words:

> For our war, for our purposes, to save American lives we have reached the point where we say that anything goes. That is what the Germans said at the beginning of the war. Once we have won our war we say that there must be international law. Undoubtedly. When it is created, Germans, Japanese, and Americans will remember with horror the days of their shame.[13]

On the other hand, the available public-opinion data suggests that, in early polls, 80 to 85 per cent of Americans, most 'good Christians', endorsed use of the atomic bomb,[14] *pace* the expressed views of leading articulators of the just-war position. According to Paul Boyers, letters to the editor at the time of the bombings frequently expressed regret 'that atomic bombs had not been used to destroy all human life in Japan. A Milwaukee woman expressed her genocidal impulses this way: "When one sets out to destroy vermin, does one try to leave a few alive in the nest? Certainly not!" A letter in the *Washington Post* on August 17 from a woman who said the atomic bomb made her ashamed to be an American elicited a torrent of bitter, abusive letters.'[15] Exterminationist rhetoric was rife, and support for a policy of annihilation against the Japanese was widespread. One 1943 'best-seller stated that the fight against Japan had to continue "until not alone the body but the soul ... is annihilated, until the land ... is plowed with salt, its men dead and its women and children divided and lost among other people." Carthage, sacked and razed by the Romans struck the more historically minded as an apt model for Japan ... *Collier's* ran an editorial entitled "Delenda est Japonia"'.[16]

How to explain this popular savagery? In part, it stems from the crusading impulse lurking in the interstices of just-war discourse. The language of good and evil, just and unjust, may, under conditions that invite total war, turn people out as judges who sometimes become executioners. Should this happen, the preponderant force of 'official' just-war discourse may not have sufficient strength to hold in check the 'heretical' crusading offshoot. In a pithy critique of the moral absolutism of pacifists, Reinhold Niebuhr argues that the Christian faith 'ought to persuade us that political controversies are always conflicts between sinners and not between righteous men and sinners. It ought to mitigate the self-righteousness which is an inevitable concomitant of all human conflict'.[17] Hitler, or rather our collective and ongoing reactions to him, continually imperil such recognitions. Hitler gave the Allied countries permission, so to speak, to indulge in collective selfrighteousness. Constructed as the *incarnation* of Evil, a kind of mirror-image demiurge of the 'good god', Hitler worked, and works, wonderfully whenever we want to reconfirm our benign sense of ourselves. By 1945, we were morally inured to obliteration of cities, and use of the atomic bomb was an extension of what had become standard war policy.

The force of these reflections is not to suggest that just-war prohibitions must go by the board given war excesses, but that they are under terrible pressure to succumb. Presupposing the possibility of civic virtue (partly) disarmed, just-war teaching presumes that all human beings can and should attempt to thread their way through the violent currents of the past, present, and projected future.

To make more secure contact on the level of 'lived life', to enter into the fray from the ground up rather than descending from the lofty pinnacle of a 'morality system', just-war thinkers would do well to retrieve Augustine's way of thinking as part of an effort to capture the living textures within which limited human beings think and act. Augustine deflates rather than builds up the possibility that we might one day control events. No human being can foreordain endings, happy or otherwise. We cannot even safely foretell what we shall do 'on the morrow'. Augustine's awareness of the fragility of life in the *saeculum* — no tidied-up world of foreordained, abstract duties and obligations, but a hothouse of conflicting pressures — his way of *evoking* bitter conflicts between real protagonists, his biting irony, and his lyrical descriptions — all speak to his attunement to human shortcomings and tragedies.

Inviting neither total relativism nor despairing withdrawal, Augustine's tragic recognitions point to modes of moral thinking stripped of the demand for triumphant moral heroism. He seeks to limit the damage done, by oneself and others, rather than to preach an unattainable counsel of perfection that invites smugness and despair. The distance that separates Augustine from the Catholic bishops or Walzer is not merely a question of chronology but a matter of where one *locates* one's hopes and what these hopes require. Walzer presumes and requires that human beings act as moral judges who weigh the consequences of their deeds against the magnitude of others' acts, arriving at judgments of blame or (relative) innocence. The bishops presume and require that human beings be prepared to do the 'right thing' even when others have done them wrong.

Is this degree of civic virtue possible in the modern world? Are most human beings in the West open to such constructions and prepared to take them on as their own? Just-war analysts would say human beings in the West have already taken them on — thus justifying their (these analysts') arguments. But suppose the analysts are wrong, at least as the propositions are usually stated. It was from a strongly felt moral perspective that Robert Kennedy — as attorney general, the President's brother, and a member of the team handling the October 1962 confrontation between the United States and the Soviet Union over the latter's moves to install ballistic missiles in Cuba — urged caution during the Cuban missile crisis, specifically arguing against a US air strike on Cuba. This stance was later called by the former secretary of state Dean Acheson, who had been brought in as an adviser attending the meetings, 'emotional intuitive responses more than . . . the trained lawyer's analysis'. Kennedy did *not* offer his caveats as a just-war perspective or in those terms; rather, he insisted that a 'surprise attack by a large nation on a small one, entailing many civilian casualties, would go against America's traditions'.[18] Just-war moral principles (non-combatant immunity) seeped into his pronouncements to become resonant and compelling only because, as a 'Pearl Harbor' in reverse, the proposed air strike would cut against the *American* grain. Where some members of the crisis team advocated a surprise air attack against Cuban missile sites, Robert Kennedy passed a note to the President which read: 'I now know how Tojo felt when he was planning Pearl Harbor.'[19]

This example suggests that the structure of a particular nation's history and experience will be more salient to political decision makers who enter into debates of moral principles than will be finely honed ethical systems.

NOTES

1 See Richard Niebanck, *Conscience, War and the Selective Objector* (Board of Social Ministry, Lutheran Church of America, 1972).
2 There isn't much of a female presence on the professional side of these developments for reasons that need no explaining. Female voices were *heard* by the Catholic bishops as they conjured with their 1983 pastoral 'The Challenge of Peace' but were not, by definition, among its *authors*.
3 This scenario is probably fanciful – not because a lust to annihilate one's tormentors would not arise, but because it seems unlikely that there would exist the mechanisms for, or the possibility of, citizen reaction feeding into decisions by statements and women in the disordered aftermath of a nuclear attack. By the time the citizens had gotten over the shock and registered their vehemence, the deed would no doubt have been done.
4 Michael Walzer *Just and Unjust Wars* (New York: Basic Books, 1977), pp. 256–7.
5 John Paul II, 'The UN Address', *Origins* 9 (11 Oct, 1979): 266.
6 Located at the heart of the Gospel message, forgiveness is mostly forgotten in the political affairs of men – and women. Hannah Arendt calls forgiveness Jesus of Nazareth's most radical and important teaching – 'the exact opposite of vengeance', which sets in motion chain reactions. Jesus' teaching contains a message of freedom, 'freedom from vengeance, which encloses both doer and sufferer in the relentless automatism of the action process'. Hannah Arendt, *The Human Condition* (Chicago: University of Chicago Press, 1958), pp. 238–42.
7 Freeman Dyson, *Weapons and Hope* (New York: Harper & Row, 1984), pp. 4–5.

8   Michael Walzer, *Just and Unjust Wars* (New York: Basic Books, 1977), p. xv.

9   Ibid., p. 274.

10 Ibid., p. 264.

11 The same criticism can be leveled at the bishops' pastoral letter, but the letter can more readily be translated into homey reflections than can Walzer's often schematized discourse. I here tap some of the concerns and criticisms my students have expressed upon reading Walzer's book, and am especially grateful for the thoughts of Ken Bertsch, my graduate teaching assistant.

12 See, for example, 'What Does Church Teach on War, Peace, Nuclear Arms?', *The Pilot* (26 February 1983): 8. (*The Pilot* is the paper of the Catholic Archdiocese of Boston.) See also Kenneth A. Briggs, 'Bishops Taking the Letter on Atomic War to the Parishes', *New York Times*, 16 December 1983.

13 Paul Boyers, *The Bomb's Early Light* (New York: Parthenon Books, 1985), pp. 228, 218.

14 Ibid., pp. 183—4. At the same time, my mother was among the small minority (some 15 percent) who disapproved of the dropping of the bomb, and she still thinks it was wrong. My father, no warrior, had mixed feelings at the time, but figured the bomb's use was dictated by military necessity, that thousands of American boys would have died if we had had to attack the Japanese mainland.

15 Ibid., pp. 184—85.

16 John W. Dower, *War Without Mercy: Race and Power in the Pacific War* (New York: Parthenon Books, 1986), p. 54, tells the whole sorry tale from both sides.

17 Reinhold Niebuhr, *Christianity and Power Politics* (New York: Archon Books, 1969), p. 23.

18 Robert F. Kennedy, *Thirteen Days* (New York: W. W. Norton, 1969), p. 31.

19 See Gregory S. Kavka, 'Morality and Nuclear Politics: Lessons of the Missile Crisis', in Steven Lee and Avner Cohen (eds) *Nuclear Weapons and the Future of Humanity* (Totowa, NJ: Rowman & Allanheld, 1986), p. 233—254.

Index

From the moment when Allied Forces implemented 'Desert Storm', in January 1991, following a United Nations resolution requiring Saddam Hussein's forces to withdraw from Kuwait, the phrase a 'just war' proliferated throughout the western media. While US and British politicians in particular proclaimed a 'just war', Saddam countered with the call for a 'holy war' justified by a wholly different set of criteria.

This indispensable collection of readings examines the crucial questions which lie behind this rhetoric: when can war be said to be 'just', and what means are or are not acceptable even in the course of a 'just war'? Moving beyond the theological just war tradition, the readings in this volume delineate the importance of the debates around just war theory for political and social theorists, military strategists, philosophers, and anyone concerned with the use of force in the relation between states.

Jean Bethke Elshtain is Centennial Professor of Political Science and Professor of Philosophy at Vanderbilt University, USA.

Readings in Social and Political Theory
Edited by William Connolly and Steven Lukes

This series brings together a carefully edited selection of the most influential and enduring articles on central topics in social and political theory. Each volume contains around ten articles and an introductory essay by the editor.

Feminism and Equality
Edited by Anne Phillips

Interpreting Politics
Edited by Michael T. Gibbons

Legitimacy and the State
Edited by William Connolly

Liberalism and Its Critics
Edited by Michael J. Sandel

Rational Choice
Edited by Jon Elster

Power
Edited by Steven Lukes

The Self and the Political Order
Edited by Tracy B. Strong

Social Contract Theory
Edited by Michael Lessnoff

Cover design by Martin Miller

NEW YORK UNIVERSITY PRESS

Washington Square
New York, NY 10003

ISBN 0-8147-2187-7